Modern Chinese Complex Sentences III

This book is the third volume of a four-volume set on modern Chinese complex sentences, with a focus on adversative complex sentences and their relevant forms.

Complex sentences in modern Chinese are unique in formation and meaning. The author proposes a tripartite classification of Chinese complex sentences according to the semantic relationships between the clauses, i.e., coordinate, causal, and adversative. This volume analyzes representative forms of adversative types, including the prototype, the clauses linked by connectives referring to "otherwise", the combinations of clause structures and certain adversative conjunctions or linking adverbs indicating an adversative relationship, the adversative factors and relationship in two typical progressive sentences, factive sentences, and concessive forms. It also discusses the adversative type in the broad sense, classifying the different forms and analyzing the semantic meaning, pragmatic value, and implications for research and language teaching.

The book will be a useful reference for scholars and learners in Chinese grammar and language information processing.

XING Fuyi is a renowned Chinese linguist and a senior professor at Central China Normal University. He has been devoted to the studies of modern Chinese grammar and has initiated the clause-pivotal approach for modern Chinese grammar studies. His other major publications include *Modern Chinese Grammar: A Clause-Pivot Approach* and *Three Hundred Qs & As about Chinese Grammar*.

Chinese Linguistics

Chinese Linguistics series selects representative and frontier works in linguistic disciplines including lexicology, grammar, phonetics, dialectology, philology and rhetoric. Mostly published in Chinese before, the selection has had far-reaching influence on China's linguistics and offered inspiration and reference for the world's linguistics. The aim of this series is to reflect the general level and latest development of Chinese linguistics from an overall and objective view.

Titles in this series currently include:

A Brief History of the Chinese Language IV
Old Chinese Lexicon
Xi Xiang

A Brief History of the Chinese Language V
Middle Chinese Lexicon 1
Xi Xiang

A Brief History of the Chinese Language VI
Middle Chinese Lexicon 2
Xi Xiang

A Brief History of the Chinese Language VII
Modern Chinese Lexicon 1
Xi Xiang

A Brief History of the Chinese Language VIII
Modern Chinese Lexicon 2
Xi Xiang

Modern Chinese Complex Sentences III
Adversative Type
XING Fuyi

For more information, please visit https://www.routledge.com/Chinese-Linguistics/book-series/CL

Modern Chinese Complex Sentences III
Adversative Type

XING Fuyi

LONDON AND NEW YORK

This book is published with financial support from the Chinese Fund for the Humanities and Social Sciences

First published in English 2023
by Routledge
4 Park Square, Milton Park, Abingdon, Oxon OX14 4RN

and by Routledge
605 Third Avenue, New York, NY 10158

Routledge is an imprint of the Taylor & Francis Group, an informa business

© 2023 XING Fuyi

Translated by WANG Yuhong, YI Honggen

The right of XING Fuyi to be identified as author of this work has been asserted in accordance with sections 77 and 78 of the Copyright, Designs and Patents Act 1988.

All rights reserved. No part of this book may be reprinted or reproduced or utilised in any form or by any electronic, mechanical, or other means, now known or hereafter invented, including photocopying and recording, or in any information storage or retrieval system, without permission in writing from the publishers.

Trademark notice: Product or corporate names may be trademarks or registered trademarks, and are used only for identification and explanation without intent to infringe.

English Version by permission of The Commercial Press.

ISBN: 978-1-032-44650-9 (hbk)
ISBN: 978-1-032-44853-4 (pbk)
ISBN: 978-1-003-37423-7 (ebk)

DOI: 10.4324/9781003374237

Typeset in Times New Roman
by Apex CoVantage, LLC

Contents

Diagrams	vi
Tables	vii

1 "*p, dànshì q*" and relevant forms   1

2 "*p, fǒuzé q*" and relevant forms   28

3 Occurrence of *dàn* or its synonym in "*jì p, yòu q*" and relevant forms   59

4 Occurrence of *dàn* or its synonym in "*wúlùn p, dōu q*"   75

5 Occurrence of *què* in "*jìrán p, jiù q*"   95

6 Occurrence of *què* in "*rúguǒ shuō p, nàme q*"   115

7 Occurrence of *què* in "*yuè p, yuè q*"   124

8 "*bùdàn bù p, fǎn'ér q*" and its adversative relationship   153

9 Progressive *gèng*-sentences and adversative *gèng*-sentences   181

10 Factive "*jíshǐ p, yě q*"   217

11 Investigation into concessive complex sentence forms   243

12 Outline of adversative sentence forms   269

Index   300

Diagrams

8.1   Formation of "*bùdàn bù p, fǎn'ér q*"   165

11.1   Position of *suīrán*-sentences and *jíshǐ*-sentences in tripartite classification   247

12.1   Steps of checking whether *què* can be present in hypothetical sentences with *rúguǒ*   297

Tables

2.1	Sub-forms of "*p, fǒuzé q*"	57
9.1	"gèng" complex sentences in modern Chinese	214
11.1	Commonalities among concessive sentences	244
11.2	Inconsistency in classification	245
11.3	Conflicts between classification criteria	246
11.4	Subtypes of concessive complex sentences	256

1 "*p, dànshì q*" and relevant forms

This chapter is devoted to the discussions of some particular forms of adversative complex sentences, with "... *dànshì*..." ('but') being the typical marker of the prototypical adversative sentences.

The chapter is divided into three sections: i) "*p, dànshì q*" ('*p*, but *q*'); ii) "*p, bùguò q*" ('*p*, though *q*'); iii) comparisons between "*p, dànshì q*" and "*suīrán p, dànshì q*" ('*although *p*, but *q*').

1.1 "*p, dànshì q*"

As a prototypical form of adversative complex sentences, "*p, dànshì q*" indicates that an adversative relationship exists between the anterior and the posterior clauses, without any foreshadowing adversative indicators.

1.1.1 About dànshì

The connective *dànshì* is used to form the most typical adversative complex sentences in the strict sense. The following are three examples:

(1) 外国的经验可以借鉴，<u>但是</u>绝对不能照搬。
Wàiguó   de jīngyàn   kěyǐ jièjiàn,   <u>dànshì</u> juéduì   bù
foreign country SP experience can use for reference but   definitely NEG
néng zhàobān.
can   copy
{Foreign experience can be used for reference, but definitely cannot be copied.}

(2) 前进的道路并不平坦，<u>但是</u>我们相信这十年好的形势能够继续发展下去。
Qiánjìn de dàolù bìng   bù   píngtǎn, <u>dànshì</u> wǒ-men xiāngxìn zhè shí
advance SP road indeed NEG smooth but   we   believe   this ten
nián hǎo de xíngshì   nénggòu jìxù   fāzhǎn-xiàqù.
year good SP situation can   continue continue to develop
{The road ahead is indeed not smooth, but we believe that the good situation in the past decade will continue to gain momentum.}

DOI: 10.4324/9781003374237-1

2 "p, dànshì q" and relevant forms

(3) 她想笑，<u>但是</u>笑不出。

Tā xiǎng xiào, <u>dànshì</u> xiào bù chū.
she want smile but cannot smile
{She wanted to smile, but she couldn't.}

The word *dàn* often occurs in the position of *dànshì*, as in the following example:

(4) 邮差是信使，<u>但</u>真正快乐的天使是她。

Yóuchāi shì xìnshǐ, <u>dàn</u> zhēnzhèng kuàilè de tiānshǐ shì tā.
postman COP messenger but real happy SP angle COP her
{Mailmen are messengers, but the real happy angel is her.}

In some cases, although *dàn* precedes *shì*, *dàn* and *shì* do not form the word *dànshì*. This happens when *shì* is a copular verb and followed by a noun phrase, as in the following example:

(5) 中国是个贫弱国家，<u>但</u>是个独立自主的国家。

*Zhōngguó shì gè pínruò guójiā, <u>dàn</u> **shì** gè dúlì-zìzhǔ de guójiā.*
China COP CL poor and weak country but COP CL independent SP country
{China is a poor and weak country, but it is an independent one.}

In the above example, "*dàn shì*" means "*dànshì shì*" ('*but be'), thus (5) could be rewritten as (6):

(6) 中国是个贫弱国家，<u>但是</u>，是个独立自主的国家。

*Zhōngguó shì gè Pínruò guójiā, <u>dànshì</u>, **shì** gè dúlì-zìzhǔ de*
China COP CL poor and weak country but COP CL independent SP
guójiā.
country
{China is a poor and weak country, but it is an independent one.}

Synonyms of *dànshì* that can be used as adversative markers include *kěshì* ('but'), *kě* ('but'), *rán'ér* ('but'), *bùguò* ('though'), *zhǐshì* ('only'), *jiùshì* ('only'), *què* ('however'), and so on. The following are seven examples:

(7) 本来潘树林打完了可以跑，<u>可是</u>有孙燕在场他就不能跑了。

Běnlái Pān Shùlín dǎ-wán-le kěyǐ pǎo, <u>kěshì</u> yǒu
originally PAN Shulin finish fighting-PEF can run away but there be
Sūn Yàn zàichǎng tā jiù bù néng pǎo le.
SUN Yan be present he then NEG can run away MP
{PAN Shulin would have been able to run away after the fight, but he couldn't because SUN Yan was there.}

"p, dànshì q" and relevant forms   3

(8)   许哥本不愿这样，<u>可</u>他实在没办法。
Xǔ gē   běn   bù   yuàn   zhèyàng, <u>kě</u> tā shízài méi   bànfǎ.
XU brother originally NEG want to this   but he really not have way
{Brother XU didn't want to do this, but he really had no other way.}

(9)   女儿话里的辛辣味儿令她反感，<u>然而</u>不能说这些话没有一点道理。
Nǚ'ér   huà-lǐ   de xīnlà wèir   lìng tā   fǎngǎn, <u>rán'ér</u> bù   néng
daughter in words SP spicy flavor make her disgust but   NEG   can
shuō zhèxiē huà   méiyǒu   yīdiǎn dàolǐ.
say   these words there not be a little truth
{The pungency of her daughter's remarks repelled her, but there was some truth
in what she said.}

(10) 张二娃对"早点"这个词是很陌生的，<u>不过</u>，他猜想"早点"大概就是早饭吧！
Zhāng Èrwá   duì   "zǎodiǎn" zhè gè cí   shì hěn mòshēng de, <u>bùguò</u>,
ZHANG Erwa with breakfast   this CL word COP very unfamiliar SP though
tā cāixiǎng "zǎodiǎn" dàgài   jiù shì zǎofàn   ba!
he guess   breakfast probable just COP morning meal MP
{ZHANG Erwa was unfamiliar with the word "breakfast", though he guessed that
"breakfast" was probably the morning meal!}

(11) 你有问必答就是了，<u>只是</u>不要冒犯她的忌讳。
Nǐ   yǒuwèn-bìdá   jiùshìle, <u>zhǐshì</u> bùyào màofàn tā   de jìhuì.
you answer all the questions MP   only   do not offend she SP taboo
{Just answer all the questions, only don't touch her sore point.}

(12) 妈连开飞机的胆都有，<u>就是</u>没有闲工夫，……
Mā   lián... dōu... kāi   fēijī   de dǎn   dōu yǒu, <u>jiùshì</u> méiyǒu
mother even ...   operate airplane SP courage   have but   not have
xián gōngfu ...
free time
{Mom even has the guts to fly a plane, but she has no spare time. . .}

(13) 她眼里含着泪花，<u>却</u>勉强笑着。
Tā yǎn-lǐ hán-zhe   lèihuā, <u>què</u>   miǎnqiǎng   xiào-zhe.
she in eye hold-PRG tear   however managing with an effort smile-PRG
{With tears in her eyes, she managed to smile.}

Among all the markers mentioned above, *dànshì*, *kěshì*, and *rán'ér* are conjunctions, and they often collocate with the linking adverb *què* in the posterior
clause, as in the following two examples:

4 *"p, dànshì q" and relevant forms*

(14) 您为我操劳，含辛茹苦，<u>但</u>您<u>却</u>从未想到，有些事本该是我自己做的呀。

Nín wèi wǒ cāoláo,   hánxīn-rúkǔ,   <u>dàn</u> nín <u>què</u>   cóngwèi
you for me work hard endure all kinds of hardships but you however never
xiǎng-dào, yǒuxiē shì   běn   gāi   shì wǒ zìjǐ   zuò de ya.
think of   some   thing originally should COP me oneself do MP MP
{You've worked so hard and put up so much for me, but it has never occurred to
you that there are things I should do by myself.}

(15) 我没来过这山村，<u>但</u>对连贯这一带村子的这条山区铁路<u>却</u>很熟悉。

Wǒ méi   lái-guò   zhè shāncūn,   <u>dàn</u> duì   liánguàn zhè yīdài
I   NEG come-EXP this mountain village but with connect   this area
cūnzi de   zhè tiáo   shānqū   tiělù   <u>què</u>   hěn shúxī.
village SP this CL mountain area railway however very familiar
{I have never been to this mountain village, but I am very familiar with the
mountain railroad that connects the villages in this area.}

1.1.2 Semantic basis for "p, dànshì q"

In general, the semantic bases for "*p, dànshì q*" are the contrast and opposition
between *p* and *q*, and the bases fall into three types.

First, direct contrast. In this type, *p* and *q* respectively denote two opposing
matters or situations, as in the following two examples:

(16) 画家都应该是勤于观察的，<u>但</u>也有一些闭门造车的画家。

Huàjiā dōu yīnggāi shì   qín   yú guānchá de, <u>dàn</u> yě   yǒu   yīxiē
painter all   should   COP diligent in observe MP but also there be some
bìmén-zàochē   de huàjiā.
shut oneself up in a room making a cart SP painter
{Painters are supposed to be diligent observers, but there are some painters who
paint only by imagination.}

(17) 事实明摆着，这孙大拿是假货，<u>可</u>共产党是真的。

Shìshí míngbǎizhe, zhè Sūn Dàná shì   jiǎhuò,   <u>kě</u> Gòngchǎndǎng shì
truth be obvious this SUN Dana COP dishonest but Communist Party COP
zhēn de.
honest SP
{It is obvious that SUN Dana is dishonest, but the Communist Party is honest.}

Second, contrastive causality. In this type, *q* can be regarded as the opposite
of the effect caused by *p*. To be more accurate, if *p* is understood as the cause in
an instance of the cause-effect relationship, *q* is the opposite of the effect in that
relationship. The following are two examples:

(18) 他白发如雪，<u>但</u>精神矍铄。

Tā bái   fà   rú   xuě,   <u>dàn</u> jīngshén-juéshuò.
he white hair be like snow but hale and hearty
{His hair is as white as snow, but he is hale and hearty.}

"p, dànshì q" and relevant forms   5

(19) 他的作品我见得很少，<u>但</u>每幅都给我留下了相当深的印象。

Tā   de   zuòpǐn   wǒ   jiàn   de   hěn   shǎo,   <u>dàn</u>   měi   fú   dōu   gěi   wǒ
he   SP   work   I   see   SP   very   few   but   every   CL   all   on   me

liúxià-le   xiāngdāng   shēn   de   yìnxiàng.
leave-PEF   considerable   deep   SP   impression

{I have seen very few of his works, but each of those I have seen left a deep impression on me.}

Third, slight contrast. In this type, *p* and *q* coexist with a slight contrast but without major opposition. In sentences in the form of *"p, dànshì q"*, *q* modifies or supplements *p*, as in the following two examples:

(20) 改革中，可能会出现这样那样的小毛病，<u>但是</u>不要紧。

Gǎigé-zhōng,   kěnéng   huì   chūxiàn   zhèyàng   nàyàng   de   xiǎo   máobìng,   <u>dànshì</u>
in reform   may   will   occur   this   that   SP   minor   problem   but

bùyàojǐn.
unimportant

{In the course of the reform, there may occur minor problems of one kind or another, but that doesn't matter.}

(21) "一国两制"，是从我们自己的实际提出来的，<u>但是</u>这个思路可以延伸到某些国际问题的处理上。

"Yīguó-liǎngzhì",   shì   cóng   wǒ-men   zìjǐ   de   shíjì   tí-chūlái
one country, two system   COP   from   our   oneself   SP   reality   put forward

de,   <u>dànshì</u>   zhè   gè   sīlù   kěyǐ   yánshēn-dào   mǒu   xiē   guójì   wèntí   de
SP   but   this   CL   idea   can   extend to   certain   CL   international   issue   SP

chǔlǐ   shàng.
handle   LOC

{The initiative of "One country, two systems" was put forward on the basis of our own reality, but this idea can be extended to the handling of some international issues.}

1.1.3   Differences between adversative conjunctions and què

In some cases, the linking adverb *què* can be used interchangeably with the adversative conjunction *dànshì* or any of its synonyms, such as *kěshì* and *rán'ér*. The following are two examples:

(22) 您对我的生活关怀得无微不至，<u>却</u>很少询问我的思想情况。

Nín   duì   wǒ   de   shēnghuó   guānhuái   de   wúwēi-bùzhì,   <u>què</u>   hěn   shǎo
you   for   I   SP   life   care   SP   meticulous   however   very   seldom

xúnwèn   wǒ   de   sīxiǎng   qíngkuàng.
ask   I   SP   thought   situation

{You care for every aspect of my life, but rarely ask me about my thoughts.}

6 *"p, dànshì q" and relevant forms*

(23) 婉本能地伸出双手去抓房脊，<u>却</u>没抓牢，结果朝房下滚去。

Wǎn běnnéng   de shēn-chū shuāngshǒu qù zhuā fángjǐ,   <u>què</u>   méi
Wan instinctively SP stretch out both hands go grasp roof ridge however NEG

zhuā-láo,   jiéguǒ cháo   fáng-xià   gǔn-qù.
hold tightly so that toward under roof roll

{Wan instinctively stretched out her hands to grab the roof ridge, but failed to hold it firmly, so she rolled and fell off the roof.}

The connective *dàn* can occur in place of *què* in either of these two examples, but there are still a number of differences between them.

First, differences in usage. If the posterior clause includes the subject or an adverbial denoting location, time, or recipient of the action, or consists of a construction indicating when or in what sense, the word *què* needs to follow these elements and cannot be replaced by *dàn*. The following are two examples:

(24) 他身上有那么多刺，我<u>却</u>喜欢和他在一起。

Tā shēn-shàng yǒu   nàme duō cì,   wǒ <u>què</u>   xǐhuān hé   tā
he on body   there be so   many thorn I   however like   with him

zài   yīqǐ.
at   together

{He is so rebellious, but I enjoy being with him.}

(25) 我能下地了，做田里活<u>却</u>不便了。

Wǒ néng xiàdì   le, zuò tián-lǐ huó <u>què</u>   bù   biàn le.
I   can   get out of bed MP do in field work however NEG easy MP

{I can get out of bed now, but can't easily do farm work.}

In (24) and (25), *dàn* cannot occur in place of *què*. The following are four more examples:

(26) 他平时口才很好，这会儿<u>却</u>结结巴巴讲不出话来。

Tā píngshí   kǒucái   hěn hǎo, zhèhuìr   <u>què</u>   jiējiē-bābā
he ordinary times oral expression very good this moment however stammer

jiǎng bù chū huà   lái.
cannot speak   DP

{He is usually very eloquent, but now he is stammering and unable to speak.}

(27) 他平时口才很好，在领导面前<u>却</u>不敢开口。

Tā píngshí   kǒucái   hěn hǎo, zài lǐngdǎo miànqián <u>què</u>   bù
he ordinary times oral expression very good at   leader   before face however NEG

gǎn   kāikǒu.
dare   speak

{He is usually very eloquent, but dare not speak in front of his boss.}

"*p, dànshì q*" and relevant forms   7

(28)　他平时口才很好，对她却像一个不善于表达的小学生。

Tā píngshí　　kǒucái　　 hěn hǎo, duì tā què　 xiàng yī gè
he ordinary times oral expression very good to her however be like one CL
bù　 shànyú　 biǎodá　 de xiǎoxuéshēng.
NEG be good at express SP elementary school student
{He is usually very eloquent, but when speaking to her, he is like an elementary school kid who is not good at expressing himself.}

(29)　他平时口才很好，讲起课来却总是条理不清。

Tā　 píngshí　　 kǒucái　　　 hěn　 hǎo, jiǎng qǐ kè lái
he　 ordinary times　 oral expression　 very　 good start and continue to teach
què　　 zǒngshì　 tiáolǐ　　　 bù　 qīng.
however always　 train of thought　 NEG　 clear
{He is usually very eloquent, but becomes incoherent whenever he starts to teach.}

The word *què* cannot be substituted by *dàn* in any of the aforementioned examples.

Second, differences in function. The word *què* marks the turning point in meaning, but *dànshì* and its synonyms highlight the boundary of the contrast between the two clauses. The following is an example:

(30)　地方不大，布置得却精致匀称。

Dìfāng　 bù　　 dà,　 bùzhì　　 de　 què　　 jīngzhì　　 yúnchèn.
area　　 NEG　 big　 decorate　 SP　 however　 delicate　　 well balanced
{(Its) area isn't big, but its decoration is exquisite and well balanced.}

In the above example, *què*, which precedes the complement "*jīngzhì yúnchèn*" ('exquisite and well balanced'), marks the turning point. The following are five examples with the cooccurrence of *què* and *dànshì*:

(31)　她已经多年不出远门，感到什么都有点新奇，但有时却又忘了是在旅行中。

Tā yǐjīng　 duō nián bù　　 chū yuǎn mén, gǎndào shénme　 dōu yǒudiǎn
she already many years NEG travel far　　 feel　　 anything　 all　 a little
xīnqí, dàn yǒushí　 què　　 yòu　　　　　　 wàng-le　 shì　 zài
novel but sometimes however on the other hand forget-PEF COP at
lǚxíng-zhōng.
during trip
{She hasn't traveled far for many years, so everything looks a bit novel to her, but sometimes she forgets that she is traveling.}

(32)　她端坐在那儿，一动也未动，但在脑海里却忽然掀起一片片疑云。

Tā duānzuò zài nàr, yī-dòng yě wèi-dòng, dàn zài nǎohǎi-lǐ què　　 hūrán
she sit up　 at there not move at all　　　 but at in mind however suddenly

8 *"p, dànshì q" and relevant forms*

xiān-qǐ yī piàn-piàn yíyún.
rise one CL-REDP cloud of suspicion
{She sat upright there, motionless, but suddenly clouds of suspicion arose in her mind.}

(33) 大怪物只须一踏，就可轧扁它们，<u>然而</u>它们置身于大怪物之前<u>却</u>异常镇静，毫无顾忌，真令人惊讶。

Dà guàiwù zhǐ xū yī tà, jiù kě yà-biǎn tā-men, <u>rán'ér</u> tā-men
big monster only need one step on then can squash them but they
zhìshēnyú dà guàiwù zhī qián <u>què</u> yìcháng zhènjìng, háo wú gùjì,
put oneself at big monster SP front however unusual calm a bit NEG scruple
zhēn lìng rén jīngyà.
really make person surprised
{The big monster can squash them with a single step, but they are surprisingly calm and fearless in front of the big monster.}

(34) 他反对我流"咸水"，<u>但</u>说起这些事情，我<u>却</u>发现他的眼眶会突然潮湿起来。

Tā fǎnduì wǒ liú "xiánshuǐ", <u>dàn</u> shuō-qǐ zhèxiē
he oppose me shed salty water but start and continue to talk about those
shìqing, wǒ <u>què</u> fāxiàn tā de yǎnkuàng huì tūrán cháoshī-qǐlái.
thing I however discover he SP rim of the eye will sudden start to be moist
{He objected to me shedding "salty water", but when we were talking about those things, I found that his eyes would suddenly get moist.}

(35) 他也许有点婆婆妈妈，有点儿女情长，<u>但</u>在工作上，他要认准了怎么干，<u>却</u>是轻易不动摇的。

Tā yěxǔ yǒudiǎn pópó-māmā, yǒudiǎn érnǚ-qíngcháng, <u>dàn</u> zài
he perhaps a little womanishly fussy a little overvaluing emotions but at
gōngzuò-shàng, tā yào rènzhǔn-le zěnme gàn, <u>què</u> shì qīngyì bù
at work he once firmly believe-PEF how do however COP easily NEG
dòngyáo de.
shake MP
{He may be a little fussy like a woman and may overvalue emotions, but workwise once he has an idea about how to do something, he won't change his mind easily.}

In the five aforementioned examples, *dànshì* or its synonym occurs and indicates that there is an adversative relationship between the two clauses. However, following the adverbial of time or location, or the predicative structure, *què* marks the turning point and highlights what exactly the antithesis is. In other words, *dànshì* and its synonyms mark the boundary of the opposition, whereas *què* exhibits the opposition. The following is another example:

(36) 有人提出冷占国，<u>但是</u>大多数委员不同意，<u>却</u>选择了胡万通。

Yǒu rén tíchū Lěng Zhànguó, <u>dànshì</u> dàduōshù wěiyuán
there be person nominate LENG Zhanguo but majority committee member

"*p, dànshì q*" and relevant forms   9

| bù | tóngyì, | *què* | xuǎnzé-le | Hú Wàntōng. |
| NEG | agree | however | choose-PEF | HU Wantong |

{Some people nominated LENG Zhanguo, but most of the committee members disagreed and chose HU Wantong instead.}

In the aforementioned example, *dànshì* marks the boundary of the opposition between "some people nominated LENG Zhanguo" and "most of the committee members disagreed and chose HU Wantong instead", whereas *què* exhibits the content of the opposition, i.e., "chose HU Wantong".

Third, differences in range of application. Generally, *què* can be used on more occasions than *dànshì*. In some cases, *què* is equivalent to *fǎn'ér* ('on the contrary'), and in these cases it cannot be replaced by *dàn*. The following is an example:

(37) 昨晚，从医院看了罗先敏出来，他没有去女儿家，却一头钻进了矿井里，和做夜班的矿工们一起，在电煤钻的呼啸声中过了一夜。

| *Zuówǎn,* | *cóng yīyuàn* | *kàn-le* | *Luó Xiānmín* | *chūlái,* | *tā méiyǒu* | *qù* |
| last night | from hospital | see-PEF | LUO Xianmin | come out | he NEG | go |

| *nǚ'ér jiā,* | *què* | *yītóu* | *zuān-jìn-le* | *kuàngjǐng-lǐ,* | *hé* | *zuò yèbān* |
| daughter's home | however | headlong | go into-PEF | in pit | and | do night shift |

| *de kuànggōng-men yīqǐ,* | *zài diànméizuàn* | *de* | *hūxiàoshēng-zhōng* |
| SP miner-PL | together | at electric coal drill | SP | in roar |

| *guò-le* | *yī* | *yè.* |
| spend-PEF | one | night |

{Last night, after visiting LUO Xianmin in the hospital, instead of going to his daughter's house, he went headlong for the pit, and spent the night in the roar of the electric coal drills with the miners on night shift.}

In the aforementioned example, *què* can be replaced by *fǎn'ér*, but not by *dàn*. The following is an example:

(38) 一个市委书记的千金小姐，怎么会看中一个下贱的罪犯，却反而看不上省委书记的儿子？

| *Yī* | *gè* | *shìwěi* | *shūjì* | *de* | *qiānjīn xiǎojiě,* | *zěnme* | *huì* |
| one | CL | municipal party committee | secretary | SP | daughter | why | can |

| *kàn-zhòng yī* | *gè* | *xiàjiàn de* | *zuìfàn,* | *què* | *fǎn'ér* | *kàn bù shàng* |
| prefer | one | CL lowly | SP criminal | however | on the contrary | despise |

| *shěngwěi* | *shūjì* | *de* | *érzi?* |
| provincial party committee | secretary | SP | son |

{How could the daughter of a municipal Party Secretary prefer a lowly criminal, but despise the son of a provincial Party Secretary?}

In the aforementioned example, *què* and *fǎn'ér* cooccur, with almost the same function. Between the two words, *què* emphasizes the direct contrast, whereas *fǎn'ér* stresses the counter-expectation, but either of them can be deleted with the meaning of the sentence remaining the same. In this sentence, *què* cannot be substituted by *dàn*.

10 *"p, dànshì q"* and relevant forms

1.2 *"p, bùguò q"*

The form *"p, bùguò q"* is a sub-class of *"p, dànshì q"*. However, the contrast indicated by the former is slighter by the contrast indicated by the latter.

1.2.1 About bùguò

There are two different cases in which *bùguò* indicates a slight contrast.

First, *bùguò* indicates a partial contrast. In sentences in the form of *"p, bùguò q"*, the posterior clause modifies the anterior clause in a certain aspect or from a certain perspective. Some modal words, such as *bàle* and *jiùshìle*, can occur at the end of the posterior clause to highlight "to a certain degree". The following are three examples:

(39)　小孟也来了，<u>不过</u>她来得迟得多。

Xiǎo Mèng　yě　lái-le,　　<u>bùguò</u>　tā　lái　　de　chí　de　duō.
little MENG　also　come-PEF　though　she　come　SP　late　SP　much
{Little MENG also came, though much later.}

(40)　钱先生果真下了牢，<u>不过</u>还没有受刑。

Qián xiānshēng　guǒzhēn　xià-le láo,　　　bùguò　hái　méiyǒu
QIAN mister　　indeed　be put in prison-PEF　though　still　NEG
shòuxíng.
receive corporal punishment
{Mr. Qian has indeed been put in prison, though he hasn't suffered corporal punishment yet.}

(41)　我也曾有过一位"有方"的老师，<u>不过</u>她不是什么有名的人物，只是一个大我几岁的女孩子。

Wǒ　yě　céng　yǒu-guò　yī　wèi "yǒufāng"　　de lǎoshī, bùguò tā
I　also　once　have-EXP　one　CL　have proper method SP teacher though she
bù　shì　shénme yǒumíng de rénwù, zhǐ shì yī gè dà wǒ jǐ　suì de
NEG COP any　　famous　SP figure　only COP one CL old me several year SP
nǚháizi.
girl
{I once had a teacher who was very good (at teaching), though she was not a famous person but just a girl a few years older than me.}

These three examples respectively indicate a partial contrast in time, manner, and age. Either *bàle* or *jiùshìle* can be present at the end of each example. The following are another two examples:

(42)　······省委业已批准，<u>不过</u>没有下文<u>罢了</u>。

... shěngwěi　　　yèyǐ　pīzhǔn, bùguò méiyǒu xiàwén　　bàle.
provincial party committee already approve though NEG　issue a document MP
{… it has been approved by the provincial Party Committee, though the document hasn't been issued yet.}

"p, dànshì q" and relevant forms   11

(43)　"望气"、取得"感性认识"什么的，我也有这种经验，<u>不过</u>没有你说的那样明白<u>就是了</u>。

"Wàngqì", qǔdé "gǎnxìng rènshi" 　　　 *shénmede,　wǒ　yě　　yǒu　zhè　zhǒng*
observe Qi　gain　perceptual knowledge　and the like　I　also　have　this　kind
jīngyàn,　　bùguò　　méiyǒu　　nǐ　　shuō　de　nàyàng　míngbai　jiùshìle.
experience　though　not have　you　say　SP　that　clear　MP
{I also have the experience of "observing Qi", gaining "perceptual knowledge", and the like, though I can't verbalize it as clearly as you do.}

In (42), *bàle* occurs at the end; so does *jiùshìle* in (43).

If *bàle* or *jiùshìle* is absent in a sentence in the form of *"p, bùguò q"*, the posterior clause only modifies the anterior clause; if *bàle* or *jiùshìle* is present, the posterior clause emphasizes the firm tone in what is stated in the anterior clause apart from modifying the anterior clause. The following is an example:

(44)　……箱子底下压了多少人民币，甚至连五元的有多少张，十元的有多少张，老汉心里都清楚得像镜子，还用得着瞒吗？<u>不过</u>他不打算向儿子说破这一层<u>罢了</u>。

... xiāngzi díxià　　yā-le　　duōshǎo　rénmínbì, shènzhì lián... dōu... wǔ
cabinet　bottom　press-PEF　how much　RMB　even　even　　five
yuán de yǒu　　duōshǎo　zhāng, shí yuán de yǒu　　duōshǎo　zhāng,
yuan SP there be　how many　CL　ten yuan SP there be　how many　CL
lǎohàn　xīn-lǐ　dōu qīngchǔ de xiàng　jìngzi,　hái　yòng de zháo mán
old man　in heart　clear　SP be like glass　still　need　conceal
ma? Bùguò　tā　bù　dǎsuàn xiàng érzi shuō-pò　zhè yī　céng bàle.
MP　though　he NEG intend to　son be explicit this one CL　MP
{… the old man knows clearly how much cash is hidden at the bottom of the cabinet, even how many five-*yuan* notes and how many ten-*yuan* notes, though he doesn't want to make it explicit to his son. Therefore, there is no need for the son to conceal it from the father.}

The above example is a sentence group, but it can be rewritten as a complex sentence, as in the following:

(45)　这一切老汉心里都清楚得像镜子，<u>不过</u>他不打算向儿子说破这一层<u>罢了</u>。

Zhè yīqiè　　lǎohàn xīn-lǐ　dōu qīngchǔ de xiàng jìngzi, bùguò tā bù
this everything old man in heart all　clear　SP be like glass　though he NEG
dǎsuàn xiàng érzi shuō-pò　zhè yī　céng bàle.
intend　to　son be explicit this one CL　MP
{The old man knows everything clearly, though he doesn't want to make it explicit to his son.}

In (45), with the presence of *bàle*, the posterior clause supplements "the old man knows everything clearly" and meanwhile it emphasizes that "the old man undoubtedly knows everything clearly"; without *bàle*, the posterior clause would only supplement the anterior clause.

12 *"p, dànshì q"* and relevant forms

Second, *bùguò* marks a reduced contrast. In other words, a sharp contrast exists between the two clauses, but the use of *bùguò* softens the tone, hence the contrast is reduced. In sentences where *bùguò* marks a reduced contrast, *bàle* or *jiùshìle* cannot be present. The following are two examples:

(46) 他俩都知道这个事弄不好会掉脑袋，<u>不过</u>俩人都毫不迟疑地把担子担了起来。

Tā liǎ   dōu zhīdào zhè gè shì   nòng bù hǎo   huì diào nǎodai,
the two of them both know this CL matter not handled properly will get beheaded
bùguò liǎ rén   dōu háo bù   chíyí   de bǎ dànzi   dān-le   qǐlái.
though two person both a bit NEG hesitate SP BA responsibility take-PEF DC
{Both of them knew that they would get beheaded if they couldn't handle the matter properly, though they both took the responsibility without hesitation.}

(47) 这些年来，你吃了不少苦；<u>不过</u>，总算挺过来了。

Zhèxiē nián lái,   nǐ   chī-le   bùshǎo kǔ;   bùguò, zǒngsuàn
these   year since you suffer-PEF many   hardship but   eventually
tǐng-guòlái   le.
come through PEF
{You suffered a lot over the years, though eventually you've come through.}

In (46), it is a sharp contrast between "knowing that they would get beheaded if they couldn't handle the matter properly" and "taking the responsibility without hesitation". If *dànshì* or *rán'ér* was present, the sharp contrast would be manifested; however, *bùguò* reduces the sharp contrast. In (47), there exists a strong contrast between "suffering a lot over the years" and "coming through", but *bùguò* lessens the contrast by transferring the emphasis to the relief of all the hardships. Therefore, *bàle* or *jiùshìle* cannot be used in (46) or (47).

In conclusion, *bùguò* indicates a slight contrast in terms of degree or in tone.

1.2.2 *"p, zhǐshì q" and "p, bùguò q"*

The form *"p, zhǐshì q"* marks a partial contrast, with the modal particle *bàle* or *jiùshìle* occurring at the end of the posterior clause in some cases. The following are two examples:

(48) 数目都能报销，<u>只是</u>要经过单位会计仔细盘查<u>罢了</u>。

Shùmù dōu néng bàoxiāo, zhǐshì yào jīngguò dānwèi kuàijì   zǐxì
amount all can reimburse only need by   company accountant careful
pánchá bàle.
check   MP
{All the expenses can be reimbursed, only they have to be carefully checked by the accountant of the company.}

"p, dànshì q" and relevant forms 13

(49) 蹬凤凰牌单车一样活着，<u>只是</u>没有那样神气<u>罢了</u>！
Dēng Fènghuáng pái dānchē yīyàng huó-zhe, <u>zhǐshì</u> méiyǒu nàyàng shénqì <u>bàle!</u>
ride Phoenix brand bicycle same live-PRG only NEG so proud MP
{One can still get around by riding a Phoenix bicycle, only they don't have that air of pride!}

The modal particle *bàle* occurs at the end of both aforementioned examples. Even if *bàle* or its synonym is absent in a sentence marking a partial contrast, it can be added and placed at the end of the sentence. The following are two examples:

(50) 他们就这样相爱，<u>只是</u>爱的方式与一般在校大学生不一样，（不张扬，不黏乎，不疯傻。）
Tā-men jiù zhèyàng xiāng'ài, <u>zhǐshì</u> ài de fāngshì yǔ yībān zàixiào
they just so love each other only love SP way as general at college
dàxuéshēng bù yīyàng, (bù zhāngyáng, bù niánhu, bù
college student NEG same NEG make widely known NEG clinging NEG
fēngshǎ.)
crazy and silly
{They just love each other this way, only their way of love is different from college students in general: low key, not clinging to each other all day long, or crazy, or silly.}

(51) 两个人依旧来往，<u>只是</u>贴心话比以前少了。
Liǎng gè rén yījiù láiwǎng, <u>zhǐshì</u> tiēxīn huà bǐ yǐqián shǎo le.
two CL person still be in contact only intimate words than before few MP
{The two are still in contact, only they are not as intimate as before.}

In the two examples above, *bàle* or *jiùshìle* can be respectively added and placed at the end of the posterior clause.

The two forms, "*p, zhǐshì q*" and "*p, bùguò q*", differ in the following two aspects.

First, "*p, zhǐshì q*" does not indicate a reduced contrast, but "*p, bùguò q*" can. Modal particles, such as *bàle* and *jiùshìle*, can only be present in sentences in the form of "*p, zhǐshì q*".

Second, both "*p, zhǐshì q*" and "*p, bùguò q*" can mark partial contrast, but the contrast in "*p, zhǐshì q*" is even less sharp than that in "*p, bùguò q*". If the subject in a sentence in the form of "*p, zhǐshì q*" is a person, the comment sounds generous and benevolent. If the sentence is used to persuade someone, the persuasion sounds tactful and diplomatic. The following are two examples:

(52) 老崔热情淳厚，有组织才能，<u>只是</u>对知识不求甚解。
Lǎo Cuī rèqíng chúnhòu, yǒu zǔzhī cáinéng, <u>zhǐshì</u> duì
old CUI warm-hearted simple, honest and kind have organize ability only of

14 *"p, dànshì q" and relevant forms*

zhīshi   bùqiúshènjiě.
knowledge be content with superficial understanding
{Old CUI is warm-hearted, simple, honest, kind, and has organizational skills, only he is content with superficial understanding of knowledge.}

(53) 你做得对，<u>只是</u>不应该吵架。

Nǐ   zuò   de   duì,   <u>zhǐshì</u>   bù   yīnggāi   chǎojià.
you do   SP   right   only   NEG   should   quarrel
{You did it right, only you shouldn't have quarreled.}

With *zhǐshì*, the speaker of (52) touches on the subject' shortcoming but with the implication of understanding and sympathy. In (53), with *zhǐshì*, the speaker's advice sounds gentle and tactful.

In some cases, *zhǐshì* and *bùguò* can be combined into a phrasal word *"zhǐ bùguò"* ('only'), which can also mark a partial contrast. Modal particles such as *bàle* and *jiùshìle* can occur at the end of the posterior clause in sentences in the form of *"p, zhǐ bùguò q"*. The following are three examples:

(54) 其实，我并不是有心栽蒲公英的，<u>只不过</u>任它繁殖<u>罢了</u>。

Qíshí,   wǒ   bìng   bù   shì   yǒuxīn zāi   púgōngyīng de,   <u>zhǐ bùguò</u> rèn tā
actually I   indeed NEG COP intend plant dandelion   MP   only   let it
fánzhí   <u>bàle</u>.
reproduce MP
{In fact, I didn't mean to raise the dandelions, only I just let them reproduce.}

(55) 他还是从前那样，矜持、骄傲、目空一切，<u>只不过</u>现在的心更狠些<u>罢了</u>。

Tā   háishi cóngqián nàyàng, jīnchí,   jiāo'ào,   mùkōngyīqiè,   <u>zhǐ bùguò</u>
he   still   before   that   reserved conceited arrogant   only
xiànzài de   xīn   gèng   hěn   xiē   <u>bàle</u>.
now   SP   heart more ruthless a bit MP
{He is as reserved, conceited, and arrogant as before, only he is more ruthless.}

(56) 我们的纺织工业向来是习惯大批量生产，利润大，麻烦小，<u>只不过</u>打不进国际市场<u>罢了</u>。

Wǒ-men de   fǎngzhī gōngyè xiànglái shì   xíguàn   dàpīliàng shēngchǎn, lìrùn
we   SP   textile   industry always COP be used to mass   production profit
dà,   máfan   xiǎo,   <u>zhǐ bùguò</u> dǎ bù jìn   guójì   shìchǎng   <u>bàle</u>.
high   trouble little   only   cannot enter international market   MP
{Our textile industry has always been accustomed to mass production, with high profits and little trouble, only it just can't enter the international market.}

The modal particle *bàle* occurs at the end of each example, and *"zhǐ bùguò"* in each of them can be replaced by *zhǐshì* or *bùguò*.

1.2.3 Comparisons between "*p, jiùq*" and "*p, zhǐshì q*" / "*p, bùguò q*"

In some cases, "*p, jiùshì q*" indicates a partial contrast. Compare the following sentences:

(57) 这孩子不错，<u>就是</u>不怎么聪明。
     Zhè   háizi   bùcuò,   <u>jiùshì</u>   bù   zěnme   cōngmíng.
     this   child   quite good   but   NEG   to a certain degree   smart
     {This kid is quite good, but not so smart.}

(58) 这孩子不错，<u>只是</u>不怎么聪明。
     Zhè   háizi   bùcuò,   <u>zhǐshì</u>   bù   zěnme   cōngmíng.
     this   child   quite good   only   NEG   to a certain degree   smart
     {This kid is quite good, only he's not so smart.}

(59) 这孩子不错，<u>不过</u>不怎么聪明。
     Zhè   háizi   bùcuò,   <u>bùguò</u>   bù   zěnme   cōngmíng.
     this   child   quite good   though   NEG   to a certain degree   smart
     {This kid is quite good, though not so smart.}

The three aforementioned examples are practically the same in meaning.

However, *jiùshì* highlights what is stated in the posterior clause even though the contrast between *p* and *q* is not a sharp one. For instance, in (57), the child's disadvantage of not being so smart is brought to light by the word *jiùshì*, but this is not the case for (58) or (59). The following is another example:

(60) 你这人，啥都好，<u>就是</u>脾气赖坏了事。
     Nǐ   zhè   rén,   shá   dōu   hǎo,   <u>jiùshì</u>   píqì   lài   huài-le   shì.
     you   this   person   everything   all   good   but   temper   bad   ruin-PEF   matter
     {You are good in all aspects, but your bad temper often messes things up.}

In the aforementioned example, the speaker uses "*p, jiùshì q*" to indicate a partial and slight contrast between the listener's merit and demerit in the hope that the listener can take the criticism. Thus, the word *jiùshì* reveals the speaker's intention to highlight the listener's defect in the character for him/her to face it.

1.2.4 *zhǐshì, bùguò, zhǐbùguò* as adverbs

In some cases, *zhǐshì* is used an adverb. As a conjunction, *zhǐshì* is synonymous with *dànshì*, *kěshì*, and so on. Although *zhǐshì*, *dànshì*, and *kěshì* differ in tone when indicating a contrast, they can be used interchangeably. However, as an adverb, *zhǐshì* does not indicate a contrast and therefore can only be used interchangeably with *zhǐ*. The following is an example:

16 *"p, dànshì q" and relevant forms*

(61) 大爷像没看见，<u>只是</u>用筷子指指碗、盘，示意我吃菜、吃糕。

Dàye xiàng méi kànjiàn, <u>zhǐshì</u> yòng kuàizi zhǐ-zhǐ wǎn, pán, shìyì
uncle as if NEG see just use chopstick point-REDP bowl plate indicate

wǒ chī cài, chī gāo.
me eat food eat cake

{Uncle didn't seem to notice it, and just motioned me to eat the dishes and cakes by pointing to the bowls and plates with his chopsticks.}

In the above example, *zhǐshì* can be replaced by *zhǐ*.

The adverb *zhǐshì* can collocate with *bàle* or its synonyms in some cases, in which *zhǐshì* can also be replaced by *zhǐ*, as in the following example:

(62) 她的离开，对他来说，<u>只是</u>证明金钱并不是他想象的那样力量无限<u>罢了</u>。

Tā de líkāi, duì... láishuō tā láishuō, <u>zhǐshì</u> zhèngmíng jīnqián bìng bù
she SP leave to him just prove money indeed NEG

shì tā xiǎngxiàng de nàyàng lìliàng wúxiàn <u>bàle</u>.
COP he imagine SP that power infinite MP

{Her departure, to him, only proves that money is not as omnipotent as he imagined.}

The adverb *zhǐshì* is always immediately adjacent to the predicate. If the subject is present in the sentence, the adverb *zhǐshì* follows the subject and can be replaced by *zhǐ*, as in the following example:

(63) 这时，老倔随同大冯赶来了，他<u>只是</u>激动地和石铁握手，紧紧握手。

Zhèshí, lǎo Juè suí tóng dà Féng gǎn-lái-le, tā <u>zhǐshì</u> jīdòng de hé
this moment old JUE follow big FENG come-PEF he just excited SP with

Shí Tiě wòshǒu, jǐn-jǐn wòshǒu.
SHI Tie shake hands tight-REDP shake hands

{At this moment, Old JUE came along with Big FENG, and he just shook hands with SHI Tie excitedly and firmly.}

In this example, *zhǐshì* follows the subject *tā* ('he') and can be replaced by *zhǐ*.

In some cases, *bùguò* and *"zhǐ bùguò"* can also be used as an adverb or an adverbial phrasal word, which can be used in the same way as *zhǐshì*. The following are two examples. In (64), *bùguò* is an adverb, and in (65) *zhǐ bùguò* is an adverbial phrasal word, both of which can be substituted by *zhǐ*.

(64) 对我来说，这<u>不过</u>是一件算不得意外的意外<u>罢了</u>。

Duì... láishuō wǒ láishuō, zhè <u>bùguò</u> shì yī jiàn suàn bù dé
to me this just COP one CL cannot be regarded as

yìwài de yìwài <u>bàle</u>.
unexpected SP accident MP

{To me, this was just a not-so-surprising accident.}

"p, dànshì q" and relevant forms   17

(65)   他本来压根不想给传辉介绍什么对象，<u>只不过</u>把这作为一种助兴的话题<u>而已</u>。

Tā   běnlái   yàgēn bù   xiǎng gěi Chuánhuī jièshào   shénme duìxiàng,
he   originally ever   NEG want to   Chuanhui introduce any   girlfriend

zhǐ bùguò   bǎ   zhè   zuòwéi   yī   zhǒng zhùxìng   de huàtí éryǐ.
just   BA   this   regard as   one   kind   liven things up SP topic MP

{He had no intention of playing matchmaker for Chuanhui, only regarding this as a topic of amusement.}

1.3   Comparisons between *"p, dànshì q"* and *"suīrán p, dànshì q"*

Although *"p, dànshì q"* and *"suīrán p, dànshì q"* can often be used interchangeably, they differ in certain aspects.

1.3.1   About *"suīrán p, dànshì q"*

The conjunction *"suīrán... dànshì..."* is a typical marker for concessive complex sentences, and other markers for concessive complex sentences include *"jíshǐ... yě..."*, *"wúlùn... dōu..."*, *"nìngkě... yě..."*, and so forth. Two points need to be clarified before the discussion of the differences between sentences in the forms of *"suīrán p, dànshì q"* and *"p, dànshì q"*.

First, *"suīrán p, dànshì q"* indicates that in a cause-effect relationship, *q* turns out to be the opposite of the assumed effect caused by *p*. In other words, *q* occurs in spite of *p*. The logical basis for *"suīrán p, dànshì q"* is contrastive causality. Compare the following two examples:

(66)   <u>因为</u>黑夜笼罩着他，<u>所以</u>我看不到他脸上的忧伤。

Yīnwèi   hēiyè lǒngzhào-zhe tā,   suǒyǐ   wǒ kàn bù dào tā liǎn-shàng de
because   night shroud-PRG him   therefore I   cannot see his on face   SP

yōushāng.
sadness

{I couldn't see the sadness on his face because he was in the dark of night.}

(67)   <u>虽然</u>，黑夜笼罩着他，<u>但</u>我仍看到了他脸上的忧伤。

Suīrán,   hēiyè lǒngzhào-zhe tā,   dàn wǒ réng kàn-dào-le tā liǎn-shàng de
although   night shroud-PRG him   but I   still see-PEF   his on face   SP

yōushāng.
sadness

{Although he was in the dark of night, I still saw the sadness on his face.}

In (66), "him being in the dark of night" is the cause of "me being unable to see the sadness on his face". However, in (67), the action of "me seeing the sadness on his face" occurs despite "him being in the dark of night". Thus, the relationship between the two clauses in (67) is contrastive causality.

18 *"p, dànshì q" and relevant forms*

In actual language use, there are two types of contrastive causal relationships on which sentences in the form of *"suīrán p, dànshì q"* are based.

The first type of contrastive causal relationship exists between p and q, i.e., q is the opposite of the effect of p. Therefore, *"suīrán p, dànshì q"* of this type can be understood as "in spite of p, q". For example, (67) can be rewritten as (68):

(68) 虽然黑夜笼罩着他，但我并不因为黑夜笼罩着他而看不到他脸上的忧伤。
Suīrán   hēiyè lǒngzhào-zhe tā, dàn wǒ bìng   bù   <u>yīnwèi</u> hēiyè lǒngzhào-zhe
although night shroud-PRG him but I   indeed NEG because night shroud-PRG
tā,   ér   kàn-bù-dào tā liǎn-shàng de yōushāng.
him therefore cannot see his on face   SP sadness
{Although he was in the dark of night, I didn't fail to see the sadness on his face because of the darkness.}

Compare the following two examples:

(69) <u>虽然</u>这种人在党内外都是极少数，<u>但是</u>应该重视他们的作用。
<u>Suīrán</u> zhè zhǒng rén zài dǎng-nèiwài   dōu shì jí
although this kind person at inside and outside the party both COP extremely
shǎoshù, <u>dànshì</u> yīnggāi zhòngshì   tā-men de zuòyòng.
minority but   should   seriously consider they   SP role
{Although such people are a tiny minority both inside and outside the Party, their role should be considered seriously.}

(70) <u>虽然</u>这几种人在党内外都是极少数，<u>但是</u>不能因为他们是极少数而忽视他们的作用。
<u>Suīrán</u> zhè jǐ   zhǒng rén zài dǎng-nèiwài   dōu shì
although this several kind   person at inside and outside the party both COP
jí   shǎoshù, <u>dànshì</u> bù néng yīnwèi tā-men shì jí   shǎoshù
extremely minority but   NEG can because they   COP extremely minority
ér   hūshì   tā-men de zuòyòng.
then neglect they SP role
{Although such people are a tiny minority both inside and outside the Party, their role shouldn't be neglected only because they are a tiny minority.}

Semantically, (69) and (70) are the same, but the latter displays and highlights the contrastive causal relationship between p and q at the word level.

The second type of contrastive causal relationship does not exist between p and the visible q, but between p and an invisible q, which is an implied effect of the visible q. For the sake of clarity, the visible q is referred to as q_1 and the invisible q as q_2. Therefore, *"suīrán p, dànshì q"* of this type can be understood as "although p, (but) because q_1, then q_2". In this type of contrastive causal relationship, q_2 is a natural result of q_1 but contrasting with p. For example:

"p, dànshì q" and relevant forms **19**

(71) 这种衣料<u>虽然</u>很贵，<u>但</u>质量是上乘的。

Zhè zhǒng yīliào   <u>*suīrán*</u> *hěn guì,*   <u>*dàn*</u> *zhìliàng shì* *shàngchéng de.*
this kind dress material although very expensive but quality COP superb   SP
{This kind of dress material is very expensive, but the quality is superb.}

In the aforementioned example, "superb quality" is not in an opposition to "expensive dress material", but the sentence implies that the dress is still worth buying or that the speaker would like to buy it, thus the sentence can be paraphrased as (72) and (73):

(72) 这种衣料<u>虽然</u>很贵<p>，<u>但</u>质量是上乘的<q_1>，还是很值得买的<q_2>。

Zhè zhǒng yīliào   <u>*suīrán*</u>   *hěn guì* <p>, <u>*dàn*</u> *zhìliàng shì*   *shàngchéng*
this kind   dress material although very expensive but quality COP superior
de <q_1>, *hái shì* *hěn zhídé mǎi de* <q_2>.
MP   still COP very worth buy MP
{Although this material is expensive, (the dress) is of excellent quality, so it is well worth buying.}

(73) 这种衣料<u>虽然</u>很贵<p>，<u>但</u>质量是上乘的<q_1>，我还是想买<q_2>。

Zhè zhǒng yīliào   <u>*suīrán*</u>   *hěn guì* <p>, <u>*dàn*</u> *zhìliàng shì*
this kind   dress material although very expensive but quality COP
shàngchéng de <q_1>, *wǒ hái shì* *xiǎng mǎi* <q_2>.
superior   SP   I still COP want to buy
{Although this material is expensive, (the dress) is of excellent quality, so I still want to buy it.}

"Wanting to buy the dress" is a natural result of "the excellent quality", but it is the opposite of the result of "the expensive material". Therefore, the logical basis for (71) or (72) is still contrastive causality, for only this relationship is invisible.

Second, in terms of linguistic form, concessive connectives, such as *suīrán* and the like, often collocate with adversative connectives, for example, *dànshì*. In this regard, the following three points need to be noted.

To begin with, the concessive connective *suīrán* can precede or follow the subject in the anterior clause, as in the following two examples:

(74) <u>虽然</u>过去我们已经进行了多年的社会主义建设，<u>但是</u>我们仍然有足够的理由说，这是一个新的历史发展阶段的开端。

<u>*Suīrán*</u> *guòqù wǒ-men yǐjīng* *jìnxíng -le*   *duō* *nián de shèhuìzhǔyì*
although past we   already carry out-PEF many year SP socialism
jiànshè,   <u>*dànshì*</u> *wǒ-men réngrán yǒu zúgòu*   *de lǐyóu shuō, zhè shì*
construction but   we   still   have sufficient SP reason say this COP
yī *gè* *xīn de* *lìshǐ* *fāzhǎn*   *jiēduàn de kāiduān.*
one CL new SP history developmental stage   SP start
{Although our socialist construction has been going on for many years, we still have every reason to say that this is the beginning of a new stage of historical development.}

20 "*p, dànshì q*" and relevant forms

(75) 目前我们同各种反革命分子、严重破坏分子、严重犯罪分子、严重犯罪集团的斗争，<u>虽然</u>不都是阶级斗争，<u>但是</u>包含阶级斗争。

Mùqián   wǒ-men   tóng   gè   zhǒng   fǎngémìng fènzǐ,   yánzhòng
at present   we   against   each   kind   counter-revolutionary   serious

pòhuài fènzǐ, yánzhòng fànzuì fènzǐ, yánzhòng fànzuì jítuán   de   dòuzhēng,
saboteur   serious criminal   serious criminal syndicate SP   struggle

<u>*suīrán*</u>   *bù   dōu   shì   jiējí dòuzhēng,* <u>*dànshì*</u> *bāohán jiējí dòuzhēng.*
although   NEG   all   COP   class struggle   but   include class struggle

{At present, although our struggle against all kinds of counter-revolutionaries, serious saboteurs, serious criminals, and serious criminal syndicates is not exclusively class struggle, it includes class struggle.}

The word *suīrán* can be used interchangeably with *suī* ('although') or *suīshuō* ('although'), and *jǐnguǎn* ('even though') or *gùrán* ('admittedly') can occur in place of *suīrán*, as in the following three examples:

(76) 这个小寨<u>虽</u>被我军先拆毁，<u>但</u>敌人昨天下午到达后又连夜改修，加上地形复杂，易守而不易攻。

Zhè gè xiǎo zhài <u>*suī*</u> *bèi   wǒ jūn xiān chāihuǐ,* <u>*dàn*</u> *dírén*
this CL small castle although PASSIVE our army first pull down but   enemy

zuótiān   xiàwǔ   dàodá hòu yòu liányè   gǎixiū, jiāshàng
yesterday   afternoon   arrive after and at that very night rebuild in addition

dìxíng fùzá,   yì   shǒu ér bù yì   gōng.
terrain complex easy defend but NEG easy capture

{Although this small castle was pulled down by our army, the enemy rebuilt it overnight after they arrived yesterday afternoon. In addition, the complex terrain makes it easy to defend but difficult to capture.}

(77) <u>尽管</u>彭德怀同志也有缺点，<u>但</u>对彭德怀同志的处理是完全错误的。

<u>*Jǐnguǎn*</u>   *Péng Déhuái tóngzhì   yě   yǒu   quēdiǎn,* <u>*dàn*</u> *duì*
although   PENG Dehuai comrade   also   have   shortcomings but   to

Péng Déhuái tóngzhì   de   chǔlǐ   shì   wánquán   cuòwù   de.
PENG Dehuai comrade   SP   treat   COP   completely wrong   MP

{Although comrade PENG Dehuai had shortcomings, the treatment he received was completely wrong.}

(78) 日耳曼人<u>固然</u>一般比较庄重严肃，<u>不过</u>倒也很热情好客。

*Rìěrmànrén   * <u>*gùrán*</u> *yībān   bǐjiào   zhuāngzhòng yánsù,*
Germanic peoples admittedly general to a certain extent solemn   serious

<u>*bùguò*</u> *dào   yě   hěn   rèqíng-hàokè.*
but   unexpectedly also very hospitable

{Germanic peoples are generally solemn and serious, but they are also very hospitable.}

The connective *suī* is often present between two occurrences of the same adjective to indicate tolerance and concession, as in the following two examples:

"p, dànshì q" and relevant forms 21

(79) 少<u>虽</u>少，拎在手里，<u>却</u>像偷来的一样，生怕人看见，左右不是味道。

Shǎo <u>suī</u>   shǎo, līn   zài shǒu-lǐ, <u>què</u>   xiàng... yīyàng tōu-lái de
few   although few   carry at in hand however be like   steal   SP

yīyàng,   shēngpà rén   kànjiàn,   zuǒyòu   bù   shì   wèidào.
      fear   person see   anyway NEG COP taste

{Although (the peanuts in his hand were) few, he felt as if he had stolen them, so he was afraid of being seen by others and didn't know what to do.}

(80) 穷<u>虽</u>穷，<u>可</u>那是她的家啊！

Qióng   <u>suī</u>   qióng,   <u>kě</u>   nà   shì   tā   de   jiā   a!
poor   although   poor   but   that COP she   SP   home   MP

{Poor as it is, it is her own family!}

Both *suīrán* and *jǐnguǎn* indicate concession. In cases where there are two concessive sentences in a row, one of the two words can be used in one sentence and the other in the other sentence to avoid simple repetition. The following is an example:

(81) 过去那个郑诚，<u>虽</u>遥隔这么多年，<u>可</u>谭谟对他是熟悉的。然而眼前这个郑诚，<u>尽管</u>近在咫尺，却是陌生的。

Guòqù nà gè Zhèng Chéng, <u>suī</u>   yáo gé   zhème duō nián, <u>kě</u>
past   that CL ZHENG Cheng although far separate so   many year but
Tán Mó duì tā shì shúxī de. Rán'ér yǎn-qián zhè gè Zhèng Chéng,
TAN Mo with him COP familiar SP however before eyes this CL ZHENG Cheng
<u>*jǐnguǎn*</u>   *jìnzài-zhǐchǐ,*   <u>*què*</u>   *shì   mòshēng de.*
even though   a very short distance away   however COP unfamiliar SP

{In the past, TAN Mo was familiar with ZHENG Cheng, though they were far apart for many years. However, the present ZHENG is strange to him, though he is just in front of him.}

Next, adversative connectives that can collocate with *suīrán* and its synonyms include *dànshì, dàn, kěshì, kě, rán'ér, búguò,* and *què,* but not *zhǐshì* or *jiùshì.* The following are four examples:

(82) 父亲<u>虽然</u>能干、精悍，<u>可</u>极不聪明地把自己的全部乃至生命都系结在极不可靠的名誉和钱财上。

Fùqīn <u>suīrán</u>   nénggàn, jīnghàn, <u>kě</u> jí   bù   cōngmíng de bǎ zìjǐ
father although capable   shrewd   but extremely NEG wise   SP BA oneself
de quánbù nǎizhì shēngmìng dōu xìjié zài jí   bù   kěkào de
SP whole   even   life   all   tie   at extremely NEG reliable SP
míngyù   hé   qiáncái shàng.
reputation and money LOC

{Capable and shrewd as he is, Father is extremely unwise to tie everything he has, and even his life to reputation and money, which are extremely unreliable.}

22 *"p, dànshì q" and relevant forms*

(83) 这里的茶叶，<u>虽然</u>比不上太湖洞庭山的碧螺春，<u>然而</u>临近黄天荡，自有独特的色和香。

Zhèlǐ de cháyè, <u>suīrán</u> bǐ bù shàng Tài Hú Dòngtíng Shān de
here SP tea   although not be as good as Lake Tai Dongting Mountain SP
Bìluóchūn, <u>rán'ér</u> línjìn Huángtiān Dàng, zì yǒu dútè de
Biluochun Tea however be close to Huangtian Lake   oneself have unique SP
sè hé xiāng.
color and scent
{Although the tea produced here is not as good as Biluochun, made in Dongting Mountain of Taihu Lake, it has its unique color and fragrance since it's close to Huangtian Lake.}

(84) 料<u>虽然</u>砸断了，<u>不过</u>嘛，想想办法，或者会变成一根好料呢！

Liào <u>suīrán</u> zá-duàn-le, <u>bùguò</u> ma, xiǎng-xiǎng bànfǎ, huòzhě huì biànchéng
timber although break-PEF but   MP think-REDP way   maybe can become
yī gēn hǎo liào ne!
one CL good timber MP
{The timber is broken, but let's see what we can do. Perhaps we can turn it into a piece of good timber.}

(85) 他<u>虽然</u>只有三十六岁，<u>却</u>已经在球场上打了十八、九年了。

Tā <u>suīrán</u> zhǐ yǒu sānshíliù suì, <u>què</u> yǐjīng zài qiúchǎng-shàng
he although only have thirty-six year however already at on court
dǎ-le shíbā-jiǔ nián le.
play-PEF eighteen or nineteen year MP
{Although he is only thirty-six years of age, he has been playing (volleyball) for eighteen or nineteen years.}

Last, such words as *suīrán* and *jǐnguǎn* indicate a concession and foreshadow an opposition between the two clauses. Therefore, as long as *suīrán*, *jǐnguǎn*, or a synonym is present in the anterior clause, the sentence is a concessive one regardless of whether *dànshì* or its synonym occurs in the posterior clause. In other words, adversative connectives can be absent in sentences with *suīrán*. The following are three examples:

(86) 他<u>虽然</u>笨，也晓得共产党历来主张集体化。

*Tā <u>suīrán</u> bèn, **yě** xiǎode Gòngchǎndǎng lìlái zhǔzhāng*
he although stupid also be aware Communist Party always advocate
jítǐhuà.
collectivization
{Although he is stupid, he is aware that the Communist Party has always advocated collectivization.}

(87) 我们这些卖票的，开车的，<u>虽说</u>有个职业，其实全是"在业游民"。

*Wǒ-men zhèxiē màipiàode, kāichēde, <u>suīshuō</u> yǒu gè zhíyè, **qíshí** quán*
we   these ticket seller driver   although have CL occupation actually all

shì "zàiyè yóumín".
COP employed vagrant
{We ticket sellers and drivers, although being employed, are all "vagrants in employment", as a matter of fact.}

(88) 尽管周红娜事先打过招呼，孙燕还是觉得潘树林怎么那么黑呀。

Jǐnguǎn   *Zhōu Hóngnà*   *shìxiān*   *dǎ-guò zhāohu,*   *Sūn Yàn*   **háishi**
even though ZHOU Hongna in advance give a heads-up-EXP SUN Yan still

juéde   *Pān Shùlín*   *zěnme*   *nàme*   *hēi*   *ya.*
feel   PAN Shulin   how   so   dark   MP

{Even though ZHOU Hongna has given Sun Yan a heads-up, she is still surprised that PAN Shulin is so dark-skinned.}

1.3.2 Differences between "suīrán p, dànshì q" and "p, dànshì q"

Sentences in the two forms of "*suīrán p, dànshì q*" and "*p, dànshì q*" differ in the following four aspects.

First, there are more semantic constraints upon the logical basis for sentences in the form of "*suīrán p, dànshì q*". If there is no obvious or implied contrastive causality between *p* and *q*, "*suīrán... dànshì...*" cannot be used. Compare the following two examples:

(89) （我亲眼看见）有三个同志坐下来抱在一起想暖和一下，<u>但</u>他们再也没有站起来。

(Wǒ qīnyǎn   *kànjiàn) yǒu*   *sān*   *gè*   *tóngzhì*   *zuò-xiàlái*   *bào*
I   with one's own eyes see   there be three CL comrade sit down cuddle

zài   *yīqǐ*   *xiǎng*   *nuǎnhuo-yīxià,*   <u>*dàn*</u>   *tā-men*   *zài yě méiyǒu*   *zhàn-qǐlái.*
at   together   want   get warm   but   they   no longer   stand up

{[I saw with my own eyes that] three comrades sat down and cuddled each other to get warm, but they could never stand up.}

(90) *（我亲眼看见）有三个同志<u>虽然</u>坐下来抱在一起想暖和一下，<u>但</u>他们再也没有站起来。

(Wǒ qīnyǎn   *kànjiàn) yǒu*   *sān*   *gè*   *tóngzhì*   <u>*suīrán*</u>   *zuò-xiàlái*
I   with one's own eyes see   there be three CL comrade although sit down

bào   *zài*   *yīqǐ*   *xiǎng*   *nuǎnhuo-yīxià,*   <u>*dàn*</u> *tā-men zài yě méiyǒu zhàn-qǐlái.*
cuddle at together want get warm   but   they   no longer   stand up

Between the two examples, (89) is well-formed, but (90) is illogical, because there is no contrastive causality between what is stated in the two clauses, i.e., "not being able to stand up again" is not an opposition to what would be caused by "siting down and cuddling each other to get warm". For the same reason, *suīrán* cannot occur in the anterior clause in the following two sentences:

24 *"p, dànshì q" and relevant forms*

(91) 今后你就与妈妈一起活吧，<u>但</u>会活得很苦很难的。

Jīnhòu nǐ jiù yǔ māma yīqǐ huó ba, <u>dàn</u> huì huó de hěn kǔ hěn
future you just with mother together live MP but will live SP very hard very

nán de.
difficult MP

{From now on, you will live with your mother, but it will be very hard.}

(92) "是城市吗?"我问道，<u>但</u>立即为自己的饶舌而发窘了，……

"Shì chéngshì ma?" wǒ wèndào, <u>dàn</u> lìjí wèi zìjǐ de ráoshé
COP city MP I ask but immediately for oneself SP be garrulous

ér fājiǒng-le, ...
therefore feel embarrassed-PEF

{"Is it a city?" I asked, but immediately realized that I was being garrulous and therefore felt embarrassed . . .}

Second, *suīrán* foreshadows an opposition between the clauses, thus the contrast in "*suīrán p, dànshì q*" is foreboded when *suīrán* occurs, whereas the opposition or contrast in "*p, dànshì q*" is relatively abrupt due to the absence of *suīrán*. In short, "*suīrán p, dànshì q*" differs from "*p, dànshì q*" in that the former entails a concession and the latter involves an abrupt opposition. Compare the following two examples:

(93) 他<u>虽然</u>身材瘦小，长得<u>却</u>很机灵，……

Tā <u>suīrán</u> shēncái shòuxiǎo, zhǎng de <u>què</u> hěn jīling,...
he although build thin and small appear SP however very clever

{Although he is small and thin, he looks very clever...}

(94) "保长"身上很热，<u>但</u>又不敢用力扇扇子。

"Bǎozhǎng" shēn-shàng hěn rè, <u>dàn</u> yòu bù gǎn yònglì shān
village head on body very hot but on the contrary NEG dare hard fan

shànzi.
fan

{The "village head" felt very hot, but he did not dare to fan himself too hard.}

Due to the presence of *suīrán* in (93), the anterior clause indicates that an opposition will occur in the posterior clause. By contrast, the reader of (94) does not know that there is an opposition until the word *dàn* occurs at the beginning of the posterior clause.

Third, with regard to the communication effect, "*suīrán p, dànshì q*" concedes *p* but highlights *q*, whereas "*p, dànshì q*" only shows the opposition between *p* and *q*. The following are two examples:

(95) (甚至也没和他谈过心，)客观原因<u>虽</u>是战斗频繁，主观原因<u>却</u>是我没注意他，压根没注意他。

(Shènzhì yě méi hé tā tánxīn guò xīn,) kèguān
even either NEG with him have a heart-to-heart talk EXP objective

yuányīn *suī* shì zhàndòu pínfán, zhǔguān yuányīn *què* shì
reason although COP fight frequent subjective reason however COP
wǒ méi zhùyì tā, yàgēn méi zhùyì tā.
I NEG pay attention him ever NEG notice him
{[(I) hadn't even talked with him.] Although the objective reason was the frequent battles, the subjective reason was that I didn't pay attention to him at all.}

(96) 本来今天是来听会的，<u>但是</u>选拔培养中青年干部这个问题太大了，还是讲几句。

Běnlái *jīntiān* *shì* *lái* *tīnghuì* *de*, <u>*dànshì*</u> *xuǎnbá péiyǎng*
originally today COP come sit in on a meeting MP but select train
zhōngqīngnián *gànbù zhè gè wèntí tài dà* *le, háishi jiǎng*
young and middle-aged cadre this CL matter too important MP still say
jǐ *jù.*
several words
{(I) was going to come and sit in on this meeting today, but the topic of selection and training of young and middle-aged cadres is extremely important, so (I) would still like to say a few words.}

Example (95) stresses "the subjective reason" by conceding "the objective factor", whereas (96) only shows that there is an adversative relationship between "sitting in on the meeting" and "saying a few words", without an indication of a concession.

Fourth, in terms of sentence structure, if *dànshì* is removed from sentences in the form of "*suīrán p, dànshì q*", the order of the two clauses can be reversed. However, the positions of the two clauses in sentences in the form of "*p, dànshì q*" cannot be swapped. The following are two examples:

(97) 她中文说得很好，<u>虽然</u>她从未上过哪个学校的中文系。

Tā *zhōngwén shuō* *de hěn hǎo,* <u>*suīrán*</u> *tā* *cóngwèi shàng-guò* *nǎ*
she Chinese speak SP very good although she never attend-EXP any
gè *xuéxiào* *de* *zhōngwénxì.*
CL university SP Chinese department
{She speaks really good Chinese, though she has never studied in the Chinese department at any university.}

(98) 党章规定，党员必须执行党的决议，<u>虽然</u>在执行中有权保留自己的意见。

Dǎngzhāng *guīdìng, dǎngyuán* *bìxū zhíxíng* *dǎng de juéyì,*
party constitution stipulate party member must implement party SP resolution
<u>*suīrán*</u> *zài zhíxíng-zhōng* *yǒu quán bǎoliú zìjǐ* *de yìjiàn.*
although at during implementation have right reserve oneself SP opinion
{The Party Constitution stipulates that party members must implement party resolutions, although they are entitled to have reservations during implementation.}

The postpositional concessive clause not only complements the preceding clause, but also attracts the attention of the listener or reader. The concessive

26 *"p, dànshì q"* and relevant forms

clause in other forms of concessive sentences can also be postpositioned, such as *"jíshǐ p, yě q"* and *"wúlùn p, dōu q"*, as in the following:

(99) 在原则问题上，我郑维中从来是不含糊的，<u>即使</u>是对你！
Zài yuánzé wèntí-shàng, wǒ Zhèng Wéizhōng cónglái shì bù hánhu de,
on principle on matter I ZHENG Weizhong ever COP NEG vague SP
<u>jíshǐ</u> shì duì nǐ!
even if COP to you
{On matters of principle, I, ZHENG Weizhong, have never been vague, even when they involve you!}

In the aforementioned example, the concessive clause introduced by *jíshǐ* is postpositioned. The following is an example with postpositional concessive clauses introduced respectively by *wúlùn* and *bùguǎn*:

(100) 每天，珠珠都起这么早，到二路车终点站去乘车上班，<u>无论</u>天气好坏。
Měitiān, Zhūzhū dōu qǐ zhème zǎo, dào èrlù chē zhōngdiǎnzhàn qù
every day Zhuzhu all get up so early go to 2nd route bus terminal go
chéng chē shàngbān, <u>wúlùn</u> tiānqì hǎo huài.
take bus go to work no matter weather good bad
{Every day, Zhuzhu gets up so early and goes to the terminal of Bus Route 2 to take the bus to work, be the weather good or bad.}

(101) 反正我是老老实实地报，<u>不管</u>将来碰到什么问题。
Fǎnzhèng wǒ shì lǎolǎo-shíshí de bào, <u>bùguǎn</u> jiānglái pèngdào shénme
anyway I COP honest SP report no matter... future meet any
wèntí.
problem
{Anyway, I will report honestly, no matter what problems will be encountered in the future.}

Summary

First, *"p, dànshì q"* is the prototypical form of adversative complex sentences. In this form, the adversative predictor is absent in the anterior clause. Due to the absence of the adversative predictor, the opposition/contrast between clauses is unforeseen, and consequently the adversativity is direct or abrupt between *p* and *q*.

Second, *"p, bùguò q"* also shows a direct or abrupt contrast, but the contrast is relatively slight. In sentences in the form of *"p, bùguò q"*, *bàle*, *jiùshì*, and so on, can occur at the end of the posterior clause. In terms of function, synonyms of *bùguò* include *zhǐshì* and *jiùshì*.

Third, *"suīrán p, dànshì q"* and *"p, dànshì q"* can often be used interchangeably, but they differ more or less in logical basis, the pattern of change in tone, communicative effect, and sentence structure.

NB Some examples in this chapter are cited from literary works, political essays, articles, and so on. The sources are listed as follows:

1 *Baihuazhou* (《百花洲》) 1983(4), including Examples (49), (55), (62), and (94);
2 *Changcheng* (《长城》) 1982(1), including (10), (81), and (84); 1983(3), including (9), (11), (15), (17), (48), (51), (61), (63), and (64);
3 *Chinese* for Junior High School Students, Book 1, including (14), (22), (30), and (89); Book 3, including (76) and (87); Book 4, including (41);
4 *Chinese* for Senior High School Students, Book 1, including (33) and (54);
5 *Chunfeng* (《春风》) 1982(1), including (52);
6 *Dangdai* (《当代》) 1982(3), including (24) and (39); 1982(4), including (78) and (99); 1983(2), including (34); 1983(3), including (32);
7 *Dispute* (《纠纷》) by Xirong (西戎), including (60);
8 *Fiction Monthly* (《小说月报》) 1982(2), including (25); 1982(3), including (3); 2000(2), including (4), (7), (8), and (88);
9 *Flower City* (《花城》) 1983(2), including (31) and (93); 1983(4), including (12);
10 *Harvest* (《收获》) 1982(4), including (16), (67), and (92); 1983(4), including (44), (56), and (97);
11 *Health Times* (《健康时报》), 2000(February 3), including (91);
12 *Lotus* (《芙蓉》) 1982(3), including (37);
13 *October* (《十月》) 1982(1), including (19); 1982(2), including (40) and (46); 1982(3), including (18), (47), (53), (83), and (95); 1982(4), including (13); 1983(3), including (100); 1983(4), including (35);
14 *People's Literature* (《人民文学》) 1982(1), including (85); 1982(3), including (36), (79), (80), and (86);
15 *Qingming* (《清明》) 1983(3), including (38);
16 *Selected Works of DENG Xiaoping* (《邓小平文选》), including (70), (74), (75), and (77);
17 *Selected Works of DENG Xiaoping* (1975–1982) (《邓小平文选(1975–1982年)》), including (1), (2), (5), (20), (21), (96), and (98);
18 *Short Stories Since the Foundation of People's Republic of China* (《建国以来短篇小说》), including (101);
19 *Xiao Shuo Jia* (《小说家》) 1983 (2), including (42) and (43);
20 *Zhongpian Xiaoshuo Xuankan* (《中篇小说选刊》) 1999(6), including (23) and (50);
21 *Zhongshan* (《钟山》) 1983(4), including (65) and (82).

2 *"p, fǒuzé q"* and relevant forms

"p, fǒuzé q" ('*p*, otherwise *q*') is a form of adversative complex sentences in which the clauses are linked by the connective *fǒuzé* or one of its synonyms, which include *bùrán, yàobùrán, yàobù, ruòbù*, and so forth.

This chapter mainly discusses sentences in the following forms:

xìngkuī p, fǒuzé q	('fortunately *p*, otherwise *q*')
kěxī p, fǒuzé q	('unfortunately *p*, otherwise *q*')
yīnwèi p, fǒuzé q	('*because p*, otherwise *q*')
xiǎnglái p, fǒuzé q	('*presumably p*, otherwise *q*')
chúfēi p, fǒuzé q	('*unless p*, otherwise *q*')
yàome p, fǒuzé q	('*p*, otherwise *q*')
háishì p ba, fǒuzé q	('you'd better *p*, otherwise *q*')
bù néng p, fǒuzé q	('*cannot p*, otherwise *q*')
bù néng bù p, fǒuzé q	('*must p*, otherwise *q*')

LV Shuxiang focused on the analysis of posterior clauses introduced by *fǒuzé* and its synonyms. For example, he wrote, "the posterior clause (introduced by *fǒuzé*) is the result inferred from the anterior clause, or a different choice". [1] He also claimed that "(*bùrán* is used to) introduce the result clause or the conclusion clause . . . and to introduce an alternative situation to the one from the preceding context". [2] However, this chapter places the emphasis on the observation and analysis of anterior clauses in an attempt to reveal the relationship between the two clauses in various sentence forms in which the clauses are linked by *fǒuzé*.

Most examples used in this chapter are complex sentences, but a few of them are sentence groups.

2.1 *"xìngkuī p, fǒuzé q"*

Sentences in the form of *"xìngkuī p, fǒuzé q"* indicate a cause and a result. In the sentences the result is contrary to the assumed effect of the cause. The sentences emphasize that an unsatisfactory or unusual result has been avoided for a specific reason.

DOI: 10.4324/9781003374237-2

"p, fǒuzé q" and relevant forms 29

2.1.1 Anterior clause in "xìngkuī p, fǒuzé q"

In sentences in the form of *"xìngkuī p, fǒuzé q"*, the anterior clause, either in the affirmative or negative form, presents the reason, which is a realis event. In the anterior clause, *xìngkuī* highlights the realis event with an implication of being lucky. The following are three examples:

(1)　幸亏脂肪极其丰满，否则就伤及血管、骨头或神经了。
Xìngkuī　zhīfáng jíqí　　fēngmǎn, fǒuzé　　jiù　shāng jí　xuèguǎn,
fortunately fat　　extremely thick　otherwise then injure arrive blood vessel
gǔtou　huò　shénjīng le.
bone　　or　　nerve　　MP
{Fortunately, the fat layer is extremely thick, otherwise the blood vessels, bones, or nerves would have been damaged.}

(2)　幸亏这家伙没吃，否则这笑话就闹大了。
Xìngkuī　zhè jiāhuo méi　chī, fǒuzé　zhè nàoxiàohua　　　jiù
fortunately this guy　　NEG eat otherwise this make a fool of oneself then
nàodà　le.
serious　MP
{Fortunately, this guy didn't eat it, otherwise he would have made a complete fool of himself.}

(3)　幸亏河水是污浊的，不然，映出她的脸一定很难看。
Xìngkuī　héshuǐ　shì　wūzhuó　　de, bùrán,　yìng-chū tā de liǎn
fortunately river water COP dirty and turbid MP otherwise reflect　she SP face
yīdìng　hěn　nánkàn.
definitely very bad looking
{Fortunately, the river is dirty and turbid, otherwise her face—reflected in the water—would be terrible looking.}

The word *xìngkuī* can be replaced by other words of the same meaning, such as *xìnghǎo, kuīdé* ('fortunately'), *duōkuī* ('fortunately'), *hǎozài* ('fortunately'), and so on. The following is an example:

(4)　幸好"四人帮"打倒了，幸好冯局长是个明白人，否则，他起码也是一
　　个"肖伯仲的黑后台、大红伞"……
Xìnghǎo　"sìrénbāng"　dǎ-dǎo-le,　xìnghǎo　Féng júzhǎng　shì　gè
fortunately Gang of Four defeat-PEF fortunately FENG director COP CL
míngbai rén,　fǒuzé,　tā qǐmǎ　yě　shì　yī　gè　"Xiāo Bózhòng
sensible person otherwise he at least also COP one CL XIAO Bozhong
de hēi　hòutái,　dà hóng sǎn"...
SP black　person behind big red　umbrella
{Fortunately, "the Gang of Four" was defeated and Director FENG was a sensible person, otherwise he would have been a "behind-the-scenes supporter of and protective umbrella for XIAO Bozhong" at least . . .}

30 *"p, fŏuzé q" and relevant forms*

2.1.2 Posterior Clause in "xìngkuī p, fŏuzé q"

In sentences in the form of "*xìngkuī p, fŏuzé q*", *q* denotes a result contrary to the fact, or a result contrasting with what would be caused by *p*, or an unpleasant result. In such sentences, *fŏuzé* or its synonym reveals the contrastive causality between *p* and *q*. As a matter of fact, the posterior clause is used as counter-evidence to prove that *p* is decisive in the occurrence of the event stated in the posterior clause. The following is an example:

(5)　　幸亏四辈儿改行得早，不然非失业不可。

Xìngkuī　　*Sìbèir*　　*găiháng*　　　　*de*　　*zăo,*　　*bùrán*　　*fēi . . . bùkĕ*
fortunately　Sibei'er　change occupation　SP　　early　　otherwise　definitely

shīyè　　*bùkĕ.*
lose job

{Fortunately, Sibei'er changed her occupation early, otherwise she would surely have been unemployed.}

In the aforementioned example, as can be seen, *fŏuzé* introduces *q*, a counter-factual result. In other words, the actual result is the opposite of *q*. The anterior clause indicates that the occurrence of *p* is fortunate, but *q* is an unsatisfactory result contrary to the actual result; therefore, *fŏuzé* signals contrastive casualty. The word *fŏuzé* also emphasizes that it is just because of the occurrence of *p* that the unpleasant result has been avoided. Thus, the avoidance of the unpleasant or undesirable result or consequence is taken as counterevidence to highlight the reason and prove that the reason is critical to the actual fact. Compare the following two examples:

(6)　　幸亏他及时地抓住了床沿，才没掉到地板上。

Xìngkuī　　*tā*　*jíshí*　　*de*　*zhuā-zhù*　　*le*　　*chuángyán,*　*cái*　*méi*　*diào-dào*
fortunately　he　in time　SP　catch hold of　PEF　edge of bed　just　NEG　fall to

dìbăn-shàng.
on floor

{Fortunately, he caught hold of the edge of the bed just in time to avoid falling to the floor.}

(7)　　幸亏他及时抓住了床沿，不然就掉到地板上了。

Xìngkuī　　*tā*　*jíshí*　　*zhuā-zhù*　　*le*　　*chuángyán,*　*bùrán*　*jiù*　*diào-dào*
fortunately　he　in time　catch hold of　PEF　edge of bed　otherwise　then　fall to

dìbăn-shàng　*le.*
on floor　　MP

{Fortunately, he caught hold of the edge of the bed in time, otherwise he would have fallen to the floor.}

Example (6) is in the form of "*xìngkuī p, cái q*" and shows a cause-effect relationship, whereas (7) is in the form of "*xìngkuī p, bùrán q*" and indicates

"p, fǒuzé q" and relevant forms 31

contrastive causality. The two are practically the same in meaning, but the latter includes counterevidence.

2.1.3 "xìngkuī p, fǒuzé q" and "yàobùshì p, jiù q"

Sentences in the form of *"xìngkuī p, fǒuzé q"* can be rewritten as *"yàobùshì p, jiù q"*. For example:

(8)   a 幸亏脂肪极其丰满，否则就伤及血管、骨头或神经了。

Xìngkuī   zhīfáng   jíqí   fēngmǎn, fǒuzé   jiù   shāng jí   xuèguǎn,
fortunately fat   extremely thick   otherwise then injure arrive blood vessel
gǔtou   huò   shénjīng   le.
bone   or   nerve   MP
{Fortunately, the fat layer is extremely thick, otherwise the blood vessels, bones, or nerves would have been damaged.}

→b 要不是脂肪极其丰满，   就伤及血管、骨头或神经了。

Yàobùshì   zhīfáng   jíqí   fēngmǎn, jiù   shāng jí   xuèguǎn,
if not   fat   extremely thick   then injure arrive blood vessel
gǔtou   huò   shénjīng   le.
bone   or   nerve   MP
{But for the extremely thick fat layer, the blood vessels, bones, or nerves would have been damaged.}

In actual language use, quite a number of sentences in the form of *"yàobùshì p, jiù q"* can be rewritten as *"xìngkuī p, fǒuzé q"*. For instance, (9) can be rewritten as (10):

(9)   要不是预先听你讲了，我会以为他是个劳改犯。

Yàobùshì yùxiān   tīng nǐ   jiǎng-le, wǒ huì   yǐwéi tā   shì   gè   láogǎifàn.
if not   in advance hear you say-PEF I   will think he COP CL prisoner
{If I hadn't heard what you had said, I would have mistakenly thought that he was a prisoner.}

(10) 幸亏预先听你讲了，要不，我会以为他是个劳改犯。

Xìngkuī   yùxiān   tīng nǐ   jiǎng-le, yàobù,   wǒ huì   yǐwéi tā
fortunately in advance hear you say-PEF otherwise I   will think he
shì   gè   láogǎifàn.
COP CL prisoner
{Fortunately I had heard what you had said, otherwise I would have mistakenly thought that he was a prisoner.}

2.2   "kěxī p, fǒuzé q"

Sentences in the form of *"kěxī p, fǒuzé q"* indicate a cause and a result. In these sentences the result is contrary to the assumed effect of the cause. These sentences emphasize that a desirable result has not been achieved for a specific reason.

32 *"p, fǒuzé q" and relevant forms*

2.2.1 *Anterior clause in "kěxī p, fǒuzé q"*

In sentences in the form of *"kěxī p, fǒuzé q"*, the anterior clause, either in the affirmative or negative form, presents the reason, which is a realis event. In the anterior clause, *kěxī* highlights the realis event with an implication of being unlucky. The following are three examples:

(11) 可惜师伯那时不在，否则令狐大哥也不会身受重伤了。

Kěxī   shībó nàshí bù   zài,   fǒuzé   Línghú dàgē   yě   bù
unfortunately uncle then   NEG be there otherwise LINGHU brother indeed NEG

huì   shēnshòu zhòngshāng   le.
will   suffer   serious injury   MP

{Unfortunately, Uncle was not there then, otherwise Brother LINGHU would not have been seriously injured.}

(12) 可惜他们不懂得绘画，否则要给免费画一副素描肖像赠送。

Kěxī   tā-men bù   dǒngde huìhuà, fǒuzé   yào gěi miǎnfèi   huà
unfortunately they   NEG know   painting otherwise will for not charge draw

yī   fù   sùmiáo xiàoxiàng zèngsòng.
one CL sketch portrait   give as a present

{It's a pity that they know nothing about painting, otherwise they would paint a portrait sketch (for him) for free and give it (to him) as a present.}

The word *kěxī* can be rephrased as *zhǐ kěxī* ('unfortunately'), which gives greater emphasis to the cause, as in the following example:

(13) 只可惜天上没有神灵，若不，我得哀求神灵保佑你······

Zhǐ kěxī   tiān-shàng méiyǒu   shénlíng, ruòbù,   wǒ děi āiqiú
unfortunately in sky   there not be god   otherwise I   need entreat

shénlíng bǎoyòu nǐ . . .
god   bless   you

{It's a pity that there are no gods, otherwise I would beg gods to bless you . . .}

2.2.2 *Posterior clause in "kěxī p, fǒuzé q"*

In sentences in the form of *"kěxī p, fǒuzé q"*, *q* is a result contrary to the fact, or a result contrasting with what would be caused by *p*, and can be used as counter-evidence to prove that *p* is decisive in the occurrence of the event stated in the posterior clause. Usually, *q* is something pleasant or desirable. The following is an example:

(14) 可惜我手上无权，我自己的帽子也还没有摘掉，要不然，我一定要做了这件好事。

Kěxī   wǒ shǒu-shàng wú   quán, wǒ zìjǐ   de màozi yě   hái
unfortunately I   in hand   not have power I   oneself SP hat   also still

"p, fǒuzé q" and relevant forms 33

méiyǒu zhāi-diào, yàobùrán, wǒ yīdìng yào zuò le zhè jiàn hǎoshì.
NEG take off otherwise I definitely will do MP this CL good deed
{Unfortunately I have no power and my own label hasn't been removed yet, otherwise I would definitely do this good deed.}

In the aforementioned example, *kěxī* introduces the reason, and *yàobùrán*, a synonym of *fǒuzé*, indicates the contrastive causality. The whole sentence, while indicating that a certain cause has prevented a desirable result from being achieved, emphasizes that *p* plays a decisive role.

The form "*xìngkuī p, fǒuzé q*" indicates that the speaker is content with the result, whereas "*kěxī p, fǒuzé q*" shows that the speaker feels sorry for the result. Thus, in both sentence forms *q* and *q* oppose the actual result in terms of whether they are satisfactory. Compare the following two examples:

(15) 幸亏他没当教练，不然我肯定不能参加甲级队。
Xìngkuī tā méi dāng jiàoliàn, bùrán wǒ kěndìng bùnéng cānjiā
fortunately he NEG be coach otherwise I definitely cannot join
jiǎjí duì.
A level team
{Fortunately, he wasn't the coach, otherwise I wouldn't have been able to join an A-level team.}

(16) 可惜他没当教练，不然我肯定能够参加甲级队。
Kěxī tā méi dāng jiàoliàn, bùrán wǒ kěndìng bùnéng cānjiā
unfortunately he NEG be coach otherwise I definitely cannot join
jiǎjí duì.
A level team
{Unfortunately, he wasn't the coach, otherwise I would definitely have been able to join an A-level team.}

It should be noted that regardless of whether *xìngkuī* is used to indicate a satisfactory or unsatisfactory result, the word only reflects the speaker's stance, attitude, or emotion, and does not necessarily have to do with the subject of *p* or *q*. Compare the following two examples:

(17) 幸亏小张力气小，不然吴华跑不了。
Xìngkuī Xiǎo Zhāng lìqi xiǎo, bùrán Wú Huá pǎo bù liǎo.
fortunately little ZHANG strength small otherwise WU Hua cannot run away
{Fortunately, Little ZHANG wasn't very strong, otherwise WU Hua couldn't have escaped.}

(18) 可惜小张力气小，不然吴华跑不了。
Kěxī Xiǎo Zhāng lìqi xiǎo, bùrán Wú Huá pǎo bù liǎo.
unfortunately little ZHANG strength small otherwise WU Hua cannot run away
{Unfortunately, Little ZHANG wasn't strong enough, otherwise WU Hua couldn't have escaped.}

34 *"p, fǒuzé q"* and relevant forms

2.2.3 *"kěxī p, fǒuzé q"* and *"yàobùshì p, jiù q"*

Sentences in the form of *"kěxī p, fǒuzé q"* can be rewritten as *"yàobùshì p, jiù q"*. For example:

(19)   a 可惜我手上无权，我自己的帽子也还没有摘掉，要不然，我一定要做了这件好事。

      Kěxī   wǒ shǒu-shàng wú   quán, wǒ zìjǐ   de màozi yě   hái
      unfortunately I in hand   not have power I   oneself SP hat   also still
      méiyǒu zhāi-diào, yàobùrán, wǒ yīdìng   yào zuò le   zhè jiàn hǎoshì.
      NEG   take off   otherwise I   definitely will do MP this CL good deed
      {Unfortunately I have no power and my own label hasn't been removed yet, otherwise I would definitely do this good deed.}

      →b 要不是我手上无权，我自己的帽子也还没有摘掉，我一定要做了这件好事。

      Yàobùshì wǒ shǒu-shàng wú   quán, wǒ zìjǐ   de màozi yě   hái
      if not   I in hand   not have power I   oneself SP hat   also still
      méiyǒu zhāi-diào, wǒ yīdìng   yào zuò le zhè jiàn hǎoshì.
      NEG   take off   I   definitely will do   MP this CL   good deed
      {If it wasn't for my powerlessness and my own unremoved label had been removed, I would definitely do this good deed.}

    Sentences in the form of *"yàobùshì p, jiù q"* implying that the speaker feels sorry or regretful can all be rewritten as *"kěxī p, fǒuzé q"*. The following are two examples:

(20)   a <u>要不是</u>下班时间到了，他还想跟我再杀几盘。

      <u>*Yàobùshì*</u> *xiàbān   shíjiān dào-le,   tā hái xiǎng gēn wǒ zài shā jǐ*
      if not   get off work time   come-PEF he still want with me again play several
      pán.
      CL
      {If it wasn't time to get off work, he would like to play a few more games (of chess) with me.}

      →b <u>可惜</u>下班时间到了，<u>否则</u>他还想跟我再杀几盘。

      <u>*Kěxī*</u>   *xiàbān   shíjiān dào-le,   *<u>*fǒuzé*</u>   *tā hái xiǎng gēn wǒ*
      unfortunately get off work time   come-PEF otherwise he still want with me
      zài   shā jǐ   pán.
      again play several CL
      {Unfortunately, it is time to get off work, otherwise he would play a few more games (of chess) with me.}

(21)   a ······ <u>若不是</u>眼下有急事，他真想坐下来休息一下。

      ... <u>ruòbùshì</u> yǎnxià   yǒu   jíshì,   tā zhēn xiǎng zuò-xiàlái xiūxi
      if not   the present there be urgent matter he really want sit down rest

yīxià.
briefly
{He would really like to sit down and have a rest if it wasn't for the urgency at the moment.}

→b 可惜眼下有急事，<u>否则</u>他真想坐下来休息一下。

Kěxī yǎnxià yǒu jíshì, <u>fǒuzé</u> tā zhēn xiǎng
unfortunately the present there be urgent matter otherwise he really want
zuò-xiàlái xiūxi yīxià.
sit down rest briefly
{Unfortunately, there is an urgency at the moment, otherwise he would really like to sit down and have a rest.}

2.3 "*yīnwèi p, fǒuzé q*"

Sentences in the form of "*yīnwèi p, fǒuzé q*" indicate a cause and a result. In these sentences, the result is contrary to the assumed effect of the cause. Compared with the previous two sentence forms, "*yīnwèi p, fǒuzé q*" carries an objective tone.

2.3.1 Anterior clause in "*yīnwèi p, fǒuzé q*"

In sentences in the form of "*yīnwèi p, fǒuzé q*", the anterior clause includes a conjunction, such as *yīnwèi* or *yóuyú*, which formally indicates that what follows has caused something to occur. The following are three examples:

(22) 她和沙马耳虎<u>因为</u>化了装，<u>不然</u>，进城难出城也难。
*Tā hé Shāmǎěrhǔ yīnwèi huà*zhuāng *le zhuāng, <u>bùrán,</u> jìnchéng*
she and Shamaerhu because disguise oneself PEF otherwise go into town
nán chūchéng yě nán.
difficult go out of town also difficult
{She and Shamaerhu disguised themselves, otherwise it would have been difficult for them to enter and leave the city.}

(23) 只是<u>因为</u>他们早已把我许配给查家，<u>要不</u>他们也会 ⋯⋯
Zhǐshì <u>yīnwèi</u> tā-men zǎoyǐ bǎ wǒ xǔpèi gěi Zhājiā, <u>yàobù</u>
only because they long ago BA me betroth to ZHA family otherwise
tā-men yě huì ...
they also will
{It's just because they have arranged for me to marry into the ZHA family long ago, otherwise they would also ...}

(24) "加拿大只答允贷一千五百万美元与我们；而美国人原来露出口风愿贷五千万元与我们，只是<u>由于</u>孔祥熙在其中作怪，<u>否则</u>⋯⋯"他摇了摇头，显示深有感触的样子。
"*Jiānádà zhǐ dāyǔn dài yīqiān wǔbǎi wàn měiyuán yǔ wǒ-men; ér*
Canada only agree lend 15 million US dollar to us while

36 *"p, fǒuzé q"* and relevant forms

měiguórén	*yuánlái*	*lùchū*	*kǒufēng*	*yuàn*		*dài*	*wǔqiān wàn*	*yuán*	*yǔ*
American	originally	show	intention	be willing		lend	50 million	dollar	to

wǒ-men,	*zhǐshì*	*yóuyú*	*Kǒng Xiángxī*	*zài qízhōng zuòguài,*	*fǒuzé . . ."*
us	only	because	KONG Xiangxi	at inside make trouble	otherwise

Tā	*yáo-le-yáo tóu,*	*xiǎnshì*	*shēnyǒugǎnchù*	*de yàngzi.*
he	shake-PEF-shake head	show	have a strong feeling	SP appearance

{"Canada only agreed to lend us US$15 million, while the Americans were willing to lend us US$50 million, only KONG Xiangxi made trouble, otherwise . . ." He shook his head with a deep feeling.}

In some cases, the conjunction is absent in the anterior clause. The following are two examples:

(25) 都是海棠那死丫头插一杠子，<u>要不</u>俺妹子和长锁是多好的一对呀！

Dōushì	*Hǎitáng*	*nà*	*sǐ yātou*	*chā yī gàngzi,*	*yàobù*	*ǎn*	*mèizi*	
because	Haitang	that	wicked girl	meddle	otherwise	my	younger sister	

hé	*Chángsuǒ*	*shì*	*duō*	*hǎo*	*de yī*	*duì*	*ya!*
and	Changsuo	COP	how	good	SP one	couple	MP

{What a nice couple my younger sister and Changsuo would have made if Haitang, the wicked girl, hadn't meddled in their relationship!}

(26) 我真冻坏了，<u>要不</u>我去砸您的窗户吗？

Wǒ	*zhēn*	*dòng-huài*		*le,*	*yàobù*	*wǒ qù zá*	*nín de chuānghu ma?*	
I	really	be frozen to death		PEF	otherwise	I go pound	you SP window	MP

{I was frozen to death, otherwise would I have pounded on your window?}

In both examples above, *yīnwèi* or *yóuyú* can be added and placed before the subject in each anterior clause.

2.3.2 Posterior clause in *"yīnwèi p, fǒuzé q"*

In sentences in the form of *"yīnwèi p, fǒuzé q"*, *q* is a result contrary to the fact and contrasting with what would be caused by *p*. The posterior clause can be regarded as counterevidence to prove that *p* is the cause. There are commonalities among *"yīnwèi p, fǒuzé q"*, *"xìngkuī p, fǒuzé q"*, and *"kěxī p, fǒuzé q"*.

For example, *yīnwèi* in (22) can be replaced by *xìngkuī*, and *yóuyú* in (24) can be replaced by *kěxī*.

If *"xìngkuī p, fǒuzé q"* indicates that the speaker feels happy with the result and *"kěxī p, fǒuzé q"* implies that the speaker regrets the result, then *"yīnwèi p, fǒuzé q"* shows that the speaker is neutral about the result. The form *"yīnwèi p, fǒuzé q"* does not indicate whether the speaker is happy with or sorry for the result, but only reveals the contrastive causality between *p* and *q* in an objective manner, for example:

(27) <u>只因</u>（几个年轻人）还不了解昨晚发生在松毛林子中的事，<u>不然</u>他会挨一顿好打……

Zhǐ	*yīn*	*(jǐ*	*gè*	*niánqīngrén)*	*hái*	*bù*	*liǎojiě zuówǎn*	*fāshēng*	*zài*
only	because	several	CL	youth	still	NEG	know last night	happen	at

"p, fǒuzé q" and relevant forms 37

sōngmáo línzi-zhōng de shì,   *bùrán*   *tā huì ái yī   dùn hǎodǎ . . .*
in pine woods   SP incident otherwise he will get one CL good beating
{Just because [those young people] are not aware of what happened in the pine
forest last night yet, otherwise he would get a good beating . . .}

In this example, whether the speaker feels happy or sorry is unknown. The
sentence can be rewritten either as *"xìngkuī p, bùrán q"* or *"kěxī p, bùrán q"*,
depending on whether the speaker is on "his" side.

2.3.3 *"yīnwèi p, fǒuzé q" and "yàobùshì p, jiù q"*

Sentences in the form of *"yīnwèi p, fǒuzé q"* can be rewritten as *"yàobùshì p,
jiù q"*.

It should be noted that *xìngkuī* and *kěxī* need to be removed if a sentence in
the form of *"xìngkuī p, fǒuzé q"* or of *"kěxī p, fǒuzé q"* is rewritten as *"yàobùshì
p, jiù q"*, whereas *yīnwèi* or its synonym can be retained if *"yīnwèi p, fǒuzé q"* is
rewritten as *"yàobùshì p, jiù q"*. For instance, (22) can be rephrased as (28), and
(24) can be rewritten as (29).

(28) 她和沙马耳虎<u>要不是</u>因为化了装，不然，进城难出城也难。
      *Tā hé Shāmǎěrhǔ <u>yàobùshì</u> **yīnwèi** huàzhuāng   le   zhuāng, <u>bùrán,</u>*
      she and Shamaerhu if not   because disguise oneself PEF   otherwise
      jìnchéng   nán   chūchéng   yě   nán.
      go into town difficult go out of town also difficult
      {If she and Shamaerhu had not disguised themselves, it would have been difficult
      for them to enter the city and leave the city.}

(29) "……<u>要不是</u>由于孔祥熙在其中作怪，就……"他摇了摇头，显示深有感触
      的样子。
      *"... <u>yàobùshì</u> **yóuyú**   Kǒng Xiángxī   zài   qízhōng zuòguài,   <u>jiù...</u>"*
      if not   because KONG Xiangxi at   inside make trouble then
      Tā   yáo-le-yáo tóu,   xiǎnshì   shēnyǒugǎnchù   de   yàngzi.
      he   shake-PEF-shake head show   have a strong feeling SP appearance
      {"... if KONG Xiangxi had not made trouble, it would . . ." He shook his head
      with a deep feeling.}

There are sentences in the form of *"yào bùshì yīnwèi p, jiù q"* in actual language use, and they can be rewritten as *"yīnwèi p, fǒuzé q"*. The following are
two examples:

(30) ……<u>要不是</u>因为出了这场斗殴事件，人们也许早把他忘个一干二净了。
      *... <u>yàobùshì</u> **yīnwèi** chū-le   zhè chǎng dòu'ōu shìjiàn, rén-men yěxǔ*
      if not   because happen-PEF this CL   brawl incident people perhaps
      zǎo   bǎ tā   wàng gè   yīgān-èrjìng le.
      early BA him forget CL complete   MP
      {. . . If it had not been for the brawl he might have been completely forgotten.}

38 *"p, fǒuzé q" and relevant forms*

(31) 因为出了这场斗殴事件，否则人们也许早把他忘个一干二净了。

Yīnwèi chū-le zhè chǎng dòu'ōu shìjiàn, fǒuzé rén-men yěxǔ zǎo
because happen-PEF this CL brawl incident otherwise people perhaps early
bǎ tā wàng gè yīgān-èrjìng le.
BA him forget CL complete MP
{But for the brawl, he might have been completely forgotten.}

2.4 *"xiǎnglái p, fǒuzé q"*

Sentences in the form of *"xiǎnglái p, fǒuzé q"* indicate a cause and a result. In these sentences, the result is contrary to the assumed effect of the reason. However, this sentence form is used to prove a speculated cause rather than a realis cause. If the previous three sentence forms, i.e., *"xìngkuī p, fǒuzé q"*, *"kěxī p, fǒuzé q"*, and *"yīnwèi p, fǒuzé q"*, aim to explain the cause, the form *"xiǎnglái p, fǒuzé q"* is used to infer the cause.

2.4.1 *Anterior clause in "xiǎnglái p, fǒuzé q"*

In sentences in the form of *"xiǎnglái p, fǒuzé q"*, the cause indicated in the anterior clause is an irrealis event, and such annotative expressions as *xiǎnglái* ('assume'), *kànlái* ('seem'), "X *cāixiǎng*" ('someone speculates'), or "X *huáiyí*" ('someone doubts') can occur at the beginning of a sentence to imply that *p* is a speculation. The following are two examples:

(32) 看来，姑娘的外貌给了憨嫂非常非常深刻的印象，要不她怎么会叨唠个没完。

Kànlái, gūniang de wàimào gěi-le Hānsǎo fēicháng fēicháng shēnkè de
seem girl SP appearance give-PEF Hansao very very deep SP
yìnxiàng, yàobù tā zěnme huì dāolao gè méiwán.
impression otherwise she why will chatter CL keep on
{It seems that the girl's appearance left a very deep impression on Hansao, otherwise she wouldn't talk (about her) endlessly.}

(33) 她猜想一定发生了什么意外，否则黄成宾不会不来。

Tā cāixiǎng yīdìng fāshēng-le shénme yìwài, fǒuzé
she guess definitely happen-PEF certain accident otherwise
Huáng Chéngbīn bù huì bù lái.
HUANG Chengbin NEG will NEG come
{She guessed that something must have happened, otherwise HUANG Chengbin would not be absent.}

In some cases where the annotative expression is absent, the anterior clause often includes words such as *kěndìng* ('definitely'), *yīdìng* ('definitely'), *shuōbùdìng* ('perhaps'), *xīngxǔ* ('perhaps'), and so on, or the anterior clause *p* is a question expressing doubt. The following are three examples:

"p, fǒuzé q" and relevant forms   **39**

(34)　……他们<u>肯定</u>把那天的事讲给同学们听了，<u>不然</u>为什么同学们喊她玩时没以前热情呢？

　　..._tā-men **kěndìng**　bǎ　nà　tiān　de　shì　jiǎng gěi tóngxué-men tīng　le,_
　　they　　　definitely BA that day SP matter tell　to　classmate-PL listen PEF
　　**bùrán**　wèishénme tóngxué-men hǎn　tā　wán shí　méi　yǐqián rèqíng ne?
　　otherwise why　　　classmate-PL invite her play time NEG before warm　MP
　　{They must have told their classmates about what happened that day, otherwise
　　why didn't they invite her to play with them as warmly as before?}

(35)　……<u>兴许</u>哪句话叫人抓住辫子，<u>不然</u>决不会处分他。

　　..._**xīngxǔ**　nǎ　　jù　huà　jiào　rén　zhuā-zhù_
　　perhaps　certain CL　words　make　person　catch
　　biànzi,　　　　　　　　　　　　**bùrán**　　jué
　　mistake that can be used as an excuse for attacking　otherwise　definitely
　　bù　huì　chǔfèn tā.
　　NEG　will　punish　him
　　{Perhaps some of his words had become an excuse for others to attack him,
　　otherwise he would definitely not have been punished.}

(36)　难道那个卞秃头把他们的私下交易都说出来了？<u>要不然</u>，姓周的怎么会如此强硬呢？

　　Nándào　　　　　nà　gè　Biàn tūtóu　　bǎ tā-men de sīxià　jiāoyì dōu
　　could it be said that that CL BIAN bald head BA they　SP private deal　all
　　shuō-chūlái le? Yàobùrán, xìng　　Zhōu de zěnme huì rúcǐ qiángyìng ne?
　　spell out　MP otherwise surname be ZHOU SP why　will so　tough　MP
　　{Could it be that Bald Head BIAN spelled out all their private deals? Otherwise,
　　how could ZHOU be so tough?}

2.4.2　_Posterior clause in "xiǎnglái p, fǒuzé q"_

In sentences in the form of _"xiǎnglái p, fǒuzé q"_, q is a result contrary to the fact or
to the assumed effect of the cause stated in the anterior clause. In these sentences,
q can be a pleasant or unpleasant result. In this respect, _"xiǎnglái p, fǒuzé q"_ is the
same as _"yīnwèi p, fǒuzé q"_ but different from _"xìngkuī p, fǒuzé q"_ and _"kěxī p,_
fǒuzé q". Compare the following two examples:

(37)　想来风向有变化，<u>不然</u>，张胖子会重用他的。

　　Xiǎnglái　fēngxiàng　yǒu　　biànhuà,　**bùrán,**　　Zhāng pàngzi　huì
　　presume　situation　there be　change　otherwise　ZHANG fatty　will
　　zhòngyòng　　　　　　　　　　tā　de.
　　put someone in an important position　him　MP
　　{Presumably the situation has changed, otherwise Fatty ZHANG would have put
　　him in an important position.}

40 *"p, fǒuzé q" and relevant forms*

(38) 想来风向有变化，<u>不然</u>，张胖子不会重用他的。

<u>*Xiǎnglái*</u> *fēngxiàng yǒu   biànhuà,   <u>bùrán,</u>   Zhāng pàngzi   bù   huì*
presume situation   there be change   otherwise   ZHANG fatty   NEG   will

zhòngyòng   tā   de.
put someone in an important position   him   MP

{Presumably, the situation has changed, otherwise Fatty ZHANG wouldn't have put him in an important position.}

In these two examples, the anterior clauses have the same wording. For *tā* ('him'), *q* in (37) is pleasant but contrary to the reality (being put in an important position), whereas *q* in (38) is unpleasant but contrary to the fact (not being put in an important position).

2.4.3 "xiǎnglái p, fǒuzé q" and "jìrán fēi p, jiù yīdìng shì q"

The form of *"xiǎnglái p, fǒuzé q"* is used to infer a particular cause on the basis of a particular fact, thus sentences in this form can be rewritten as a general inferential form *"jìrán fēi p, jiù yīdìng shì q"* ('since not *p*, then must *q*'). For instance, (39) can be rewritten as (40):

(39) 一定发生了什么意外，否则黄成宾不会不来。

Yīdìng   fāshēng-le shénme yìwài,   fǒuzé   Huáng Chéngbīn   bù   huì
definitely occur-PEF certain   accident otherwise HUANG Chengbin NEG   will

bù   lái.
NEG   come

{Something must have happened, otherwise HUANG Chengbin would not be absent.}

(40) 既然黄成宾没来，就一定是发生了什么意外。

Jìrán   Huáng Chéngbīn   méi   lái,   jiù   yīdìng   shì   fāshēng-le
now that HUANG Chengbin   NEG   come then definitely COP   occur-PEF

shénme   yìwài.
certain   accident

{Since HUANG Chengbin is absent, something must have happened.}

If a sentence in the form of *"jìrán p, jiù q"* is used to infer the cause based on the effect, it can be rewritten as *"xiǎnglái p, fǒuzé q"*. The following are two examples:

(41) 但是他又想，<u>既然党组织叫他联系</u>，（就）一定没有问题。

Dànshì tā yòu xiǎng, <u>jìrán</u>   dǎng zǔzhī   jiào tā   liánxi, (jiù) yīdìng
but   he again think   now that party organization ask   him contact then certainly

méiyǒu   wèntí.
there not be   problem

{But then he thought that since the Party asked him to make contact, it must be all right.}

"p, fǒuzé q" and relevant forms 41

(42) 想来一定没有问题，<u>不然</u>，党组织不会叫他联系。

Xiǎnglái yīdìng méiyǒu wèntí, <u>bùrán</u>, dǎng zǔzhī bù huì
presume certainly there not be problem otherwise party organization NEG will

jiào tā liánxi.
ask him contact

{Presumably it must be all right, otherwise the Party would not have asked him to make contact.}

Similarly, sentences in the form of "*xiǎnglái p, fǒuzé q*" can be rewritten as "*yàobùshì p, jiù q*". The following example is a rewrite of (39).

(43) 要不是发生了什么意外，黄成宾就不会不来。

Yàobùshì fāshēng-le shénme yìwài, Huáng Chéngbīn jiù bù huì bù
if not occur-PEF certain accident HUANG Chengbin then NEG will NEG

lái.
come

{Something must have happened, otherwise HUANG Chengbin would not be absent.}

However, the transformed sentence can be misunderstood if "*wǒ xiǎng*" ('I think') is not included or if the context is not clear enough, i.e., the speculation might be mistaken as a fact in some cases. Between the following two examples, (45) is a rewrite of (44). Without "*wǒ xiǎng*" or a clear context in (45), "her unawareness" might be misunderstood as a fact.

(44) 她<u>一定</u>还不晓得她的心上人走失，<u>否则</u>不会那么愉快。

Tā <u>yīdìng</u> hái bù xiǎode tā de xīnshàngrén zǒushī, <u>fǒuzé</u> bù
she definitely still NEG be aware she SP sweetheart be missing otherwise NEG

huì nàme yúkuài.
will so happy

{She must be unaware that her sweetheart is missing, otherwise she would not be as happy as that.}

(45) 她要不是还不晓得她的心上人走失，就不会那么愉快。

Tā yàobùshì hái bù xiǎode tā de xīnshàngrén zǒushī, jiù bù huì
she if not still NEG be aware she SP sweetheart be missing then NEG will

nàme yúkuài.
so happy

{She wouldn't be as happy as that if she knew that her sweetheart is missing.}

2.5 *"chúfēi p, fǒuzé q"*

As a form of conditional complex sentences, "*chúfēi p, fǒuzé q*" indicates a condition and a result contrary to the result of the condition.

42 *"p, fǒuzé q" and relevant forms*

2.5.1 Anterior clause in "chúfēi, fǒuzé q"

In the anterior clause, the word *chúfēi* introduces the condition and emphasizes that the condition is indispensable. The condition introduced by *chúfēi* can be a requirement or a reason. Both types of conditions are irrealis or unproven.

First, if the anterior clause of a sentence in the form of *"chúfēi p, fǒuzé q"* introduces the *p* as a required condition, then *p* is an indispensable condition. Thus, *"chúfēi p, fǒuzé q"* can be rewritten as *"fēi p bùkě, fǒuzé q"* ('*p* is indispensable, otherwise *q*'). The following three examples, (46a), (47a), and (48a), are in the form of *"chúfēi p, fǒuzé q"*, all of which can be rewritten in respectively as (46b), (47b), and (48b), the form of *"fēi p bùkě, fǒuzé q"*.

(46)　a 于书记还说，<u>除非</u>你到克山病区去，<u>否则</u>不会放你。

  Yú shūjì　　*hái*　*shuō,*　*chúfēi*　*nǐ*　*dào*　*kèshānbìng qū*　　　　*qù,*
  YU secretary also say　unless you go to endemic area of Keshan disease DC

  fǒuzé　　*bù*　　*huì*　*fàng*　*nǐ.*
  otherwise NEG will release you

  {Secretary Yu also said that you will not be released unless you go to (work in) the endemic area of Keshan disease.}

  → b 你非到克山病区去不可，否则不会放你。

  Nǐ　*fēi . . . bùkě dào*　*kèshānbìng qū*　　　　　*qù bùkě, fǒuzé*　*bù*
  you must　　　go to endemic area of Keshan disease DC　　otherwise NEG

  huì　*fàng*　*nǐ.*
  will release you

  {You must go to (work in) the endemic area of Keshan disease, otherwise you will not be released.}

(47)　a <u>除非</u>这一剑先将他刺死，<u>否则</u>自己下盘必被击中。

  Chúfēi zhè yī　*jiàn*　*xiān jiāng tā*　*cì-sǐ,*　　　*fǒuzé*　*zìjǐ*
  unless this one sword first BA　him stab to death otherwise oneself

  xiàpán　　　　　*bì*　　*bèi*　　*jī-zhòng.*
  lower part of the body definitely PASSIVE hit

  {My lower part will surely be hit unless I kill him first with this thrust of the sword.}

  → b 这一剑非先将他刺死不可，否则自己下盘必被击中。

  Zhè yī　*jiàn*　*fēi . . . bùkě xiān jiāng tā*　*cì-sǐ*　　　*bùkě, fǒuzé*　*zìjǐ*
  this one sword must　　first BA him stab to death　　otherwise oneself

  xiàpán　　　　　*bì*　　*bèi*　　*jī-zhòng.*
  lower part of the body definitely PASSIVE hit

  {I must kill him first with this one thrust of the sword, otherwise my lower part will surely be hit.}

"p, fǒuzé q" and relevant forms 43

(48) a 当今之世，<u>除非</u>是师父下山，<u>否则</u>不知还有谁能胜得过他。

Dāngjīn zhī shì, <u>chúfēi</u> shì shīfu xiàshān, <u>fǒuzé</u> bù zhī hái
today's world   unless COP master descend mountain otherwise NEG know else
yǒu shuí néng shèng de guò tā.
there be who can can defeat him
{In today's world, I wonder whether anyone else can defeat him if Master does not descend the mountain.}

→ b 当今之世，非师父下山不可，<u>否则</u>不知还有谁能胜得过他。

Dāngjīnzhī shì, fēi … bùkě shīfu xiàshān bùkě, <u>fǒuzé</u> bù zhī
today's world must   master descend mountain   otherwise NEG know
hái yǒu shuí néng shèng de guò tā.
else there be who can can defeat him
{In today's world, Master must descend the mountain, otherwise I wonder whether anyone else can defeat him.}

Sentences in the form of "*fēi p bùkě, fǒuzé q*" are commonly used. The following is an example:

(49) 你非给我指出人来<u>不可</u>，<u>要不</u>跟你没完！

Nǐ <u>fēi … bùkě</u> gěi wǒ zhǐ-chūlái rén lái <u>bùkě</u>, <u>yàobù</u> gēn nǐ méiwán!
you must   for me name   person DC   otherwise with you keep on
{You must name the person for me, otherwise I will go on with you!}

This example can be rewritten as one in the form of "*chúfēi p, fǒuzé q*", as follows:

(50) 除非你给我指出人来，要不跟你没完！

Chúfēi nǐ gěi wǒ zhǐ-chū rén lái, yàobù gēn nǐ méiwán!
unless you for me name person DC otherwise with you keep on
{I will go on with you unless you name that person for me!}

In actual language use, sentences in the form of "*zhǐyǒu p, fǒuzé q*" occasionally occur, which means the same as "*chúfēi p, fǒuzé q*". The following is an example:

(51) <u>只有</u>快快逃离了这个地方，<u>不然</u>会发疯的。

<u>Zhǐyǒu</u> kuài-kuài táolí le zhè gè dìfang, <u>bùrán</u> huì fāfēng de.
only   quickly-REDP escape MP this CL place   otherwise will go mad MP
{(We) must quickly get out of this place, or (we) will go crazy.}

The aforementioned example can be rewritten as (52) or (53):

(52) 除非快快逃离了这个地方，<u>不然</u>会发疯的。

<u>Chúfēi</u> kuài-kuài táolí le zhè gè dìfang, <u>bùrán</u> huì fāfēng de.
unless quickly-REDP escape MP this CL place otherwise will go mad MP
{(We) will go crazy unless (we) quickly get out of this place.}

44 *"p, fǒuzé q" and relevant forms*

(53) 非快快逃离这个地方不可，不然会发疯的。

Fēi . . . bùkě kuài-kuài   *táolí*   *le*   *zhè gè dìfang* ***bùkě,*** ***bùrán***   *huì*
must   quickly-REDP   escape   MP   this   CL   place   otherwise   will

fāfēng   *de.*
go mad   MP

{(We) must quickly get out of this place, otherwise (we) will go crazy.}

Second, the anterior clause of a sentence in the form of *"chúfēi p, fǒuzé q"* introduces *p* as a condition, meaning "unless (due to) *p*". For this reason, a sentence in the form of *"chúfēi p, fǒuzé q"* can be rewritten as *"chúfēi yīnwèi p, fǒuzé q"*. The following two examples, (54a) and (55a), can be rewritten respectively as (54b) and (55b), in the form of *"chúfēi yīnwèi p, fǒuzé.*

(54)   a 报告会上除非被逼得没有办法，否则，还是隐讳一点为好吧。

Bàogàohuì-shàng   *chúfēi bèi*   *bī*   *de méiyǒu*   *bànfǎ,*   ***fǒuzé,***
at the report meeting   unless   PASSIVE   force   SP   not have   method   otherwise

háishì . . . wéi hǎo   *yǐnhuì*   *yīdiǎn*   *wéi*   *hǎo*   *ba.*
had better   gloss over   a little   MP

{(When presenting your report) at the meeting, it is better not to be too straightforward, unless you are forced to be.}

→ b 除非因为被逼得没有办法，否则，还是隐讳一点为好。

Chúfēi yīnwèi bèi   *bī*   *de méiyǒu*   *bànfǎ,*   ***fǒuzé,***   *háishì . . . wéi hǎo*
unless   because   PASSIVE   force   SP   not have   method   otherwise   had better

yǐnhuì   *yīdiǎn wéi hǎo.*
gloss over   a little

{(When presenting your report) at the meeting, it is better not to be too straightforward, unless you are forced to be.}

(55)   a 你干完自己的活儿，除非有人请你帮忙，否则情愿呆在一旁游手好闲。

Nǐ   *gàn-wán zìjǐ*   *de huór,* ***chúfēi*** *yǒu*   *rén*   *qǐng nǐ*   *bāngmáng,*
you   finish   oneself   SP   work   unless   there be   person   ask   you   help

fǒuzé   *qíngyuàn dāi*   *zài*   *yīpáng yóushǒu-hàoxián.*
otherwise   be willing   stay   at   side   do nothing

{After you finish your work, it's best to stay there and do nothing unless someone asks you for help.}

→b 你干完自己的活儿，除非因为有人请你帮忙，否则情愿呆在一旁游手好闲。

Nǐ   *gàn-wán zìjǐ*   *de huór, chúfēi yīnwèi yǒu*   *rén*   *qǐng nǐ*
you   finish   oneself   SP   work   unless   because   there be   person   ask   you

bāngmáng,   *fǒuzé*   *qíngyuàn dāi*   *zài*   *yīpáng yóushǒu-hàoxián.*
help   otherwise   be willing   stay   at   side   do nothing

{After you finish your work, it's best to stay there and do nothing unless someone asks you for help.}

2.5.2 Posterior clause in "chúfēi p, fǒuzé q"

In sentences in the form of "*chúfēi p, fǒuzé q*", *q* is an irrealis result contrary to the result of the condition *p*.

If the condition denoted by *p* is a requirement, *q* is used as counterevidence to prove that *p* is crucial and indispensable. The posterior clause is often a negative statement, a rhetorical question, or in some cases, a "*zhǐnéng . . .*" construction in the affirmative form or "*yīdìng (zhǔn) . . .*" construction in the affirmative form. The following are four examples:

(56) 除非你离开这儿，否则他不会放过你。

Chúfēi   nǐ   líkāi   zhèr,   fǒuzé   tā   bù   huì   fàng-guò   nǐ.
unless   you   leave   here   otherwise   he   NEG   will   let go   you
{He won't let you go unless you leave here.}

(57) 除非你离开这儿，否则他怎么会放过你？

Chúfēi   nǐ   líkāi   zhèr,   fǒuzé   tā   zěnme   huì   fàng-guò   nǐ?
unless   you   leave   here   otherwise   he   how   will   let go   you
{How can he let you go if you don't leave here?}

(58) 除非你离开这儿，否则你只能整天躲着！

Chúfēi   nǐ   líkāi   zhèr,   fǒuzé   nǐ   zhǐ   néng   zhěngtiān   duǒ-zhe!
unless   you   leave   here   otherwise   you   only   can   all day   hide-PRG
{Unless you leave here, you have to hide all day!}

(59) 除非你离开这儿，否则你一定要挨打！

Chúfēi   nǐ   líkāi   zhèr,   fǒuzé   nǐ   yīdìng   yào   áidǎ!
unless   you   leave   here   otherwise   you   definitely   will   be beaten
{Unless you leave here, you will get beaten up!}

If the condition denoted by *p* is a reason, *q* is used as counterevidence to prove that *p* is a crucial condition and the only possible cause. The posterior clause is often a negative statement or a rhetorical question, or sometimes a "*yīdìng (zhǔn) . . .*" construction in the affirmative form, but not a "*zhǐnéng . . .*" construction in the affirmative form. The following are three examples:

(60) 除非没赶上班车，不然他不会迟到。

Chúfēi   méi   gǎn-shàng   bānchē,   bùrán   tā   bù   huì   chídào.
unless   NEG   catch   bus   otherwise   he   NEG   will   be late
{He won't be late unless he has missed the bus.}

(61) 除非没赶上班车，不然他怎么会迟到？

Chúfēi   méi   gǎn-shàng   bānchē,   bùrán   tā   zěnme   huì   chídào?
unless   NEG   catch   bus   otherwise   he   how   will   be late
{How can he be late if he hasn't missed the bus?}

46 *"p, fǒuzé q"* and relevant forms

(62) 除非没赶上班车，不然他两点钟准到。

Chúfēi méi gǎn-shàng bānchē, bùrán tā liǎng diǎn zhōng zhǔn dào.
unless NEG catch bus otherwise he two o'clock definitely arrive
{He will definitely arrive at two o'clock unless he has missed the bus.}

2.5.3 Expanded form

In sentences in the form of *"chúfēi p, fǒuzé q"*, another clause, *"cái . . ."*, can be inserted between the existing clauses. With *cái*, the inserted clause indicates the assumed result (+ *q*) of the condition *p*, whereas with *fǒuzé*, *q* in the original posterior clause is a result contrary to the assumed result (– *q*) of *p*. Thus, "+ *q*" is exactly the opposite of "–*q*" in meaning, even if it is not exactly opposite in wording. For example, (63a) can be expanded to (63b), and (64a) can be expanded to (64b).

(63) a 除非你到克山病区去，否则不会放你。

Chúfēi nǐ dào kèshānbìng qū qù, fǒuzé bù huì
unless you go to endemic area of Keshan disease DC otherwise NEG will
fàng nǐ.
release you
{You will not be released unless you go to (work in) the endemic area of Keshan disease.}

→b 除非你到克山病区去，才会放你，否则不会放你。

Chúfēi nǐ dào kèshānbìng qū qù, cái huì fàng nǐ,
unless you go to endemic area of Keshan disease DC then will release you
fǒuzé bù huì fàng nǐ.
otherwise NEG will release you
{You will be released only if you go to (work in) the endemic area of Keshan disease, otherwise you won't.}

(64) a 除非是师父下山，否则不知还有谁能胜得过他。

Chúfēi shì shīfu xiàshān, fǒuzé bù zhī hái yǒu shuí
unless COP master descend mountain otherwise NEG know else there be who
néng shèng de guò tā.
can can defeat him
{I wonder whether anyone else can defeat him if Master does not descend the mountain.}

→b 除非是师父下山，才能取胜，否则不知还有谁能胜得过他。

Chúfēi shì shīfu xiàshān, cái néng qǔshèng, fǒuzé bù zhī
unless COP master descend mountain then can win otherwise NEG know
hái yǒu shuí néng shèng de guò tā.
else there be who can can defeat him
{He can be defeated only if Master descends the mountain, otherwise I wonder whether anyone else can defeat him.}

"p, fǒuzé q" and relevant forms 47

2.5.4 *fǒuzé*

In some sentences in the form of *"chúfēi p, q"*, *fǒuzé* is absent, but it can be added.

In sentences where *fǒuzé* is absent, the posterior clause is often in the negative form, as in the following example:

(65) ……除非我召集你们，或者有人认为十分必要，你们不要这样成群打伙地来找我。

　　 . . . <u>chúfēi</u> wǒ zhàojí   nǐ-men, huòzhě yǒu   rén   rènwéi shífēn bìyào,
　　 unless I summon you-PL or   there be person deem very   necessary
　　 nǐ-men bùyào zhèyàng chéngqún-dǎhuǒ de lái   zhǎo wǒ.
　　 you-PL do not so   in groups   SP come see   me
　　 {Don't come to see me in such a big group unless I summon you or you think you really need to.}

2.6 *"yàome p, fǒuzé q"*

"yàome p, fǒuzé q" is a form of alternative sentences, indicating options or alternation between situations.

2.6.1 *"yàome p, yàome q" and "yàome p, fǒuzé q"*

Sentences in the form of *"yàome p, fǒuzé q"* can be rewritten as *"yàome p, yàome q"*, but they have different semantic emphases. The following is an examples:

(66) 要么是十六结婚，<u>不然</u>就——拉倒！

　　 <u>Yàome</u> shì shíliù   jiéhūn, <u>bùrán</u>   jiù— lādǎo!
　　 either COP sixteenth day of a month marry otherwise just forget about it
　　 {The wedding will be held on the 16th or forget about it!}

The aforementioned example means that one must make a choice between *p* and *q*; therefore, it can be rewritten as a *"yàome . . . yàome . . ."* sentence. However, in sentences in the form of *"yàome p, yàome q"*, *p* and *q* are parallel, whereas in *"yàome p, fǒuzé q"*, *p* is essential and *q* is supplementary.

Some sentences in the form of *"yàome p, fǒuzé q"* indicate that there is an opposition between the condition *p* and the result *q*, whereas other sentences in this form indicate that *p* and *q* are parallel situations. Thus, *"yàome p, fǒuzé q"* transforms the alternative relationship between *p* and *q* into the adversative relationship and highlights the adversative feature. If the adversative relationship does not need to be emphasized, sentences in the form of *"yàome p, fǒuzé q"* can be rewritten as *"yàome p, yàome q"*. Compare the following two examples:

(67) 要么照我的意思办，<u>否则</u>，我饶不了你！

　　 <u>Yàome</u> zhào   wǒ de yìsi   bàn, <u>fǒuzé,</u>   wǒ ráo bù liǎo   nǐ!
　　 either according to I SP intention do   otherwise I   cannot forgive you
　　 {Follow my order, or I'll never forgive you!}

48   *"p, fǒuzé q" and relevant forms*

(68)   <u>要么</u>照我的意思办，<u>不然</u>，就照你三哥的意思办！

<u>*Yàome*</u> *zhào*   *wǒ de yìsi*   *bàn,* <u>*bùrán,*</u>   *jiù*   *zhào*   *nǐ*
either   according to I   SP intention   do   otherwise then according to your

sāngē   *de yìsi*   *bàn!*
third brother   SP   intention   do
{Follow my order, or as your third brother wishes!}

Example (67) is an alternative sentence implying an opposition between the condition and the result, whereas (68) is an alternative sentence listing two parallel options.

2.6.2   *Expanded form*

The form "*yàome p, fǒuzé q*" can be expanded to "*yàome p₁, yàome p₂, fǒuzé q*", in which two choices are introduced by *yàome*, and this expanded form makes it even clearer that *q* is supplementary. For instance, (66) can be expanded to (69).

(69)   要么本月十六结婚，要么下月十六结婚，不然就——拉倒！

Yàome   *běn*   *yuè*   *shíliù*   *jiéhūn,*   *yàome*   *xià*
either   this   month   sixteenth day of a month   marry   or   next
yuè   *shíliù*   *jiéhūn,*   *bùrán*   *jiù—*   *lādǎo!*
month   sixteenth day of a month   marry   otherwise   just   forget about it
{The wedding will be held on the 16ᵗʰ of this month or the 16ᵗʰ of next month, otherwise forget about it!}

The following example is in the expanded alternative form indicating a general alternative relationship:

(70)   （既然不少人在叫喊，其中就定有原因：）<u>要么</u>就是李春山讲的统购任务过大了；<u>要么</u>就是昨天柳永凤说的，有娃娃鱼在暗里兴妖作怪。<u>再不然</u>，就是粮食本来是够吃的，但一部分人不会计划，胡乱浪费了，现在出现了窟窿。

(*Jìrán*   *bùshǎo rén*   *zài*   *jiàohǎn, qízhōng jiù*   *dìng*   *yǒu*
now that   many   person in progress shout   inside   then certainly there be
yuányīn:) <u>*yàome*</u> *jiù*   *shì*   *Lǐ Chūnshān jiǎng de tǒnggòu*   *rènwù*
reason   either   just COP   LI Chunshan say   SP monopolize purchase task
guò   *dà*   *le;*   <u>*yàome*</u> *jiù*   *shì*   *zuótiān*   *Liú Yǒngfèng shuō de, yǒu*
over   big   MP   or   just   COP   yesterday   LIU Yongfeng say   MP there be
wáwayú   *zài*   *àn-lǐ*   *xīngyāo-zuòguài.* <u>*Zàibùrán,*</u> *jiù*   *shì*
giant salamander in progress in secret make trouble   otherwise   just COP
liángshi běnlái   *shì*   *gòu*   *chī de,*   *dàn yībùfen rén*   *bùhuì*
food   originally COP   enough   eat   MP   but   a part   person   be unable
jìhuà,   *húluàn*   *làngfèi-le,*   *xiànzài chūxiàn-le kūlong.*
plan   at will   waste-PEF   now   occur-PEF shortage
{[Since many people are complaining, there must be reasons:] The amount of the monopolized purchase might be too big, as LI Chunshan said; or, as LIU Yongfeng

"*p, fǒuzé q*" *and relevant forms*   49

claimed yesterday, some giant salamanders were making trouble in secret; or there was originally enough food, but some people were not good at planning and wasted it at will, which has caused food shortages.}

A sentence in the form of "*yàome p_1, yàome p_2, fǒuzé q*" can also be rewritten as "*huòzhě p_1, huòzhě p_2, fǒuzé q*" or "*bùshì p_1, jiùshì p_2, fǒuzé q*", as in the following two examples:

(71) <u>或者</u>把他的节目全部都挪到十一点之前；<u>或者</u>给他增加工资，使他每天能吃像样的晚餐。<u>否则</u>，我就要到别的饭馆去给他找一个早一点收工的工作。

Huòzhě bǎ tā de jiémù   quánbù dōu nuó-dào shíyī diǎn   zhīqián;
either BA he SP performance whole all move to eleven o'clock before
huòzhě gěi tā zēngjiā gōngzī, shǐ tā měitiān néng chī xiàngyàng de
or   for him increase salary allow him every day can eat decent SP
wǎncān. Fǒuzé, wǒ jiù yào dào biéde fànguǎn qù gěi tā zhǎo
dinner otherwise I then will go to other restaurant DC for him look for
yī gè zǎo yīdiǎn shōugōng de gōngzuò.
one CL early a little finish work SP work
{Either move all his performance to before eleven o'clock; or increase his salary so that he can eat a decent dinner every day. Otherwise, I will go to other restaurants to find him a job that finishes a bit earlier.}

(72) （这些日子来，他常常夜里出去。）<u>不是</u>借口开会，<u>就是</u>借口去同志家坐坐，<u>要不就</u>干脆什么也不说，吃罢晚饭就匆匆走了。

(Zhèxiē rìzi lái, tā cháng-cháng yè-lǐ chū-qù.) Bùshì...jiùshì...
these   day during he often-REDP at night go out if not... then...
jiēkǒu   kāihuì, jiùshì jiēkǒu   qù tóngzhì jiā
use ... as an excuse have a meeting use ... as an excuse go comrade's home
zuò-zuò, yàobù jiù gāncuì shénme yě bù shuō, chī-bà wǎnfàn jiù
sit-REDP otherwise just simply whatever NEG say finish eating dinner then
cōng-cōng zǒu   le.
hurried   leave MP
{[These days, he often goes out at night,] either on the pretext of attending a meeting or visiting a comrade, or simply leaves in a hurry after dinner without saying anything.}

Example (71) is an expanded alternative sentence with an implied opposition between the conditions and the result, whereas (72) is a general alternative sentence in the expanded form.

2.6.3 *Absence of yàome*

Sentences indicating a general alternative relationship can be in the form of "*p, fǒuzé q*", and *fǒuzé* or its synonym can be replaced by *zàibùrán* ('otherwise') or *zàibù* ('otherwise'). The following are two examples:

50 *"p, fŏuzé q" and relevant forms*

(73) 你说呀，爸爸！……要不，你就点点头吧，爸爸！

Nǐ   shuō   ya,   bàba!   ...Yàobù,   nǐ   jiù   diǎn-diǎn   tóu   ba,   bàba!
you   say   MP   dad   otherwise   you   just   nod-REDP   head   MP   dad
{Speak, Dad . . . Otherwise just nod your head, Dad!}

(74) 准是鬼点灯，要不，就是你的眼花了。

Zhǔn   shì   guǐdiǎndēng,   yàobù,   jiù   shì   nǐ   de   yǎn   huā-le.
definitely COP phosphorus fire otherwise just COP you SP eye dazzled-PEF
{It must be phosphorus fire (in the cemetery), otherwise your eyes were dazzled.}

In the two aforementioned examples, the absence of *yàome* does not affect the intrinsic alternative relationship between the two clauses, and *yàobù* in each sentence can be replaced by *zàibùrán* or *zàibù*. The following are two examples:

(75) 有空，到街上遛遛，散散心，再不，花上两毛钱，看上场电影。

Yǒu   kòng,   dào   jiē-shàng liùliù,   sànsànxīn,   zàibù,   huā-shàng
have free time go to on street take a walk enjoy a diversion otherwise spend
liǎng   máo   qián,   kàn-shàng   chǎng   diànyǐng.
two   ten cents   money   watch   CL   movie
{If (you) have time, go for a walk on the street to have some relaxation, or spend 20 cents on a movie.}

(76) 我看那个情景，不是个老倌子，就是个病人子，再不，就是跛子、瘫子。

Wǒ kàn nà gè qíngjǐng, bùshì gè lǎoguānzi, jiùshì gè bìngrénzi, zàibù,
I   see that CL situation if not CL old man   then   CL patient   otherwise
jiùshì bǒzi,   tānzi.
then   cripple   paralytic
{From what I have seen, he must be a sick man if not an old man or otherwise, a cripple or a paralytic.}

In (75), *yàome* is absent in the anterior clause, and *zàibù* is present between *p* and *q*, whereas in (76) "*bùshì . . . jiùshì . . .*" is used within the anterior clause, and *zàibù* is placed between *p* and *q*.

2.7 *"háishì p ba, fŏuzé q"*

Sentences in the form of *"háishì p ba, fŏuzé q"* are imperative ones showing a request or a piece of advice and the consequence of the request or advice being rejected.

2.7.1 *Anterior clause in "háishì p ba, fŏuzé q"*

The anterior clause can be in the imperative form of *"háishì p ba, fŏuzé q"*, or *"háishì p, fŏuzé q"*, or *"p ba, fŏuzé q"*, or *"p, fŏuzé q"*, in all of which *p* is a request or a piece of advice.

"p, fǒuzé q" and relevant forms   51

In some cases, *háishì* and *ba* cooccur, as in the following example:

(77) 你还是来吧，要不我想你。

| Nǐ | háishì | lái | ba, | yàobù | wǒ | xiǎng | nǐ. |
| you | had better | come | MP | otherwise | I | miss | you |

{You'd better come, or I'll miss you.}

In some cases, only *háishì* or *ba* is present, or neither of them are present, as in the following three examples:

(78) 你还是早点杀了它，要不客人一来就忙不赢了。

| Nǐ | háishì | zǎo | diǎn | shā-le | tā, | yàobù | kèrén yī... jiù... lái | jiù |
| you | had better | early | a bit | butcher-PEF | it | otherwise | guest as soon as | arrive |

máng bù yíng le.
too busy to cope MP

{You'd better butcher it early, or you won't have time to do it after the guests have arrived.}

(79) 快卖了吧，要不人家可走啦！

| Kuài | mài | le | ba, | yàobù | rénjiā | kě | zǒu | la! |
| quickly | sell | MP | MP | otherwise | other people | really | leave | MP |

{Sell it quickly before they leave!}

(80) 请别这样激动，否则我就证实了他是对的。

| Qǐng | bié | zhèyàng | jīdòng, | fǒuzé | wǒ jiù | zhèngshí | le | tā | shì |
| please | do not | so | excited | otherwise | I then | be convinced | MP | he | COP |

duì de.
right SP

{Please don't be so excited, or I will be convinced that he is right.}

In (78), *háishì* is used, and *ba* can be added; in (79) *ba* is present, and *háishì* can be supplemented; in (80) neither *háishì* nor *ba* occurs, but both can be added.

The anterior clause can be in the affirmative or negative form, and in some cases, both an affirmative imperative clause and a negative one occur, as in the following example:

(81) ……要走马上就走，别耽搁，要不，我会忍不住让他给我留起来的。

| ...yào zǒu | mǎshàng | jiù | zǒu, | bié | dān'ge, | yàobù, | wǒ huì | rěn bù zhù |
| if | go right away | early | go | do not | delay | otherwise | I | will cannot help |

ràng tā gěi wǒ liú-qǐlái de.
ask him for me keep MP

{If you will leave, then leave quickly and don't delay, or I can't help but ask him to keep (it) for me.}

52 *"p, fǒuzé q" and relevant forms*

The anterior clause in the aforementioned example is a combination of an affirmative form and a negative form, i.e., "leave quickly" + "don't delay".

2.7.2 *Posterior clause in "háishì p ba, fǒuzé q"*

In sentences in the form of *"háishì p ba, fǒuzé q"*, *q* is the consequence of *p* being rejected, and it can, at the same time, be understood as another option, i.e., an unpleasant choice if *p* is rejected. The following is an example:

(82) 春生，你把种鸡舍那个洞补补吧！要不，鸡都丢光。
> *Chūnshēng, nǐ   bǎ   zhǒngjī shè   nà   gè   dòng   bǔ-bǔ   ba!*
> Chunsheng you BA breeding chicken coop that CL hole   repair-REDP MP
> *Yàobù,   jī   dōu diū-guāng.*
> otherwise chicken all   be lost
> {Chunsheng, why don't you mend the hole in the breeding chicken coop? Otherwise all the chickens will get lost.}

In this example, "all the chickens getting lost" is the unfavorable result of the advice "mending the hole in the breeding chicken coop" being rejected. If "Chunsheng" chooses not to mend the hole in the breeding chicken coop, he has to face the unpleasant consequence of allowing all the chickens to get lost.

In some cases, the anterior clause *q* is in an interrogative form that shows a disadvantaged result or an unfavorable selection, as in the following example:

(83) 走吧，阿雪，要不，我们怎么办？
> *Zǒu   ba,   Āxuě,   yàobù,   wǒ-men   zěnme   bàn?*
> go   MP   Axue   otherwise we   how   do
> {Axue, let's go, otherwise what can we do?}

2.7.3 *Paraphrase of "háishì p ba, fǒuzé q"*

The form of *"háishì p ba, fǒuzé q"* can be paraphrased as "either *p* or *q*, and since *q* isn't good, you'd better *p*". For example, (82) can be paraphrased as follows:

(84) 要么你把种鸡舍那个洞补补，要么鸡都丢光；鸡都丢光不好，所以，还是把
种鸡舍那个洞补补为好。
> *Yàome . . . yàome . . .   nǐ   bǎ   zhǒngjī shè   nà   gè   dòng*
> either . . . or . . .   you   BA   breeding chicken coop that   CL   hole
> *bǔ-bǔ,   yàome jī   dōu diū-guāng; jī   dōu diū-guāng bù   hǎo.*
> repair-REDP chicken all be lost   chicken all be lost   NEG good
> *suǒyǐ,   háishì . . . wéi hǎo   bǎ   zhǒngjī shè   nà   gè   dòng*
> therefore   had better   BA   breeding chicken coop that   CL   hole
> *bǔ-bǔ   wéi hǎo.*
> repair-REDP be   good
> {Either you mend the hole in the breeding chicken coop, or allow all the chickens to get lost. Since losing all the chickens is bad, you'd better mend the hole in the breeding chicken coop.}

"p, fǒuzé q" and relevant forms 53

Between "*yàome p, fǒuzé q*" and "*háishì p ba, fǒuzé q*", the former is a simple alternative form, whereas the latter includes disjunctive reasoning. Compare the following two examples:

(85) 要么杀了它，不然，就卖掉它！
Yàome shā le tā, bùrán, jiù mài-diào tā!
either kill MP it otherwise just sell it
{Either kill it or sell it!}

(86) 还是杀了它吧，不然，大家都不得安宁！
Háishì shā le tā ba, bùrán, dàjiā dōu bù dé ānníng!
had better kill MP it MP otherwise everyone all NEG get peace
{Let's kill it, otherwise no one can be at peace!}

Example (85) is in an alternative complex sentence implying an opposition between *p* and *q*, so it can only be rewritten as (87), whereas (86) is imperative, thus it can be paraphrased as (88).

(87) 要么杀了它，要么就卖掉它！
Yàome ... yàome ... shā le tā, yàome jiù mài-diào tā!
either ... or ... kill MP it just sell it
{Either kill it or sell it!}

(88) 要么杀了它，要么大家都不得安宁；大家都不得安宁不好，所以，还是杀了它为好！
Yàome ... yàome ... shā le tā, yàome dàjiā dōu bù dé ānníng; dàjiā
either ... or ... kill MP it everyone all NEG get peace everyone
dōu bù dé ānníng bù hǎo, suǒyǐ, háishì ... wéi hǎo shā le tā wéi hǎo!
all NEG get peace NEG good therefore had better kill MP it be good
{Either kill it, or no one can be at peace. It is not good that no one can be at peace, so it is better to kill it!}

2.8 *"bù néng p, fǒuzé q"* and *"bù néng bù p, fǒuzé q"*

The sentence forms "*bù néng p, fǒuzé q*" and "*bù néng bù p, fǒuzé q*" both express a need and the result of the need being unmet. A salient feature of these two forms is the inclusion of an auxiliary verb in the anterior clause, thus they can be termed as auxiliary sentence forms.

2.8.1 *Anterior clause in "bù néng p, fǒuzé q"*

With "*bù néng*", the anterior clause of "*bù néng p, fǒuzé q*" points out the necessity and requirement of a matter in a negative form. The following is an example:

54 "p, fǒuzé q" and relevant forms

(89) <u>不能</u>在错误面前退却，<u>不然</u>这种无组织无纪律的行为，会像病菌那样继续蔓延传染的。

<u>Bù</u> <u>néng</u> zài cuòwù miànqián tuìquè, <u>bùrán</u> zhè zhǒng wú zǔzhī
NEG can at mistake front retreat otherwise this kind disorganized
wú jìlǜ de xíngwéi, huì xiàng bìngjūn nàyàng jìxù mànyán chuánrǎn de.
undisciplined SP behavior will like germ such continue spread infect MP
{(We) can't accommodate mistakes, otherwise this kind of disorganized and undisciplined behavior will continue to spread like germs.}

In some cases, what is in the position of "*bù néng*" is its synonym, such as "*bù yīng*" ('should not'), "*bù kě*" ('must not'), and so on. The following is an example:

(90) 这种女人绝<u>不应</u>是对现代伦理有清醒知觉，对现代文明有热烈向往的那种女性，<u>否则的话</u>，格格不入的追求，就会使情感发生危机，使先天的悲剧愈演愈惨。

Zhè zhǒng nǚrén jué <u>bù</u> <u>yīng</u> shì duì xiàndài lúnlǐ yǒu qīngxǐng
this kind woman absolutely NEG should COP of modern ethics have clear
zhījué, duì xiàndài wénmíng yǒu rèliè xiàngwǎng de nà zhǒng nǚxìng,
sense for modern civilization have enthusiastic yearn SP that kind female
<u>fǒuzé</u> <u>dehuà</u>, gégé-bùrù de zhuīqiú, jiù huì shǐ qínggǎn fāshēng wēijī,
otherwise MP incompatible SP pursue then will make emotion occur crisis
shǐ xiāntiān de bēijù yùyǎn-yùcǎn.
make congenital SP tragedy become even more miserable
{This kind of woman should never be the kind of woman who has a clear awareness of modern ethics and a passionate yearning for modern civilization, otherwise, the incompatible pursuit will cause emotional crisis and make the congenital tragedy worse.}

2.8.2 Anterior clause in "bùnéng bù p, fǒuzé q"

With "*bù néng bù*", the anterior clause of "*bù néng bù p, fǒuzé q*" points out the necessity and requirement of a matter in a double-negative form. The following are two examples:

(91) 细妹她娘，我<u>不能不走</u>，<u>要不</u>，我对不住你，也对不住春牛！

Xìmèi tā niáng, wǒ <u>bù</u> <u>néng</u> <u>bù</u> zǒu, <u>yàobù</u>, wǒ duìbùzhù nǐ, yě
Ximei's mother I NEG can NEG go otherwise I be unfair to you also
duìbùzhù Chūnniú!
be unfair to Chunniu
{Ximei's mom, I must go, otherwise it would be unfair to you, as well as to Chunniu!}

(92) 作为一个人，又<u>不能不看</u>，<u>不能不想</u>，<u>否则</u>，她的头脑里就会一片空白，她的神经就无法忍受，她会疯的！

Zuòwéi yī gè rén, yòu <u>bù</u> <u>néng</u> <u>bù</u> kàn, <u>bù</u> <u>néng</u> <u>bù</u> xiǎng,
as one CL person indeed NEG can NEG look NEG can NEG think

fǒuzé, tā de tóunǎo-lǐ jiù huì yī piàn kòngbái, tā de shénjīng jiù
otherwise she SP in mind just will one CL blank she SP nerve just
wúfǎ rěnshòu, tā huì fēng de!
cannot endure she will go crazy MP
{As a person, she can't stop looking, nor can she stop thinking; otherwise her
mind will go blank and her nerves won't be able to stand it—she'll go crazy!}

The alternative to the double-negative form is the affirmative form, therefore
"bù néng bù" can be rephrased as *děi* ('need'), *bìxū* ('must'), *yīnggāi* ('should'),
and so forth. Thus, *"děi (yào, bìxū, yīnggāi) p, fǒuzé q"* carries approximately the
same meaning as *"bù néng bù p, fǒuzé q"* does. The following are two examples:

(93) 就像种子一样，到了一定时候就<u>得</u>更新换代，<u>不然</u>就退化了，老化了。

    Jiù xiàng . . . yīyàng zhǒngzi yīyàng, dào le yīdìng shíhou jiù <u>děi</u>
    just like   seed   come to MP certain time then need

    gēngxīn-huàndài, <u>bùrán</u> jiù tuìhuà le, lǎohuà le.
    regenerate   otherwise then degenerate MP age MP
    {Just like seeds, (it) has to be updated at a certain time, otherwise (it) will degen-
    erate and age.}

(94) 这话<u>该</u>说了，<u>否则</u>会让莹莹太难堪。

    Zhè huà <u>gāi</u> shuō le, <u>fǒuzé</u> huì ràng Yíngyíng tài nánkān.
    this words should say MP otherwise will make Yingying too embarrassed
    {It's time to say that, otherwise Yingying will be too embarrassed.}

2.8.3 Posterior clause in *"bù néng (bù) p, fǒuzé q"*

The posterior clause in *"bù néng (bù) p, fǒuzé q"* indicates the result of the need
or requirement being unmet, and it can also be understood as the opposite choice
of the need or requirement, thus the whole sentence can be paraphrased as "either
cannot (must) *p*, or *q*, and *q* is not good, therefore cannot (must) *p*". For example,
(91) can be paraphrased as follows:

(95) 要么我不能不走，要么我对不住你和春牛；对不住你和春牛不好，所以，我
    不能不走。

    Yàome . . . yàome . . . wǒ bù néng bù zǒu, yàome wǒ duìbùzhù nǐ hé
    either . . . or . . . I NEG can NEG go I be unfair to you and

    Chūnniú; duìbùzhù nǐ hé Chūnniú bù hǎo, suǒyǐ, wǒ bù néng bù zǒu.
    Chunniu be unfair to you and Chunniu NEG good therefore I NEG can NEG go
    {Either I must go, or it would be unfair to you as well as to Chunniu. It is not
    good to be unfair to you and Chunniu, so I must go.}

Although similarities exist between *"bù néng (bù) p, fǒuzé q"* and *"háishì p
ba, fǒuzé q"*, differences also exist. First, most of the anterior clauses in sentences
in the form of *"bù néng (bù) p, fǒuzé q"* are declarative clauses, whereas all the

56 *"p, fǒuzé q"* and relevant forms

anterior clauses in *"háishì p ba, fǒuzé q"* are imperative clauses. Second, in some cases the anterior clause in *"bù néng (bù) p, fǒuzé q"* can be imperative, but it puts more emphasis on the analysis of the subjective and the objective need, and cannot be worded as *"háishì bù néng (bù) p wéi hǎo"*. Compare:

(96) 割草可<u>不能</u>碰了坏天气呀，<u>不然</u>要泡汤的。

Gē cǎo kě <u>bù</u> <u>néng</u> pèng le huài tiānqì ya, <u>bùrán</u> yào
cut grass really NEG can meet MP bad weather MP otherwise will

pàotāng de.
fall through MP
{If the weather happens to be bad, the mowing plan will fall through.}

(97) 割草<u>还是</u>注意一下天气吧，<u>不然</u>要泡汤的。

Gē cǎo <u>háishì</u> zhùyì-yīxià tiānqì ba, <u>bùrán</u> yào pàotāng de.
cut grass had better pay attention weather MP otherwise will fall through MP
{One had better watch the weather when making a mowing plan, otherwise the plan may fall through.}

It would sound awkward if the anterior clause in (96) was rephrased as *"gē cǎo háishì bù néng pèng le huài tiānqì wéi hǎo"* ('in mowing, the weather had better not happen to be bad'), but it would sound natural if the wording was changed into *"gē cǎo háishì zhùyì yīxià tiānqì wéi hǎo"* ('one had better watch the weather before mowing').

If the anterior clause in a sentence in the form of *"děi p, fǒuzé q"* is an imperative clause, it is quite close to *"háishì p ba, fǒuzé q"*, but it cannot be rewritten as *"háishì děi p ba"* because the mood would change. The following is an example:

(98) 这年头，脑瓜<u>得</u>活点，<u>要不</u>，得处处碰壁呢！

Zhè niántou, nǎoguā <u>děi</u> huó diǎn, <u>yàobù</u>, děi chù-chù
this year brain need flexible a little otherwise must everywhere

pèngbì ne!
run into a wall MP
{Nowadays (you) need to act according to changing circumstances, otherwise (you) will constantly find yourself banging your head against walls!}

If the last example was rewritten with the retainment of the auxiliary verb *děi* and the addition of *"háishì ... ba"*, as in (99), the original imperative mood would turn into a questioning tone:

(99) 这年头，脑瓜还是<u>得</u>活点吧，······

Zhè niántou, nǎoguā háishì <u>děi</u> huó diǎn ba, ...
this year brain had better need flexible a little MP
{Nowadays, is it better (for you) to act according to changing circumstances ...?}

Summary

First, a number of sub-forms of "*p, fŏuzé q*" have been discussed in this chapter. As they differ in semantic relationship, they can be rewritten as different forms, as listed in the following table for reference:

Table 2.1 Sub-forms of "*p, fŏuzé q*"

	Typical sub-forms	*Main rephrased forms*
Reason explaining	*xìngkuī p, fŏuzé q*; *kĕxī p, fŏuzé q*; *yīnwèi p, fŏuzé q*;	*yàobùshì p, jiù q* (*zhīsuŏyĭ fēi p, jiù yīnwèi shì q*)
Reason inferring	*xiănglái p, fŏuzé q*	*yàobùshì p, jiù q* (*jìrán fēi p, jiù kĕndìng shì q*)
Conditional	*chúfēi p, fŏuzé q*	*chúfēi p, cái + q, fŏuzé—q* (*fēi p bùkĕ, fŏuzé q*) (*chúle yīnwèi p, fŏuzé q*)
Alternative	*yàome p, fŏuzé q*	*yàome p, yàome q*
Imperative	*háishì p ba, fŏuzé q*	*yàome p, yàome q, q bù hăo, suŏyĭ háishì p wéi hăo*
Auxiliary	*bùnéng p, fŏuzé q*; *bùnéngbù p, fŏuzé q*	*yàome bù néng (bù) p, yàome q, q bù hăo, suŏyĭ bù néng (bù) p*

Second, the semantic relationships between *p* and *q* in different sub-forms of "*p, fŏuzé q*" are different, but they share some similarities, i.e., *p* and *q* are contradictory. In general, *q* is a result contrary to the assumed result of *p*; however, the alternative sub-form (i.e., *yàome p, fŏuzé q*) is an exception in the sense that in this sub-form *q* is an alternative—rather than a result—contrary to *p*.

Third, in general, "*p, fŏuzé q*" places the semantic emphasis on *p*. The reason explaining form and the reason inferring form both emphasize that the reason *p* is crucial. The condition form emphasizes that the condition *p* is indispensable. The alternative form highlights *p* as the preferred option. The imperative form and the auxiliary form emphasize that *p* as advice needs to be followed or that *p* as requirement needs to be met. Only the conditional form highlights *q*, for it emphasizes that the occurrence of *q* is independent on everything but *p*.

Fourth, a connective, such as *fŏuzé* or its synonym, links the contrasting anterior clause and posterior clause. Consequently, the connective needs to be present in most cases, except in the conditional form.

Fifth, even though both *fŏuzé* and *dànshì* can indicate opposition, they are not the same. With *fŏuzé*, the opposition is formed after the affirmation of what is said later based on the hypothesis that what is said earlier is negated. By comparison, *dànshì* and its synonyms simply introduce an abrupt and direct contrast. Thus, *fŏuzé* and *dànshì* mark different types of oppositions. Therefore, adversative complex sentences often refer to those marked by connective *dàn* or one of its synonyms, even though the complex sentences marked by *fŏuzé* or its synonyms

58 *"p, fǒuzé q" and relevant forms*

indicating a hypothetical opposition between the clauses are a subtype of adversative complex sentences.

NB Some examples in this chapter are cited from literary works, political essays, articles, and so on. The sources are listed as follows:

1 *Baihuazhou* (《百花洲》) 1982(6), including Examples (9) and (14); 1983(1), including (30); 1983(3), including (32);
2 *Changjiang Literature* (《长江》) 1982(4), including (78); 1983(1), including (24), (33), (36), and (91); 1983(2), including (25), (74), (82), and (94);
3 *Changcheng* (《长城》) 1982(1), including (75) and (98);
4 *Chinese* for Junior High School Students, Book 1, including (41),
5 *Dangdai* (《当代》) 1982(3), including (72), (79), (81), and (93); 1982(6), including (65) and (77); 1983(1), including (44) and (54a); 1983(2), including (4); 1985(5), including (23);
6 *Fiction Monthly* (《小说月报》) 1982(2), including (12) and (66); 1982(3), including (83); 1982(7), including (90); 1983(3), including (49); 1996(12), including (2);
7 *Flower City* (《花城》) 1983(2), including (92);
8 *Harvest* (《收获》) 1982(1), including (71); 1982(6), including (80);
9 *Kunlun* (《昆仑》) 1983(1), including (21a), (22), and (89);
10 *Lotus* (《芙蓉》) 1982(3), including (13);
11 *October* (《十月》) 1982(1), including (46a); 1982(3), including (3); 1982(4), including (6); 1983(2), including (35);
12 *People's Literature* (《人民文学》) 1982(12), including (34) and (73);
13 *Qingming* (《清明》) 1983(1), including (27) and (76);
14 *Revolution* (《春潮急》) by Kefei (克非), including (70);
15 *Selected Stories* (《小说选刊》) 1996(11), including (1) and (20a);
16 *State of Divinity* (《笑傲江湖》) by JIN Yong (金庸), including (11) and (47a);
17 *The Heaven Sword and Dragon Saber* (《倚天屠龙记》) by JIN Yong (金庸), including (48a);
18 *Zhongpian Xiaoshuo Xuankan* (《中篇小说选刊》) 1994(6), including (26); 1995(2), including (55a); 1997(4), including (5);
19 *Zuopin yu Zhengming* (《作品与争鸣》) 1982(7), including (96).

Bibliogpraphy

[1] LV Shuxiang (吕叔湘). *Eight Hundred Words in Modern Chinese* (《现代汉语八百词》). The Commercial Press, 1980, p. 183.
[2] LV Shuxiang (吕叔湘). *Eight Hundred Words in Modern Chinese* (《现代汉语八百词》). The Commercial Press, 1980, p. 82.

3 Occurrence of *dàn* or its synonym in *"jì p, yòu q"* and relevant forms

dàn and its synonyms refer to conjunctions and linking adverbs indicating an adversative relationship. These words include *dàn, dànshì, kě, kěshì, què,* and so on.

This chapter discusses complex sentences in which *dàn* or its synonyms can be present. These sentences are in the forms of *"jì p, yòu q"*, *"yīfāngmiàn p, lìng yīfāngmiàn q"*, *"jíshǐ p, yě q"*, *"níngkě p yě q"*, and so on.

3.1 Occurrence of *dàn* or its synonym in *"jì p, yòu q"*

The correlative conjunction *"jì . . . yòu . . ."* marks a coordinate relationship, and hence is used to form coordinate complex sentences. In some cases, *dàn* or its synonym can be present in sentences in the form of *"jì p, yòu q"*. The following are two examples:

(1) 陈毅说的<u>既</u>是微妙的外交辞令，<u>但又</u>是率真的大实话，⋯⋯

Chén Yì   shuō de <u>jì</u>...<u>yòu</u>...   shì   wēimiào de wàijiāo   cílìng,   **dàn**
CHEN Yi say   SP both...and... COP subtle   SP diplomatic language but

<u>yòu</u> shì   shuàizhēn de dà   shíhuà, . . .
    COP frank   SP real truth

{The words that CHEN Yi used were subtle and diplomatic, but frank and honest as well . . .}

(2) 他<u>既</u>希望周奉宛能办成此事，却<u>又</u>怕她弄不好捅出麻烦来⋯⋯

Tā <u>jì</u>...<u>yòu</u>...   xīwàng Zhōu Fèngwǎn   néng bàn-chéng cǐ shì,
he both...and... hope   ZHOU Fengwan can   accomplish this matter

què <u>yòu</u> pà   tā   nòng bù hǎo   tǒng-chū máfan   lái . . .
however   be afraid she cannot do well make   trouble DP

{He hoped that ZHOU Fengwan could accomplish this, but he was also afraid that she might cause trouble if she failed . . .}

These two examples each employ *"jì . . . yòu . . ."* and *dàn/què*, i.e., Example (1) is in the form of *"jì p, dàn yòu q"*, and (2) is in *"jì p, què yòu q"*. The two forms can be used interchangeably for these two examples. Without *dàn* or *què*, the two

DOI: 10.4324/9781003374237-3

60 *Occurrence of dàn or its synonym and relevant forms*

sentences would be coordinate complex sentences, but the occurrence of *dàn* or *què* defines the nature of the sentences as adversative. The following are two examples:

(3) 我既感到摆脱了一种负担的轻松，却又有一种相形见绌的沉重。
    Wǒ jì . . . yòu . . .   *gǎndào bǎituō-le yī zhǒng fùdān de qīngsōng,* **què**
    I both . . . and . . . feel   rid-PEF one kind burden SP light   however
    yòu yǒu yī zhǒng xiāngxíng-jiànchù   *de chénzhòng.*
    have one kind   be inferior by comparison SP heavy
    {I have a sense of relief from a burden, but I also feel heavy hearted because of my inferiority to others.}

(4) 对于林冲，我们既寄以满腔的同情，却又深惜其认识不够；……
    Duìyú Lín Chōng, wǒ-men jì . . . yòu . . .   *jìyǐ mǎnqiāng de tóngqíng,*
    for LIN Chong we   both . . . and . . . give heart be filled SP sympathize
    què   *yòu shēn xī*   *qí rènshi bù   gòu; . . .*
    however   deep feel sorry he know NEG enough
    {For LIN Chong, we are full of sympathy, but we also feel deeply sorry for him for his insufficient understanding . . .}

Examples (3) and (4) not only use "*jì . . . yòu . . .*" but also *què*, which can be replaced by *dàn*.

A synonymous form of "*jì p, yòu q*" is "*jì p, yě q*", in which *dàn* or its synonym can also occur, as in the following three examples:

(5) 她既没有踊跃赞同，但也没有露出一丝不愿的样子。
    Tā jì . . . yě . . .   *méiyǒu yǒngyuè   zàntóng,* **dàn** *yě méiyǒu lù-chū yīsī*
    she both . . . and . . . NEG   enthusiastic agree   but   NEG   show a little
    bù yuàn   de yàngzi.
    NEG be willing SP appearance
    {She did not enthusiastically agree, but nor did she show any sign of reluctance.}

(6) 爱情既是一首优美的歌曲，但也是难谱的乐章，难弹的琴……
    Àiqíng jì . . . yě . . .   *shì yī shǒu yōuměi de gēqǔ,* **dàn** *yě shì nán*
    love   both . . . and . . . COP one CL beautiful SP song but   COP difficult
    pǔ   de yuèzhāng, nán   tán de qín . . .
    compose SP movement difficult play SP piano
    {Love is a beautiful song, but it is also a piece of music difficult to compose and play.}

(7) 这么些年，既听不到他们一点点自我批评，可也听不到他们一句互相埋怨的话，……
    Zhème xiē nián, jì . . . yě . . .   *tīng bù dào tā-men yīdiǎndiǎn zìwǒ pīpíng,*
    so   CL year both . . . and . . . cannot hear they a little   self-criticize
    kě *yě* *tīng bù dào yī jù   hùxiāng mányuàn de huà, . . .*
    but   cannot hear one CL   mutually complain SP words

Occurrence of dàn or its synonym and relevant forms 61

{Over the years, not a little bit of self-criticism has been heard from them, but nor can a word of complaint against each other be heard . . .}

The three aforementioned examples employ both "*jì . . . yě . . .*" and *dàn/kě*, which can be replaced by *què*.

In sentences in the form of "*jì p, yòu q*", there are two different relationships between the clauses: a simple coordinate relationship and an implied adversative relationship. In the following two examples the relationship is purely coordinate:

(8) 你爸回来了，既有实权，又有威望，求他给秀芳办办不可以吗？

Nǐ   bà   huílái   le,   jì . . . yòu . . .   yǒu shíquán, yòu yǒu wēiwàng,
your father come back PEF both . . . and . . . have real power have prestige

qiú   tā   gěi   Xiùfāng   bàn-bàn   bù   kěyǐ   ma?
beg   him   for   Xiufang   do-REDP   NEG   can   MP
{Your dad's back. He has both real power and prestige. Can't you ask him to do it for Xiufang?}

(9) 他们三三两两在村头上转游，既卖这里缺少的土产，又讲他们近两年来的变化。

Tā-men sānsān-liǎngliǎng zài cūntóu-shàng zhuànyou, jì . . . yòu . . .   mài zhèli
they   by twos and threes at in village   wander   both . . . and . . . sell here

quēshǎo de tǔchǎn,   yòu jiǎng tā-men jìn   liǎng nián lái   de biànhuà.
lack   SP local product talk they   recent two   year since SP change
{They wandered about the village in twos and threes, selling their local products that were lacking here, and talking of the changes in their place over the last couple of years.}

In each of the aforementioned examples, the relationship between the clauses is purely coordinate, for instance, between "*yǒu shíquán*" ('having real power') and "*yǒu wēiwàng*" ('having prestige') in (8). Since there is no opposition between the clauses, *dàn* or any of its synonyms cannot be present. In the following two examples, there exists an implied adversative relationship between the clauses:

(10) 我想着你，既想马上见到你，又怕马上见到你。

Wǒ xiǎng-zhe nǐ,   jì . . . yòu . . .   xiǎng mǎshàng   jiàndào nǐ,   yòu pà
I   miss-PRG you both . . . and . . . want immediately see   you   be afraid

mǎshàng   jiàndào nǐ.
immediately see   you
{I miss you. I want to see you right away, but afraid to see you right away as well.}

(11) 哪个单位出个先进人物，既是哪个单位领导的光荣，又是哪个单位领导的包袱。

Nǎ   gè dānwèi chū   gè xiānjìn   rénwù, jì . . . yòu . . .   shì
whichever CL unit   emerge CL advanced figure both . . . and . . . COP

62 *Occurrence of dàn or its synonym and relevant forms*

nǎ   gè   dānwèi lǐngdǎo de guāngróng, yòu shì   nǎ   gè   dānwèi
whichever CL unit   leader   SP glory   COP whichever CL unit

lǐngdǎo de bāofu.
leader   SP burden

{The emergence of a role model in any unit is the honor of the leadership of that unit, but their burden, too.}

Apparently in both the aforementioned examples, there is a contradiction between the two clauses, i.e., between "want to see" and "afraid to see" in (10), and between "an honor" and "a burden" in (11). Consequently, *dàn* or its synonym can be present in these sentences. In the following three examples, *dàn* or *què* can also be used.

(12) 我荣升"大姐级"的同时，既为自己是公司的元老而自豪，又暗暗感慨时光不饶人。

Wǒ róngshēng "dàjiě   jí   de tóngshí, jì ... yòu ...   wèi zìjǐ   shì
I   promote   big sister level SP same time both ... and ... for oneself COP

gōngsī   de yuánlǎo ér   zìháo, yòu àn-àn   gǎnkǎi shíguāng bù
company SP veteran therefore proud secretly sigh   time   NEG

ráo   rén.
spare person

{When I was promoted to the "Big Sister Level", I felt proud of being a veteran of the company on the one hand, and, on the other hand, I secretly lamented that time spares no one becoming old.}

(13) 这使我既感到欣慰，又体会到某种凄凉。

Zhè shǐ wǒ jì ... yòu ...   gǎndào xīnwèi, yòu tǐhuì-dào mǒu   zhǒng
this make me both ... and ... feel   gratified realize certain type

qīliáng.
desolation

{It made me feel gratified, but gave me a sense of desolation as well.}

(14) 你真的疯狂就好了，红娣也会这样想的。可惜，你既疯狂，又不疯狂！

Nǐ   zhēnde fēngkuáng jiù hǎo le, Hóngdì yě   huì zhèyàng xiǎng de.
you really crazy   then good MP Hongdi also will so   think MP

Kěxī,   nǐ jì ... yòu ...   fēngkuáng, yòu bù   fēngkuáng!
unfortunately you both ... and ... crazy   NEG crazy

{I wish you were really crazy, and so does Hongdi. Unfortunately, you are both crazy and not crazy!}

To sum up, there are two different logical bases for "*jì p, yòu q*". One is a coordinate relationship. In sentences based on the coordinate relationship, the correlative conjunction "*jì ... yòu ...*" is employed to mark that relationship. The other is a combination of a coordinate relationship and an adversative relationship. In sentences based on this combined relationship, "*jì ... yòu ...*" indicates the coordination, and *dàn* or its synonym, if present, marks the contradiction. Thus, "*jì p, dàn yòu q*"

Occurrence of dàn or its synonym and relevant forms   63

indicates the combined relationship and highlights the adversative component, with *dàn* transforming a coordinate complex sentence into an adversative one.

3.2 Occurrence of *dàn* or its synonym in "*yīfāngmiàn p, lìng yīfāngmiàn q*"

The correlative connective "*yīfāngmiàn . . . lìng yīfāngmiàn . . .*" is used to show two parallel situations, therefore "*yīfāngmiàn p, lìng yīfāngmiàn q*" is a form of coordinate complex sentences. In some cases, *dàn* or its synonym can be present in this form, hence "*yīfāngmiàn p, dàn lìng yīfāngmiàn q*". The following are four examples:

(15) 一方面，他们不能禁止自己不犯已经知道的错误，他们明知故犯；但另一方面，他们又要禁止别的党员向党向上级报告及在会议上批评他们。

Yīfāngmiàn,   tā-men bùnéng jìnzhǐ zìjǐ   bù   fàn   yǐjīng zhīdào de
on the one hand they   cannot stop oneself NEG make already know SP
*cuòwù, tā-men míngzhī-gùfàn;   **dàn** lìng yīfāngmiàn, tā-men yòu yào jìnzhǐ*
mistake they intentionally violate but on the other hand they   also will stop
biéde dǎngyuán   xiàng dǎng xiàng shàngjí bàogào jí   zài huìyì-shàng
other party member to   party to   superior report and at   at meeting
pīpíng tā-men.
criticize them
{On the one hand, they can't stop themselves from intentionally making the mistakes that they are already aware of; on the other hand, they prevent other party members from reporting the mistakes to their superiors and criticizing them at meetings.}

(16) 在目前，我们一方面应当动员群众向国民党政府提出要求，允许救国会的公开，允许各种非法团体的登记，允许言论、集会、罢工的自由；但是另一方面，我们还应当利用各种灰色的团体去组织群众，加入各种已有的合法团体去进行工作。

Zài mùqián, wǒ-men yīfāngmiàn   yīngdāng dòngyuán qúnzhòng xiàng
at   present we   on the one hand should   mobilize the masses to
Guómíndǎng zhèngfǔ   tíchū yāoqiú, yǔnxǔ Jiùguóhuì
Kuomintang government make request allow National Salvation Association
de gōngkāi, yǔnxǔ gè   zhǒng fēifǎ tuántǐ   de dēngjì, yǔnxǔ yánlùn,
SP be public allow each kind illegal organization SP register allow speech
*jíhuì,   bàgōng de zìyóu;   **dànshì** lìng yīfāngmiàn, wǒ-men hái*
assembly strike SP freedom but   on the other hand we   still
yīngdāng lìyòng gè   zhǒng huīsè de tuántǐ   qù zǔzhī   qúnzhòng,
should use   each kind gray SP organization go organize the masses
jiārù gè   zhǒng yǐ   yǒu de héfǎ tuántǐ   qù jìnxíng gōngzuò.
join each kind already exist SP legal organization go carry out work
{At present, on the one hand, we should mobilize the masses to request the Kuomintang government to allow public activities of the National Salvation Association, to allow various illegal organizations to be registered as legal ones, and

64 Occurrence of dàn or its synonym and relevant forms

to allow freedom of speech, assemblies, and strikes; but on the other hand, we should also use various gray groups to organize the masses to join various existing legal groups to carry out the work.}

(17) ……蒋介石又发表了一个谈话，<u>一方面</u>是承认我们，可是<u>另一方面</u>，还是说要取消红军，取消苏区。

... *Jiǎng Jièshí   yòu   fābiǎo-le   yī   gè   tánhuà,   yīfāngmiàn*
CHIANG Kai Shek   again   make-PEF   one   CL   speech   on the one hand
shì   chéngrèn   wǒ-men,   kěshì   lìng yīfāngmiàn,   háishì   shuō   yào   qǔxiāo
COP   recognize   us   but   on the other hand   still   say   will   abolish
hóngjūn,   qǔxiāo   Sūqū.
the Red Army   abolish   Chinese Soviet area (Red Army's bases)
{. . . CHIANG Kai Shek made another speech. In the speech, on the one hand, he recognized us, but on the other hand, he still said that the Red Army and its bases would be abolished.}

(18) 许多人都有一种好奇的心理，他<u>一方面</u>说你是"无巧不成书"，<u>另一方面</u>却又"无巧不看书"。

Xǔduō rén   dōu yǒu yī   zhǒng hàoqí de xīnlǐ, tā   yīfāngmiàn   shuō nǐ
many   person   all   have one kind   curious SP mind he on the one hand say   you
shì   "wúqiǎobùchéngshū",   lìng yīfāngmiàn   què   yòu
COP   there be no stories without coincidences   on the other hand   however   also
"wúqiǎobùkànshū".
not to read books without stories of coincidence
{Many people are full of curiosity. On the one hand, they accuse writers of fabricating fanciful stories, but on the other hand, they wouldn't read any books without fanciful stories.}

All the four aforementioned examples include "*yīfāngmiàn . . . lìng yīfāngmiàn . . .*" and *dàn* or its synonym. Some conjunctions, such as *dàn*, *dànshì*, and *kěshì*, precede "*lìng yīfāngmiàn*", whereas the linking adverb *què* follows "*lìng yīfāngmiàn*". If only "*yīfāngmiàn . . . lìng yīfāngmiàn . . .*" occurs, the sentence is clearly marked as a coordinate one, but the presence of *dàn* or its synonym shifts the focus of the intrinsic coordinate relationship, hence marking the originally coordinate sentence as an adversative one.

Besides, "*yīmiàn . . . yīmiàn . . .*" is similar to "*yīfāngmiàn . . . lìng yīfāngmiàn . . .*", therefore *dàn* or its synonym can be present within the structure. The following are three examples:

(19) 朱洪武建造了世界上围墙最大的城市，这<u>一面</u>是他的丰功伟绩，<u>另一面</u>却是他穷奢极欲的心理裸现。

Zhū Hóngwǔ   jiànzào le   shìjiè- shàng wéiqiáng zuì   dà de chéngshì, zhè
ZHU Hongwu   build   PEF in world   wall   most big SP city   this
yīmiàn   shì   tā   de   fēnggōng-wěijì,   lìng yīmiàn   què
on the one hand   COP   he   SP   valiant record   on the other hand   however

Occurrence of dàn or its synonym and relevant forms 65

shì tā qióngshē-jíyù de xīnlǐ luǒxiàn.
COP he be lapped in luxury SP mind nakedness
{ZHU Hongwu built the world's largest walled city, which on the one hand was
his great achievement, but on the other hand was the blunt psychological expression of his extravagance.}

(20) 老孟一面用了十分敬畏的神情朝老太太看，一面却悄悄地跑到派出所去找户籍警老刘同志作了秘密报告。

Lǎo mèng *yīmiàn* yòng-le shífēn jìngwèi de shénqíng cháo lǎotàitai
old MENG on the one hand use-PEF very revere SP expression at old lady
kàn, *yīmiàn* **què** qiāoqiāo de pǎo-dào pàichūsuǒ qù zhǎo
look on the other hand but secretly SP run to police station go find
hùjíjǐng lǎo Liú tóngzhì zuò-le mìmì bàogào.
household registrar police officer old LIU comrade make-PEF secret report
{Old MENG looked at the old lady in awe, but then he quietly ran to the police
station to find the household registrar police officer, Comrade Old LIU, to make
a secret report.}

(21) 军阀对红军曾三次"会剿"，每次都含着两方面的意义：一面固然是在共同进攻革命势力，一面却又是军阀为了准备自己战争，必须先求解决红军以固后防……

Jūnfá duì hóngjūn céng sān cì "huìjiǎo", měi cì dōu
warlord against the Red Army once three time jointly suppress every time all
hán-zhe liǎng fāngmiàn de yìyì: *yīmiàn* **gùrán** shì zài
have-PRG two aspect SP meaning on the one hand certainly COP in progress
gòngtóng jìngōng gémìng shìlì, *yīmiàn* **què** yòu shì
jointly attack revolutionary force on the other hand however also COP
jūnfá wèile zhǔnbèi zìjǐ zhànzhēng, bìxū xiān qiú jiějué hóngjūn
warlord for prepare oneself war must first seek destroy the Red Army
yǐ gù hòufáng . . .
to consolidate defense from rear attacks
{The warlords' three "joint suppressions" against the Red Army all had two purposes: on the one hand, they were undoubtedly jointly attacking the revolutionary
forces; on the other hand, the warlords must first destroy the Red Army to consolidate their defense from rear attacks in order to prepare for their own wars.}

Among the three aforementioned examples, *què* is used in (19) and (20), and
"*gùrán . . . què . . .*" is used in (21). These connectives highlight the adversative
relationship, and meanwhile play down the coordinate relationship between the
clauses in each sentence, thus sentences in the form of "*yīmiàn p, (lìng) yīmiàn
què q*" are marked as adversative ones.

Similar to "*jì p, yòu q*", the logical basis of "*yīfāngmiàn p, lìng yīfāngmiàn q*" is
a purely coordinate relationship in some cases. In these cases, sentences in the form
of "*yīfāngmiàn p, lìng yīfāngmiàn q*" cannot be rewritten as "*yīfāngmiàn p, dàn lìng
yīfāngmiàn q*". In the following two examples, *dàn* or its synonym cannot occur.

66 *Occurrence of dàn or its synonym and relevant forms*

(22) 一方面，我们已用事实证明给老百姓看，我们有力量打倒蒋介石；另一方面，老百姓也不要蒋介石……

Yīfāngmiàn, *wǒ-men* *yǐ* *yòng* *shìshí* *zhèngmíng* *gěi* *lǎobǎixìng*
one aspect we already with fact prove to common people
kàn, *wǒ-men* *yǒu* *lìliang* *dǎ-dǎo* *Jiǎng Jièshí;* *lìng yīfāngmiàn,*
look we have strength defeat CHIANG Kai Shek another aspect
lǎobǎixìng *yě* *bù* *yào* *Jiǎng Jièshí . . .*
common people also NEG want CHIANG Kai Shek

{We have shown to the general public with facts that we are strong enough to defeat CHIANG Kai-shek; and the general public doesn't want CHIANG Kai-shek, either.}

(23) 自从父亲病故后，看透了世态炎凉。一方面自己一心想学点本事有个出路，另一方面有些愤世嫉俗同情弱者。

Zìcóng fùqin bìnggù *hòu, kàn-tòu* *le* *shìtài-yánliáng.*
since father die of illness after see through PEF inconstancy of human relationships
Yīfāngmiàn zìjǐ *yīxīn* *xiǎng xué diǎn běnshi yǒu gè chūlù,*
one aspect oneself wholeheartedly want learn a little skill have CL way of living
lìng yīfāngmiàn yǒuxiē fènshì-jísú *tóngqíng* *ruòzhě.*
another aspect some be critical of society sympathize with the weak

{Since (his) father died of illness, (he) has seen through the world. (He) was keen to learn some skills so as to make a living, and meanwhile (he) was a little cynical and sympathetic to the weak.}

In each of the two aforementioned examples, the coordinate relationship between the clauses is formally manifested by "*yīfāngmiàn . . . lìng yīfāngmiàn . . .*". By comparison, there is no adversative relationship between the clauses; therefore *dàn* or its synonyms cannot be present in these sentences.

In some sentences, the two clauses in "*yīfāngmiàn p, lìng yīfāngmiàn q*" are two opposing sides of the same matter, thus *dàn* or its synonyms can be present, i.e., "*yīfāngmiàn p, dàn lìng yīfāngmiàn q*". The following are three examples:

(24) 他一方面侈谈工业化的计划经济，另一方面又憧憬于《礼运》大同之篇……

Tā *yīfāngmiàn* *chǐtán* *gōngyèhuà* *de* *jìhuà jīngjì,* *lìng yīfāngmiàn*
he on the one hand talk glibly industrialize SP planned economy on the other hand
yòu *chōngjǐng* *yú* *"lǐyùn"* *dàtóng* *zhī* *piān . . .*
also look forward to *Conveyance of Rites* great unity SP article

{On the one hand, he talked glibly of the planned economy of industrialization; on the other hand, he longed for the great commonwealth of peace and prosperity described in the article *The Conveyance of Rites . . .*}

(25) 一方面他觉得苏青很爱他，另一方面他又觉得苏青说不爱他就可能不爱他了。

Yīfāngmiàn *tā juéde Sū Qīng hěn* *ài* *tā,* *lìngyīfāngmiàn*
on the one hand he feel SU Qing very much love him on the other hand

Occurrence of dàn or its synonym and relevant forms 67

tā yòu juéde Sū Qīng shuō bù   ài   tā   jiù   kěnéng bù   ài   tā   le.
he but feel   SU Qing say   NEG love him indeed probably NEG love him MP
{On the one hand he thinks that SU Qing loves him very much, on the other hand, he is afraid that if SU Qing says that she doesn't love him, she means what she says.}

(26) 一方面作为一个有事业心的厂长，他要把东风厂办成一流的企业，（另）一方面，对大阳厂的感情又牵扯着他，他时刻关心着大阳厂的利益。

Yīfāngmiàn   zuòwéi yī   gè   yǒu   shìyèxīn   de chǎngzhǎng,   tā
on the one hand as   one CL   have   career ambition SP factory director he
yào   bǎ   Dōngfēng Chǎng   bàn-chéng yīliú   de   qǐyè,   (lìng)yīfāngmiàn,
will BA Dongfeng Factory build into   first-rate SP enterprise on the other hand
duì Dàyángchǎng   de gǎnqíng yòu qiānchě-zhe tā, tā shíkè   guānxīn-zhe
for Dayang Factory SP feeling   also tug at-PRG him he constantly care-PRG
Dàyángchǎng   de lìyì.
Dayang Factory SP interest
{On the one hand, as an ambitious factory director, he wants to build Dongfeng Factory into a first-class enterprise, on the other hand, his feelings for Dayang Factory always make him care about the interests of Dayang Factory.}

In these examples, the connective "*yīfāngmiàn . . . lìng yīfāngmiàn . . .*" indicates the coexistence of the two sides of the same matter and marks the sentences as coordinate; however, the opposition between the two sides makes possible the occurrence of *dàn*, *què*, or their synonyms, and the occurrence would highlight the opposition and mark the original coordinate complex sentences as adversative ones. The presence of the adversative connective not only indicates the two sides of a matter or situation, but also highlights the opposition between the two of them.

3.3   Occurrence of *dàn* or its synonym in "*jíshǐ p, yě q*"

Sentences in the form of "*jíshǐ p, yě q*" are hypothetical ones indicating concession. It is generally understood that *jíshǐ* can collocate with *yě*, *hái*, and so on, but not with *dàn*, *què*, and so forth. For example, LV Shuxiang pointed out that "*jǐnguǎn* or *suīrán* can be followed by *kěshì*, *dànshì*, *rán'ér*, and so on, but *jíshǐ* cannot".[1] However, there are, in fact, quite a number of sentences in the form of "*jíshǐ p, dàn yě q*". The following are three examples:

(27) 如果她承袭了这笔财产，即使是合法的，但也不光彩。

Rúguǒ tā   chéngxí-le zhè bǐ   cáichǎn, jíshǐ . . . yě . . . shì   héfǎ de, dàn yě
if   she inherit-PEF this CL wealth   even if   COP legal MP but
bù   guāngcǎi.
NEG graceful
{If she inherited the wealth, even if it was legal, it would be inglorious.}

68   *Occurrence of dàn or its synonym and relevant forms*

(28) 即使自己有很多对的意见，但是还要听人家的意见，把人家的好意见吸取过来……

*Jíshǐ   zìjǐ   yǒu   hěnduō   duì   de   yìjiàn,   **dànshì** hái   yào   tīng*
even if oneself have many   right SP opinion but   still need listen
rénjiā   de   yìjiàn,   bǎ   rénjiā   de   hǎo   yìjiàn   xīqǔ-guòlái . . .
other people SP opinion BA other people SP good opinion accept
{Even if you have many good ideas, you should still listen to others' opinions and accept the good ones.}

(29) 即使人山人海，男人们的目光却总是一眼就能看到灵秀。

*Jíshǐ   rénshān-rénhǎi,   nánrén-men de   mùguāng   **què**   zǒngshì*
even if huge crowds of people man-PL   SP sight   however always
yī   yǎn   jiù   néng   kàn-dào Língxiù.
one glance early can   see   Lingxiu
{Even if Lingxiu is in a sea of people, men can always spot her at one glance.}

Among the three aforementioned examples, (27) is in the form of "*jíshǐ p, dàn yě q*", (28) is in the form of "*jíshǐ p, dànshì hái p*", and (29) is a "*jíshǐ . . . què . . .*" sentence. In some cases, synonyms of *jíshǐ*, such as *nǎpà* and *jiùsuàn*, can also collocate with *dàn* or its synonyms. The following are four examples:

(30) 我甚至觉得男人都是骗子，哪怕恋爱的时候说得再动听，但只要结了婚，孩子一生，爱情也就褪色了。

Wǒ shènzhì juéde nánrén dōu shì   piànzi, nǎpà   liàn'ài   de shíhou shuō de
I   even   feel   man   all COP liar   even if be in love SP time   say SP
*zài   dòngtīng, **dàn** zhǐyào . . . jiù . . . jiéhūn-le hūn, háizi yī   shēng, àiqíng*
more moving   but as long as   marry-PEF   child once be born love
yě   jiù tuìsè   le.
also   fade MP

{I even think that men are all liars. Even though their words may sound very touching before marriage, love will fade away as soon as they marry you and have a family.}

(31) 就算这话不假，可南边是南边，翰林府是翰林府，天南地北的，哪能拉到一根弦上？

*Jiùsuàn zhè huà   bù   jiǎ, **kě** nánbiān shì   nánbiān, Hànlínfǔ*
even if this statement NEG false but south   COP south   Hanlin mansion
shì   Hànlínfǔ,   tiānnán-dìběi   de, nǎ   néng lā-dào yī   gēn xián-shàng?
COP Hanlin mansion far from each other SP how can   pull to one CL on string
{Even if this statement is true, the south and the Hanlin Mansion can't be compared as they are far apart!}

(32) 就算他酒量当真无底，肚量却总有底，……

Jiùsuàn tā jiǔliàng   dàngzhēn wú   dǐ,   dùliàng
even if   his drinking capacity really   there not be limit stomach capacity

Occurrence of dàn or its synonym and relevant forms 69

què   zǒng   yǒu   dǐ, . . .
however   after all   there be   limit
{Even if his drinking capacity is really unlimited but, his stomach capacity, after all, is limited . . .}

(33)   记得韩非子曾经教人以竞马的要妙，其一是 "不耻最后"。即使慢，驰而不息，纵令落后，纵令失败，但一定可以达到他所向的目标。

Jìde   Hánfēizǐ céngjīng jiāo rén   yǐ   jìngmǎ   de yàomiào,
remember Hanfeizi once   teach others with horse race SP secret of success
qíyī   shì "bù chǐ   zuìhòu". Jíshǐ   màn, chí   ér bù   xī,
one of them COP NEG ashamed last   even if slow gallop but NEG cease
*zòng_lìng luòhòu,   zòng_lìng shībài,   **dàn** yīdìng   kěyǐ dádào tā suǒ*
even if   fall behind even if   lose   but definitely can   achieve he PAP
xiàng de   mùbiāo.
go   SP goal
{(I) remember that Hanfeizi once taught people the secret of horse racing, and one of his tips was "do not be ashamed of being the last". Even if one is slow, they should still keep going; so even if they fall behind or even come last, they will definitely achieve their goal eventually.}

Among the four aforementioned examples, (30) is in the form of "*nǎpà p, dàn q*", (31) is in the form of "*jiùsuàn p, kě q*", (32) uses "*jiùsuàn . . . què . . .*", and (33) uses "*zònglìng . . . zòngjìng . . . dàn . . .*".

Since the innate relationship between the clauses in "*jíshǐ . . . yě . . .*" is first-concessive-then-adversative, what is wrong with the occurrence of *dàn* or its synonyms in "*jíshǐ . . . yě . . .*" sentences?

If a sentence is syntactically complicated, the occurrence of *dàn* or its synonym not only highlights the adversative relationship between the clauses, but can also clearly mark the boundary between the opposing items. The following are four examples:

(34)   我猜想：即使在这风雪迷茫的黑夜，工人、工人的妻子和工人的孩子，谁也看不清谁，可是他们一定能感觉到相互深切的鼓舞和期待。

Wǒ   cāixiǎng: jíshǐ   zài zhè fēngxuě   mímáng   de hēiyè,
I   guess   even if in   this snowstorm vast and hazy SP night
gōngrén, gōngrén de qīzǐ hé gōngrén de háizi, shuí   yě   kàn bù qīng
worker worker SP wife and worker SP child anyone also cannot see clearly
*shuí,   **kěshì** tā-men yīdìng   néng gǎnjué-dào xiānghù shēnqiè de*
anyone but   they   definitely can   feel   mutually deep SP
gǔwǔ   hé   qīdài.
encourage and   expect
{I suppose that even if in this dark and snowy night, the workers, their wives, and their children could not see one another clearly, they definitely could feel a deep encouragement and expectation from each other.}

70 Occurrence of *dàn* or its synonym and relevant forms

(35) 即使无人豢养，饿的精瘦，变成野狗了，但还是遇见所有的阔人都驯良，遇
见所有的穷人都狂吠的，（不过这时它就愈不明白谁是主子了。）

Jíshǐ   wú   rén   huànyǎng, è   de jīngshòu, biànchéng yěgǒu
even if there not be person feed   hungry SP wiry   become   wild dog

*le, **dàn** háishì yùjiàn suǒyǒu de kuòrén dōu xùnliáng, yùjiàn suǒyǒu de qióngrén*
PEF but still meet all   SP the rich all gentle   meet all   SP the poor

dōu kuángfèi   de, (bùguò zhèshí   tā jiù yù   bù   míngbai shuí
all   bark furiously MP however this time it then more NEG know   who

shì   zhǔzi le.)
COP master MP

{Even if ("a running dog") has been deserted, lean and hungry, and has become
a stray dog, whenever it meets a rich person, it is gentle, and whenever it meets
a poor one, it barks furiously, [but at this time it will become more confused as
to who is its master.]}

(36) 尽管他精通生产，有敏锐的智力，即使在他的坏脾气中也时常显现出智慧的
异彩，但是他的坏脾气毁了他的智慧，人们只知道他脾气坏，不承认他有智
慧。

Jǐnguǎn   tā   jīngtōng   shēngchǎn, yǒu mǐnruì de
although he   have a profound knowledge of production have acute   SP

zhìlì,   jíshǐ   zài tā de huài píqi   zhōng yě   shícháng xiǎnxiàn-chū
intelligence even if at he SP bad temper LOC also often   show

*zhìhuì de yìcǎi,   **dànshì** tā de huài píqi   huǐ-le   tā de zhìhuì,*
wisdom SP splendor but   he SP bad temper destroy-PEF he SP wisdom

rén-men zhǐ zhīdào tā píqi   huài, bù   chéngrèn tā yǒu zhìhuì.
people   only know   his temper bad   NEG recognize he have wisdom

{He has a profound knowledge of production and an acute mind, and often shows
great wisdom even when he is in a bad temper, but his bad temper has destroyed
his wisdom, that is, he is known only for his bad temper but not considered wise.}

(37) 他们，尤其是妈，即使对我的不回去觉得失望，但是因为我是他们的儿子，
他们会慢慢原谅我的。

Tā-men, yóuqí   shì mā,   jíshǐ   duì wǒ de bù   huíqù   juéde
they   particularly COP mother even if with I   SP NEG go back feel

*shīwàng,   **dànshì** yīnwèi wǒ shì tā-men de érzi, tā-men huì*
be disappointed but   because I   COP they SP son they   will

màn-màn   yuánliàng wǒ de.
slowly-REDP forgive   me MP

{Even though my parents are disappointed that I'm not coming home, especially
my mother, they will eventually forgive me because I'm their son.}

In (34), the clause introduced by *jíshǐ* is relatively long and complicated in
syntactic structure. In (35), *jíshǐ* is followed by more than one clause and so is
dàn. In (36), before *dàn* is a *jǐnguǎn*-clause and a *jíshǐ*-clause, and after *dàn* there
is more than one clause. In (37), though the *jíshǐ*-clause is not complicated in
structure, the *dàn*-clause is acted by a causal complex sentence. In conclusion,

Occurrence of dàn or its synonym and relevant forms 71

dàn and its synonyms in these sentences that stress the adversative relationship mark the turning point.

3.4 Occurrence of *dàn* or its synonym in "*nìngkě p, yě q*"

"*nìngkě p, yě q*" is generally taken as a form of alternative complex sentences. In this form, the connective *nìngkě* ('would rather'), or its synonym—such as *nìng, nìngkěn, or nìngyuàn*—introduces *p*, and *yě* introduces *q* either in the affirmative form or the negative form. The following are four examples:

(38) 我宁可受穷，也不跟他们学！

Wǒ	*nìngkě . . . yě*	*shòuqióng,*	*yě*	*bù*	*gēn*	*tā-men*	*xué!*
I	would rather . . .	live in poverty	NEG	from	them	learn	

{I would rather be poor than learn from them!}

(39) 她宁可坐在马路边，也决不肯一个人耽在里面。

Tā	*nìngkě . . . yě . . .*	*zuò*	*zài*	*mǎlù*	*biān,*	*yě jué*	*bù*	*kěn*	*yī*
she	would rather . . .	sit	on	road	side	definitely NEG	be willing	one	

gè rén dān zài lǐmiàn.
CL person stay on inside

{She would rather sit by the side of the road than stay inside by herself.}

(40) 为了滋补他，我宁愿自己平时吃饭再节省一些，也要尽量把星期日全天的野餐准备得丰富可口。

Wèile	*zībǔ*	*tā,*	*wǒ*	*nìngyuàn . . . yě . . .*	*zìjǐ*	*píngshí*	*chīfàn zài*
in order to nourish		him	I	would rather . . .	oneself	normal times	eat more

jiéshěng yīxiē, yě yào jìnliàng bǎ xīngqīrì quántiān de yěcān zhǔnbèi
save some will try one's best BA Sunday whole day SP picnic prepare

de fēngfù kěkǒu.
SP abundant delicious

{To nourish him, I would rather spend on my own food as sparingly as I can, and try my best to prepare an abundant and delicious picnic for him on Sunday.}

(41) 她宁肯自己挨饿，也要把公有的几升米匀给贫苦的农友。

Tā	*nìngkěn . . . yě . . .*	*zìjǐ*	*ái'è,*	*yě yào bǎ gōngyǒu*	*de jǐ*
she	would rather . . .	oneself	starve	will BA the public owns	SP several

shēng mǐ yún-gěi pínkǔ de nóngyǒu.
liter rice distribute poor SP fellow farmer

{She would rather distribute the few liters of communal rice among her poor fellow farmers (than keep the rice to herself) even if she went hungry.}

In (38) and (39) the posterior clauses introduced by *yě* are in the negative form, whereas in (40) and (41) the posterior clauses introduced by *yě* are in the affirmative form, which has the same function as the double-negative form.

72 *Occurrence of dàn or its synonym and relevant forms*

In a sentence in the form of "*nìngkě p, yě q*", *dàn* or its synonym can be present, but the word *yě* cannot be present if *dàn* or its synonym is. The following are three examples:

(42) 宁可慢些，但要好些！

     *Nìngkě   màn xiē,   **dàn** yào hǎo   xiē!*

     would rather slow some but need good some

     {It is better to be slow to ensure quality.}

(43) （芬酷爱花）她宁可几年不添一件新衣服，可房里决不能断了花卉，……

     (Fēn kù'ài   huā) tā <u>nìngkě</u>   jǐ   nián bù   tiān yī

     Fen be very fond of flower she would rather several year NEG add one

     *jiàn xīn yīfu, **kě** fáng-lǐ jué   bùnéng duàn   le huāhuì, . . .*

     piece new clothes but in room definitely cannot discontinue MP flower

     {(Fen loves flowers so much that) she would rather have no new clothes for a few years than have no flowers for a moment in her room . . .}

(44) 我宁看《红楼梦》，却不愿看新出的《林黛玉日记》，它一页能够使我不舒服小半天。

     *Wǒ <u>nìng</u>   kàn 'Hónglóumèng',   **què** bù   yuàn   kàn*

     I would rather read *Dream of the Red Chamber* however NEG be willing read

     xīn   chū   de 'Lín Dàiyù rìjì', tā yī yè nénggòu shǐ wǒ bù

     recently publish SP *Diary of LIN Daiyu* it one page can   make me NEG

     shūfu   xiǎo bàntiān.

     comfortable almost half a day

     {I would rather read *Dream of the Red Chamber* than read the newly published *Diary of LIN Daiyu*, a page in which would make me uncomfortable for almost half a day.}

Among these three examples cited from literary works, "*nìngkě . . . dàn . . .*" is used in (42), "*nìngkě . . . kě . . .*" in (43), and "*nìng . . . què . . .*" in (45). If these citations were classified as alternative complex sentences, it would be extremely difficult to justify the occurrence of *dàn* and its synonyms.

First, admittedly sentences in the form of "*nìngkě p, yě q*" are based on a selective relationship between *p* and *q*, i.e., after consideration *p* is adopted and *q* is abandoned. The anterior clause, with the word *nìngkě*, identifies the adopted or preferred option *p*, and the posterior clause either directly rejects the opposing option *q* with a negative statement or indirectly abandons *q* with an affirmative expression of a goal to achieve.

Second, it should be noted that there exists an adversative relationship between *p* and *q* in "*nìngkě p, yě q*". As *nìngkě* has the implication of "taking the somewhat less unpleasant of two poor choices", the so-called adopted or preferred option *p* is not an ideal one. In other words, the adoption of *p* is making a concession, for instance, "being poor" in (38) and "going hungry" in (41). As can be seen, in these sentences, a concession comes the first, and an opposition follows.

Last, "*nìngkě p, yě q*" and "*jíshǐ p, yě q*" are similar in meaning. The following are two examples:

(45) 我宁愿打一辈子光棍，也决不办这桩事！

    Wǒ   *nìngyuàn* . . . *yě*   *dǎ guānggùn*   *yī bèizi*   *guānggùn,*   *yě jué*
    I   would rather . . . remain a bachelor all one's life   definitely

    bù   *bàn*   *zhè*   *zhuāng*   *shì!*
    NEG   do   this   CL   matter
    {I'd rather remain single all my life than do this!}

(46) ……宁肯不吃饭，也得满满小酒壶。

    . . . *nìngkěn* . . . *yě* . . .   *bù*   *chīfàn,*   *yě*   *děi*   *mǎn-mǎn*   *xiǎo*   *jiǔhú.*
    would rather . . .   NEG   eat   must   full-REDP   small   flagon
    {. . . (he) would rather drink a full flask than have a meal.}

Both *nìngyuàn* in (45) and *nìngkěn* in (46) can be replaced by *jíshǐ* without any drastic change in meaning, though the concessive tone will be weakened if *jíshǐ* occurs in place of *nìngyuàn* or *nìngkěn*. As an adversative sentence form, "*nìngkě p, yě q*" does not reject the occurrence of *dàn* or its synonyms, but usually *dàn* or its synonyms are absent in "*nìngkě . . . yě . . .*" unless the opposition between two clauses needs to be stressed.

Summary

This chapter deals with the following four phenomena:

i)   Occurrence of *dàn* or its synonym in "*jì p, yòu q*";
ii) Occurrence of *dàn* or its synonym in "*yīfāngmiàn p, lìng yīfāngmiàn q*";
iii) Occurrence of *dàn* or its synonym in "*jíshǐ p, yě q*";
iv) Occurrence of *dàn* or its synonym in "*nìngkě p, yě q*".

In the first two phenomena, *dàn* or its synonym occur in a non-adversative complex sentence, thus they are rephrased as an adversative one. However, in the other two phenomena, *dàn* or its synonym is included in an adversative complex sentence to highlight the innate adversative relationship.

NB Some examples in this chapter are cited from literary works, political essays, articles, and so on. The sources are listed as follows:

1 *Baihuazhou* (《百花洲》) 1998(3), including Example (19);
2 *Changcheng* (《长城》) 1982(3), including (38) and (46);
3 *Chinese* for Junior High School Students, Book 2, including (34); Book 5, including (41);
4 *Chinese* for Senior High School Students, Book 5, including (4);
5 *Chunfeng* (《春风》) 1982(1), including (8) and (10);

6 Complete Works of LU Xun (《鲁迅全集》), including (33), (35), and (44);
7 *Fiction Monthly* (《小说月报》) 1996(11), including (29); 1996(12), including (13);
8 *Harvest* (《收获》) 1982(1), including (40); 1982(4), including (39); 1982(2), including (3); 1983(1), including (2); 1983(3), including (6);
9 *Legends of the Condor Heroes 1: A Hero Born* (《射雕英雄传》) by JIN Yong (金庸), including (32);
10 *Lotus* (《芙蓉》) 1983(2), including (20);
11 *October* (《十月》) 1982(3), including (27); 1982(4), including (23); 1983(4), including (42); 1983(5), including (7);
12 *People's Literature* (《人民文学》) 1982(3), including (9) and (36);
13 *Selected Works of LIU Shaoqi* (《刘少奇选集》), including (16);
14 *Selected Works of ZHOU Enlai* (《周恩来选集》), including (22), (24), and (28);
15 *The Palm Tree* (《又见棕榈，又见棕榈》) by YU Lihua (於梨华), including (37);
16 *Xiao Shuo Jia* (《小说家》) 1998(4), including (1); 1997(3), including (26);
17 *Zhongpian Xiaoshuo Xuankan* (《中篇小说选刊》) 1997(3), including (14) and (25); 1997(4), including (12);
18 *Zhongshan* (《钟山》) 1982(3), including (18); 1983(4), including (43).

Note

1 LV Shuxiang (吕叔湘). *Eight Hundred Words in Modern Chinese* (《现代汉语八百词》). The Commercial Press, 1980.

4 Occurrence of *dàn* or its synonym in *"wúlùn p, dōu q"*

The form *"wúlùn p, dōu q"* is an unconditional complex sentence form, in which the marker *wúlùn/búlùn/bùguǎn* ('no matter') usually occurs in the anterior clause, and the marker *dōu* ('all')/*yě* ('also')/*quán* ('all')/*zǒng* ('always'), often occurs in the posterior clause. In some cases, no markers occur in the posterior clause.

The form of *"wúlùn p, dōu q"* involves adversative relationships that vary in degree or in nature; therefore some sentences in this form do not exclude the occurrence of *dàn* or its synonyms. This chapter discusses the occurrence of *dàn* or its synonyms in this form.

4.1 Subdivisions of *"wúlùn p, dōu q"*

There are three subdivisions of sentences in the form of *"wúlùn p, dōu q"* according to the characteristics of the anterior clause: Subdivision I, in which the anterior clause lists two or more situations; Subdivision II, in which the anterior clause summarizes two or more situations with a generic expression; Subdivision III, in which the anterior clause condenses one single situation with variations in degree.

4.1.1 Subdivision I

In Subdivision I, the anterior clause lists two or more situations linked by such words as *háishì* ('or'), *huòzhě* ('or'), and so on. The situations can be listed in the following three patterns: coordinated pattern, i.e. "A + B + C"; affirmative-negative pattern, i.e., "A + *bù* ('not') A", and bipolar pattern, i.e., "A + Z". Each of the following three sentences respectively exemplifies one of the three patterns:

(1) <u>不论整顿领导班子</u>，整顿作风，整顿政治机关，没有一股子劲头不行。

Bùlùn   zhěngdùn lǐngdǎo bānzi, zhěngdùn zuòfēng, zhěngdùn zhèngzhì
no matter ... rectify   leader   group rectify   behavior rectify   political

jīguān,   méiyǒu yī   gǔzi   jìntóu bù   xíng.
organ   not have one CL   energy NEG   work

{It won't work without much energy, no matter it is to rectify the leading group, the work behavior, or the political organs.}

DOI: 10.4324/9781003374237-4

76 *Occurrence of dàn or its synonym in "wúlùn p, dōu q"*

(2) 不管你信不信，他做到了！

    Bùguǎn   *nǐ*   *xìn*   *bù*   *xìn,*   *tā*   *zuò-dào*   *le!*
    no matter ... you believe NEG believe he achieve PEF
    {He made it, believe it or not!}

(3) 认识的，不管事急事缓，都要坐下喝口水才去。

    Rènshi de, bùguǎn ... dōu ... shì   *jí*   *shì*   *huǎn,*   *dōu yào zuò-xià*
    know SP no matter ...   matter urgent matter nonurgent will sit down
    hē   *kǒu*   *shuǐ*   *cái*   *qù.*
    drink mouth water then leave
    {(At his place,) people who knew (him) would always sit down and have a drink first, no matter they were in a hurry or not.}

Among the three examples, (1) is in the pattern of "A + B + C", (2) is in "A + *bù* A", and (3) is in "A + Z".

4.1.2 *Subdivision II*

In Subdivision II, the anterior clause uses a generic expression to summarize two or more situations.

The generic expression refers to any interrogative pronoun with a general denotation, such as *shuí* ('who'), *shénme* ('what'), *nǎlǐ* ('where'), and so on. The following are two examples:

(4) 不管是谁搞错的，我们都得向院里写个检查。

    Bùguǎn ... dōu ... shì **shuí** *gǎo-cuò*   *de, wǒ-men dōu děi*   *xiàng*
    no matter ...   COP who make a mistake SP we   must to
    yuàn-li   *xiě*   *gè*   *jiǎnchá.*
    in hospital write CL review
    {Whoever made the mistake, we must submit a review to the hospital.}

(5) 大婶，你无论说什么，我都不会生你的气。

    Dàshěn, nǐ **wúlùn** *... dōu ... shuō* **shénme**, *wǒ dōu bù*   *huì* *shēng nǐ de qì.*
    aunt   you no matter ...   say what I   NEG will get angry with you
    {Aunt, I won't get angry with you whatever you say.}

Subdivision I illustrates the situations by listing a few specific examples, whereas Subdivision II summarizes the situations with "infinite variations".[1] However, the two subdivisions can be interchangeable if the wording is changed. For example, (4) can be rewritten as (6), an instance of Subdivision I:

(6) 不管是老张搞错的，还是小李搞错的，我们都得向院里写个检查。

    Bùguǎn ... dōu ... shì   *lǎo Zhāng*   *gǎo-cuò de, háishì xiǎo Lǐ gǎo-cuò*
    no matter ...   COP old ZHANG mistake SP or   little LI make a mistake

Occurrence of dàn or its synonym in "wúlùn p, dōu q" 77

de, wǒ-men *dōu* děi xiàng yuàn-li xiě gè jiǎnchá.
SP we must to in hospital write CL review
{We must submit a review to the hospital no matter the mistake was made by Old ZHANG or Little LI.}

4.1.3 Subdivision III

In Subdivision III, the anterior clause uses a generic expression to condense a situation with variations in degree.

The anterior clause contains such structures as "*zěnme* (*zěnyàng/rúhé*) + head", or "*duōme* (*duō*) + head", or "*duōshǎo* + head". The head denotes a particular situation or defines the range of a particular situation, and the generic expression, such as *zěnme* ('how'), *duōme* ('how'), *duōshǎo* ('how many/how much'), and so on, sums up the various degrees inherent in the situation. The following are three examples:

(7) 不管姐姐怎么数落、怨恨，小伙子只是低着头，不敢还腔。
Bùguǎn jiějiě **zěnme** *shǔluò, yuànhèn, xiǎohuǒzi zhǐshì dī-zhe*
no matter . . . elder sister how scold complain lad only lower-PRG
tóu, bù gǎn huánqiāng.
head NEG dare talk back
{No matter how his elder sister scolded and blamed him, the young man just kept his head lowered and did not dare to talk back.}

(8) （这是她在学校时养成的习惯，）无论晚上睡得多迟，早晨总是六点钟起床。
(Zhè shì tā zài xuéxiào shí yǎng-chéng de xíguàn,) wúlùn wǎnshàng
this COP she at school time develop SP habit no matter night
shuì de **duō** *chí, zǎochén zǒngshì liù diǎn zhōng qǐchuáng.*
sleep SP how late morning always six o'clock get up
{No matter how late she goes to bed at night, she always gets up at six in the morning, [which is a habit that she developed when she was a student].}

(9) ⋯⋯ 这项工作，无论有多少困难，我们都敢于承担。
. . . zhè xiàng gōngzuò, wúlùn . . . dōu . . . yǒu **duōshǎo** *kùnnán, wǒ-men dōu*
this CL work no matter . . . have how many difficult we
gǎnyú chéngdān.
have the courage undertake
{. . . no matter how many difficulties there may be in this work, we have the courage to undertake it.}

In Subdivision III, the anterior clause also uses an interrogative pronoun to denote a general situation with infinite variations, just as in Subdivision II. However, these two subdivisions differ in some respects. First, the interrogative pronoun in "*wúlùn p, dōu q*" of Subdivision III often serves as a modifier—in

78 Occurrence of dàn or its synonym in "wúlùn p, dōu q"

particular, an adverbial—rather than the subject, object, or predicate. The only exception is *duōshǎo*, which can act as an attribute. Second, in Subdivision III the word *duōme* is no longer an interrogative but should be regarded as an adverb of degree. Third, unlike Subdivision II, Subdivision III is difficult to be transformed into Subdivision I.

4.2 Occurrence of *dàn* or its Synonyms in Subdivision III

Sentences in the form of *"wúlùn p, dōu q"* of Subdivision III entail an adversative relationship between the clauses, thus *dàn* or one of its synonyms can be present.

4.2.1 *Adversative relationship between p and q*

In sentences in the form of *"wúlùn p, dōu q"* of Subdivision III, no matter how the degree of *p* varies, there is always an adversative relationship between *p* and *q*.

Sentences in the form of *"wúlùn (zěnme) p, dōu q"* can be rewritten as *"suīrán p, dànshì q"* or *"jíshǐ p, yě q"*. For example, (7) and (8) can be respectively rewritten as (10) and (11):

(10) 虽然姐姐怎么数落、怨恨，但小伙子只是低着头，不敢还腔。

Suīrán   jiějiě   zěnme shǔluò, yuànhèn, dàn xiǎohuǒzi zhǐshì dī-zhe
although elder sister how   scold   complain but lad   only   lower-PRG

tóu,   bù   gǎn   huánqiāng.
head NEG dare   talk back

{Though his elder sister scolded and blamed him, the young man just kept his head lowered and did not dare to talk back.}

(11) 即使晚上睡得再迟，早晨也总是六点钟起床。

Jíshǐ . . . yě . . . wǎnshàng shuì de zài   chí, zǎochén yě zǒngshì liù diǎn zhōng
even if   night   sleep SP how late morning   always six o'clock

qǐchuáng.
get up

{Even if she goes to bed late at night, she always gets up at six in the morning.}

The following are three more examples:

(12) ……不管春哥说的话多么难听，他（培南）还是笑咪咪的。

*. . . bùguǎn   Chūn gē   shuō de huà   **duōme**   nántīng,*
no matter . . . Chun brother say   SP words how   unpleasant to the ears

tā (Péinán) háishì   xiàomīmī de.
he (Peinan) still   smile   MP

{. . . no matter how bad Brother Chun's words sounded, he [Peinan] kept smiling.}

Occurrence of dàn or its synonym in "wúlùn p, dōu q" 79

(13) 他虽然笨，也晓得共产党历来主张集体化。

Tā suīrán bèn, yě xiǎode Gòngchǎndǎng lìlái zhǔzhāng
he although dumb also be aware Communist Party always advocate

jítǐhuà.
collectivization

{Dumb as he is, he knows that the Communist Party always advocates collectivization.}

(14) 即使她有多高超的音乐素养，也决不会给观众留下太多美感的东西。

Jíshǐ...yě... tā yǒu duō gāochāo de yīnyuè sùyǎng, yě jué
even if she have how superb SP music accomplishment definitely

bù huì gěi guānzhòng liúxià tài duō měigǎn de dōngxi.
NEG will with audience leave too many aesthetic feeling SP thing

{However high level her musical attainment is, she will never leave the audience with many things of aesthetic feeling.}

In (12), the connective *bùguǎn* introduces *p* and stresses that the occurrence of *q* is unconditional. If the stress of the sentence is on the tolerance of the fact, (12) can be rewritten as (15a). If the stress of the sentence is on the indulgence of the condition, (12) can be rewritten as (15b). In (13), *suīrán* introduces *p* and stresses the tolerance of the fact. If the stress is to be shifted to the unconditionality of *q*, (13) can be rewritten as (16). In (14), *jíshǐ* is used to introduce *p* and stresses the indulgence of the condition. If the emphasis is to be shifted to the unconditionality of *q*, (14) can be rewritten as (17).

(15) a 虽然春哥说的话十分难听，他还是笑咪咪的。

Suīrán Chūn gē shuō de huà shífēn nántīng, tā háishì
no matter Chun brother say SP words very unpleasant to the ears he still

xiàomīmī de.
smile MP

{Although Brother Chun's words sounded very bad, he kept smiling.}

b 即使春哥说的话十分难听，他也是笑咪咪的。

Jíshǐ...yě... Chūn gē shuō de huà shífēn nántīng, tā yě
even if Chun brother say SP words very unpleasant to the ears he

shì xiàomīmī de.
COP smile MP

{Even if Brother Chun's words sounded very bad, he still kept smiling.}

(16) 不管他怎么笨，也晓得共产党历来主张集体化。

Bùguǎn tā zěnme bèn, yě xiǎode Gòngchǎndǎng lìlái zhǔzhāng
no matter he how dumb also know Communist Party always advocate

jítǐhuà.
collectivization

{No matter how dumb he is, he knows that the Communist Party always advocates collectivization.}

80 Occurrence of dàn or its synonym in "wúlùn p, dōu q"

(17)　不管她有多高超的音乐素养，也决不会给观众留下太多美感的东西。

Bùguǎn…yě… tā yǒu duō gāochāo de yīnyuè sùyǎng,　　yě jué
no matter…　　she have how superb SP music accomplishment　definitely
bù　huì　gěi　guānzhòng liúxià tài duō　měigǎn　de dōngxi.
NEG　will　with audience　leave too　many aesthetic feeling SP thing
{No matter how high her musical attainment level is, she will never leave the audience with many things of aesthetic feeling.}

4.2.2　Logical basis for the occurrence of dàn or its synonyms

Just like sentences in the form of "*jíshǐ p, yě q*", sentences in the form of "*wúlùn p, dōu q*" of Subdivision III entail a logical basis for the occurrence of *dàn* or its synonyms. For this reason, Example (7) can be rewritten as (18), (8) as (19), (9) as (20), and (12) as (21).

(18)　不管姐姐怎么数落、怨恨，小伙子（却）只是低着头，不敢还腔。

Bùguǎn　jiějiě　zěnme shǔluò, yuànhèn, xiǎohuǒzi (què)　zhǐshì
no matter…elder sister how　scold　complain lad　　however only
dī-zhe　tóu, bù　gǎn　huánqiāng.
lower-PRG head NEG dare talk back
{No matter how his elder sister scolded and blamed him, the young man just kept his head lowered and did not dare to talk back.}

(19)　无论晚上睡得多迟，早晨（却）总是六点钟起床。

Wúlùn　　wǎnshàng shuì　de duō　chí, zǎochén què　　zǒngshì
no matter…　night　　sleep SP how　late　morning however always
liù diǎn zhōng qǐchuáng.
six o'clock　get up
{No matter how late she goes to bed at night, she always gets up at six in the morning.}

(20)　无论有多少困难，（但）我们都敢于承担。

Wúlùn…dōu… yǒu　　duōshǎo　kùnnán, (dàn) wǒ-men dōu
no matter…　there be how many difficult but　we　but
gǎnyú　　chéngdān.
have the courage undertake
{No matter how many difficulties there may be, we have the courage to undertake it.}

(21)　不管春哥说的话多么难听，他（却）还是笑咪咪的。

Bùguǎn　Chūn gē　shuō de huà　duōme nántīng,　　　tā
no matter…Chun brother say　SP words how　unpleasant to the ears he
(què)　háishì　xiàomīmī de.
however still　smile　MP
{No matter how bad Brother Chun's words sounded, he kept smiling.}

Compare the following two examples:

(22) 不管他此时心情如何沉重、压抑、失望、悲哀，但他不能不去看看那块人工雕成的石柱……

*Bùguǎn   tā cǐshí   xīnqíng **rúhé** chénzhòng, yāyì,   shīwàng,*
no matter . . . he this moment mood   how heavy   depress disappointed
bēi'āi, <u>dàn</u> tā bù   néng bù   qù kàn-kàn   nà kuài réngōng diāo-chéng de
grieved but he NEG can   NEG go see-REDP that CL artificial carve   SP
shízhù . . .
stone pillar
{No matter how heavy-hearted, depressed, disappointed, and sorrowful he felt at the moment, he couldn't help going there to have a look at that artificial stone pillar . . .}

(23) 不管她如何地勤俭、刻苦、自励，日子总是过得十分艰难。

*Bùguǎn   tā **rúhé** de qínjiǎn,   kèkǔ,   zìlì,   rìzi*
no matter . . . she how SP diligent and thrifty assiduous encourage oneself life
zǒngshì guò de shífēn jiānnán.
always   live SP very hard
{No matter how industrious and thrifty, assiduous and self-motivated she is, life has always been very hard.}

The two aforementioned examples are in the same form, i.e., "*bùguǎn + rúhé + a parallel structure*". The adversative connective *dàn* is present in (22), but it can be removed. In (23), *dàn* is absent, but it can be present.

4.2.3 *Functions of occurrence of dàn or its synonyms*

In sentences in the form of "*wúlùn p, dōu q*" of Subdivision III, *dàn* or its synonym is usually used to highlight the adversative relationship between the clauses and to mark the boundary between the two clauses in some cases. The following are two examples:

(24) 实际情况是，不管我们的现实生活多么平庸而沉闷，但是它所缺少的从来也不是戏剧性。

*Shíjì   qíngkuàng shì, **bùguǎn** . . . yě . . . wǒ-men de xiànshí shēnghuó **duōme***
actual situation   COP no matter . . .   we   SP reality life   how
píngyōng ér chénmèn, <u>dànshì</u> tā suǒ quēshǎo de cónglái yě bù   shì xìjùxìng.
ordinary and dreary   but   it PAP lack SP ever   NEG COP drama
{The truth is that no matter how ordinary and dreary our life is, what it lacks is never drama.}

(25) "阳历年"——那算什么年？不管你给它起了多好听的名儿叫什么"元旦"，可中国人从来不把它当"年"看待。

*"Yánglìnián"   —nà suàn shénme nián?   **Bùguǎn***
solar calendar New Year's Day that count what   New Year's Day no matter . . .

82 *Occurrence of dàn or its synonym in "wúlùn p, dōu q"*

nǐ	gěi	tā	qǐ-le	**duō**	hǎotīng		de	míng'ér	jiào	shénme
you	to	it	give-PEF	how	pleasant to the ears		SP	name	call	what

"*yuándàn*", <u>*kě*</u> *zhōngguórén cónglái bù bǎ tā dāng* "*nián*" *kàndài.*
first day but Chinese ever NEG BA it treat as New Year's Day regard

{"Solar calendar New Year's Day"? What kind of New Year's Day is that? No matter how beautiful "The First Day of the Year"—the name you gave it—sounds, the Chinese never regard it as "New Year's Day".}

The anterior and posterior clauses in the two aforementioned examples are brief and short, and the occurrence of *dàn* or its synonym highlights the contrast between the condition and the result.

The following are three more examples:

(26) <u>无论</u>我怎么发问，怎么催促她指出我可能存在的错误，<u>可是</u>她还是闭口不谈。

<u>*Wúlùn*</u> *wǒ* **zěnme** *fāwèn,* **zěnme** *cuīcù tā zhǐ-chū wǒ kěnéng cúnzài*
no matter ... I how ask how urge her point out I possible exist
de cuòwù, <u>*kěshì*</u> *tā háishì bìkǒu-bùtán.*
SP mistake but she still refuse to say anything

{No matter what questions I asked her, or how I urged her to point out my possible mistakes, she wouldn't respond.}

(27) 笑话我吧，珊姐！……<u>不管</u>我在社会上看到过多少阴郁的、可憎的事情，<u>但</u>只要想到你，心地便纯真了。

Xiàohuà wǒ ba, Shān jiě! ... <u>*Bùguǎn*</u> *wǒ zài shèhuì-shàng kàn-dào-guò*
laugh at me MP Shan sister no matter ... I at in society see-EXP
duōshǎo *yīnyù de, kězēng de shìqing,* <u>*dàn*</u> *zhǐyào* ... *biàn* ...
how many gloomy SP detestable SP matter but as long as
xiǎng-dào nǐ, xīndì biàn chúnzhēn le.
think about you heart pure MP

{Sister Shan, you are laughing at me, aren't you! ... No matter how many gloomy and detestable things I have seen in society, my heart will become pure as long as I think about you.}

(28) 一个人<u>不管</u>职务多高，权势多重，身分多么显赫，<u>但</u>只要他做了亏心事，做了见不得人的事，那他所摆出来的任何样子，都只能是虚的，假的，都只能是外强中干、色厉内荏！

Yī gè rén <u>*bùguǎn*</u> ... *dōu* ... *dōu* ... *zhíwù* **duō** *gāo, quánshì* **duō** *zhòng,*
one CL person no matter ... position how high power how great
shēnfèn **duōme** *xiǎnhè,* <u>*dàn*</u> *zhǐyào tā zuò-le kuīxīn shì, zuò-le*
status how prominent but as long as he do-EXP feeling guilty deed do-PEF
jiàn bù de rén de shì, nà tā suǒ bǎi-chūlái de rènhé yàngzi, dōu zhǐ
cannot be revealed SP deed then he PAP put on SP any appearance only
néng shì xū-de, jiǎ-de, dōu zhǐ néng shì wàiqiáng-zhōnggān,
can COP false fake only can COP strong in appearance but weak in reality

sèlǐ-nèirěn!
be tough outwardly but timid inwardly

{No matter how high a person's position is, how powerful he is, or how prominent his status is, as long as he has something on his conscience or has done something shameful, whatever he puts on can only be false and fake—tough outwardly but timid inwardly!}

In (26), two mutually explanatory *zěnme*-structures are used in the anterior clause. In the posterior clause, *kěshì* not only emphasizes the adversative relationship between the two clauses but also clearly shows that the two *zěnme*-structures belong to the anterior clause. In (27), the posterior clause is a "*zhǐyào . . . biàn . . .*" conditional clause. Dividing the sentence into two parts, *dàn* highlights the adversative relationship between them and clearly shows that the conditional clause acts as the second part. In (28), the anterior clause at the first layer is complex in the sense that it is made up of three coordinated structures. The posterior clause consists of a second-layer "*zhǐyào . . . jiù . . .*" conditional clause, which makes it even more complex. The word *dàn* marks the boundary between the two first-level clauses and highlights the adversative relationship between them.

4.3 Occurrence of *dàn* or its Synonyms in Subdivisions I and II

Different than "*wúlùn p, dōu q*" of Subdivision III, "*wúlùn p, dōu q*" of Subdivisions I and II covers multiple situations, thus there are various relationships between the two clauses—it is hard to determine whether the relationship is adversative or non-adversative. Therefore, whether *dàn* or its synonyms can be present in the sentences depends on the specific relationship.

4.3.1 *Partial adversative relationship*

In sentences in the form of "*wúlùn p, dōu q*" of Subdivisions I and II, *p* and *q* are in a partial adversative relationship.

"Partial" means the adversative relationship only exists between the posterior clause and some of the situations stated in the anterior clause. For example, *p* includes two situations, A and B. If A contradicts *q*, then B does not. The reverse is also true. The following are two groups of examples:

Group A

(29) a 不管天冷不冷，他总穿着大棉袄。（no matter A or not A）

Bùguǎn	*tiān*	*lěng*	*bù*	*lěng,*	*tā*	*zǒng*	*chuān-zhe*	*dà*
no matter . . .	weather	cold	NEG	cold	he	always	wear-PRG	big

mián'ǎo.
cotton-padded jacket

{Whether it is cold or not, he is always wearing a big cotton-padded jacket.}

84 *Occurrence of dàn or its synonym in "wúlùn p, dōu q"*

    b 别说天冷，即使天不冷，他也穿着大棉袄。

Biéshuō	*tiān*	*lěng, jíshǐ . . . yě . . .*	*tiān*	*bù*	*lěng,*	*tā yě*
not to mention	weather	cold even if	weather	NEG	cold	he

chuān-zhe dà mián'ǎo.
wear-PRG big cotton-padded jacket

{He wears a big cotton-padded jacket even if it is not cold, not to mention when it is cold.}

(30)   a 不管天冷不冷，他从来不穿棉袄。（no matter A or not A）

Bùguǎn tiān lěng bù lěng, tā cónglái bù chuān mián'ǎo.
no matter . . . weather cold NEG cold he ever NEG wear cotton-padded jacket

{Whether it is cold or not, he never wears a cotton-padded jacket.}

    b 别说天不冷，即使天冷，他也不穿棉袄。

Biéshuō tiān bù lěng, jíshǐ . . . yě . . . tiān lěng, tā yě bù chuān
not to mention weather NEG cold even if weather cold he NEG wear

mián'ǎo.
cotton-padded jacket

{He never wears a cotton-padded jacket even if it is cold, not to mention when it isn't.}

(31)   a 不管天热天冷，他总穿着大棉袄。（no matter A or Z）

Bùguǎn tiān rè tiān lěng, tā zǒng chuān-zhe dà
no matter . . . weather hot weather cold he always wear-PRG big

mián'ǎo.
cotton-padded jacket

{Whether it is hot or cold, he is always wearing a big cotton-padded jacket.}

    b 别说天冷，即使天热，他也穿着大棉袄。

Biéshuō tiān lěng, jíshǐ . . . yě . . . tiān rè, tā yě chuān-zhe dà
not to mention weather cold even if weather hot he wear-PRG big

mián'ǎo.
cotton-padded jacket

{He is always wearing a big cotton-padded jacket even if it is hot, not to mention when it is cold.}

(32)   a 不管天热天冷，他从来不穿棉袄。（no matter it is A or Z）

Bùguǎn tiān rè tiān lěng, tā cónglái bù chuān mián'ǎo.
no matter . . . weather hot weather cold he ever NEG wear cotton-padded jacket

{Whether it is hot or cold, he never wears a cotton-padded jacket.}

    b 别说天热，即使天冷，他也不穿棉袄。

Biéshuō tiān rè, jíshǐ . . . yě . . . tiān lěng, tā yě bù chuān
not to mention weather hot even if weather cold he NEG wear

mián'ǎo.
cotton-padded jacket
{He never wears a cotton-padded jacket even if it is cold, not to mention when it is hot.}

(33) a 不管在冬天，还是在春天和秋天，还是在夏天，他总穿着大棉袄。（no matter A, or B, or C）
Bùguǎn   zài dōngtiān, háishì zài chūntiān hé   qiūtiān, háishì zài xiàtiān,
no matter ... in winter   or   in spring   and autumn or   in summer
tā zǒng   chuān-zhe   dà   mián'ǎo.
he always wear-PRG big cotton-padded jacket
{No matter in winter, or in spring and fall, or in summer, he is always wearing a big cotton-padded jacket.}

b 别说在冬天，也别说在春天和秋天，即使在夏天，他也穿着大棉袄。
Biéshuō   zài dōngtiān, yě   biéshuō   zài chūntiān hé qiūtiān,
not to mention in winter   also not to mention in spring   and autumn
jíshǐ . . . yě . . . zài xiàtiān, tā yě chuān-zhe dà miánǎo.
even if   in summer   he wear-PRG big cotton-padded jacket
{He is wearing a big cotton-padded jacket even in summer, not to mention in winter, or in spring, or in fall.}

(34) a 不管在冬天，还是在春天和秋天，还是在夏天，他从来不穿棉袄。（no matter A, or B, or C）
Bùguǎn   zài dōngtiān, háishì zài chūntiān hé   qiūtiān, háishì zài xiàtiān,
no matter ... in winter   or   in spring   and autumn or   in summer
tā cónglái bù   chuān mián'ǎo.
he ever   NEG wear cotton-padded jacket
{Whether it is in winter, or in spring, or in fall, or in summer, he never wars a cotton-padded jacket.}

b 别说在夏天，也别说在春天和秋天，即使在冬天，他也不穿棉袄。
Biéshuō   zàixiàtiān, yě biéshuō   zàichūntiānhé qiūtiān,jíshǐ . . . yě . . .
not to mentionin summeralsonot to mentionin spring   andautumn even if
zài dōngtiān, tā yě bù   chuān mián'ǎo.
in   winter   he yě NEG wear cotton-padded jacket
{He never wears a cotton-padded jacket even in winter, not to mention in summer, or in spring, or in fall.}

Group B

(35) a 不管在哪个季节，他总穿着大棉袄。
Bùguǎn   zài nǎ   gè jìjié,   tā zǒng   chuān-zhe dà mián'ǎo.
no matter ... in which CL season he always wear-PRG big cotton-padded jacket
{No matter what season it is, he is always wearing a big cotton-padded jacket.}

86 *Occurrence of dàn or its synonym in "wúlùn p, dōu q"*

b 不管在冬天，还是在春天和秋天，还是在夏天，他总穿着大棉袄。

Bùguǎn   zài dōngtiān, háishì zài chūntiān hé qiūtiān, háishì zài xiàtiān, tā
no matter . . . in winter   or   in spring   and autumn or   in summer he
zǒng   chuān-zhe dà mián'ǎo.
always wear-PRG big cotton-padded jacket
{Whether in winter, or in spring, or in fall, or in summer, he is always wearing
a big cotton-padded jacket.}

c 别说在冬天，也别说在春天和秋天，即使在夏天，他也穿着大棉袄。

Biéshuō   zài dōngtiān, yě biéshuō   zài chūntiān hé qiūtiān,
not to mention in winter   also not to mention in spring   and autumn
jíshǐ . . . yě . . . zài xiàtiān, tā yě chuān-zhe dà mián'ǎo.
even if   in summer he   wear-PRG big cotton-padded jacket
{He wears a big cotton-padded jacket even in summer, not to mention in winter,
or in spring, or in fall.}

(36) a 不管在哪个季节，他从来不穿棉袄。

Bùguǎn   zài nǎ   gè jìjié, tā cónglái bù   chuān mián'ǎo.
no matter . . . in which CL season he ever   NEG wear cotton-padded jacket
{No matter what season it is, he never wears a cotton-padded jacket.}

b 不管在冬天，还是在春天和秋天，还是在夏天，他从来不穿棉袄。

Bùguǎn   zài dōngtiān, háishì zài chūntiān hé qiūtiān, háishì zài xiàtiān,
no matter . . . in winter   or   in spring   and autumn or   in summer
tā cónglái bù   chuān mián'ǎo.
he ever   NEG wear cotton-padded jacket
{Whether it is in winter, or in spring, or in fall, or in summer, he never wears a
cotton-padded jacket.}

c 别说在夏天，也别说在春天和秋天，即使在冬天，他也不穿棉袄。)

Biéshuō   zài xiàtiān, yě biéshuō   zài chūntiān hé qiūtiān,
not to mention in summer also not to mention in spring   and autumn
jíshǐ . . . yě . . . zài dōngtiān, tā yě bù   chuān mián'ǎo.
even if   in winter   he NEG wear cotton-padded jacket
{He never wears a cotton-padded jacket even in winter, not to mention in summer,
or in spring, or in fall.}

In Group A, the six examples, from (29a) to (34a), are all in the form of "*wúlùn
p, dōu q*" of Subdivision I, and the two clauses in each of them are in a partial
adversative relationship. Thus, all the sentences can be rewritten as "*biéshuō . . .
jíshǐ . . . yě*" sentences,[2] i.e., from (29b) to (34b) respectively, in which what follows *jíshǐ* contradicts *q*. In Group B, however, the two examples, (35a) and (36a),
are in the form of "*wúlùn p, dōu q*" of Subdivision II, which can be transformed
into Subdivision I. After the transformation, the partial adversative relationship
between *p* and *q* becomes more visible.

Usually, *dàn* or its synonym cannot be present in sentences where only a partial adversative relationship exists between *p* and *q*. However, in face-to-face communication, *dàn* can be present if the speaker intends to emphasize that the occurrence of *q* is independent of the condition *p*, regardless of to what extent *p* is true. The following are two examples:

(37) 不管你是不是指我，但不许你这样说！
Bùguǎn *nǐ* **shì bù shì** *zhǐ* *wǒ*, *dàn* *bù* *xǔ* *nǐ* *zhèyàng shuō!*
no matter you whether . . . or not refer to me but NEG allow you so say
{Whether you refer to me or not, you are not allowed to say so!}

(38) 不管第一次恋爱是不是成功，但必须都得讲真的，⋯⋯
Bùguǎn *dìyī* *cì* *liàn'ài* **shì bù shì**
no matter first time have a romantic relationship whether . . . or not
chénggōng, *dàn* *bìxū* *dōu* *děi* *jiǎng* *zhēn* *de*, . . .
succeed but must both must talk truth SP
{Whether the first relationship will be successful or not, both must be sincere.}

The speaker of (37) severely rebukes the listener and emphasizes that "the listener is not allowed to say that" even if the condition *p* is completely untrue. The speaker of (38) prescribes the listener's behavior and emphasizes that "the listener must be sincere" even if the condition *p* is completely true. The use of *dàn* in both examples further emphasizes the unconditionality of *p*'s occurrence.

4.3.2 Total or none adversative relationship

In some cases, there is no adversative relationship between *p* and *q* in "*wúlùn p, dōu q*" of Subdivision I and Subdivision II, whereas in some cases, there exists a total adversative relationship between *p* and *q*. Compare the following four examples:

(39) （小张和小李都很不错。）无论选小张还是选小李，他都同意。（no matter A or B）
(Xiǎo Zhāng *hé* *xiǎo Lǐ* *dōu* *hěn* *bùcuò.)* *Wúlùn* . . . *dōu* . . . *xuǎn*
little ZHANG and little LI both very good no matter . . . choose
xiǎo Zhāng *háishì* *xuǎn* *xiǎo Lǐ*, *tā* *dōu* *tóngyì.*
little ZHANG or choose little LI he agree
{[Both Little ZHANG and Little LI are quite good.] Either of them being selected will be fine with him.}

(40) （小张和小李都很不错。可是，）无论选小张还是选小李，他都不同意。（no matter A or B）
(Xiǎo Zhāng *hé* *xiǎo Lǐ* *dōu* *hěn* *bùcuò. Kěshì,)* *wúlùn* . . . *dōu* . . . *xuǎn*
little ZHANG and little LI both very good but no matter . . . choose

88 *Occurrence of dàn or its synonym in "wúlùn p, dōu q"*

xiǎo Zhāng   háishì xuǎn   xiǎo Lǐ, tā dōu bù   tóngyì.
little ZHANG or   choose little LI he   NEG agree

{[Although both Little ZHANG and Little LI are quite good,] he doesn't agree to select either of them.}

(41)　（几位候选人都不错。）无论选哪一位，他都同意。

(Jǐ   wèi hòuxuǎnrén dōu bùcuò.) Wúlùn … dōu … xuǎn   nǎ   yī   wèi, tā
several CL   candidate   all good   no matter …   choose which one CL he
dōu   tóngyì.
        agree

{[All the candidates are quite good.] Any of them being selected will be fine with him.}

(42)　（几位候选人都不错。可是，）无论选哪一位，他都不同意。

(Jǐ   wèi hòuxuǎnrén dōu bùcuò. Kěshì,) wúlùn … dōu … xuǎn   nǎ
several CL   candidate   all good   but   no matter …   choose which
yī   wèi, tā   dōu bù   tóngyì.
one CL he   NEG agree

{[Although all the candidates are quite good,] he doesn't agree to select any of them.}

Examples (39) and (40) are instances of Subdivision I. In (39) there is no adversative relationship between *p* and *q*, but in (40) there is a total adversative relationship. Examples (41) and (42) are instances of Subdivision II. In (41) there is no adversative relationship between *p* and *q*, but in (40) there is a total adversative relationship.

The adversative relationship is implicit in "*wúlùn p, dōu q*" of Subdivision III, but this relationship in sentences of Subdivisions I and II is even more implicit. Whether there is a total adversative relationship or no adversative relationship at all depends on the context or the occasion for which the speech is made. In some cases, though, whether or not there is such a relationship is self-evident because the reader/listener has a pre-existing opinion about what is stated in the sentence. The following are two examples:

(43)　无论留校当助教还是分到报社当编辑，他都没意见。

Wúlùn … dōu … liú   xiào   dāng zhùjiào   háishì fēn-dào
no matter …   stay university be   teaching assistant or   assign to
bàoshè   dāng biānji, tā dōu méi   yìjiàn.
newspaper be   editor he   not have different opinion

{He's happy with either staying on as a teaching assistant or being assigned to a newspaper as an editor.}

(44)　无论留校当助教还是分到报社当编辑，他都有意见。

Wúlùn … dōu … liú   xiào   dāng zhùjiào   háishì fēn-dào
no matter …   stay at university be   teaching assistant or   assign to

bàoshè	dāng biānji,	tā	dōu	yǒu	yìjiàn.
newspaper	be editor	he		have	different opinion

{He's unhappy with either staying on as a teaching assistant or being assigned to a newspaper as an editor.}

There is no adversative relationship between the two clauses in (43), while there is such a relationship between the two clauses in (44). This judgment is based on a common understanding that staying on as a teaching assistant or being assigned to a newspaper as an editor is a good thing for a college graduate. Nevertheless, some sentences in the form of *"wúlùn p, dōu q"* in Subdivisions I and II entail a total adversative relationship, just like sentences in the form of *"wúlùn p, dōu q"* in Subdivision III. For this reason, *"wúlùn p, dōu q"* of Subdivisions I and II can be transformed into *"wúlùn p, dōu q"* of Subdivision III or into *"jíshǐ p, yě q"*. For instance, (44) can be rewritten as (45) or (46). If the adversative relationship needs to be highlighted, *dàn* or its synonym can be used, as in (47):

(45)　无论给他分配多么好的工作，他都有意见。

Wúlùn . . . dōu . . . gěi tā fēnpèi duō hǎo de gōngzuò, tā dōu yǒu
no matter . . . 　to　him　assign　how　good　SP　job　　he　　have

yìjiàn.
different opinion

{No matter how good a job is assigned to him, he's unhappy.}

(46)　即使留校当助教或分到报社当编辑，他也有意见。

Jíshǐ . . . yě . . . liú xiào dāng zhùjiào huò fēn-dào
even if　　　　stay at　university　be　teaching assistant　or　assign to

bàoshè dāng biānji, tā yě yǒu yìjiàn.
newspaper　be　editor　he　　have　different opinion

{He's unhappy even with staying on as a teaching assistant or being assigned to a newspaper as an editor.}

(47)　无论留校当助教还是分到报社当编辑，他却都有意见。真不像话！

Wúlùn . . . dōu . . . liú xiào dāngzhùjiào háishìfēn-dào
no matter . . .　stay atuniversitybe teaching assistantor assign to

bàoshè dāng biānji, tā dōu yǒu yìjiàn. Zhēn bùxiànghuà!
newspaper　be　editor　he　　have　different opinion　really　nonsensical

{He's unhappy with either staying on as a teaching assistant or being assigned to a newspaper as an editor. What a shame!}

In some sentences of Subdivisions I and II, there are two *wúlùn*-clauses, one in the form of Subdivision I and the other in the form of Subdivision II. The two *wúlùn*-clauses are mutually explanatory. In these sentences, *dàn* or its synonyms can be present between *p* and *q*, just as in *"wúlùn p, dōu q"* of Subdivision III. For example:

90 *Occurrence of dàn or its synonym in "wúlùn p, dōu q"*

(48) 贾大哥呀，<u>无论</u>你说了我什么，<u>无论</u>因为你的话，我遭了多少难堪的境遇，<u>但</u>我一点不怨恨你。

Jiǎ dàgē   ya, wúlùn   nǐ   shuō-le wǒ shénme, wúlùn   yīnwèi
JIA brother MP no matter . . . you say-PEF me what   no matter . . . because

nǐ   de huà,   wǒ zāo-le   duōshǎo nánkān   de jìngyù,   dàn wǒ
you SP words I   suffer-PEF how many embarrassed SP situation but I

yīdiǎn bù   yuànhèn nǐ.
a little NEG   resent   you

{Brother JIA, no matter what you have said about me, no matter how much I have suffered because of your words, I don't resent you at all.}

In the aforementioned example, "what you have said about me" refers to "the bad things you have said about me", which conflicts with "I don't resent you at all". After the coordinated structures—"what you have said about me" and "how much I have suffered"—and before "I don't resent you at all", the word *dàn* marks the boundary between *p* and *q* and stresses the opposition between them.

4.4 Clarifications

Some clarifications need to be made.

4.4.1 *Adversative relationship in unconditional sentences*

To be precise, unconditional sentences should be termed as unconditional concessive complex sentences.

In sentences in the form of *"wúlùn p, dōu q"*, the anterior clause presents all the alternative conditions, but then disregards all of them with *wúlùn* or its synonym. This indicates that the speaker first admits the conditions, deliberately making concessions to them, and then turns around. As previously discussed, in some cases there is a total or partial opposition between *p* and *q* in *"wúlùn p, dōu q"*. Even in some cases where there is no direct opposition between *p* and *q*, the sentence still involves a contradiction, which can be shown by (49), a rewrite of (39).

(49) 选小张他同意，但选小李他也同意。

Xuǎn   xiǎo Zhāng   tā tóngyì, dàn xuǎn   xiǎo Lǐ tā yě   tóngyì.
choose little ZHANG he agree   but choose little LI he also agree
{He agrees with the selection of Little ZHANG, but he also agrees with the selection of Little LI.}

In other words, even though "Condition A + Condition B" does contradict with *q*, there is a contradiction between "Condition A + *q*" and "Condition B" + *q* because they exclude each other. To sum up, all unconditional concessive complex sentences contain oppositions, which vary in degree or in nature if observed from the perspective of the relationship between *p* and *q* or the overall meaning of the sentence.

4.4.2 Ill-formed "bùguǎn . . . dàn/què . . ." sentences

Some "*bùguǎn . . . dàn/què . . .*" sentences are ill-formed. However, they are ill-formed not because of the inclusion of *dàn* or its synonyms, but due to the ungrammatical structure of the anterior clause. Some scholars claim that *bùguǎn* or its synonyms cannot collocate with *dàn*, which is obviously a misunderstanding.[3] In the discussion *of bùguǎn* and *jǐnguǎn*, LV Shuangxiang and Zhu Dexi have cited the following two examples[4]:

(50) 不管艾奇逊喜欢重弹戈培尔博士的老调，在华盛顿的参议院绅士们却在招供。

Bùguǎn   Àiqíxùn   xǐhuān   chóngtán Gēpéi'ěr bóshì   de   lǎodiào,   zài
no matter Acheson   like   repeat   Goebbels doctor   SP   platitude   in
Huáshèngdùn de cānyìyuàn shēnshì-men què   zài   zhāogòng.
Washington   SP   senate   gentleman-PL however in progress confess
{No matter how much Acheson liked to repeat Dr. Goebbel's platitudes, the gentlemen in the Senate in Washington were confessing.}

(51) 五四时代的白话文是一个革命的运动，不管其中有部分的人是软弱妥协，但它却是要革文言文的命。

Wǔsì   shídài de báihuàwén   shì yī gè gémìng   de
May 4th Movement era   SP vernacular Chinese COP one CL revolution SP
yùndòng, bùguǎn   qízhōng yǒu   bùfen de rén   shì ruǎnruò tuǒxié,
movement no matter inside   there be part SP person COP weak   compromise
dàn tā què   shì   yào gé wényánwén   de mìng.
but it however COP   will end classical Chinese SP life
{The vernacular language of the May Fourth era was a revolutionary movement, and no matter how many people were weak and compromising, it was meant to revolutionize Classical Chinese.}

According to LV and Zhu, if *zěnyàng* occurs before *xǐhuān* in (50) and *duōshǎo* is used in place of "*bùfèn de*" in (51), *bùguǎn* can be present in each anterior clause. Otherwise, only *jǐnguǎn* can be used. However, they did not claim that *dàn/què* cannot be used in the posterior clause if *bùguǎn* is present in the anterior clause. If *zěnyàng* is added and placed before *xǐhuān* in (50) and *duōshǎo* is used in place of "*bùfèn de*" in (51), the two sentences will be in the form of Subdivision III, in which *dàn* or *què* can remain intact.

4.4.3 Cases where dàn or its synonyms cannot be present

If the anterior clause in an unconditional concessive sentence is subjectless but acted by such expressions as "*wúlùn rúhé*" ('no matter how'), "*bùguǎn zěnyàng*" ('no matter how'), and "*bùguǎn zěnme shuō*" ('no matter what'), *dàn* or its synonym cannot be present between the two clauses. The following are three examples:

92 Occurrence of dàn or its synonym in "wúlùn p, dōu q"

(52) （如果再受刑，那就还要咬牙忍住。……）无论如何，我们不能向敌人屈
服，……

(*Rúguǒ . . . jiù . . . zài   shòuxíng,   nà   jiù   hái   yào*
if   again receive corporal punishment then   still must
yǎoyá   rěnzhù. . . .) Wúlùn rúhé, wǒ-men bùnéng xiàng dírén   qūfú.
grit one's teeth hold on   in any case we   cannot to enemy give in
{[If we receive corporal punishment again, we must grit our teeth and hold on . . .]
In no case shall we give in to the enemy . . .}

(53) （人做事要凭良心 …… 你忍心让大家饿得红天黑日头？）不管怎样，你起
码要放两个月限期……

(*Rén   zuòshì yào   píng   liángxīn. . . Nǐ rěnxīn   ràng dàjiā*
person act   must base on conscience you be hardhearted make everyone
è   de hóng tiān hēi rìtou?) Bùguǎn zěnyàng, nǐ   qǐmǎ yào fàng liǎng
hungry SP red sky and black sun in any case   you at least must extend two
gè   yuè   xiànqī. . .
CL   month deadline

{[One must behave with conscience. . . . Do you have the heart to make everyone
starve to faint?] In any case, you have to extend the deadline until at least two
months from now . . .}

(54) 不管怎么说，打，总是要打的吧？
Bùguǎn zěnme shuō, dǎ,   zǒngshì yào   dǎ   de   ba?
in any case   fight against always must fight against SP   MP
{In any case, we must fight against (economic crimes), right?}

"*wúlùn rúhé*" is a set phrase,[5] and "*bùguǎn zěnyàng*" is a colloquialism for
"*wúlùn rúhé*".[6] "*bùguǎn zěnme shuō*" is also a set phrase, which has the same
meaning as "*wúlùn rúhé*" and "*bùguǎn zěnyàng*". Even though "*bùguǎn zěnme
shuō*" is in the form of "*zěnme* + head", the head *shuō* does not refer to a real
action. Unconditional concessive complex sentences with "*bùguǎn zěnme shuō*"
acting as the anterior clause are clearly different from "*wúlùn p, dōu q*" of Subdivision III.

If there is an agent acting as the subject of "*bùguǎn zěnme shuō*", and the word
shuō denotes the action of saying, the sentence is usually one of Subdivision III.
For example:

(55) 不管人们怎么说，她都没有明显的反应。
Bùguǎn . . . dōu . . . rén-men zěnme shuō, tā   dōu méiyǒu míngxiǎn de fǎnyìng.
no matter   person-PL how say   she not have obvious SP reaction
{No matter what they say, she has no obvious reaction.}

This example is of Subdivision III, in which *shuō* means "to talk about", *rén-
men* acts as the subject, and *dàn* can be present. Thus, the aforementioned example can be rephrased as following:

Occurrence of *dàn* or its synonym in *"wúlùn p, dōu q"*   93

(56) 不管人们怎么说，她却都没有明显的反应。

<u>*Bùguǎn*</u> ... *dōu* ... *rén-men*   *zěnme*   *shuō*, *tā*   *què*   *dōu*   *méiyǒu*   *míngxiǎn*
no matter   person-PL how   say   she   but   not have obvious
de fǎnyìng.
SP reaction
{No matter what they say, she still has no obvious reaction.}

4.4.4   Beyond the scope of this discussion

This chapter focuses on complex sentences; therefore, no attention is to be paid to whether *dàn* or its synonyms can be present in simple sentences in the *"wúlùn . . . dōu . . ."* structure.

Summary

First, the sentence form *"wúlùn p, dōu q"* entails adversative relationships that vary in degree and nature, hence *dàn* or its synonyms can be present in some sentences in this form.

Second, this form can be divided into three subdivisions: Subdivision I, in which the anterior clause lists two or more situations; Subdivision II, in which the anterior clause uses a generic expression to summarize two or more situations; Subdivision III, in which the anterior clause uses a generic expression to condense a situation with variations in degree.

Third, Subdivision III involves a total adversative relationship, hence *dàn* or its synonyms can be present if necessary.

Fourth, Subdivisions I and II cover multiple situations, thus there are various relationships between *p* and *q*. Therefore, whether *dàn* or its synonyms can be present needs to be considered on a case-by-case basis.

NB Some examples in this chapter are cited from literary works, political essays, articles, and so on. The sources are listed as follows:

1 *Baihuazhou* (《百花洲》) 1984(1), including Example (53);
2 *Changcheng* (《长城》) 1982(1), including (7);
3 *Chinese* for Junior High School Students, Book 5, including (52);
4 *Dangdai* (《当代》) 1983(3), including (4) and (9);
5 *Fiction Monthly* (《小说月报》) 1982(2), including (2);
6 *Flower City* (《花城》) 1983(3), including (5); 1983(4), including (37); 1983(6), including (48);
7 *Harvest* (《收获》) 1983(2), including (22); 1983(4), including (8); 1983(6), including (54) and (55);
8 *October* (《十月》) 1982(3), including (23); 1983(4), including (14); 1983(6), including (12), (26), and (27);

94 *Occurrence of dàn or its synonym in "wúlùn p, dōu q"*

9 *People's Literature* (《人民文学》) 1982(2), including (13); 1982(3), including (25);
10 *Selected Stories* (《小说选刊》) 1997(1) (supplement), including (28);
11 *Selected Works of DENG Xiaoping* (1975–1982) (《邓小平文选 (1975–1982 年)》), including (1);
12 *Works* (《作品》) 1999(4) (supplement), including (24);
13 *Xiao Shuo Jia* (《小说家》) 1997 (3), including (38);
14 *Zhongshan* (《钟山》) 1982(3), including (3).

Bibliography

1 LV Shuxiang (吕叔湘). *Sketches of Chinese Grammar* (《中国文法要略》). The Commercial Press, 1956, p. 450.
2 ibid., p. 448.
3 Editorial Office of Zhongguo Yuwen (Ed). *Selections of Chinese Short Reviews* (《语文短评选辑》). Zhonghua Book Company, 1959, p. 105.
4 LV Shuxiang (吕叔湘) and ZHU Dexi (朱德熙). *Lrectures on Grammar and Rhetoric* (《语法修辞讲话》). Kaiming Book Co., 1952.
5 LV Shuxiang (吕叔湘). *Eight Hundred Words in Modern Chinese* (《现代汉语八百词》). The Commercial Press, 1980, p. 490.
6 Department of Chinese Language and Literature, Peking University (Ed.). *Interpretations of Grammatical Words in Modern Chinese* (《现代汉语虚词例释》). The Commercial Press, 1982, p. 435.

5 Occurrence of *què* in "*jìrán p, jiù q*"

Sentences in the form of "*jìrán p, jiù q*", or *jìrán*-sentences, are inferential-causal complex sentences. The connective "*jìrán . . . nàme (/ jiù) . . .*" ('since . . . then . . .') is the typical marker for these sentences. In some cases, *jìrán* can be abbreviated to *jì*. This form is used to infer the causality between matters by taking a fact as the reason or basis.

In most cases, the adversative connective *què* cannot occur in *jìrán*-sentences. The following are two pairs of examples:

(1)　　a 既然他有能力，那么应该重用他！（＋）
　　　　Jìrán　　tā　yǒu　nénglì, *nàme* yīnggāi zhòngyòng　　　　　　　　*tā!*
　　　　now that　he　have　ability　then　should　put someone in an important position　him
　　　　{Since he has the ability, he should be put in an important position!}

　　　　b 既然他有能力，那么却应该重用他！（－）
　　　　Jìrán　　tā　yǒu　nénglì, *nàme* **què**　　*yīnggāi*
　　　　now that　he　have　ability　then　however　should
　　　　zhòngyòng　　　　　　　　　*tā!*
　　　　put someone in an important position　him

(2)　　a 既然他没能力，那么不应重用他！（＋）
　　　　Jìrán　　tā　méi　　nénglì, *nàme* bù　　yīng
　　　　now that　he　not have　ability　then　NEG　should
　　　　zhòngyòng　　　　　　　　　*tā!*
　　　　put someone in an important position　him
　　　　{Since he isn't capable, he shouldn't be put in any important position!}

　　　　b 既然他没能力，那么却不应重用他！（－）
　　　　Jìrán　　tā　méi　　nénglì, *nàme* **què**　　bù　　yīng
　　　　now that　he　not have　ability　then　however　NEG　should
　　　　zhòngyòng　　　　　　　　*tā!*
　　　　put someone in an important position　him

DOI: 10.4324/9781003374237-5

96   *Occurrence of* què *in "*jìrán p, jiù q*"*

Nonetheless, *què* is present in the posterior clause in some *jìrán*-sentences, as in the following two examples:

(3)   既然他有能力，那么为什么却不重用他呢？

    Jìrán   tā   yǒu   nénglì,   nàme   wèishénme   què   bù
    now that he have ability then why   however NEG
    zhòngyòng   tā   ne?
    put someone in an important position him MP
    {Since he is capable, why wasn't he put in any important position?}

(4)   既然他没能力，那么为什么却重用了他呢？

    Jìrán   tā   méi   nénglì,   nàme   wèishénme   què
    now that he not have ability then why   however
    zhòngyòng-le   tā   ne?
    put someone in an important position-PEF him MP
    {Since he wasn't capable, why was he put in an important position?}

In actual language use, "*jìrán . . . què . . .*" sentences are not uncommon. The following are two examples:

(5)   （十二岁的马夫，甚至不明白，）妈妈既然有过一个开着桂花的美丽的家，却为什么要搬到这破烂拥挤的小杂院来居住。

    (Shí'èr suì   de Mǎfū, shènzhì bù   míngbai,)   māma   jìrán   yǒu-guò
    twelve year of age SP Mafu even   NEG understand mother now that have-EXP
    yī gè kāi-zhe   guìhuā   de měilì   de jiā,   què   wèishénme yào
    one CL bloom-PRG osmanthus SP beautiful SP home however why   will
    bān-dào zhè pòlàn   yōngjǐ   de xiǎo záyuàn
    move to this dilapidated crowded SP small compound with many households
    lái   jūzhù.
    come live
    {[The 12-year-old Mafu doesn't even understand] why his mom moved to live in this shabby and crowded small courtyard complex since she once had a beautiful home with Osmanthus flowers.}

(6)   美容院既（然）能将她旧日粗糙的皮肤改换得如同纸张般细腻，却为什么没能除去她隔着厚厚的貂皮短大衣和羊毛围巾仍然张牙舞爪地向我袭来的那股酸腥味？

    Měiróngyuàn jì(rán)   néng jiāng tā   jiùrì   cūcāo de pífū gǎihuàn de
    beauty salon now that can BA him former day rough SP skin change SP
    rútóng . . . bān . . . zhǐzhāng bān xìnì,   què   wèishénme méi néng chúqù
    be like   paper   delicate however why   NEG can remove
    tā gé-zhe   hòu-hòu   de diāopí duǎn dàyī hé yángmáo wéijīn réngrán
    her separate-PRG thick-REDP SP mink short coat and wool scarf still
    zhāngyá-wǔzhǎo   de xiàng wǒ xí-lái de nà gǔ suānxīng wèi?
    bare fangs and brandish claws SP to me attack SP that CL sour and fishy smell

{Since the beauty salon can turn her old rough skin into skin as delicate as paper, why can't they get rid of the sour and fishy smell that lashes me through her thick mink coat and woolen scarf?}

On what occasion can *què* be present in *jìrán*-sentences? What are the rules? What is its pragmatic significance? This chapter aims to analyze the phenomenon and find out the law, along with discussions on the adversative connective *kě* ('but').

5.1 *jìrán*-sentences inferring the cause

Adversative connective *què* cannot occur in *jìrán*-sentences inferring the cause.

It is generally assumed that the reason often relates to the cause and the conclusion relates to the effect, but this assumption is not always true. In some cases, the reason does not refer to the cause, nor does the conclusion refer to the effect. Compare the following two examples:

(7) 既然奖金这么多，报名的人一定不少。

    Jìrán   jiǎngjīn zhème duō,   bàomíng de   rén   yídìng   bù   shǎo.
    now that prize   so   much sign up SP person definitely NEG few
    {Since the prize money is such a big amount, there must be a lot of people who have signed up.}

(8) 既然报名的人这么多，奖金一定不少。

    Jìrán   bàomíng de   rén   zhème duō,   jiǎngjīn yídìng   bù   shǎo.
    now that sign up SP person so   many prize   definitely NEG little
    {Since there are a lot of people who have signed up, the prize money must be a big amount.}

Between the two matters stated in these sentences, it is understood that "the generous prize money" is the cause, and "the large number of people signing up" is the effect. Consequently, in (7) the reason is the cause and the conclusion is the effect, whereas in (8) the reason is the effect and the conclusion is the cause.

In all *jìrán*-sentences, the anterior clause presents the reason or basis for the inference, and the posterior clause gives the conclusion or assertion. Based on the relationship between the anterior clause and the posterior clause, *jìrán*-sentences fall into two subtypes: inferring the effect and inferring the cause. In sentences that infer the effect, the inference is based on the realis cause and the conclusion is about the effect; in other words, the reason refers to the cause and the conclusion refers to the effect. In sentences that infer the cause, the realis effect is taken as the grounds to infer the cause; that is, the reason refers to the effect and the conclusion refers to the cause. This has been already discussed in Chapter 4, Volume I. The following are four examples:

98 Occurrence of què in "jìrán p, jiù q"

(9) 市委<u>既然</u>点名要我们注意祁时飞，<u>就</u>一定掌握了情况。

Shìwěi   *jìrán*   *diǎnmíng*   *yào wǒ-men*
municipal party committee   now that   mention one's name   ask   us
zhùyì   *Qí Shífēi*,   *jiù*   *yīdìng*   *zhǎngwò-le*   *qíngkuàng*.
pay attention   QI Shifei   then   definitely   know well-PEF   situation
{Since the Municipal Party Committee asked us to keep an eye on QI Shifei, they must have understood the situation very well.}

(10) 市委<u>既然</u>指示我们注意，<u>那</u>肯定是有问题。

Shìwěi   *jìrán*   *zhǐshì*   *wǒ-men*   *zhùyì*,   <u>*nà*</u>
municipal party committee   now that   instruct   us   pay attention   then
kěndìng   *shì*   *yǒu*   *wèntí*.
definitely   COP   there be   problem
{Since the Municipal Party Committee instructed us to be on alert, there must be problems.}

(11) 你<u>既然</u>来找我，<u>就</u>是相信我。

Nǐ   <u>*jìrán*</u>   *lái*   *zhǎo*   *wǒ*,   <u>*jiù*</u>   *shì*   *xiāngxìn*   *wǒ*.
you   now that   come   call on   me   then   COP   trust   me
{Since you've called on me, you surely trust me.}

(12) 她<u>既然</u>能使你爱，总还有她好的地方。

Tā <u>*jìrán*</u>   *néng shǐ*   *nǐ*   *ài*,   *zǒng*   *hái yǒu*   *tā*   *hǎo*   *de*   *dìfang*.
she now that can   make you love   after all   still have   she   good   SP   quality
{Since you have fallen in love with her, she must have some good qualities.}

These four sentences all infer the cause according to the effect. Since the posterior clause in each sentence is related to the cause, a relationship marker—for instance, "*yīdìng shì yīnwèi*" ('surely because')—can be used. For example, (9)–(12) can be rewritten as (13)–(16) respectively:

(13) 市委既然点名要我们注意祁时飞，就一定是因为掌握了情况。

Shìwěi   *jìrán*   *diǎnmíng*   *yào wǒ-men zhùyì*
municipal party committee   now that   mention one's name   ask   us   pay attention
Qí Shífēi,   *jiù*   *yīdìng*   *shì*   *yīnwèi*   *zhǎngwò-le*   *qíngkuàng*.
QI Shifei   then   definitely   COP   because   know well-PEF   situation
{Since the Municipal Party Committee asked us to keep an eye on QI Shifei, they must have understood the situation very well.}

(14) 市委既然指示我们注意，那一定是因为有问题。

Shìwěi   *jìrán*   *zhǐshì*   *wǒ-men*   *zhùyì*,   *nà*
municipal party committee   now that   instruct   us   pay attention   then
yīdìng   *shì*   *yīnwèi*   *yǒu*   *wèntí*.
definitely   COP   because   there be   problem
{Since the Municipal Party Committee instructed us to be on alert, there must be problems.}

Occurrence of què in "jìrán p, jiù q" 99

(15) 你既然来找我，就一定是因为相信我。

Nǐ   jìrán   lái   zhǎo   wǒ, jiù   yīdìng   shì   yīnwèi   xiāngxìn wǒ.
you now that come call on me then definitely COP because trust   me
{Since you've called on me, you surely trust me.}

(16) 她既然能使你爱，一定是因为还有她好的地方。

Tā jìrán   néng shǐ   nǐ   ài,   yīdìng   shì   yīnwèi   hái yǒu   tā   hǎo
she now that can   make you love definitely COP because still have she good
de   dìfang.
SP   quality
{Since you have fallen in love with her, she must have some good qualities.}

In actual language use, "*jìrán . . . shì yīnwèi . . .*" sentences can be found. The following is an example, in which "*shì yīnwèi*" occurs in the posterior clause:

(17) 我既然请你看，就是因为不怕你看。

Wǒ jìrán   qíng nǐ   kàn,   jiù   shì   yīnwèi   bù   pà   nǐ   kàn.
I   now that ask   you watch just COP because NEG fear you watch
{Since I've asked you to watch it, I don't fear you watching it.}

In this example, "*shì yīnwèi*" is used to formally stress that what the posterior clause infers is a conclusion about the cause. If *yīnwèi* is absent, then what the conclusion is about will be implicit.

In some *jìrán*-sentences inferring the cause, *kějiàn* ('thus it is clear that') can occur in the posterior clause to emphasize that the cause can be inferred from the effect. The following is an example:

(18) 既然他那么小心翼翼地翻身，可见他不愿她知道他睡不着，不愿她知道他在想心事。

Jìrán   tā nàme xiǎoxīn-yìyì de fānshēn, kějiàn   tā bù   yuàn tā
now that he so   careful   SP turn over thus it is clear that he NEG want she
zhīdào tā shuì bù zháo, bù   yuàn tā zhīdào tā zài   xiǎng xīnshì.
know he cannot sleep NEG want she know he in progress think about something
{Since he turned over so gently, it's clear that he didn't want her to know that he was thinking about something and couldn't sleep.}

In the aforementioned example with *kějiàn*, "*shì yīnwèi*" can be present, as in the following one:

(19) 既然他那么小心翼翼地翻身，可见是因为他不愿她知道他睡不着……

Jìrán   tā nàme xiǎoxīn-yìyì de fānshēn, kějiàn   shì   yīnwèi
now that he so   careful   SP turn over it is thus clear that COP because
tā bù   yuàn tā zhīdào tā shuì bù zháo . . .
he NEG want she know he cannot sleep
{Since he turned over so gently, it's clear that it was because he didn't want her to know that he couldn't sleep . . .}

100 *Occurrence of què in "jìrán p, jiù q"*

In all, *jìrán*-sentences inferring a cause do not have any semantic conditions for the occurrence of *què*, so the occurrence of *què* is impermissible.

5.2 *jìrán*-sentences inferring the effect

Adversative connective *què* cannot occur in basic *jìrán*-sentences inferring the effect.

A basic *jìrán*-sentence inferring an effect is made up of two semantic segments, A and B, in which Segment B presents a subsequent effect of Segment A. The word *què* cannot be used between A and B. The following are two examples:

(20)　既然放权，就不要管他们的那些权限以内的事情。

Jìrán　　*fàngquán*,　　　　　*jiù*　*bùyào guǎn*　　　*tā-men de*
now that　delegate power to a lower level　then　do not　bother with　they　SP

nàxiē quánxiàn yǐnèi　de　shìqing.
those　within authority　SP　matter

{Since (you) have delegated (your) power, (you) shouldn't bother with those matters within their authority.}

(21)　姐夫既然做主，这事就算成了。

Jiěfu　　　　　　*jìrán*　*zuòzhǔ*, *zhè shì*　*jiù*　*suàn*　*chéng-le*.
elder sister's husband　now that　decide　this thing　then　regard　be settled-PEF

{Since (my) brother-in-law has made a decision, the matter is now settled.}

These two examples are basic *jìrán*-sentences inferring an effect. In such sentences where B presents a subsequent effect of A, the occurrence of *què* is impossible.

However, basic *jìrán*-sentences can be expanded to include a third semantic segment, i.e., "*fēi* B" ('not B'). If the structure of basic *jìrán*-sentences is "*jìrán A, nàme B*", the structure of expanded *jìrán*-sentences is "*jìrán A, nàme B, kěshì què fēi B*", in which "not B" is the opposite of the effect of A—in other words, "not B" is the opposite of B. Only in the expanded *jìrán*-sentences can the adversative connective *què* occur. The following are three groups of examples:

(22)　a　既然他有能力①，那么应该重用他②！

Jìrán　　*tā yǒu　nénglì*①, *nàme yīnggāi zhòngyòng*
now that　he　have　ability　　then　should　put someone in an important position

*tā*②*!*
him

{Since he is capable, he should be put in an important position!}

　　　b　既然他有能力①，那么应该重用他②，可是你却不重用他③！

Jìrán　　*tā yǒu　nénglì*①, *nàme yīnggāi zhòngyòng*
now that　he　have　ability　　then　should　put someone in an important position

Occurrence of què *in "*jìrán p, jiù q*"* 101

tā②,	kěshì	nǐ	què	bù	zhòngyòng				tā③!
him	but	you	however	NEG	put someone in an important position				him

{Since he is capable, you should put him in an important position, but you didn't!}

→c 既然他有能力①，那么你为什么却不重用他呢③?

Jìrán	tā	yǒu	nénglì①,	nàme	nǐ	wèishénme	què	bù
now that	he	have	ability	then	you	why	however	NEG

zhòngyòng				tā	ne③?
put someone in an important position				him	MP

{He is capable, but why didn't you put him in an important position?}

(23) a 既然他没能力①，那么不应重用他②!

Jìrán	tā	méi	nénglì①,	nàme	bù	yīng
now that	he	not have	ability	then	NEG	should

zhòngyòng				tā②!
put someone in an important position				him

{Since he isn't capable, he shouldn't be put in any important position!}

b 既然他没能力①，那么不应重用他②，可是你却重用他③!

Jìrán	tā	méi	nénglì①,	nàme	bù	yīng
now that	he	not have	ability	then	NEG	should

zhòngyòng				tā②,	kěshì	nǐ	què
put someone in an important position				him	but	you	however

zhòngyòng				tā③!
put someone in an important position				him

{Since he isn't capable, you shouldn't put him in any important position, but you did!}

→c 既然他没能力①，那么你为什么却重用他呢③?

Jìrán	tā	méi	nénglì①,	nàme	nǐ	wèishénme	què
now that	he	not have	ability	then	you	why	however

zhòngyòng				tā	ne③?
put someone in an important position				him	MP

{He isn't capable, but why did you put him in an important position?}

(24) a 既然奖金这么多①，那么报名的人一定不少②。

Jìrán	jiǎngjīn	zhème	duō①,	nàme	bàomíng	de	rén	yīdìng	bù	shǎo②.
now that	prize	so	much	then	sign up	SP	person	definitely	NEG	few

{Since the prize money is such a big amount, there must be a lot of people who have signed up.}

b 既然奖金这么多①，那么报名的人一定不少②，可是实际上却很少③。

Jìrán	jiǎngjīn	zhème	duō①,	nàme	bàomíng	de	rén	yīdìng	bù	shǎo②,
now that	prize	so	much	then	sign up	SP	person	definitely	NEG	few

kěshì shíjìshàng què hěn shǎo③.
but actually however very few
{Since the prize money is such a big amount, there must be a lot of people who have signed up, but actually very few.}

→c 既然奖金这么多①，那么报名的人为什么却很少呢③？
Jìrán jiǎngjīn zhème duō①, nàme bàomíng de rén wèishénme què
now that prize so much then sign up SP person why however
hěn shǎo ne③?
very few MP
{The prize money is such a big amount, but why are there so few people who have signed up?}

Two conclusions can be drawn from the analysis of these sentences:
First, "*jìrán . . . què . . .*" sentences are a compact version of expanded *jìrán*-sentences, which include three semantic segments: A, B, and "not B". In the compact version, only A and "not B" remain. The following is an example:

(25) 既然是军人，就应该死在战场上。
Jìrán shì jūnrén, jiù yīnggāi sǐ zài zhànchǎng-shàng.
now that COP soldier then should die at on battlefield
{Since (they) are soldiers, (they) should die on the battlefield.}

The aforementioned example is a basic *jìrán*-sentence in the form of "A + B", which can be expanded to include the third segment "*not B*", exemplified by the following sentence:

(26) 既然是军人，就应该死在战场上，可是他却枪声一响就逃跑了！
Jìrán shì jūnrén, jiù yīnggāi sǐ zài zhànchǎng-shàng, kěshì tā què
now that COP soldier then should die at on battlefield but he however
qiāngshēng yī . . . jiù . . . xiǎng jiù táopǎo-le!
gunshot as soon as ring out run away-PEF
{Since he is a soldier, he should die on the battlefield, but he ran away as soon as gunshots rang out!}

As can be seen, (26) is in the expanded adversative form "A + B + not B", which can be rewritten as (27) with B left out. In other words, (27) is in the compact version of (26).

(27) 既然是军人，为什么却枪声一响就逃跑了呢？
Jìrán shì jūnrén, wèishénme què qiāngshēng yī . . . jiù . . . xiǎng jiù
now that COP soldier why however gunshot as soon as ring out
táopǎo-le ne?
run away-PEF MP
{(He) was a soldier, but why did (he) run away as soon as gunshots rang out?}

Occurrence of què in "jìrán p, jiù q" 103

Second, if *p* and *q* respectively stand for the anterior and posterior clauses in *jìrán*-sentences inferring the effect, there are two different relationships between *p* and *q*: i) *q* is the subsequent effect of *p*, and ii) *q* is the opposite of the subsequent effect of *p*, i.e.,

> *Jìrán p + nàme q*
> → [1] *Jìrán A + nàme B.*
> → [2] *Jìrán A + nàme fēi B.*

Compare the following two examples:

(28)　既然李秋打来电话，（那么）我们就不能置之不理！

Jìrán　Lǐ Qiū dǎ-lái diànhuà,　(nàme) wǒ-men jiù　bù　néng zhìzhībùlǐ!
now that LI Qiu make a phone call　then　we　then NEG can　ignore
{Since LI Qiu called, we can't ignore (him)!}

(29)　既然李秋打来电话，（那么）你为什么却置之不理呢？

Jìrán　Lǐ Qiū dǎ-lái diànhuà,　(nàme) nǐ　wèishénme què　zhìzhī-bùlǐ ne?
now that LI Qiu make a phone call　then　you why　however ignore　MP
{LI Qiu called, but why did you ignore (him)?}

Both (28) and (29) are in the form of "*jìrán p, nàme q*". However, (28) is an instance of "*jìrán A, nàme B*", which involves no contradiction, whereas (29) is an instance of "*jìrán A, nàme fēi B*", which entails an opposition.

It is just the opposition in the compact version of *jìrán*-sentences that lays the logical basis and provides the semantic condition for the occurrence of *què*. In other words, the structure "*jìrán . . . què . . .*" is only for sentences with such a logical basis and semantic condition.

5.3　"*wèishénme*" in "*jìrán p, jiù q*"

The compact version of *jìrán*-sentences is not a simple combination of A and "not B". In form, the posterior clause requires the occurrence of *wèishénme* ('why') to form a question and the occurrence of the modal particle *ne* at the end of the question. Compare the following:

(30)　a　既然他有能力，那么应该重用他，可是你却不重用他！

Jìrán　tā yǒu nénglì, nàme yīnggāi zhòngyòng　　　　　　　tā,
now that he have ability　then　should　put someone in an important position him
kěshì nǐ　què　bù　zhòngyòng　　　　　　　　　tā!
but　you however NEG　put someone in an important position　him
{Since he is capable, you should have put him in an important position, but you didn't!}

104 Occurrence of què in "jìrán p, jiù q"

→b 既然他有能力，那么你却不重用他！（-）

Jìrán tā yǒu nénglì, nàme nǐ què bù
now that he have ability then you however NEG

zhòngyòng tā!
put someone in an important position him

→c 既然他有能力，那么你为什么却不重用他呢？（+）

Jìrán tā yǒu nénglì, nàme nǐ wèishénme què bù
now that he have ability then you why however NEG

zhòngyòng tā ne?
put someone in an important position him MP

{He is capable, but why didn't you put him in any important position?}

Example (30b) indicates that a simple combination of A and "not B" results in ungrammatical sentences, while (30c) reveals that if "not B" is slightly modified with the occurrence of *wèishénme*, the combination of "A" and "not B" will produce a grammatically correct sentence. The following is an example:

(31) 既然这故事这样有魅力，那他应该多说、多多地说才是，可他偏偏只说两个。

Jìrán zhè gùshi zhèyàng yǒu mèilì, nà tā yīnggāi . . . cáishì . . . duō
now that this story so have attraction then he should more

shuō, duō-duō de shuō cáishì, kě tā piānpiān zhǐ shuō liǎng gè.
tell more-REDP SP tell but he deliberately only tell two CL

{Since the stories are so interesting, he should have told more, but he only told two.}

The aforementioned example consists of three semantic segments: A, B, and "not B". A simple removal of B would yield such an ungrammatical sentence as (32). What needs to be done is changing B into "not B" and placing *wèishénme* (*ne*) before "not B" to produce a well-formed sentence, as (33).

(32) 既然这故事这样有魅力，那么他却偏偏只说两个。（-）

Jìrán zhè gùshi zhèyàng yǒu mèilì, nàme tā què piānpiān zhǐ
now that this story so have attraction then he however deliberately only

shuō liǎng gè.
tell two CL

(33) 既然这故事这样有魅力，那么他为什么却偏偏只说两个呢？（+）

Jìrán zhè gùshi zhèyàng yǒu mèilì, nàme tā wèishénme què
now that this story so have attraction then he why however

piānpiān zhǐ shuō liǎng gè ne?
deliberately only say two CL MP

{The stories are so interesting, but why did he only tell two?}

Two points need further attention.

Occurrence of què in "jìrán p, jiù q" 105

First, *wèishénme* can occur at the beginning of the entire *jìrán*-sentence. In these cases, *jìrán* is implied, and *nàme* cannot occur. For example:

(34) a 既然这故事这样有魅力，那么他为什么却偏偏只说两个呢?

Jìrán   zhè gùshi zhèyàng yǒu mèilì,   nàme tā **wèishénme què**
now that this story so   have attraction then he why   however

piānpiān zhǐ shuō liǎng gè ne?
deliberately only tell two CL MP

{The stories are so interesting, but why did he only tell two?}

→b 为什么这故事这样有魅力，他却偏偏只说两个呢?

Wèishénme zhè gùshi zhèyàng yǒu mèilì,   tā **què**   piānpiān zhǐ
why   this story so   have attraction he however deliberately only

shuō liǎng gè ne?
tell two CL MP

{The stories are so interesting, but why did he only tell two?}

In actual language use, there are cases in which *wèishénme* occurs at the beginning of the sentences. The following are two examples:

(35) 为什么事实已大白于天下，事情却得不到妥善、有效和及时的处理呢?

Wèishénme shìshí yǐ   dàbái   yú tiānxià,   shìqing **què**
why   fact already be known to whole country/world matter   however

dé bù dào tuǒshàn, yǒuxiào hé jíshí de chǔlǐ ne?
cannot get proper effective and prompt SP handle MP

{The fact has come to light, but why can't this matter be properly, effectively, and timely handled?}

(36) 我为什么会嫁给你父亲? 为什么不情愿，却没有拒绝?

Wǒ wèishénme huì jià-gěi nǐ fùqin? **Wèishénme** bù qíngyuàn,
I why   will be married to your father why   NEG be willing

què méiyǒu jùjué?
however NEG refuse

{Why did I marry your father? I didn't want to (marry him), but why didn't I refuse (his proposal)?}

Apparently, (35) can be rewritten as (37), and (36) as (38).

(37) 既然事实已大白于天下，事情却为什么得不到妥善、有效和及时的处理呢?

Jìrán shìshí yǐ   dàbái   yú tiānxià,   shìqing **què**
now that fact already be known to whole country/world matter   however

wèishénme dé bù dào tuǒshàn, yǒuxiào hé jíshí de chǔlǐ ne?
why   cannot get proper effective and prompt SP handle MP

{The fact has come to light, but why can't this matter be properly, effectively, and timely handled?}

106   *Occurrence of què in "jìrán p, jiù q"*

(38)   既然不情愿，为什么却没有拒绝？

> *Jìrán   bù   qíngyuàn, **wèishénme** <u>què</u>   méiyǒu jùjué?*
> now that NEG   be willing   why   however NEG   refuse
> {I didn't want to (marry him), but why didn't I refuse (his proposal)?}

Second, in *"jìrán . . . wèishénme . . . ne"* sentences, *"wèishénme . . . ne"* either serves as an "not B" showing opposition or as "B" indicating a subsequent effect. In other words, *"wèishénme . . . ne"* is not always adversative; therefore, *què* cannot always be present. As a matter of fact, whether or not *què* can be used depends on the nature of the *wèishénme* question: whether it is a rhetorical question about a possibility or an interrogative questioning a fact.

In sentences in the form of *"jìrán A, nàme B, kěshì què fēi B"*, B denotes a subsequent effect that should have occurred but has not occurred yet, and "not B" refers to a reality that is opposite to B and that should not have been the case. If the *wèishénme* question is a rhetorical one, it is semantically a part of B; if the question is an interrogative questioning the reality, it is a part of "not B". Compare the following two examples:

(39)   既然你想考大学，明年为什么不试试呢？

> *Jìrán   nǐ   xiǎng kǎo   dàxué,   míngnián wèishénme*
> now that you want enter oneself for exams university next year why
> *bù   shìshì   ne?*
> NEG   have a try   MP
> {Since you want to take the college entrance examinations, why don't you want to have a try next year?}

(40)   既然你想考大学，为什么这么不用功呢？

> *Jìrán   nǐ   xiǎng kǎo   dàxué,   wèishénme zhème bù*
> now that you want enter oneself for exams university why   so   NEG
> *yònggōng   ne?*
> be studious MP
> {Since you want to take the college entrance examinations, why are you not studying hard?}

In (39), the second segment is a rhetorical question about the possibility of "having a try next year". The real meaning of the rhetorical question is "you should have a try next year", which is a subsequent effect of the first segment. As there is no opposition between the two segments, *què* cannot be used in the *wèishénme*-question, which explains why (41) is ill-formed. In (40), the second segment is an interrogative challenging the fact of "not studying hard", which is an opposition to the subsequent effect of the first segment. As there is a contradiction between the two segments, *què* can be used in the *wèishénme* question, as in (42).

Occurrence of què in "jìrán p, jiù q"   107

(41)   *既然你想考大学，明年为什么却不试试呢？

    Jìrán   nǐ   xiǎng kǎo   dàxué,   míngnián wèishénme

    now that you want enter oneself for an exam university next year why

    què   bù   shìshì   ne?

    however NEG   have a try MP

(42)   既然你想考大学，为什么却这么不用功呢？

    Jìrán   nǐ   xiǎng kǎo   dàxué,   wèishénme què

    now that you want enter oneself for an exam university why   however

    zhème bù   yònggōng   ne?

    so   NEG   be studious MP

    {You want to take the college entrance examinations, but why are you still so lazy?}

    Whether a "*wèishénme . . . ne*" question is a rhetorical question or not depends on the context. For example, "*Jìrán tā shēntǐ bù hǎo, wèishénme yòu dǎjiǎo tā ne?*" should be interpreted differently in (43a) and (43b).

(43)   a   别去找他！既然他身体不好，为什么又打搅他呢？

    Bié   qù zhǎo tā! Jìrán   tā shēntǐ bù   hǎo, wèishénme yòu   dǎjiǎo

    do not go call on him now that his health NEG good why   again disturb

    tā   ne?

    him MP

    {Don't call on him! He's in poor health; why are you going to disturb him again?}

    b   是你不对！既然他身体不好，为什么又打搅他呢？

    Shì nǐ   bùduì! Jìrán   tā shēntǐ bù   hǎo, wèishénme yòu   dǎjiǎo tā ne?

    COP you wrong now that his health NEG good why   again disturb him MP

    {It's your fault! He's in poor health; why did you disturb him again?}

    In (43a), "*wèishénme . . . ne*" is a rhetorical question about an irrealis result, for "disturbing" hasn't taken place yet. Using "his poor health" as the reason, the speaker of (43a) emphasizes that "he shouldn't be disturbed" with the rhetorical question. However, in (43b), "*wèishénme . . . ne*" is an interrogative about the real fact of "him being disturbed again", with which the speaker blames the listener for "having disturbed him again despite his poor health". As there is a contradiction between the segments in (43b), *què* can be used.

    In actual language use, there are many cases in which *wèishénme* acts as a rhetorical question. The following are two examples:

(44)   <u>既然</u>人类的智慧可以制造机器，制造政策，那么他们<u>为什么</u>不能造就更多回城的正大光明的理由呢？

    <u>*Jìrán*</u>   *rénlèi de zhìhuì kěyǐ zhìzào jīqì,   zhìzào zhèngcè, nàme tā-men*

    now that human SP wisdom can make machine make policy   then they

108 *Occurrence of què in "jìrán p, jiù q"*

    wèishénme bù   néng zàojiù gèng duō   huí   chéng de zhèngdà-guāngmíng
    why   NEG can   create more many return city SP open and aboveboard
    de lǐyóu ne?
    SP reason MP
    {Human wisdom can make machines and policies, why can't they create more honest and open reasons (for the educated youth) to return to cities?}

(45)   （我琢磨既然有第一条鱼来咬钩，就必定有第二条，）<u>既然</u>有第二条，我为什么不把这第二条钩上来呢？

    (Wǒ zuómo jìrán   yǒu   dìyī tiáo yú   lái   yǎo gōu, jiù   bìdìng
    I   think now that there be first CL   fish come bite hook then definitely
    *yǒu   dì'èr   tiáo,) <u>jìrán</u>   yǒu   dì'èr   tiáo, wǒ **wèishénme** bù   bǎ*
    there be second CL   now that there be second CL   I   why   NEG BA
    zhè dì'èr   tiáo gōu-shànglái   ne?
    this second CL catch something with a hook MP
    {[I think now that a fish has bitten the hook, there must be a second one,] and since there is a second one, why don't I aslo catch the second one?}

    In both examples, the posterior clause is a rhetorical question about a possibility. In other words, each question is Segment B, a subsequent effect of Segment A. In effect, the posterior clause in (44) means that "they can create more honest and open reasons (for the educated youth) to return to cities", and the posterior clause in (45) means that "I can also catch the second one". In conclusion, *què* cannot occur in rhetorical questions about a possibility.

    In actual language use, there are also many sentences in which the *wèishénme* question is an interrogative questioning something. The following are two examples:

(46)   你<u>既然</u>来这里寻我唱歌，我已唱了四首，你为什么连一首也不回？

    Nǐ <u>jìrán</u>   lái   zhèli xún   wǒ chàng gē, wǒ yǐ   chàng-le sì
    you now that come here look for me sing song I   already sing-PEF four
    *shǒu, nǐ **wèishénme** lián . . . yě . . . yī   shǒu yě bù   huí?*
    CL   you why   even . . .   one CL   NEG return
    {You've come here to sing with me, and I've sung four songs, but why haven't you returned even one?}

(47)   顾城<u>既然</u>很爱谢烨，为什么又要杀死她？

    *Gù Chéng <u>jìrán</u>   hěn ài   Xiè Yè, **wèishénme** yòu yào   shā-sǐ tā?*
    GU Cheng now that very love XIE Ye why   but want kill   her
    {GU Cheng loved XIE Ye very much, but why did he kill her?}

    In each of these two examples, which are in the form of an interrogative, the posterior clause questions the fact "not B", which is the opposite of the subsequent effect of Segment A. In both sentences, Segment B is implied, i.e., "you should return songs to me" in (46) and "he should protect her" in (47). Although *què* is present in neither of the two sentences, it can occur in both questions.

5.4 *què* in "*jìrán . . . wèishénme . . .*"

There are two possible positions for *què* in "*jìrán . . . wèishénme . . .*" sentences: before *wèishénme*, i.e., "*jìrán . . . què wèishénme . . .*" or after *wèishénme*, i.e., "*jìrán . . . wèishénme què . . .*". For instance, *què* occurs before *wèishénme* in (5) and (6), but it can be placed after *wèishénme* in each of them. The following are another two examples in which the positions of *què* and *wèishénme* are interchangeable:

(48) 既然一点也不好吃，为什么却不断地吃？

Jìrán	*yīdiǎn yě bù*	*hǎochī,*	**wèishénme**	**què**	*bùduàn*	*de*	*chī?*
now that	not at all	tasty	why	however	continue	SP	eat

{It doesn't taste good at all, but why do (you) keep eating it?}

(49) 既然一点也不好吃，却为什么不断地吃？

Jìrán	*yīdiǎn yě bù*	*hǎochī,*	**què**	**wèishénme**	*bùduàn*	*de*	*chī?*
now that	not at all	tasty	however	why	continue	SP	eat

{It doesn't taste good at all, but why do (you) keep eating it?}

In actual language use, a synonym of *wèishénme*—such as *wèihé*, *héyǐ* or *zěnme*—can occur in the place of *wèishénme*. Usually, *wèihé* and *héyǐ* are only found in contemporary novels imitating modern vernacular Chinese style because of their classical Chinese style. Even so, *què* can still occur before or after them, as in the following three examples:

(50) 你既（然）要报仇，这也是好汉的本分，却为何使这下贱诡计？

Nǐ	*jì(rán)*	*yào bàochóu,*	*zhè yě*	*shì*	*hǎohàn*	*de běnfèn,*	**què**
you	now that	will revenge	this also	COP	brave man	SP obligation	however

wèihé	*shǐ*	*zhè*	*xiàjiàn guǐjì?*
why	use	this low	trick

{You want to revenge, which is a brave man's obligation, but why did you use this cheap trick?}

(51) 你既（然）知我这脑神丹的灵效，却何以大胆吞服？

Nǐ	*jì(rán)*	*zhī*	*wǒ zhè nǎoshéndān*	*de língxiào,*	**què**	**héyǐ** *dàdǎn*
you	now that	know	my this brain magic pill	SP effect	however	why bold

tūnfú?
swallow

{You know the effect of my brain magic pills, but how come you had the guts to swallow them?}

(52) 你自己既（然）不愿意死，却怎么去杀人呢？

Nǐ	*zìyǐ*	*jì(rán)*	*bù*	*yuànyì*	*sǐ,*	**què**	**zěnme** *qù shā rén*	*ne?*
you	oneself	now that	NEG	be willing	die	however	why go kill person	MP

{You didn't want to be killed, but why did you kill?}

110   *Occurrence of què in "jìrán p, jiù q"*

In the three aforementioned examples, *què* occurs before *wèihé* in (50), before *héyǐ* in (51), and before *zěnme* in (52), but it can be placed after those synonyms of *wèishénme*. The following is an example with *què* placed after *héyǐ*:

(53) 既然师父没事，何以却有烦恼？

　　　*Jìrán   shīfu   méishì,   **héyǐ què**   yǒu   fánnǎo?*
　　　now that master   have nothing to do why   however   have   worry
　　　{Master has no work to do, but why is he upset?}

The word *què* in the the aforementioned example can be placed before *héyǐ*.

Obviously, the adversative adverb *què* is not rejected in *jìrán*-sentences if there is a contradiction between the clauses. As for other adversative connectives, according to the present author's investigation, only *kě* can occur in *jìrán*-sentences and has the same function as *què*. Other adversative connectives, such as *rán'ér*, *dànshì* or *kěshì*, are not permissible in *jìrán*-sentences. The following are three examples with *kě*:

(54) 既然寻你的姑娘这么多，可你为什么偏偏跟我过不去？

　　　*Jìrán   xún   nǐ de gūniang zhème duō, **kě** nǐ   wèishénme piānpiān*
　　　now that be after you SP girl   so   many but you why   deliberately
　　　gēn   wǒ   guò bù qù?
　　　with   me   cannot get along
　　　{There are so many girls chasing you, but why do you keep bothering me?}

(55) 既然都知道汉奸不光彩，像臭狗屎，可为什么还有那么多人就当这臭狗屎呢？

　　　*Jìrán   dōu zhīdào hànjiān bù   guāngcǎi, xiàng chòu   gǒushǐ, **kě***
　　　now that all   know   traitor NEG honorable be like stinky dog shit but
　　　wèishénme hái yǒu   nàme duō   rén   jiù dāng zhè chòu gǒushǐ ne?
　　　why   still there be so   many person just be   this stinky dog shit MP
　　　{Everyone knows that traitors are despicable like stinky dog shit, but why are there so many people who are just stinky dog shit?}

(56) 既然李剑辉不构成犯罪，可怎么立案抓人了？

　　　*Jìrán   Lǐ Jiànhuī bù   gòuchéng fànzuì, **kě** zěnme lì'àn   zhuā rén   le?*
　　　now that LI Jianhui NEG constitute crime   but why   file a suit arrest person PEF
　　　{LI Jianhui's action did not constitute a crime, but why did (they) file a suit and arrest him?}

In (54) and (55), *kě* is placed before *wèishénme*, and in (56), *kě* is placed before *zěnme*. As can be seen, *kě* only occurs at the beginning of the posterior clause. If the subject is present in the posterior clause, it follows *kě* and precedes *wèishénme* or its synonym.

5.5 Pragmatic significance of "*jìrán p, què wèishénme q*"

Based on the previous discussions, the pragmatic significance of "*jìrán p, què wèishénme q*" can be concluded as follows:

First, *wèishénme* and the like are used to ask a question about the real fact and to prepare for the entry of *què*. As *què* highlights the opposition between the facts, the strangeness or abnormality of the consequence is emphasized. Compare:

(57) a 既然吃饭都成问题，还买衣服？
  Jìrán   chīfàn   dōu   chéng   wèntí,   hái   mǎi   yīfu?
  now that eat   even   become problem still buy   clothes
  {Now that even food has become a problem (for us), (are we) still buying clothes?}

  b 既然吃饭都成问题，为什么还买衣服？
  Jìrán   chīfàn   dōu   chéng   wèntí,   wèishénme   hái   mǎi   yīfu?
  now that eat   even   become problem why   still buy   clothes
  {Now that even food has become a problem (for us), why (are we) still buying clothes?}

  c 既然吃饭都成问题，却为什么还买衣服？
  Jìrán   chīfàn dōu chéng   wèntí,   què   wèishénme hái mǎi yīfu?
  now that eat   even become problem however why   still buy clothes
  {Even food has become a problem (for us), but why (are we) still buying clothes?}

Example (57c) indicates that the word *què* can be used on occasions where the questioning about an abnormal fact needs to be highlighted, as *què* can enhance the adversative momentum. The following is an example:

(58) 但是，我既然做了错事，为什么还要错上加错，去欺骗组织，欺骗人们呢？
  Dànshì, wǒ jìrán   zuò-le   cuòshì, wèishénme háiyào cuòshàngjiācuò,
  but   I   now that make-PEF mistake why   still   compound the mistake
  qù   qīpiàn zǔzhī,   qīpiàn   rén-men ne?
  go   deceive organization deceive people   MP
  {I have already made a mistake, but why did I compound it by deceiving the organization and people?}

In (58), "compounding the mistake" is a fact, and the speaker is doing soul-searching and self-recrimination. The word *què* can be used and placed before or after *wèishénme* if the speaker deems it necessary to do so.

Second, in some cases, out of the need to highlight a tone (for instance, reproachful) or a feeling (for instance, surprised), the speaker chooses to use "*què wèishénme*" or the like, as these expressions stress the strangeness or unreasonableness of the consequence. The following are two examples:

112 *Occurrence of què in "jìrán p, jiù q"*

(59) 既然人家没惹你，你为什么却总是惹人家？（reproachful）

Jìrán   rénjiā   méi   rě   nǐ, nǐ wèishénme què   zǒngshì rě
now that other people NEG annoy you you why   however always annoy
rénjiā?
other people
{No one annoys you, but why do you always annoy them?}

(60) 既然不是海南人，你为什么却会讲海南话？(surprised）

Jìrán   bù   shì   Hǎinán rén,   nǐ wèishénme què   huì jiǎng
now that NEG COP person from Hainan you why   however can speak
Hǎinán huà?
Hainan dialect
{You are not from Hainan, but how come you speak Hainan dialect?}

There are different reasons for reproach, as can be illustrated by the following two examples:

(61) 既然说谎不对，为什么却老是说谎？（contemptuous）

Jìrán   shuōhuǎng bù   duì, wèishénme què   lǎoshì shuōhuǎng?
now that tell lies   NEG right why   however always tell lies
{It's wrong to tell lies, but why (are you) telling lies all the time?}

(62) 既然还在咳嗽，为什么却又来加班？（caring）

Jìrán   hái zài   késou, wèishénme què   yòu lái   jiābān?
now that still in progress cough why   however again come work overtime
{You're still coughing, but why did you come to work overtime again?}

The tone of reproach varies in degree, as in the following two examples:

(63) 既然没有道理，却为什么还耍无赖？（more serious）

Jìrán   méiyǒu dàolǐ,   què   wèishénme hái shuǎwúlài?
now that not have justification however why   still act shamelessly
{(You are) not in the right, but why (are you) still being unreasonable?}

(64) 既然写不出来，却为什么还要硬写？（less serious）

Jìrán   xiě bù chūlái, què   wèishénme háiyào yìng   xiě?
now that cannot write however why   still   persistently write
{(You) can't write that out, but why (do you) persist?}

Whether it is a reproachful or surprised tone, what the reason for the reproach is, and whether the reproachful tone is serious all depend on the content and context of the sentence.

Third, apart from highlighting the abnormality or unreasonableness of the consequence, "*què wèishénme*" or its synonyms can potentially challenge the authenticity of *p* as the basis for the inference. For this reason, "*què wèishénme*" can place the listener in a dilemma: either the consequence is bizarre, or the so-called cause is suspectable. The following is an example:

(65) 既然读过大学，为什么却认不得几个字？

Jìrán   dú-guò   dàxué,   wèishénme què   rèn bù dé   jǐ
now that go to-EXP university why   however cannot recognize several

gè   zì?
CL   character
{(You) went to college, but how come the characters that (you) know are so few?}

If the listener indeed went to college, it is shameful that he is virtually illiterate. If the listener did not receive higher education, then "went to college" is a blatant lie. The following is another example:

(66) 既然那么穷，为什么却天天有肉吃？

Jìrán   nàme   qióng, wèishénme què   tiāntiān yǒu ròu chī?
now that so   poor   why   however every day have meat eat
{(You are) so poor, but how can (you) afford to have meat every day?}

If the listener is truthfully poor, then it is likely that the meat he eats every day was stolen or obtained by other dishonest means. If he is not a poor person, he is a dishonest one.

Summary

First, the existence of "*jìrán . . . què . . .*" sentences is a phenomenon in which connectives denoting different relationships cooccur in the same complex sentence. This phenomenon reveals that the form of one sentence can be a mixture of different complex sentence forms and hence the meaning of one sentence can be a combination of various semantic meanings.

Second, the "*jìrán . . . què . . .*" sentence is a compact version of "*jìrán A, nàme B, kěshì què fēi B*". In "*jìrán . . . què . . .*" sentences, the contradiction is between A, the cause stated in the anterior clause, and "not B", the effect stated in the posterior clause. This opposition is semantically the essential condition for the occurrence of *què* in *jìrán*-sentences.

Third, the posterior clause in "*jìrán . . . què . . .*" sentences includes "*wèishénme . . . (ne)*", and *què* can precede or follow *wèishénme*. Synonyms of *wèishénme*, such as *wèihé*, *héyǐ*, and *zěnme*, can occur in place of *wèishénme* to question the consequence as it contradicts the cause. However, *wèishénme* or its synonym only provides the necessary condition rather than the sufficient condition for the occurrence of *què* in *jìrán*-sentences. If *wèishénme* or its synonym introduces a rhetorical question, *què* cannot be used, and hence the sentence is a general *jìrán*-sentence.

Fourth, "*jìrán . . . què . . .*" sentences have unique pragmatic significance. To be brief, they are used to stress that the consequence is bizarre or unreasonable, and can challenge or disprove the basis for the inference.

114 *Occurrence of què in "jìrán p, jiù q"*

NB Some examples in this chapter are cited from literary works, political essays, articles, and so on. The sources are listed as follows:

1 *Changpian Xiaoshuo Xuankan* (《长篇小说专辑》) 1988(1), including (46);
2 *Dangdai* (《当代》) 1983(4), including (11); 1992(5), including (44); 1993(6), including (35);
3 *Fiction Monthly* (《小说月报》) 1999(9), including (36);
4 *Flower City* (《花城》) 1984(3), including (18); 19834(4), including (17);
5 *Harvest* (《收获》) 1987(6), including (31); 1994(3), including (5);
6 *Lotus* (《芙蓉》) 1983(6), including (9) and (10);
7 *October* (《十月》) 1983(1), including (54); 1983(4), including (12); 1989(6), including (21), (25), and (28);
8 *Selected Works of CHI Li* (《池莉精品文集》), including (56);
9 *State of Divinity* (《笑傲江湖》) by JIN Yong (金庸), including (51);
10 *The Semi-Gods and Semi-Devils* (《天龙八部》) by JIN Yong (金庸), including (52);
11 *Wolongji* (《卧龙记》) by an unknown author, including (48) and (53);
12 *Woodpecker* (《啄木鸟》) 1994(2), including (47);
13 *Zhongpian Xiaoshuo Xuankan* (《中篇小说选刊》) 1988 (1), including (6);1990(2), including (45); 1991(1), including (58); 1994(6), including (55); 1995(6), including (20).

6 Occurrence of *què* in "*rúguǒ shuō p, nàme q*"

"*rúguǒ shuō p, nàme q*" is a form of hypothetical complex sentences, in which *nàme* is optional.

This chapter discusses sentences in the form of "*rúguǒ shuō p, nàme q*" with the presence of the adversative *què*. The discussion also includes the occurrence of the adversative *kě* ('but') in this sentence form.

6.1 "*rúguǒ shuō p, nàme què q*"

According to most grammar textbooks, no adversatives can occur in hypothetical complex sentences introduced by *rúguǒ*; in other words, all of these sentences with an adversative included are ill-formed ones. In general, this is true. However, the adversative *què* can, in some cases, occur in hypothetical sentences in the form of "*rúguǒ shuō p, nàme q*", i.e., "*rúguǒ shuō p, nàme què q*".

The following are three examples in the form of "*rúguǒ shuō p, nàme què q*":

(1) <u>如果说</u>，职位尚可补偿的话，<u>那么</u>青春却是逝水难复了。

<u>Rúguǒ</u> <u>shuō</u>, zhíwèi shàng kě bǔcháng dehuà, <u>nàme</u> qīngchūn **què**
if say position still can compensate MP then youth however
shì shìshuǐ-nánfù le.
COP spilled water cannot be gathered up MP
{If a position is compensable, by contrast, youth is hard to recapture.}

(2) <u>如果说</u>，大秀的心绪是可以谅解的，<u>那么</u>，……"我"和大秀停留于同一思想水平上，却是我们所不能满意的。

<u>Rúguǒ</u> <u>shuō</u> Dàxiù de xīnxù shì kěyǐ liàngjiě de, <u>nàme</u>, ..."wǒ" hé
if say Daxiu SP mood COP can understand SP then I and
Dàxiù yú tóngyī sīxiǎng shuǐpíng-shàng, **què** *shì wǒ-men suǒ*
Daxiu at same ideology on level however COP we PAP
bù néng mǎnyì de.
NEG can be satisfied MP
{If Daxiu's mood is understandable, by contrast, we can't be satisfied with "me" and Dashu staying at the same ideological level.}

DOI: 10.4324/9781003374237-6

116 *Occurrence of què in "rúguǒ shuō p, nàme q"*

(3) 如果说，一向讲究"哥儿们义气"的庞喜在那次审判事件中并没有表现出
"为朋友两肋插刀"的勇气的话，那么，在他当了"官"之后，却表现出了一
种"苟富贵，毋相忘"的大度。

Rúguǒ	*shuō,*	*yīxiàng*	*jiǎngjiū*	*"gēr-men*	*yìqì"*		*de*	*Páng Xǐ*
if	say	consistently	stress	brothers	personal loyalty		SP	PANG Xi

zài	*nà*	*cì*	*shěnpàn*	*shìjiàn-zhōng*	*bìng*		*méiyǒu*	*biǎoxiàn-chū*
at	that	CL	bring to trial	in event	indeed		NEG	display

"wèi	*péngyǒu*	*liǎnglèi-chādāo"*		*de*	*yǒngqì*	*dehuà,*	*nàme,*	*zài*
for	friend	help at the loss of one's life		SP	courage	MP	then	at

tā	*dāng-le*	*"guān"*	*zhīhòu,*	***què***	*biǎoxiàn-chū*	*le*	*yī*	*zhǒng*
he	become-PEF	official	after	however	display	PEF	one	kind

"gǒu	*fùguì,*	*wú*	*xiāng*	*wàng"*	*de*	*dàdù.*
if	rich	do not	mutually	forget	SP	magnanimous

{If PANG Xi, who had always stressed the importance of brotherhood, did not
display the courage to "risk his life to help friends" in that trial, by contrast, he
demonstrated the magnanimity of "not forgetting friends if I become wealthy or
powerful" after he became an "official".}

The following are two examples in the form of "*rúguǒ shuō p, nà què q*", in
which *nà* is synonymous with *nàme*:

(4) 如果说，袁野的冤案是有形的，那她的却是无形的；……

Rúguǒ	*shuō,*	*Yuán Yě*	*de*	*yuān'àn*	*shì*	*yǒuxíng*	*de,*	*nà*
if	say	YUAN Ye	SP	unjust case	COP	tangible	SP	then

tā	*de*	***què***	*shì*	*wúxíng*	*de; . . .*
she	SP	however	COP	intangible	SP

{If YUAN Ye's unjust case is tangible, by contrast, hers is intangible; . . .}

(5) 如果说月牙营镇秋天的繁盛占了一季山葡萄市的地利，那夏嫂的豆腐坊的真
正兴隆却不是借山葡萄的光，它真正兴隆的原因是占了天时，占了一个漫长
的寒冷而又缺乏蔬菜的天时。

Rúguǒ	*shuō*	*Yuèyáyíngzhèn*	*qiūtiān*	*de*	*fánshèng*	*zhàn-le*	*yī*	*jì*
if	say	Yueyaying town	autumn	SP	prosperous	have-PEF	one	season

shānpútao	*shì*	*de*	*dìlì,*		*nà*	*Xiàsǎo*	*de*	*dòufu*
wild grapes	market	SP	favorable geographical position		then	Xiasao	SP	tofu

fáng	*de*	*zhēnzhèng*	*xīnglóng*	***què***	*bù*	*shì*	*jièguāng*	*shānpútao*
shop	SP	real	prosperous	however	NEG	COP	benefit from	wild grapes

de	*guāng,*	*tā*	*zhēnzhèng*	*xīnglóng*	*de*	*yuányīn*	*shì*	*zhàn-le*
SP		it	real	prosperous	SP	reason	COP	have-PEF

tiānshí,		*zhàn-le*	*yī*	*gè*	*màncháng*	*de*	*hánlěng*	*ér*	*yòu*
favorable climate		have-PEF	one	CL	long	SP	cold	and	also

quēfá	*shūcài*	*de*	*tiānshí.*
lack	vegetable	SP	favorable climate

{If the prosperity of Yueyaying Town in autumn is a result of its favorable geographical
position—the wild grapes market, by contrast, the prosperity of Xiasao's tofu shop does

Occurrence of *què* in *"rúguǒ shuō p, nàme q"*   117

not actually benefit from the wild grapes. The real reason for its prosperity is that it enjoys a favorable climatic condition—a long cold winter when vegetables are scarce.}

The following are two examples in the form of *"rúguǒ shuō p, què q"*, in which *nàme* is absent but can be present:

(6) <u>如果说</u>，全村人对王刚的胡来还仅仅是指责，现在对于李崮却是深恶痛绝了！

Rúguǒ shuō, quán cūn rén duì Wáng Gāng de húlái hái jǐnjǐn
if say whole village person for WANG Gang SP mess things up still only
shì zhǐzé, xiànzài duìyú Lǐ Gù *què* shì shēnwù-tòngjué le!
COP criticize now to LI Gu however COP feel an utmost repugnance MP
{If the whole village was only criticizing WANG Gang for messing things up, by contrast, the villagers feel an utmost repugnance to LI Gu now!}

(7) <u>如果说</u>香妹对银庄的指使和专断一直使我不悦的话，她这次的言行举止却令我大为满意了。

Rúguǒ shuō Xiāngmèi duì Yínzhuāng de zhǐshǐ hé zhuānduàn yīzhí
if say Xiangmei to Yinzhuang SP instigate and act arbitrarily always
shǐ wǒ bù yuè dehuà, tā zhè cì de yánxíng jǔzhǐ
make me NEG happy MP she this time SP words and deeds behavior
què lìng wǒ dàwéi mǎnyì le.
however make me very satisfied MP
{If Xiangmei's arbitrary action towards Yinzhuang has always displeased me, by contrast, her behavior this time greatly pleased me.}

6.2   Logical basis for the occurrence of *què*

In sentences in the form *"rúguǒ shuō p, nàme q"*, the anterior clause is hypothetical, and the posterior clause is a conclusion based on the hypothesis of a statement. The two clauses can be compared to or annotated by each other. This sentence form can deepen readers' impression of the matters stated in the sentence.

However, this does not mean that the adversative *què* can occur in all sentences in this form. The sentences in this form fall into two types according to the relationship between *p* and *q*, i.e., comparison and annotation. The following are two groups of examples:

Group A

(8) <u>如果说</u>在内战时期左倾机会主义路线统治苏区和红军党的时间并不算很长，在遵义会议以后已经基本上纠正过来了的话，<u>那末</u>，左倾机会主义路线统治白区党组织的时间是很长的。

Rúguǒ shuō zài nèizhàn shíqī zuǒqīng jīhuì zhǔyì lùxiàn tǒngzhì
if say at civil war time leftward opportunism basic principles rule
Sūqū hé Hóngjūn dǎng de shíjiān
Chinese Soviet area (Red Army's bases) and Red Army party SP time

118 *Occurrence of* què *in "*rúguǒ shuō p, nàme q*"*

bìng	bù	suàn	hěn	cháng,	zài	Zūnyì Huìyì		yǐhòu	yǐjīng
indeed	NEG	count	very	long	at	Zunyi Meeting		after	already

jīběn-shàng	jiūzhèng-guòlái	le	dehua	nàme,	zuǒqīng	jīhuì zhǔyì
generally	correct-PEF	PEF	MP	then	leftward	opportunism

lùxiàn		tǒngzhì	Báiqū		dǎng
basic principles		rule	White area (Kuomintang's bases)		party

zǔzhī	de	shíjiān	shì	hěn	cháng	de
organization	SP	time	COP	very	long	SP

{If leftward opportunism did not rule the Soviet area and the (Communist) Party in the Red Army for a long time during the civil war, and it was largely corrected after the Zunyi Meeting, by contrast, leftward opportunism ruled the party organizations in the White area for a very long time.}

(9) 如果说她是反毛泽东思想，你也同样是。

<u>*Rúguǒ*</u>	<u>*shuō*</u>	*tā*	*shì*	*fǎn*	*Máo Zédōng sīxiǎng,*	*nǐ*	*yě*	*tóngyàng*	*shì.*
if	say	she	COP	oppose	Mao Zedong Thought	you	also	same	COP

{If she is against Maoism, so are you.}

Group B

(10) 如果说做学问有什么诀窍，<u>那么</u>最大的诀窍就是勤奋。

<u>*Rúguǒ*</u>	<u>*shuō*</u>	*zuò xuéwèn*	*yǒu*	*shénme juéqiào,*	<u>*nàme*</u>	*zuì*	*dà*	*de*
if	say	do scholarly work	there be	any	secret	then	most	big	SP

juéqiào	*jiù*	*shì*	*qínfèn.*
secret	just	COP	diligent

{If there is any secret to doing scholarly work, then the greatest secret is diligence.}

(11) 对于我，<u>如果说</u>也有幸福的时代，那就是在农村度过的童年岁月。

Duìyú	*wǒ,*	<u>*rúguǒ*</u>	<u>*shuō*</u>	*yě*	*yǒu*	*xìngfú de*	*shídài,*	*nà*	*jiù*	*shì*
for	me	if	say	also	there be	happy SP	era	that	just	COP

zài	*nóngcūn*	*dùguò*	*de*	*tóngnián*	*suìyuè.*
in	countryside	spend	SP	childhood	years

{If I also have had a happy time, it was precisely my childhood spent in the countryside.}

In Group A, the two sentences are comparative. In each sentence, the two clauses are used to compare and verify the statements and situations. In Group B, the two sentences are annotative. In each sentence, the anterior clause presents a statement or a situation, and the posterior clause annotates the statement or the situation.

If a sentence is annotative, *què* cannot be present in it, for there is no opposition between *p* and *q*. The two sentences (10) and (11), for example, reject the presence of *què*.

In sentences that are comparative, there are two different types of comparisons: contrast, as in (8), and analogy, as in (9). The adversative *què* can occur in sentences where a contrast is drawn. For example, (8) can be rewritten as (12):

Occurrence of què in "rúguǒ shuō p, nàme q" 119

(12) ……那末，左倾机会主义路线统治白区党组织的时间却是很长的。

| …nàme, | zuǒqīng | jīhuì zhǔyì | lùxiàn | | tǒngzhì |
| then | leftward | opportunism | basic principles | | rule |

| Báiqū | | | dǎng | zǔzhī | de | shíjiān |
| White area (Kuomintang's bases) | | | party | organization | SP | time |

| què | shì | hěn | cháng | de. |
| however | COP | very | long | SP |

{. . . by contrast, leftward opportunism ruled the party organizations in the White area for a very long time.}

However, *què* cannot occur in sentences where an analogy is drawn. For example, (9) cannot be rewritten as (13):

(13) *如果说她是反毛泽东思想，你却同样是。

| Rúguǒ | shuō | tā | shì | fǎn | Máo Zédōng sīxiǎng, | nǐ | què | tóngyàng | shì. |
| if | say | she | COP | oppose | Mao Zedong Thought | you | however | same | COP |

Compare the following two examples:

(14) 如果说他是一条龙，那么，你只是一条虫。

| Rúguǒ | shuō | tā | shì | yī | tiáo | lóng, | nàme, | nǐ | zhǐ | shì | yī | tiáo | chóng. |
| if | say | he | COP | one | CL | dragon | then | you | only | COP | one | CL | worm |

{If he is a dragon, then, you are just a worm.}

(15) 如果说他是一条龙，那么，你自然也是一条龙。

| Rúguǒ | shuō | tā | shì | yī | tiáo | lóng, | nàme, | nǐ | zìrán | yě |
| if | say | he | COP | one | CL | dragon | then | you | natural | also |

| shì | yī | tiáo | lóng. |
| COP | one | CL | dragon |

{If he is a dragon, then, certainly you are also a dragon.}

In (14), a contrast is drawn, thus it can be rephrased with *què* included, whereas in (15) an analogy is made; therefore *què* cannot be used.

6.3 Further explanation of the logical basis

Some contradictions expressed by sentences in the form of "*rúguǒ shuō p, nàme q*" show the difference between the two poles of a matter, and other contradictions demonstrate hirarchycal difference. Both types of contradictions indicate opposition, and therefore form a logical ground for adversativity. The adversative *què* can be used whenever the adversative relationship needs to be highlighted. For example, in (1), *què* is used to highlight the bipolarity of "being compensable" and "being hard to recapture". Another example is (6), in which *què* is employed to stress the hierarchical difference between "criticism" and "utmost repugnance". The following are two more examples:

120 *Occurrence of què in "rúguǒ shuō p, nàme q"*

(16) 如果说，樊福林身上集中了小镇的一面，<u>那么</u>，他身上却恰恰集中了小镇的
另一面，⋯⋯

Rúguǒ shuō. Fán Fúlín shēn-shàng jízhōng-le xiǎo zhèn de yī miàn, <u>nàme,</u>
if say FAN Fulin on body embody-PEF small town SP one side then

tā shēn-shàng **què** *qiàqià jízhōng-le xiǎo zhèn de lìng yī miàn, . . .*
he body however exactly embody-PEF small town SP another one side

{If FAN Fulin embodies one side of the town, by contrast, he embodies exactly
the other side of the town . . .}

(17) <u>如果说</u>入学之初，她与都市同学的相形之下的寒伧，使她为自己的家乡而不
平，<u>那么</u>，今天，她的寒伧却使她为自己的民族而哀痛了。

Rúguǒ <u>*shuō*</u> *rùxué zhī chū, tā yǔ dūshì tóngxué de*
if say start SP beginning she with city classmate SP
school

xiāngxíng zhī xià de hánchen, shǐ tā wèi zìjǐ de jiāxiāng ér
be compared with each other SP shabby make she for oneself SP hometown then

bùpíng, <u>*nàme,*</u> *jīntiān, tā de hánchen* **què** *shǐ tā wèi zìjǐ de*
be indignant then today she SP shabby however make she for oneself SP

mínzú ér āitòng le.
nation then sad MP

{If at the beginning of her schooling, her shabbiness in contrast with her urban
classmates made her feel indignant because of her hometown, today her shabbiness
makes her feel sad for her nation.}

The adversative *què* is used in (16) to emphasize the two opposing matters:
"one side of the town" and "the other side of the town". In (17), *què* is also
used to highlight the difference between "feeling indignant" and "feeling sad"
in degree.

In some cases, the opposition is not directly worded, as in the following
example:

(18) <u>如果说</u>，在这批镀金的学生中，于少雄谁也不放在眼里的话，<u>那么</u>杨子
丰<u>却</u>是一个例外。

Rúguǒ <u>*shuō*</u>*. zài zhè pī dùjīn*
if say at this group be gilded (go somewhere to further education for fame)

de xuéshēng-zhōng, Yú Shàoxióng shuí yě bù fàng zài yǎn-lǐ dehuà,
SP among students YU Shaoxiong no one pay attention to MP

<u>*nàme*</u> *Yáng Zǐfēng* **què** *shì yī gè lìwài.*
then YANG Zifeng however COP one CL exception

{If YU Shaoxiong doesn't pay attention to anyone among these "gilded" students,
by contrast, YANG Zifeng is an exception.}

In (18), "is an exception" is used instead of the same wording of the anterior
clause to avoid simple repetition.

Occurrence of *què* in *"rúguǒ shuō p, nàme q"* 121

6.4 *shuō* in *"rúguǒ shuō p, nàme què q"*

In some sentences in the form of *"rúguǒ p, nàme q"*, the word *shuō* is implied. For example:

(19) 对于一个知识分子来说，<u>如果</u>字如其人，<u>那么</u>，书房也如其人。

Duìyú . . . lái shuō yī gè zhīshi fènzǐ lái shuō, <u>rúguǒ</u> zì rú qí
for one CL intellectual say if character be like its

rén, <u>nàme,</u> shūfáng yě rú qí rén.
character then study also be like its person

{For an intellectual, if their handwriting reflects their personality, so does their study.}

This sentence can be rewritten as *". . . rúguǒ shuō zì rú qí rén . . ."*. In this sentence, *què* cannot occur because there is no contradiction.

Similarly, in some sentences in the form of *"rúguǒ p, nàme què q"*, the word *shuō* is implied. For example:

(20) <u>假如</u>这张脸上曾有过一些美的东西的话，今天却已经荡然无存了。

<u>Jiǎrú</u> zhè zhāng liǎn-shàng céng yǒu-guò yīxiē měi de dōngxi
if this CL on face once there be-EXP some beautiful SP stuff

*dehuà, jīntiān **què** dàngrán-wúcún le.*
MP today however everything is gone PEF

{If there used to be something beautiful on this face, by contrast, it's all gone now.}

In this sentence, *jiǎrú* is synonymous with *rúguǒ*. The sentence can be rewritten as *"Jiǎrú shuō . . ."* or *"Rúguǒ shuō . . ."*. Due to the opposition between *p* and *q*, *què* is used to emphasize the contradiction.

6.5 Adversative *kě*

The most frequently used adversative in sentences in the form of *"rúguǒ shuō p, nàme q"* is *què*, but *kě* can also be used in some cases. The following are three examples:

(21) <u>如果说</u>我们过去有点糊涂，可现在已经阵线分明，我们还能糊涂下去吗？

*<u>Rúguǒ shuō</u> wǒ-men guòqù yǒu diǎn hútu, **kě** xiànzài yǐjīng*
if say we the past there be a little confused but now already

zhènxiàn fēnmíng, wǒ-men hái néng hútu-xiàqù ma?
front clear we still can continue to be confused MP

{If we were a little confused in the past, can we still be confused now that the front is clear?}

122 *Occurrence of què in "rúguǒ shuō p, nàme q"*

(22) 如果说是工作作风问题，可我又觉得不尽然。

Rúguǒ *shuō* *shì* *gōngzuò* *zuòfēng* *wèntí*, **kě**... *yòu*... *wǒ* *yòu* *juéde*
if   say   COP   work   style   matter   but   I   feel

bù *jìnrán*.
NEG exactly so

{If it is termed as a matter of style of work, I don't think it's exactly so.}

(23) 如果说当初我在彩画车间时，与罗家驹有一点潜在的紧张，可我去了罗长贵那组，我俩的关系没有丝毫冲突。

Rúguǒ *shuō* *dāngchū* *wǒ* *zài*... *shí* *cǎihuà* *chējiān* *shí*, *yǔ*
if   say   the past   I   when   color painting   workshop   with

Luó Jiājū *yǒu* *yīdiǎn* *qiánzài* *de* *jǐnzhāng*, **kě** *wǒ* *qù-le*
LUO Jiaju   there be a little   potential   SP   tense   but   I   go-PEF

Luó Chángguì *nà* *zǔ*, *wǒ liǎ de guānxi* *méiyǒu* *sīháo* *chōngtū*.
LUO Changgui   that group we two SP relationship there not be slightest conflict

{If there was some potential tension between LUO Jiaju and me when I was (working) in the color painting workshop, by contrast, there hasn't been the slightest conflict between the two of us since I joined LUO Changgui's group.}

As a conjunction, *kě* is always placed at the beginning of the posterior clause. If *kě* is present, *nàme* cannot occur.

Summary

"*rúguǒ p, nàme (jiù) q*" is a general hypothetical complex sentence form in which a result or conclusion is inferred from a hypothesis. In sentences in this form, the posterior clause presents a subsequent effect of the hypothesis stated in the anterior clauses, thus *què* cannot occur in these sentences.

"*rúguǒ shuō p, nàme q*" is a special hypothetical complex sentence form. The adversative *què* can be present in sentences in this form if there is a contradiction between the clauses.

In addition, there is another special form of hypothetical complex sentences in which *què* can occur, but the number of the sentences in that form is very small. More details about that form can be found in Section 12.4.2, Chapter 12, Volume III.

NB Some examples in this chapter are cited from literary works, political essays, articles, and so on. The sources are listed as follows:

1   *Baihuazhou* (《百花洲》) 1983(2), including Examples (4) and (5);
2   *Changjiang Literature* (《长江》) 1983(2), including (21);
3   *Dangdai* (《当代》) 1983(4), including (7); 1985(3), including (17);
4   *Fiction Monthly* (《小说月报》) 1985(6), including (23);
5   *Flower City* (《花城》) 1982(3), including (11); 1983(2), including (2), (16) and (20); 1985(3), including (1);

6   *Harvest* (《收获》) 1982(1), including (19); 1983(2), including (3); 1985(3), including (18);
7   *Lotus* (《芙蓉》) 1982(3), including (9);
8   *October* (《十月》) 1985(1), including (6);
9   *Selected Works of LIU Shaoqi* (《刘少奇选集》), including (8).

7 Occurrence of *què* in "*yuè p, yuè q*"

The topics of this chapter include the relationship between *p* and *q* in "*yuè p, yuè q*", the words or phrases after the first *yuè* and the second *yuè*, and the occurrence of adversatives in "*yuè p, yuè q*".

Most examples in the form of "*yuè p, yuè q*" quoted in this chapter include a comma between the clauses, but some compressed sentences are also quoted for illustrative purposes.

7.1 "*yuè p*" and "*yuè q*"

"*yuè p, yuè q*" is a form of correlative conditional complex sentences, in which the correlative conjunction "*yuè* . . . *yuè* . . ." acts as the formal marker, with the anterior clause presenting the condition or ground, and the posterior clause indicating the result.[1]

7.1.1 "*yuè p*" as a sufficient condition

In most sentences in the form of "*yuè p, yuè q*", "*yuè p*" presents a sufficient condition for "*yuè q*". The form "*yuè p, (jiù) yuè q*" is generally equivalent to the form "*zhǐyào yuè p, jiù yuè q*".[2] Logically, "*yuè p, yuè q*" is a hypothetical judgment based on a sufficient condition. The following are some examples:

(1) 时间越长，成功的可能性越大。
Shíjiān yuè . . . yuè . . .   cháng, chénggōng de kěnéngxìng yuè dà.
time   the more . . . the more . . . long   succeed   SP possibility   great
{The longer the time, the more likely it is to succeed.}

Example (1) is equivalent to (2):

(2) 只要时间越长，成功的可能性就越大。
Zhǐyào . . . jiù . . . shíjiān yuè . . . yuè . . .   cháng, chénggōng de
as long as . . .   time   the more . . . the more . . . long   succeed   SP
kěnéngxìng jiù yuè dà.
possibility   great
{So long as the time is longer, it is more likely to succeed.}

DOI: 10.4324/9781003374237-7

Occurrence of què in "yuè p, yuè q" 125

(3)　时间越短，成功的可能性越小。

Shíjiān yuè ... yuè ... duǎn, chénggōng de kěnéngxìng yuè xiǎo.
time　　the more ... the more ...　short　succeed　SP possibility　　small
{The shorter the time, the less likely it is to succeed.}

Example (3) is equivalent to (4):

(4)　只要时间越短，成功的可能性就越小。

Zhǐyào ... jiù ... shíjiān yuè ... yuè ... duǎn, chénggōng de
as long as ...　　time　the more ... the more ...　short　succeed　SP
kěnéngxìng jiù yuè xiǎo.
possibility　　　　small
{So long as the time is shorter, it is less likely to succeed.}

The form "*yuè p, cái yuè q*" is a hypothetical judgment in which the condition is both necessary and sufficient. In other words, this form is equivalent to "*zhǐyào yuè p, jiù yuè q; (érqiě) zhǐyǒu yuè p, cái yuè q*" ('so long as more *p*, more *q*, (and) only if more *p*, more *q*').[3] The following are two examples:

(5)　……心想，走廊里的病人为什么不再多些？越多才越有说服力。

...xīn xiǎng, zǒuláng-lǐ de bìngrén wèishénme bù zài duō xiē?
heart　think　in corridor　SP patient　why　　NEG more many some
Yuè ... yuè ... duō cái yuè yǒu shuōfúlì.
the more ... the more ...　many then　　there be persuasiveness
{... wished that there had been even more patients in the hallway. The more patients there were, the more persuasive it would be.}

(6)　不，不，越等下去，丁叔的鳜鱼才越有滋味呢！

Bù, bù, yuè ... yuè ... děng-xiàqù, Dīngshū de
NEG NEG　the more ... the more ...　continue to wait　DING uncle　SP
guìyú cái yuè yǒu zīwèi ne!
mandarin fish then　　have　taste　MP
{No, no, the longer we wait, the more delicious uncle DING's mandarin fish will taste!}

7.1.2 *"yuè p" as a realis reason*

In some sentences in the form of "*yuè p, yuè q*", what is stated in "*yuè p*" and what is stated in "*yuè q*" are both realities, with the former acting as the ground for the inference and the latter acting as the conclusion of the inference. The following are two examples:

(7)　"相思树女子客家"的生意越兴旺，就越招地方上的人们议论。

"Xiāngsīshù nǚzǐ kèjiā" de shēngyi yuè ... yuè ...
acacia　　　woman inn　SP business　the more ... the more ...

126   *Occurrence of què in "yuè p, yuè q"*

xīngwàng,   jiù   *yuè*   zhāo   dìfang-shàng   de   rén-men   yìlùn.
prosperous   then   incur   in region   SP   people   talk about
{The more prosperous "Acacia Lady Inn" is, the more the locals talk about it.}

(8)   谁叫他们上面要瞎报产量，"放卫星"？他们上报越多，我们也就瞒产越多——不能把大人小孩子一个个活活地饿死啊！

Shuí   jiào   tā-men   shàngmiàn   yào   xiā   bào   chǎnliàng, "fàng
who   ask   them   higher authorities   ask   false   report   output   launch
wèixīng"? Tā-men   shàngbào yuè . . . yuè . . .   duō,   wǒ-men yě
satellite   they   report   the more . . . the more . . .   much   we   also
jiù   mán   chǎn   yuè duō   —bù néng bǎ   dàrén   xiǎoháizi yī gè-gè
then   conceal output   much   NEG can   BA adult   child   one after another
huóhuó   de   è-sǐ   a!
alive   SP   starve to death   MP
{Who asked (our) higher authorities to fake (our) output and "launch satellites"? The more they reported, the falser our output was—we couldn't allow the adults and children to starve!}

In sentences in the form of "*yuè p, yuè q*", whether the ground for the inference is realis depends on the context to a large extent. The inference could be interpreted as a hypothetical judgment if there is no context. For example, (8) could be possibly interpreted as (9) or (10) with no context.

(9)   他们上报越多，我们也就瞒产越多。

Tā-men   shàngbào yuè . . . yuè . . .   duō,   wǒ-men yě   jiù   mán
they   report   the more . . . the more . . .   much   we   also then conceal
chǎn   yuè duō.
output   much
{The more they report, the falser our output is. }

(10)   只要他们上报越多，我们也就瞒产越多。

Zhǐyào . . . jiù . . .   tā-men   shàngbào yuè . . . yuè . . .   duō,   wǒ-men
as long as...   they   report   the more. . . the more. . .   much   we
yě   jiù   mán   chǎn   yuè duō.
also then conceal output   much
{So long as they report more, our output will be false.}

In some sentences in the form of "*yuè p, yuè q*", the events are ongoing, for instance, (7), and in other sentences, the events took place in the past, for instance, (8). If the events are ongoing, "*yuè p, yuè q*" means the same as "*yuèláiyuè p, yīncǐ, yuèláiyuè q*". For instance, (7) can be rewritten as (11):

(11)   生意越来越兴旺，因此，越来越招地方上的人们议论。

Shēngyi   yuèláiyuè   xīngwàng,   yīncǐ,   yuèláiyuè   zhāo
business   more and more   prosperous   therefore   more and more   incur
dìfang-shàng   de   rén-men   yìlùn.
in region   SP   people   talk about

Occurrence of què in "yuè p, yuè q"   127

{As the business is becoming more and more prosperous, more and more locals are talking about it.}

The following are another two examples:

(12) 但毕竟"四人帮"都已经倒台三四年了，群众意见<u>越来越</u>大，政治影响也<u>越来越</u>差……

Dàn bìjìng "sì rén bāng" dōu yǐjīng dǎotái sān-sì nián
but after all Gang of Four even already fall from power three or four year

le, qúnzhòng yìjiàn <u>yuèláiyuè</u> dà, zhèngzhì yǐngxiǎng yě
PEF the masses complaint more and more strong politics influence also

<u>yuèláiyuè</u> chà ...
more and more bad

{But after all, it's already three or four years since the "Gang of Four" fell from power. Public complaints are growing stronger and stronger, and the political influence is getting worse and worse . . .}

(13) ……家庭<u>越来越</u>不和，他的脾气<u>越来越</u>不好。

... jiātíng <u>yuèláiyuè</u> bù hé, tā de píqi <u>yuèláiyuè</u>
family more and more NEG harmonious he SP temper more and more

bù hǎo.
NEG good

{Relations between his family members became worse and worse, and his temper became more and more hostile.}

In the two aforementioned examples, "_yuèláiyuè_ . . . _yuèláiyuè_ . . ." can be replaced by "_yuè_ . . . _yuè_ . . .".

7.1.3 Isomorphic forms of "yuè p, yuè q"

In some cases, if there are two isomorphic "_yuè p, yuè q_", with one showing a hypothesis and the other indicating the realis, then there exists a syllogism with the major premise implied, i.e.,

(_zhǐyào_) yuè p, (_jiù_) yuè q.   (major premise—hypothetical)
(_yīnwèi_) yuè p,   (minor premise—realis)
(_suǒyǐ_) yuè q.   (conclusion—realis)

If Example (12) were to be rewritten to include the implied major premise, it would be like (14):

(14) ……(只要)群众的意见越大，政治影响就越差，(事实上)群众的意见越大，（所以）政治影响也就越差。

... (_zhǐyào_) ... jiù ... qúnzhòng de yìjiàn yuè ... yuè ...
as long as the masses SP complaint the more ... the more ...

dà, zhèngzhì yǐngxiǎng jiù yuè chà, (_shìshí-shàng_) qúnzhòng de
great politics influence bad as a matter of fact the masses SP

128 Occurrence of què in "yuè p, yuè q"

yìjiàn	yuè . . . yuè . . .			dà,	(suǒyǐ)	zhèngzhì	yǐngxiǎng
complaint	the more . . . the more . . .			great	therefore	politics	influence

yě	jiù	yuè	chà.
also			bad

{As long as public complaints grow stronger and stronger, the political influence will be getting worse and worse, and as a matter of fact, public complaints are growing stronger and stronger, so the political influence is getting worse and worse.}

In all sentences like (12), where "*yuè p*" is realis, the major premise—isomorphic to the sentence itself—is invisible. On the other hand, if "*yuè p*" is irrealis, the sentence must be a general statement of a hypothetical inference based on a number of instances of the correlation between "*yuè p*" and "*yuè q*" and can be used as the implied major premise to make new judgments when applicable.

7.1.4 Correlation between "yuè p" and "yuè q"

Regardless of whether "*yuè p*" in "*yuè p, yuè q*" is realis or irrealis, it is a condition or ground with indefinite variability, and "*yuè q*" indicates a result with indefinite variability correspondingly.

In "*yuè p, yuè q*", *p* and *q* are always proportional.[4] To be precise, the correlation between *p* and *q* is either positive or negative. If it is a positive correlation, when *p* increases *q* also increases and vice versa; if it is a negative correlation, when *p* increases *q* decreases and vice versa. Compare the following examples:

(15) a 时间越长，成功的可能性越大。

Shíjiān	yuè . . . yuè . . .			cháng,	chénggōng	de	kěnéngxìng
time	the more . . . the more . . .			long	succeed	SP	possibility

yuè	dà.
	great

{The longer the time, the more likely it is to succeed.}

b 时间越长，成功的可能性越小。

Shíjiān	yuè . . . yuè . . .			cháng,	chénggōng	de	kěnéngxìng
time	the more . . . the more . . .			long	succeed	SP	possibility

yuè	xiǎo.
	small

{The longer the time, the less likely it is to succeed.}

(16) a 时间越短，成功的可能性越小。

Shíjiān	yuè . . . yuè . . .			duǎn,	chénggōng	de	kěnéngxìng
time	the more . . . the more . . .			short	succeed	SP	possibility

yuè	xiǎo.
	small

{The shorter the time, the less likely it is to succeed.}

b 时间越短，成功的可能性越大。

Shíjiān *yuè . . . yuè . . .* *duǎn,* *chénggōng* *de* *kěnéngxìng*
time the more . . . the more . . . short succeed SP possibility

yuè *dà.*
great

{The shorter the time, the more likely it is to succeed.}

There is a positive correlation between "the longer the time" and "the greater the chances" and between "the shorter the time" and "the smaller the chances". Similarly, there exisits a negative correlation between "the shorter the time" and "the greater the chances" and between "the longer the time" and "the smaller the chances". The following are two examples:

(17) 鸟不但没赶跑，反倒蚕越大，鸟越多。

Niǎo *bùdàn* *méi* *gǎn-pǎo,* *fǎndào* *cán*
bird not only NEG be chased away on the contrary silkworm

yuè . . . yuè . . . *dà,* *niǎo* *yuè* *duō.*
the more . . . the more . . . big bird many

{The birds hadn't been driven away, but, on the contrary, the bigger the silkworms, the more the birds.}

(18) 俗话说：情越多，礼越小。

Súhuà *shuō: qíng* *yuè . . . yuè . . .* *duō,* *lǐ* *yuè xiǎo.*
saying say relationship the more . . . the more . . . much gift small

{As the saying goes, the closer the relationship, the more trifling the gift.}

Example (17) indicates a positive correlation, i.e., "the size of silkworms" is in direct proportion to "the number of birds", whereas (18) shows a negative correlation, i.e., "the closeness of the friendship" is in inverse proportion to "the value of the gift".

Thus, an increase of p does not necessarily result in an increase of q, and vice versa. The sentence form "*yuè p, yuè q*" reveals that the actual relationship between matters can be as complicated as a functional relationship.[5]

Apparently, language is not mathematics, and no sentences are calculus. Sometimes, a correlation itself does not tell whether it is positive or negative. The following is an example:

(19) 你现在调回来了，这是第一步，以后的路只会越走越宽，不会越走越窄……

Nǐ *xiànzài diào-huílái* *le,* *zhè shì* *dìyī bù,* *yǐhòu de lù* *zhǐ* *huì*
you now transfer back PEF this COP first step after SP road only will

yuè . . . yuè . . . *zǒu* *yuè kuān,* *bù* *huì* *yuè . . . yuè . . .*
the more . . . the more . . . walk wide NEG will the more . . . the more . . .

zǒu *yuè zhǎi . . .*
walk narrow

{You're back now, and this is the first step. The road ahead will only get wider and wider rather narrower and narrower . . .}

130 *Occurrence of què in "yuè p, yuè q"*

It is hard to tell whether the correlation between "walking" and "the width of the road" is positive or negative. However, by comparing "the more you walk, the wider the road" and "the more you walk, the narrower the road", it can be concluded that "getting wider and wider" shows a positive correlation, and "getting narrower and narrower" shows a negative correlation.

7.1.5 *"yuè q" in "yuè p, yuè q; yuè q, yuè r"*

Regardless of whether *"yuè p"* in *"yuè p, yuè q"* is realis or irrealis, *"yuè q"* is a correlative result produced by *"yuè p"*, and it can also act as a correlative condition for *"yuè r"*, i.e., *"yuè p, yuè q; yuè q, yuè r"*. The following are two examples:

(20) 三姐妹满的欲望是难以满足的，年纪越大，受的闲气便越多；受的气越多，便越羡慕别个的命好……

Sānjiě　　　　　*Mèimǎn de yùwàng shì*　　*nányǐ*　　　*mǎnzú de, niánjì*
third elder sister Meiman SP desire　　COP　difficult to　satisfy MP age

yuè . . . yuè . . .　　　　　*dà, shòu de xiánqì*　　　*biàn yuè duō; shòu*
the more . . . the more . . . old suffer SP anger about trifles then　　much suffer

de qì　yuè . . . yuè . . .　　　　*duō, biàn yuè xiànmù biége de mìng hǎo . . .*
SP anger the more . . . the more . . . much then　　envy　others SP fate good

{Third elder sister Meiman's desire is hard to satisfy. The older she is, the easier she gets angry about trifles; and the more often she gets angry, the more she envies others' fate . . .}

(21) 愈是酗酒，愈是误村事、家事，愈是误事，愈使二贝、白银不满。

Yù shì . . . yù shì . . .　　　*xùjiǔ,*　　　　　*yù shì wù*　　　*cūn shì,*
the more . . . the more . . . drink excessively　　cause delay village matter

jiāshì,　　　*yù shì . . . yù . . .*　　　*wùshì,*　　　*yù shǐ*
household affairs the more . . . the more . . . hold things up　make

Èrbèi, Báiyín bùmǎn.
Erbei Baiyin dissatisfied

{The more he drank, the more he held up village and family affairs, and the more he delayed, the more dissatisfied Erbei and Baiyin became.}

"*yuè p, yuè q; yuè q, yuè r*" is a form of chain correlative conditional sentences, and it can be condensed into "*yuè p, yuè q, (yě) (jiù) yuè r*". The following are five examples:

(22) 她越不抬起头转过脸，男人们越不甘心，越急于想看到她模样儿。

Tā　yuè . . . yuè . . . yuè . . .　　　　　*bù　tái-qǐ tóu　zhuǎn-guò*
she　the more . . . the more . . . the more . . . NEG raise head turn around

liǎn,　nánrén-men yuè bù　gānxīn,　yuè jíyú　xiǎng kàn-dào
face　man-PL　　　　NEG be satisfied　be eager want see

Occurrence of què *in "yuè p, yuè q"* 131

tā   múyàngr.
her   looks

{The more she didn't look up and turn around, the more unreconciled the guys were, and the more eagerly they wanted to see her face.}

(23)　（阿猫这孩子，从一学会说话起就口吃。）越高兴，越着急，也越结巴。

(*Āmāo zhè háizi, cóng yī...jiù... xué-huì shuōhuà qǐ   jiù*
Amao   this   child   from as soon as   be able   speak   start and continue

kǒuchī.) yuè...yuè...yuè...   gāoxìng, yuè zháojí,
stutter   the more...the more...the more... happy   be anxious

yě   yuè jiēba.
also   stutter

{Amao has been stuttering ever since he learned to speak. The happier he is, the more anxious, and the more stuttering in turn.}

(24)　……向红的事拖的时间越长，舆论对赵大川和向红越有利，麦金万等人就越焦急。

...Xiàng Hóng   de   shì   tuō   de   shíjiān
XIANG Hong   SP   matter drag on   SP   time

Yuè...yuè...yuè...   cháng,   yúlùn   duì
the more...the more...the more...   long   public opinion to

Zhào Dàchuān   hé   Xiàng Hóng   yuè   yǒulì,   Mài Jīnwàn   děng
ZHAO Dachuan   and   XIANG Hong   favorable MAI Jinwan   etc.

rén   jiù   yuè jiāojí.
person then   anxious

{... The longer XIANG Hong's affair drags on, the more favorable the public opinion is to ZHAO Dachuan and XIANG Hong, and the more anxious Mai Jinwan and others will be.}

(25)　顶撞越多，广州人对黎子流的了解就越多，对市长的误解和闲话就越少。

Dǐngzhuàng yuè...yuè...yuè...   duō,   Guǎngzhōu rén
contradict   the more...the more...the more... much Guangzhou people

duì   Lí Zǐliú de liǎojiě jiù yuè duō, duì shìzhǎng de wùjiě
about LI Ziliu SP know   then much about mayor   SP misunderstanding

hé   xiánhuà jiù   yuè shǎo.
and gossip   then   little

{The more confrontations there are, the more Guangzhou people know about LI Ziliu, and the less misunderstanding and gossip they have about the mayor.}

(26)　他越跟陶慧贞接触，就越觉得她是一块无价之宝，也就越怕这无价之宝失落他人之手。

Tā yuè...yuè...yuè...   gēn   Táo Huìzhēn jiēchù, jiù
he   the more...the more...the more... with TAO Huizhen contact then

yuè juéde tā   shì yī   kuài wújià-zhībǎo, yě jiù yuè pà   zhè
     feel   she   COP one CL   priceless treasure also then   fear this

132 *Occurrence of què in "yuè p, yuè q"*

wújià-zhībǎo   shīluò   tārén zhī shǒu.
priceless treasure get lost others SP hand

{The more contact he had with TAO Huizhen, the more he felt that she was a priceless treasure, and the more he was afraid that this priceless treasure would get lost to others.}

The word *yīn'ér* ('as a result') can be used and placed before "*yuè r*" to emphasize that "*yuè q*" results in "*yuè r*". For example, (22) can be rewritten as (27), and (23) as (28).

(27)　她越不抬起头转过脸，男人们越不甘心，因而也就越急于想看到她模样儿。

Tā   yuè . . . yuè . . . yuè . . .   bù   tái-qǐ tóu   zhuǎn-guò
she   the more . . . the more . . . the more . . .   NEG   raise   head   turn around

liǎn, nánrén-men yuè bù   gānxīn,   yīn'ér   yě   jiù   yuè jíyú
face man-PL   NEG   be satisfied therefore also   be eager

xiǎng kàn-dào tā   múyàngr.
want   see   her   looks

{The more she didn't look up and turn around, the more unreconciled the guys were, and therefore the more eagerly they wanted to see her face.}

(28)　越高兴，越着急，因而也就越结巴。

Yuè . . . yuè . . . yuè . . .   gāoxìng,   yuè   zháojí,   yīn'ér
the more . . . the more . . . the more . . .   happy   be anxious therefore

yě   jiù   yuè   jiēba.
also then   stutter

{The happier (he is), the more anxious, and therefore the more stuttering.}

7.1.6 *"yuè p, yuè q; yuè q, yuè p"*

Some sentences in the form of "*yuè p, yuè q; yuè q, yuè p*" indicate that "*yuè p*" results in "*yuè p*", which in turn, acts as the condition for "*yuè p*", for example:

(29)　心里越烦，越做不好；越做不好，心里越烦。

Xīn-lǐ   yuè . . . yuè . . . yuè . . . yuè   fán,   yuè zuò bù   hǎo;
in heart the more . . . the more . . . the more . . .   upset   do   NEG   good

yuè zuò bù   hǎo, xīn-lǐ   yuè   fán.
      do   NEG   good in heart   upset

{The more upset (you) are, the less likely (you) can succeed; and the less likely (you) succeed, the more upset you are. }

The following are four examples:

(30)　<u>越有越</u>吝，越吝<u>越有</u>；我又不向你借，何必恐慌。

Yuè . . . yuè . . .   yǒu yuè   lìn,   yuè . . . yuè . . .   lìn
the more . . . the more . . .   have the more stingy the more . . . the more . . . stingy

Occurrence of què in "yuè p, yuè q" 133

yuè yǒu; wǒ yòu bù xiàng nǐ jiè, hébì kǒnghuāng.
have I really NEG from you borrow unnecessarily panicking
{The wealthier you are, the stingier; the stingier, the wealthier. I'm not going to borrow any money from you, so why should you panic?}

(31) 越穷越折腾，越折腾越穷。

Yuè . . . yuè . . . qióng yuè zhēteng, yuè . . . yuè . . .
the more . . . the more . . . poor squander the more . . . the more . . .

zhēteng yuè qióng.
squander poor

{The poorer someone is, the more they squander; the more they squander, the poorer they become.}

(32) 越够不着心里越急，越急越够不着。

Yuè . . . yuè . . . gòu bù zháo xīn-lǐ yuè jí,
the more . . . the more . . . can't reach in heart anxious

yuè . . . yuè . . . jí yuè gòu bù zháo.
the more . . . the more . . . anxious can't reach

{The more (someone) can't reach (something), the more anxious they are; the more anxious they are, the more they can't reach it.}

(33) 圣上护着，谁攻田文镜，立地就疑人是冲着新政，冲着自己。越攻越护，越护越攻。

Shèngshàng hù-zhe, shuí gōng Tián Wénjìng, lìdì jiù yí
His Majesty protect-PRG who attack TIAN Wenjing immediately then suspect

rén shì chòng-zhe xīnzhèng, chòng-zhe zìjǐ. Yuè . . . yuè . . .
person COP aim at-PRG new deal aim at-PRG oneself the more . . . the more . . .

gōng yuè hù, yuè . . . yuè . . . hù yuè gōng.
attack protect the more . . . the more . . . protect attack

{His Majesty is protecting (TIAN Wenjing), so, as long as someone attacks TIAN, His Majesty will immediately suspect that the attacker is aiming at the new deal and himself. The more attack, the more protection; the more protection, the more attack.}

The form "*yuè p, yuè q; yuè q, yuè p*" cannot be condensed into "*yuè p, yuè q, yuè p*". For example, neither of the two occurrences of "*yuè zuò bù hǎo*" can be omitted in (29). This also holds true for "*yuè zhēteng*" in (31).

If the second part in a sentence in the form of "*yuè p, yuè q; yuè q, yuè p*" happens to be an independent sentence of exactly the same wording, then "*yuè q, yuè p*" becomes "*yuè p, yuè q*" in that independent sentence. In other words, it is possible that "*yuè p, yuè q*" in a sentence can be the part of "*yuè q, yuè p*" in another sentence of the same wording in the form of "*yuè p, yuè q; yuè q, yuè p*". Compare the following two examples:

(34) 越伤心越哭，越哭越伤心。

Yuè . . . yuè . . . shāngxīn yuè kū, yuè . . . yuè . . .
the more . . . the more . . . heartbroken cry the more . . . the more . . .

134 *Occurrence of què in "yuè p, yuè q"*

kū   yuè   shāngxīn.
cry   heartbroken
{The more grieved (he) was, the more (he) wept, and the more (he) wept, the more grieved (he) became.}

(35) 詹姆哭了，越哭越伤心。
Zhānmǔ   kū-le,   yuè . . . yuè . . .   kū   yuè   shāngxīn.
Jaime   weep-PEF   the more . . . the more . . .   cry   heartbroken
{Jaime wept, and the more he wept, the more grieved he became.}

The section "the more he wept, the more grieved he became" acts as "*yuè q, yuè p*" in (34), but "*yuè p, yuè q*" in (35).

7.2 "*yuè*"

The word *yuè* functions as a grammatical element, as well as a semantic element. The words that follow *yuè* vary in part of speech and in function.

7.2.1 "*yuè*" as an adverb

The word *yuè* is an adverb.[6] In some cases, what occurs in the place of *yuè* is "*yuè shì*", a synonym of *yuè*. "*yuè shì*" can occur in pairs, or cooccur with *yuè*. The following are three examples:

(36) ······战争越是接近结束，越是残酷。
. . . zhànzhēng   yuèshì . . . yuè shì . . .   jiējìn   jiéshù,   yuèshì   cánkù.
War   the more . . . the more . . .   approach end   cruel
{. . . the closer the war approaches the end, the more brutal it becomes.}

(37) 经验已经证明了，你越是老实，就越有人来欺负你。
Jīngyàn   yǐjīng   zhèngmíng-le,   nǐ   yuè shì . . . yuè . . .   lǎoshi, jiù
experience already prove-PEF   you the more . . . the more . . .   honest then
yuè   yǒu   rén   lái   qīfu   nǐ.
      there be person come   bully   you
{Experience has proved that the more honest you are, the more you will be bullied.}

(38) 越近春节，匪徒越是猖獗。
Yuè . . . yuè shì . . .   jìn   chūnjié,   fěitú   yuè shì   chāngjué.
the more . . . the more . . .   approach Spring Festival bandit   rampant
{The closer the Chinese New Year is, the more rampant the bandits are.}

Generally, *yuè* or "*yuè shì*" can be used interchangeably. The collocation of "*yuè shì*" and *yuè* can be either "*yuè shì . . . yuè . . .*" or "*yuè . . . yuè shì . . .*". Usually, monosyllabic words follow *yuè* rather than "*yuè shì*". For example:

Occurrence of què in "yuè p, yuè q" 135

(39) 时间越长，问题越大。

Shíjiān *yuè . . . yuè . . .* *cháng,* *wèntí* *yuè* *dà.*
time the more . . . the more . . . long problem serious
{The longer the time, the more serious the problem.}

On the other hand, subject-predicate structures and prepositional structures usually follow "*yuè shì*" rather than *yuè*.[7] The following are two examples:

(40) 越是家境败下去，越要翻上来……

Yuè shì . . . yuè . . . *jiājìng* *bài-xiàqù,*
the more . . . the more . . . financial situation of a household decline
yuè *yào* *fān-shànglái . . .*
must come up
{The more the financial situation of a household goes down, the more it needs to come up . . .}

(41) 越是在情况紧急的时候，越（是）需要冷静。

Yuè shì . . . yuè (shì) . . . *zài* *qíngkuàng* *jǐnjí* *de* *shíhou,* *yuè (shì)*
the more . . . the more . . . at situation urgent SP time
xūyào *lěngjìng.*
need calm
{The more urgent the situation is, the more (we) need to calm down.}

In some cases, *yuèfā* or *yuèjiā*—a synonym of *yuè*—occurs in the place of *yuè* or "*yuè shì*" in the posterior clause, i.e., "*yuè/yuè shì p, yuèfā/yuèjiā q*", as in the following two examples:

(42) 可是日子越是红火，他心里就越发觉得不安。

Kěshì *rìzi* *yuè shì . . . yuèfā . . .* *hónghuǒ,* *tā* *xīn-lǐ* *jiù* *yuèfā*
but life the more . . . the more . . . prosperous he in heart then
juéde *bù'ān.*
feel uneasy
{But the more prosperous his life was, the more uneasy he felt.}

(43) 越对他亲切，他就越加痛苦。

Yuè . . . yuèjiā . . . *duì* *tā* *qīnqiè,* *tā* *jiù* *yuèjiā* *tòngkǔ.*
the more . . . the more . . . to him kind he then painful
{The more kind (others are) to him, the more painful he is.}

Another synonym of *yuè*/"*yuè shì*" is *yù*/"*yù shì*". The following are two examples:

(44) 愈往高处攀，山风愈大。

Yù . . . yù . . . *wǎng* *gāo* *chù* *pān,* *shān* *fēng* *yù* *dà.*
the more . . . the more . . . to high place climb mountain wind strong
{The higher you climb to, the stronger the wind.}

136 *Occurrence of què in "yuè p, yuè q"*

(45) ⋯⋯他愈是害怕禾禾，愈是待禾禾友好。

    . . . tā   <u>*yù shì*</u> *. . .* <u>*yù shì*</u> *. . .*   *hàipà Héhé,* <u>*yù shì*</u> *dài Héhé yǒuhǎo.*

    he   the more . . . the more . . .   fear Hehe   treat Hehe friendly

    {. . . the more fearful he was of Hehe, the more friendly he was to Hehe.}

7.2.2 *"yuè shì" as a grammatical element*

As a formal marker, the adverb *yuè*/"*yuè shì*" usually occurs in pairs, but there are also three other forms.

First, "*yuè p, gèng q*", in which *gèng* means the same as *yuè*. The following is an example:

(46) ⋯⋯ 会议沉默的时间越长，有勇气打破僵局的发言者就更少。

    . . . huìyì chénmò de shíjiān <u>*yuè*</u> *. . .* <u>*gèng*</u> *. . .*   *cháng, yǒu yǒngqì*

    meeting be silent SP time   the more . . . the more . . .   long   have courage

    dǎ-pò jiāngjú de fāyánzhě jiù <u>*gèng*</u> *shǎo.*

    break deadlock SP speaker then   few

    {. . . the longer the meeting is in silence, the fewer speakers have the courage to break the deadlock.}

Second, "*yuè p, piān/piānpiān q*", in which *piān/piānpiān* means "on the contrary". For example:

(47) 可是，我这个姑娘就有这么个鬼毛病：越禁止我做的事，我就偏要做，⋯⋯

    Kěshì, wǒ zhè gè gūniang jiù yǒu zhème gè guǐ máobìng: <u>*yuè*</u> *jìnzhǐ*

    but   I   this CL girl   just have so   CL bad shortcoming more forbid

    wǒ zuò de shì, wǒ jiù <u>*piān*</u>   *yào zuò, . . .*

    I   do SP thing I   just on the contrary will do

    {However, this daughter of mine has such a bad problem: The more I'm not allowed to do something, the more I'll do it . . .}

Third, "*. . . yuè . . .*", which is quite rare, and in which the same adjective is used in the two clauses. For example:

(48) ⋯⋯树大，招雷的可能性也越大。

    . . . shù dà, zhāo léi   *de   kěnéngxìng yě* <u>*yuè*</u>   *dà.*

    tree   big   incur thunder   SP   possibility   also   more   great

    {. . . the bigger the tree, the more likely it is to be struck by lightning.}

7.2.3 *yuè as a semantic element*

The adverb *yuè*/"*yuè shì*", together with the words that follow, shows a correlative condition (ground) or result. For this reason, *yuè*/"*yuè shì*" *is* a semantic element, which can be attested by the following two points.

Occurrence of que in "yuè p, yuè q" 137

First, if *"yuè/yuè shì . . . yuè/"yuè shì. . ."* is removed from a sentence, the form or meaning of the correlation between the two clauses will no longer exist. The following are four examples:

(49) 时间长，成功的可能性大。
     Shíjiān   cháng,   chénggōng   de   kěnéngxìng   dà.
     time   long   succeed   SP   possibility   great
     {The time is long; the chances of success are big.}

(50) 时间短，成功的可能性小。
     Shíjiān   duǎn,   chénggōng   de   kěnéngxìng   xiǎo.
     time   short   succeed   SP   possibility   small
     {The time is short; the chances of success are small.}

(51) 时间长，成功的可能性小。
     Shíjiān   cháng,   chénggōng   de   kěnéngxìng   xiǎo.
     time   long   succeed   SP   possibility   small
     {The time is long; the chances of success are small.}

(52) 时间短，成功的可能性大。
     Shíjiān   duǎn,   chénggōng   de   kěnéngxìng   dà.
     time   short   succeed   SP   possibility   great
     {The time is short; the chances of success are big.}

Second, if *"yuè/yuè shì . . . yuè/"yuè shì. . ."* is removed from a sentence, there could be no correlation of condition and result at all between *p* and *q*. The following are two examples:

(53) ……一点风丝也没有。<u>越</u>走，<u>越</u>闷得慌。
     . . . yīdiǎn   fēngsī   yě   méiyǒu.   <u>*Yuè*</u> . . . *yuè* . . .   *zǒu,*   <u>*yuè*</u>
     a little   wind   even   there not be   the more . . . the more . . .   walk
     mēn de huang.
     feel unbearably stuffy
     {. . . There was not even a breath of wind. The more I walked, the more unbearably stuffy (I) felt.}

(54) 其实她们<u>越</u>说，我就<u>越</u>不听她们那一套……
     Qíshí   tā-men <u>yuè</u> . . . <u>yuè</u> . . .   shuō, wǒ jiù <u>yuè</u> bù   tīng
     actually they   the more . . . the more . . . say   I   then   NEG listen to
     tā-men nà   yī   tào . . .
     they   that one CL
     {In fact, the more they talk, the less I listen to them . . .}

In (53), there is no correlation between "feeling unbearably stuffy" and "walking"; in other words, it does not mean that "I would feel stuffy so long as I

138 *Occurrence of què in "yuè p, yuè q"*

walked". The correlation of condition and result only lies between "more walking" and "feeling more stuffy". This also holds true for (54).

7.2.4 *Grammatical structures of yuè-clause*

There are three types of grammatical structures of *yuè*-clauses: i) "*yuè/yuè shì* + V*", in which V stands for a verb, a verbal structure, or a prepositional structure; ii) "*yuè/yuè shì* + A", in which A stands for an adjective or adjectival structure; iii) "*yuè* + V/A de N"; iv) "*yuè* + *shì* N".

First, "*yuè/yuè shì* + V" usually acts as the predicate. The subject of this structure can be present or absent. The subjects of the two "*yuè/yuè shì* + V" structures can be the same or different. The following are two examples:

(55)   我越往下读，越深切地感到马克思的书是浓缩了的人类智慧……
 Wǒ yuè . . . yuè . . .   wǎng   xià   dú, yuè   shēnqiè de
 I   the more . . . the more . . . toward position below read deep SP
 gǎndào Mǎkèsī de shū   shì   nóngsuō-le   de rénlèi   zhìhuì . . .
 feel   Marx   SP book COP   condense-PEF SP human beings wisdom
 {The further I read, the more I realized that Marx's books were condensed human wisdom . . .}

(56)   他越这样说，我越感到非帮他复习不可。
 Tā yuè . . . yuè . . .   zhèyàng shuō, wǒ yuè gǎndào fēi . . . bùkě
 he   the more . . . the more . . . So   say   I   feel   necessarily
 bāng tā   fùxí   bùkě.
 help him review lessons
 {The more he said so, the more I felt compelled to help him review his lessons.}

If "V" in "*yuè/yuè shì* + V" is acted by a prepositional structure, "*yuè/yuè shì* + prepositional structure" can only occur in the anterior clause, in which the prepositional structure acts as the adverbial. The conjunction "*yuè/yuè shì . . . yuè/yuè shì . . .*" is used to emphasize the conditional correlation between the adverbial and the head of the predicate, as in the following citation from a short story:

(57)   如果具有自觉性，人越是在艰苦的环境，释放出来的能力也越大。
 Rúguǒ jùyǒu zìjuéxìng,   rén   yuè shì . . . yuè . . .   zài jiānkǔ
 if   have self-consciousness person the more . . . the more . . . in   hard
 de huánjìng,   shìfàng-chūlái de nénglì yě   yuè dà.
 SP environment release   SP ability also   big
 {If (we) are self-conscious, the more difficult the environment is, the more capable (we are).}

Second, in some cases, "*yuè/yuè shì* + A" acts as the predicate. Similar to "*yuè/yuè shì* + V", the subject of this structure can be present or absent, and the subjects

Occurrence of *què* in *"yuè p, yuè q"*   139

of the two *"yuè/yuè shì* + A" structures can be the same or different. The following are two examples:

(58) 越高兴，越着急。

     Yuè . . . *yuè* . . .   *gāoxìng,   yuè   zháojí.*

     the more . . . the more . . .   happy   be anxious

     {The happier (he was), the more anxious (he was).}

(59) 蚕越大，鸟越多。

     Cán   yuè . . . *yuè* . . .   *dà,   niǎo   yuè   duō.*

     silkworm   the more . . . the more . . .   big   bird   many

     {The bigger the silkworms were, the more the birds.}

In some cases, *"yuè/yuè shì* + A" functions as the complement, while *"yuè/yuè shì* + V" cannot. The following are two examples:

(60) 我弹得越响，他吼得越凶。

     Wǒ   tán   de   yuè . . . *yuè* . . .   *xiǎng, tā hǒu de yuè xiōng.*

     I   play SP the more . . . the more . . . loud he roar SP   fierce

     {The louder I played (the piano), the more fiercely he roared.}

(61) 陶世光越是想说服他，他就争辩得越上劲。

     Táo Shìguāng   yuèshì . . . *yuè* . . .   *xiǎng   shuōfú   tā, tā jiù*

     TAO Shiguang   the more . . . the more . . . want   persuade he he then

     zhēngbiàn de   yuè   shàngjìn.

     argue   SP   energetic

     {The more TAO Shiguang tried to persuade him, the harder he argued.}

In (60), *"yuè xiǎng"* ('louder') and *"yuè xiōng"* ('more fiercely') serve as the complement respectively. In (61), *"yuè shàngjìn"* ('harder') also acts as the complement.

Third, *"yuè* + V/A de N" is a variant of "(N) *yuè* V/A", and it only occurs in the anterior clause, as in the following two examples:

(62) 越有胆略的干部，越受群众欢迎。

     Yuè . . . *yuè* . . .   *yǒu   dǎnlüè   de   gànbù,*

     the more . . . the more . . . have   courage and resourcefulness SP cadre

     yuè   shòu   qúnzhòng   huānyíng.

     receive   the masses   welcome

     {The more courageous and resourceful a leader is, the more popular he or she is with the masses.}

(63) 生产第一线缺人。越艰苦的岗位越空虚，⋯⋯

     Shēngchǎn   dìyīxiàn   quē   rén.   Yuè . . . *yuè* . . .   *jiānkǔ*

     production   forefront   lack   manpower   the more . . . the more . . . hard

140 *Occurrence of què in "yuè p, yuè q"*

de gǎngwèi *yuè* kōngxū, ...
SP position empty
{The forefront of industry is short of manpower. The harder the post, the more vacancies there are ...}

The following are three more examples of the same type:

(64) 越能干的人，负担越重。

Yuè ... yuè ... nénggàn de rén, fùdān yuè zhòng
the more ... the more ... capable SP person burden heavy
{The more capable a person is, the heavier his or her burden is.}

(65) 越漂亮的房子，越没人敢住。

Yuè ... yuè ... piàoliàng de fángzi, yuè méi rén gǎn zhù.
the more ... the more ... beautiful SP house NEG people dare live
{The more beautiful a house is, the fewer people dare to live in it.}

(66) 越冗长的文章，读者越不爱读。

Yuè ... yuè ... rǒngcháng de wénzhāng, dúzhě yuè bù ài dú.
the more ... the more ... lengthy SP article reader NEG love read
{The lengthier an article is, the less people like to read it.}

In "*yuè* V/A de N", what *yuè* modifies is, in fact, "V/A" only. Moreover, "*yuè* V/A de N" can be worded as "N *yuè* V/A". For instance, (67) can be rewritten as (68):

(67) 越有胆略的干部，越受群众欢迎。

Yuè ... yuè ... yǒu dǎnlüè de gànbù, *yuè*
the more ... the more ... have courage and resourcefulness SP cadre
shòu qúnzhòng huānyíng.
receive the masses welcome
{The more courageous and resourceful a leader is, the more popular he or she is with the masses.}

(68) 干部越有胆略，越受群众欢迎。

Gànbù yuè ... yuè ... yǒu dǎnlüè, *yuè*
cadre the more ... the more ... have courage and resourcefulness
shòu qúnzhòng huānyíng.
receive the masses welcome
{The more courageous and resourceful a leader is, the more popular he or she is with the masses.}

If the conjunction "*yuè* ... *yuè* ..." is removed from a sentence in the form of "*yuè* V/A de N, *yuè* V/A de N", the remaining elements will be in a subject-predicate

Occurrence of què in "yuè p, yuè q" 141

relationship. The antecedent clause acts as the condition or ground for the subsequent, and the noun structure "V/A de N" in the antecedent is taken as the tacit subject. The following are examples:

(69) a 越有胆略的干部，越受群众欢迎。

Yuè . . . *yuè* . . .   *yǒu   dǎnlüè*   *de   gànbù,*
the more . . . the more . . .   have   courage and resourcefulness SP   cadre

yuè   shòu   qúnzhòng   huānyíng.
        receive the masses   welcome

{The more courageous and resourceful a leader is, the more popular he or she is with the masses.}

→b 有胆略的干部，受群众欢迎。

Yǒu   dǎnlüè   de gànbù, shòu   qúnzhòng   huānyíng.
have   courage and resourcefulness SP cadre   receive the masses   welcome
{Courageous and resourceful leaders are popular with the masses.}

Fourth, "*yuè + shì* N" is a special form of "*yuè + V*", for the word *shì* is a judgmental verb, and "*shì* N" can be regarded as a verbal structure. "*yuè + shì* N" can only occur in the antecedent, as in the following two examples:

(70) 那个时候，越是马屁精，越受到重用。

Nà   gè   shíhou,   yuè . . . *yuè* . . .   *shì   mǎpìjīng,   yuè   shòudào*
that   CL   time   the more . . . the more . . .   COP   flatterer   receive

zhòngyòng.
put someone in an important position

{Back then, the better you were at flattery, the more important position you would be put in.}

(71) 在这种情况下，越是亲戚，越想避嫌。

Zài   zhè   zhǒng   qíngkuàng-xià,   yuè . . . *yuè* . . .   *shì   qīnqi,*
at   this   kind   under circumstances   the more . . . the more . . .   COP   relative

yuè   xiǎng   bìxián.
        want   avoid arousing suspicion

{Under this kind of circumstances, the closer the kinship is, the more they want to avoid arousing suspicion.}

The following are another three examples of the same type:

(72) 越是群众，越要关心。

Yuè . . . *yuè* . . .   *shì   qúnzhòng,   yuè   yào   guānxīn.*
the more . . . the more . . .   COP   the masses   need   care
{The more ordinary (they are), the more (we) should care about (them).}

142   *Occurrence of què in "yuè p, yuè q"*

(73)   越是领导，越为难。

      Yuè . . . yuè . . .   *shì*   *lǐngdǎo, yuè wéinán.*
      the more . . . the more . . . COP   leader   in a pickle
      {The more senior a leader is, the more difficult he or she feels.}

(74)   越是楼房，越不安全。

      Yuè . . . yuè . . .   *shì*   *lóufáng,*   *yuè bù   ānquán.*
      the more . . . the more . . . COP   storied house   NEG safe
      {The higher a storied house is, the more dangerous it is.}

In these cases, the verb *shì* must be present, and "*yuè shì*" as a whole cannot be regarded as an adverb, as it is different from "*yuè shì*" in "*yuè shì* V/A".

If "*yuè shì . . . yuè . . .*" is removed from a "*yuè shì . . . yuè . . .*" sentence, what remains will also be in a subject-predicate relationship. For this reason, the consequent also takes the antecedent as a correlative condition or ground, and "N" in the antecedent is taken as the tacit subject. The following are two examples:

(75)   越是马屁精，越受到重用。

      Yuè . . . yuè . . .   *shì*   *mǎpìjīng, yuè shòudào*
      the more . . . the more . . . COP   flatterer   receive
      zhòngyòng.
      put someone in an important position
      {The better you were at flattery, the more important position you would be put in.}

(76)   马屁精受到重用。

      Mǎpìjīng shòudào zhòngyòng.
      flatterer   receive   put someone in an important position
      {Those who are good at flattery are put in important positions.}

7.3   Occurrence of *què* in "*yuè p, yuè q*"

In some cases, the adversative connective *què* can occur in sentences in the form of "*yuè p, yuè q*". Whether *què* can occur depends on whether the correlation is positive or negative.

7.3.1   *Normal and abnormal correlation*

There are two types of correlation in terms of the result: normal and abnormal.

A normal correlation is a relationship in which the result is a subsequent effect of the condition. In other words, there is no contradiction between the condition and the result. The following are three examples:

(77)   越是爱她，越是希望她得到幸福！

      Yuè shì . . . yuèshì . . .   *ài tā, yuè shì xīwàng tā dédào xìngfú!*
      the more . . . the more . . . love her   hope her get happiness
      {The more (I) love her, the more (I) want her to be happy!}

Occurrence of què in "yuè p, yuè q" 143

(78) 人们<u>越是</u>预感到还要持续高温，就<u>越</u>向往江岸的清凉和林荫路里的静谧。

Rén-men <u>*yuè shì*</u> ... *yuè* ... *yùgǎn-dào hái yào chíxù gāo*
people the more ... the more ... forebode still will continue high

wēn, jiù <u>*yuè*</u> *xiàngwǎng jiāng àn de qīngliáng hé*
temperature then look forward to river bank SP cool and

línyīnlù-lǐ de jìngmì.
on boulevard SP quiet

{The more people feel that the heat will continue, the more they yearn for the coolness on the riverbanks and the tranquility on the boulevards.}

(79) 我呢，<u>越是</u>了解刘世雄的为人，<u>越</u>是憎恶刘家的这个小少爷。

Wǒ ne, <u>*yuè shì*</u> ... *yuè shì* ... *liǎojiě Liú Shìxióng de wéirén,* <u>*yuèshì*</u>
I MP the more ... the more ... know LIU Shixiong SP behave

zēngwù Liú jiā de zhè gè xiǎo shàoye.
loathe LIU family SP this CL young son of an aristocratic family

{As for me, the better I know LIU Shixiong as a person, the more I loathe this young master of the LIU family.}

An abnormal correlation is a relationship in which the result is opposite to the subsequent effect of the condition. In other words, there is a contradiction between the condition and the result. The following are three examples:

(80) 可不知怎么的，报上<u>越是</u>这样宣传，我心中那些莫名其妙的烦恼就<u>越</u>深重。

Kě bù zhī zěnme de, bào-shàng <u>*yuè shì*</u> ... *yuè* ...
but NEG know how MP in newspaper the more ... the more ...

zhèyàng xuānchuán, wǒ xīn-zhōng nà xiē mòmíng-qímiào de fánnǎo
so propagate I in heart that some inexplicable SP annoyance

jiù <u>*yuè*</u> *shēnzhòng.*
then heavy

{But somehow, the more the newspapers publicized it, the more my inexplicable annoyance grew.}

(81) 他抽烟抽成了气管炎，时常咳得脸红脖子胀，好像一口气倒不上来就会憋死。可<u>越</u>咳<u>越</u>要抽，他竟然学成一种特殊的本事，能靠大口的烟把咳压下去。

Tā chōuyān chōu chéng-le qìguǎnyán, shícháng ké de liǎn
he smoke cigarette smoke become-PEF tracheitis often cough SP face

hóng bózi zhàng, hǎoxiàng yī kǒu qì dǎo bù shànglái jiù huì
red neck swell as if one mouthful breath can't breathe then will

biē-sǐ. Kě <u>*yuè*</u> ... *yuè* ... *ké* <u>*yuè*</u> *yào chōu, tā jìngrán*
suffocate but the more ... the more ... cough will smoke he unexpectedly

xué-chéng yī zhǒng tèshū de běnshi, néng kào dà kǒu de
learned one kind special SP skill can depend on big mouthful SP

yān bǎ ké yā-xiàqù.
smoke BA cough suppress

{His tracheitis resulted from smoking. Often, when he coughed, his face would turn red and his neck would become thick, as if he was going to suffocate.

144 Occurrence of què in "yuè p, yuè q"

However, the more he coughed, the more he would smoke. He learned a special trick that allowed him to suppress his cough with a big mouthful of smoke.}

(82) 他不明白，为什么<u>越是</u>从小一起长大的女孩他<u>越是</u>爱不起来，⋯⋯

Tā bù míngbai, wèishénme <u>yuèshì</u>... <u>yuèshì</u>... cóng xiǎo
he NEG understand why the more... the more... from young

yīqǐ zhǎngdà de nǚhái tā <u>yuèshì</u> ài bù qǐlái, ...
together grow up SP girl he cannot love

{He doesn't understand why the more he grew up with a girl, the less likely he is to fall in love with her ...}

7.3.2 Occurrence of què in abnormal correlative sentences

If the correlation in a sentence in the form of "*yuè p, yuè q*" is abnormal, the adversative connective *què* can occur when needed, hence "*yuè p, què yuè q*". Without *què*, the abnormal correlation is implicit; with *què*, it is explicit. For example, if *què* occurs in place of *jiù* in (80), the abnormal correlation will be highlighted, and the speaker's unusual feeling of annoyance will be better depicted, which is also the case if *què* is used and placed between "*yuè ké*" ('the more he coughed') and "*yuè yào chou*" ('the more he would cough') in (81). The following is another example:

(83) 曲非烟<u>愈是</u>笑得欢畅，仪琳心头却<u>愈</u>酸楚。

Qǔ Fēiyān <u>yù shì</u>... <u>yù</u>... xiào de huānchàng, Yílín xīntóu
QV Feiyan the more... the more... laugh SP delighted Yilin heart

què <u>*yù*</u> *suānchǔ.*
however grieved

{The more heartily QV Feiyan laughed, the more grieved Yilin was.}

Example (83) is in the form of "*yù shì p, què yù shì q*", in which "*zhēn qíguài*" ('really strange') and the like can usually occur at the beginning, showing an exclamation of surprise. The following are three examples:

(84) 真奇怪，时间<u>愈</u>长，你在想象中却离我<u>越</u>近。

Zhēn qíguài, shíjiān <u>yù</u>... <u>yuè</u>... cháng, nǐ zài
really strange time the more... the more... long you at

*xiǎngxiàng-zhōng **què** lí wǒ <u>yuè</u> jìn.*
in imagination however be away from I close

{It's strange that the longer the time, the closer you are to me in my imagination.}

(85) 他这人也怪！人家越冷淡他，他却越亲热。

Tā zhè rén yě guài! Rénjiā <u>yuè</u>... <u>yuè</u>...
he this person somewhat strange other people the more... the more...

Occurrence of què in "yuè p, yuè q" 145

lěngdàn	*tā,*	*tā* **què**	*yuè qīnrè.*
treat someone with indifference	him	he however	treat someone with affection

{He is a bit strange! The more people treat him with indifference, the more affectionate he is towards them.}

(86) 人的感情实在是个复杂的函数，我<u>愈是</u>躲避袁野，心里却<u>愈是</u>更多地想到他。

Rén	*de*	*gǎnqíng*	*shízài*	*shì*	*gè*	*fùzá*	*de*	*hánshù,*	*wǒ*
person	SP	feelings	indeed	COP	CL	complex	SP	function	I

yù shì . . . *yù shì* . . .	*duǒbì*	*Yuán Yě,*	*xīn-lǐ*	**què**	*yù shì*	*gèng*
the more . . . the more . . .	avoid	YUAN Ye	in heart	however		more

duō	*de*	*xiǎngdào*	*tā.*
much	SP	think about	him

{Human feelings are indeed a complex function. The more I avoid YUAN Ye, the more I think about him.}

Connectives, such as *dànshì* and *kěshì*, can often occur in sentences with *què*, hence "*dàn yuè p, què yuè q*". The connective *què* indicates that *q* contrasts with *p*, but *dàn* indicates that there is an opposition between the current sentence and its preceding sentence. The two connectives collocate with each other and emphasize unusualness, as in the following two examples:

(87) ……真恨不得一步跨进南京城。但火车<u>越</u>近南京，我却<u>越</u>感到情怯。

. . . *zhēn*	*hènbùdé*	*yī*	*bù*	*kuà-jìn*	*Nánjīng Chéng.*	***Dàn***
really	can't wait to do something	one step	step into		Nanjing City	but

huǒchē	*yuè* . . . *yuè* . . .	*jìn*	*Nánjīng,*	*wǒ*	**què**	*yuè*
train	the more . . . the more . . .	approach	Nanjing	I	however	

gǎndào	*qíngqiè.*
feel	timid

{. . . I wish I could get to Nanjing in one step. However, the closer the train is to Nanjing, the more timid I feel.}

(88) 雯雯使劲儿点点头，心想以后再不敢忘记了。可<u>越</u>想着不忘，忘性却<u>越</u>大。

Wénwén	*shǐjìnr*	*diǎn-diǎn tóu,*	*xīn*	*xiǎng yǐhòu zài*	*bù*	*gǎn*
Wenwen	put in energy	nod-REDP head	heart	think later again	NEG	dare

wàngjì	*le.*	***Kě***	*yuè* . . . *yuè* . . .	*xiǎng-zhe*	*bù*	*wàng,*
forget	MP	but	the more . . . the more . . .	think-PRG	NEG	forget

wàngxìng	**què**	*yuè*	*dà.*
forgetfulness	however		big

{Wenwen nodded her head hard, thinking that she would never forget it again. However, the more she wanted to remember it, the more forgetful she was.}

In some cases, the two adversatives are far apart, but their functions are the same, as in the following example:

146 *Occurrence of què in "yuè p, yuè q"*

(89) 我不敢回顾过去二十多天里我的行为举止，然而像是有意惩罚我似的，有一张银幕在我眼帘内部显示出我的种种劣迹，我眼睛闭得<u>越</u>紧，银幕上的影子却<u>越</u>清晰。

Wǒ bù   gǎn   huígù guòqù èrshí   duō   tiān lǐ   wǒ de xíngwéi jǔzhǐ,
I   NEG dare recall past   twenty more day LOC I   SP behavior manner

rán'ér *xiàng . . . shìde shì   yǒuyì   chéngfá wǒ shìde, yǒu   yī   zhāng*
but   as if   COP deliberately punish me   there be one CL

yínmù zài wǒ yǎnlián nèibù xiǎnshì-chū wǒ de zhǒng-zhǒng lièjì,   wǒ
screen at my eye   inside show   I   SP kind-REDP misdeed my

yǎnjing bì   de   <u>yuè</u> . . . <u>yuè</u> . . .   jǐn,   yínmù-shàng de yǐngzi
eye   close SP the more . . . the more . . . tight on screen   SP shadow

què   <u>yuè</u>   *qīngxī.*
however   clear

{I dare not recall my behavior during the past 20-plus days. However, as if I had been intentionally punished, there was a screen inside my eyes showing all my misdeeds. The more tightly I closed my eyes, the more clearly I could see the images on the screen.}

The word *jiù* cannot occur in sentences in the form of "*yuè p, què yuè q*". Compare (90) and (91):

(90) ……他<u>越是</u>想避嫌疑，这个嫌疑就<u>越</u>会洗不清。

. . . tā   <u>yuè shì</u> . . . <u>yuè</u> . . .   xiǎng bì   xiányí, zhè gè xiányí
he   the more . . . the more . . . want avoid suspicion this CL suspicion

jiù   <u>yuè</u>   *huì   xǐ bù qīng.*
then   will   cannot be washed clean

{. . . the more he tried to avoid suspicion, the less he could.}

(91) ……他<u>越是</u>想避嫌疑，这个嫌疑却<u>越</u>会洗不清。

. . . tā   <u>yuè shì</u> . . . <u>yuè</u> . . .   xiǎng bì   xiányí, zhè gè xiányí
he   the more . . . the more . . . want avoid suspicion this CL suspicion

què   <u>yuè</u>   *huì   xǐ bù qīng.*
however   will   cannot be washed clean

{. . . the more he tried to avoid suspicion, the less he could.}

7.3.3   Cooccurrence of fǎn'ér/piānpiān and què

To emphasize the abnormal correlation, *fǎn'ér* or *piānpiān* can be used in sentences in the form of "*yuè p, yuè q*" but, even so, *què* can also be present to further highlight the abnormal correlation. The following are two examples:

(92) ……和齐克接触了半年多时间，时间<u>越</u>长，对他反而<u>越</u>感到陌生了。

...hé Qí Kè   jiēchù   le   bàn nián duō   shíjiān, shíjiān
with QI Ke be in contact with PEF half year more time   time

| *yuè* . . . *yuè* . . . | | | *cháng,* | *duì* | *tā* | **fǎn'ér** | | *yuè* | *gǎndào* |

the more . . . the more . . . long   to   him   on the contrary   feel

mòshēng   le.

strange   MP

{. . . (she) has been in contact with QI Ke for more than half a year. The more they are in contact, the stranger (she) feels that he is.}

(93) 他<u>越是</u>这样, 我偏偏主动接近他, 一如既往。

*Tā   yuè shì   zhèyàng,   wǒ   **piānpiān**   zhǔdòng   jiējìn   tā,*

he   more   so   I   on the contrary   initiatively   approach   him

yīrú-jìwǎng.

same as the past

{He behaves like that, but I take the initiative to approach him, as always.}

Example (92) is in the form of "*yuè p, fǎn'ér yuè q*", in which *fǎn'ér* emphasizes that the result is just opposite to the expectation. The adversative *què* can be used to further highlight the opposition, as in (94). Example (93) is in the form of "*yuè p, piānpiān yuè q*", in which *piānpiān* is employed to highlight the unexpectedness of the result. In this sentence *què* can be also used, as in (95).

(94) ⋯⋯时间越长, 对他却反而越感到陌生了。

. . . shíjiān yuè . . . yuè . . .   cháng,   duì   tā   què   fǎn'ér

time   the more . . . the more . . . long   to   him   however   on the contrary

yuè gǎndào mòshēng le.

feel   strange   MP

{. . . the more they are in contact, the stranger (she) feels that he is.}

(95) 他越是这样, 我却偏偏主动接近他⋯⋯

Tā yuè shì zhèyàng, wǒ què   piānpiān   zhǔdòng   jiējìn   tā . . .

he   more   so   I   however   on the contrary   initiatively   approach   him

{He behaves like that, but I take the initiative to approach him . . .}

By the same token, (47) which can be rewritten as the (96):

(96) ⋯⋯ 越禁止我做的事, 我却偏要做, ⋯⋯

. . . yuè jìnzhǐ wǒ zuò de shì,   wǒ què   piān   yào zuò, . . .

more   forbid   I   do   SP   thing   I   however   on the contrary   will   do

{. . . the more I'm not allowed to do something, the more I'll do it . . .}

To avoid repetition, *què* and *fǎn'ér* can be used alternately in a sentence. For example:

(97) 人再忙, 追求爱情的空儿还是腾得出来。<u>越</u>忙的时候可能身体里的要求却<u>越</u>为迫切, 海绵挤水一样抽出的柔情欢宴的空儿反而<u>越</u>多。

Rén   zài   máng, zhuīqiú àiqíng de kòngr háishì téng de chūlái.

person even more busy pursue love SP time still   can be allocated

148 *Occurrence of què in "yuè p, yuè q"*

Yuè . . . *yuè* . . . *yuè* . . .				*máng*	*de*	*shíhou*	*kěnéng*	*shēntǐ-lǐ*
the more . . . the more . . . the more . . .				busy	SP	time	possible	in body
de yāoqiú	***què***	*yuè*	*wéi*	*pòqiè,*	*hǎimián*	*jǐ*	*shuǐ yīyàng*	*chōu-chū*
SP need	however	COP	urgent	sponge	squeeze	water	same	draw
de	*róuqíng*	*huānyàn*	*de*	*kòngr*	***fǎn'ér***		*yuè*	*duō.*
SP	tenderness	feast	SP	time	on the contrary		much

{No matter how busy you are, there is always time to pursue love. The busier you are, the more urgent your physiological needs are, and the more time you can find for the enjoyment of the feast of intimacy—like squeezing water out of sponge.}

In this example, *què* and *fǎn'ér* occur alternately, i.e., "*yuè* . . . *què yuè* . . . *fǎn'ér yuè* . . .".

There are two points worth noting. First, in the consequent, even if *fǎn'ér* is used, *yuè* still needs to be present, whereas *yuè* can be absent if *piānpiān* occurs. Second, *què* can be placed before *fǎn'ér* or simply replace it. For instance, (94) can be rewritten as (98).

(98)   ……时间越长，对他却越感到陌生了。

... shíjiān	*yuè* . . . *yuè* . . .		*cháng,*	*duì*	*tā*	*què*	*yuè*	*gǎndào*
time	the more . . . the more . . .		long	to	him	however		feel
mòshēng	*le.*
strange	MP

{. . . the more they are in contact, the stranger (she) feels that he is.}

By comparison, *què* can be placed before *piānpiān*, but cannot replace it. For example, in (95), *què* precedes *piānpiān*, but *piānpiān* cannot be removed.

7.3.4 *Normal or abnormal correlation*

In some cases, whether the correlation is normal or abnormal depends on how the speaker views or feels about the relationship between the result and the condition, rather than the correlation itself. The following are two examples:

(99)   读书越多，脸皮愈薄。

| *Dúshū* | *yuè* . . . *yù* . . . | | *duō,* | *liǎnpí* | *yù* | *báo.* |
| do reading | the more . . . the more . . . | | much | face skin | | thin |

{The better someone is read, the thinner their skin is.}

(100)   他越是说不知道，人们就越从守口如瓶的机密劲里判断出会议的重要性。

Tā	*yuè shì* . . . *yuè* . . .		*shuō*	*bù*	*zhīdào,*	*rén-men*	*jiù*	*yuè*	*cóng*
he	the more . . . the more . . .		say	NEG	know	people	then		from
shǒukǒu-rúpíng	*de*	*jīmì*	*jìn*	*lǐ*	*pànduàn-chū*	*huìyì*	*de*
be tight-lipped	SP	secret	expression	LOC	judge	meeting	SP
zhòngyàoxìng.
importance

{The more he said he didn't know, the more people assumed that the meeting was important from his tight-lipped expression.}

Some may think the correlation in (99) is normal because well-read people are normally thin-skinned as they are knowledgeable, but others may hold the opposite view: being thin-skinned is unusual for well-educated people because they are not fearful of speaking in public. Similarly, some might think the correlation in (100) is normal, for they take for granted that there is causality between "zipped lips" and "important meeting". However, other people might think the correlation is abnormal because they think it is abnormal to continue making wild guesses about the meeting after the person has said that he knows nothing about it.

Therefore, in some complex sentences in the form of "*yuè p, yuè q*", the correlation between the condition and the result cannot reflect a unanimous view or understanding. Thus, whether the correlation is normal or abnormal is somewhat equivocal. Anyway, as long as the speaker thinks the result is abnormal or unusual, the adversative connective *què* or *fǎn'ér* can be used in sentences in the form of "*yuè p, yuè q*". The following are two examples:

(101) 读书越多，脸皮却越薄！（你这是怎么搞的？）

| *Dúshū* | *yuè* . . . *yuè* . . . | *duō,* | *liǎnpí* | *què* | *yuè* | *báo!* | *(Nǐ* |
| do reading | the more . . . the more . . . | much | face skin | however | | thin | you |

| *zhè* | *shì* | *zěnme* | *gǎo* | *de?)* |
| this | COP | how | do | MP |

{The better you are read, the thinner your skin is. (What's the matter with you?)}

(102) 他越是说不知道，人们却越从守口如瓶的机密劲里判断出会议的重要性。
（真是神经过敏！）

| *Tā* | *yuè shì* . . . *yuè* . . . | *shuō* | *bù* | *zhīdào,* | *rén-men* | *què* | *yuè* | *cóng* |
| he | the more . . . the more . . . | say | NEG | know | people | however | | from |

| *shǒukǒu-rúpíng* | *de* | *jīmì* | *jìn* | *lǐ* | *pànduàn-chū* | *huìyì* | *de* |
| be tight-lipped | SP | secret | expression | LOC | judge | meeting | SP |

| *zhòngyàoxìng.* | *(Zhēn* | *shì* | *shénjīng guòmǐn!)* |
| importance | really | COP | oversensitive |

{The more he said he didn't know, the more people assumed that the meeting was important from his tight-lipped expression. (They were really oversensitive!)}

7.3.5 *Normal vs. abnormal and positive vs. negative*

The correlation between *p* and *q* in a sentence in the form of "*yuè p, yuè q*" can be normal or abnormal and can be positive or negative. A normal correlation refers to a relationship in which the condition results in a normal result, while an abnormal correlation is one in which the subsequent result is abnormal. A positive correlation is a relationship between two variables—the condition and result in this form—move in the same direction, while a negative correlation is one in which one variable increases as the other one decreases, and vice versa.

There is no necessary connection between these two pairs of concepts.

Positive correlations can be normal or abnormal, as in the following two examples:

150   *Occurrence of què in "yuè p, yuè q"*

(103) 贡献越大，得到的荣誉也越大。

Gòngxiàn   yuè ... yuè ...   dà,   dédào de   róngyù yě   yuè dà.
contribution the more ... the more ... great get   SP honor   also   great
{The greater the contribution, the greater the honor.}

(104) 贡献越大，受到的攻击（却）也越大。

Gòngxiàn   yuè ... yuè ...   dà,   shòudào de   gōngjī (què)
contribution the more ... the more ... great receive   SP attack   however

yě   yuè dà.
also   great

{The greater the contribution, the heavier the attack.}

The correlations in both aforementioned examples are positive. However, the correlation in (103) is a normal one, thus *què* cannot be used, while the correlation in (104) is an abnormal one, thus *què* can be present.

Negative correlations can be normal or abnormal as well, as in the following two examples:

(105) 有的人，做的事情越少，受到的照顾（却）越多！

Yǒude rén,   zuò de shìqing yuè ... yuè ...   shǎo, shòudào de
some   person do SP thing   the more ... the more ... few   receive   SP

zhàogù (què)   yuè duō!
care for however   much

{The less some people do, the more they are taken care of!}

(106) 一个干部，做的事情越少，群众的意见自然会越多！

Yī   gè   gànbù, zuò de shìqing yuè ... yuè ...   shǎo, qúnzhòng
one CL cadre do SP thing   the more ... the more ... few   the masses

de yìjiàn   zìrán   huì yuè duō!
SP complaint naturally will   many

{The less a leader does, the more complaints the masses will naturally have!}

The correlations in the above two examples are negative. However, the correlation in (105) is an abnormal one, thus *què* can be used, while the correlation in (105) is a normal one, thus *què* cannot be present.

Summary

First, "*yuè p, yuè q*" indicates a conditional correlation, in which the amount of *q* changes in relation to the change of the amount of *p*.

Second, "*yuè p, yuè q*" usually shows a hypothetical judgment, but sometimes the condition in the judgment is a reality. If a hypothetical judgment is combined with an isomorphic judgment based on a condition in the realis mood, hence a

Occurrence of què in "yuè p, yuè q" 151

special form of inference—hypothetical-realis syllogism—will be formed, i.e., "*yuè p, yuè q; yuè p, yuè q*".

Third, "*yuè p, yuè q*" can be expanded forward to the form "*yuè p, yuè q; yuè q, yuè r*" or "*yuè p, yuè q; yuè q, (yě) (jiù) yuè r*", or backward to form "*yuè p, yuè q; yuè q, yuè p*".

Fourth, as a verb, *yuè* usually occurs in pairs, but in some cases, it can occur singly in the antecedent or the consequent.

Fifth, words following *yuè* differ in part of speech, function, and usage. In some cases, "*yuè shì*" acts as an adverb, and in other cases it is a combination of *yuè* and a judgmental verb.

Sixth, "*yuè p, yuè q*" can show a normal correlation or an abnormal one. The adversative connective *què* can be present in an abnormal correlation.

Seventh, either positive or negative correlation can be normal or abnormal. Whether or not *què* can be used depends on the normality of the correlation, regardless of whether the correlation is positive or negative.

Eighth, to judge whether a correlation is normal or abnormal is sometimes subjective. In other words, for the same correlation, different people may have different judgments. The word *què* won't be used by someone who views the correlation as a normal one; on the other hand, it will be used if the correlation is understood as an abnormal one and the contradiction needs to be emphasized.

NB Some examples in this chapter are cited from literary works, political essays, articles, and so on. The sources are listed as follows:

1. *Changjiang Literature* (《长江》) 1983(4), including (43); 1984(1), including (7), (12), and (20); 1984(2), including (84);
2. *Changcheng* (《长城》) 1984(1), including (53), (61), (63), (86), and (93);
3. *Eight Hundred Words in Modern Chinese* (《现代汉语八百词》), including (41);
4. *Emperor Yongzheng* (《雍正皇帝》) by Eryuehe (二月河), including (33);
5. *Fiction Monthly* (《小说月报》) 1996(12), including (82); 1997(5), including (22) and (32); 1997(6), including (97);
6. *Flower City* (《花城》) 1983(3), including (24), (37), and (77); 1984(2), including (26) and (79);
7. *Harvest* (《收获》) 1983(3), including (23) and (87); 1983(6), including (8), (47), and (54); 1984(3), including (18) and (88);
8. *Hongyan* (《红岩》) 1983(2), including (80); 1984(1), including (19);
9. *Lotus* (《芙蓉》) 1983(4), including (85); 1983(5), including (42); 1983(6), including (99);
10. *October* (《十月》) 1982(2), including (57); 1982(4), including (56); 1983(4), including (6), (46), (60), (78), and (100); 1983(5), including (81); 1984(2), including (17), (40), (45), (55), and (89); 1984(4), including (13), (21), (30), (35), and (48);
11. *Qingming* (《清明》) 1983(3), including (26) and (92);

152 *Occurrence of què in "yuè p, yuè q"*

12 *State of Divinity* (《笑傲江湖》) by JIN Yong (金庸), including (83);
13 *Xiao Shuo Jia* (《小说家》) 1984(1), including (5), (44), and (90);
14 *Zhongpian Xiaoshuo Xuankan* (《中篇小说选刊》) 1995(2), including (38); 1997(4), including (25) and (31).

Notes

1 LV Shuxiang (吕叔湘) proposed that the sentence form "*yuè p, yuè q*" shows correlative change. More details can be referred to in his *Sketches of Chinese Grammar* 《中国文法要略》, published by The Commercial Press in 1982, pp. 367–369.
2 ZHANG Zhigong (张志公) stated that "the longer the time, the better the effect is" includes the meaning that "so long as the time is longer, the effect is better" or the meaning that "no matter how long the time is, the effect is great". Details can be found in *Knowledge about Chinese* (《汉语知识》) edited by ZHANG Zhigong and published by People's Education Press in 1977, p. 226.
3 With respect to the forms of hypothetical judgment in which the condition is both necessary and sufficient conditions, more details can be found in *Knowledge about Logic and Its Application* (《逻辑知识及其应用》) written by XING Fuyi and published by Hubei People's Press in 1979, p. 87.
4 LV Shuxiang has talked about proportional relationship and functional relationship. The source is as [1], p. 367.
5 LV Shuxiang has talked about proportional relationship and functional relationship. The source is as [1], p. 367.
6 More details can be found in *Eight Hundred Words in Modern Chinese* (《现代汉语八百词》), written by LV Shuxiang and published by The Commercial Press in 1980, p. 567.
7 In some cases, *yuè* can also occur before a subject-predicate structure or before a prepositional structure.

8 *"bùdàn bù p, fǎn'ér q"* and its adversative relationship

Among Chinese complex sentences, there is a special type of progressive complex sentences that involve both reversion and progression from the anterior clause to the posterior clause, hence "reversed progressive sentences". Due to the reversion, those sentences have some of the features of adversative complex sentences. The typical form of reversed progressive sentences is *"bùdàn bù p, fǎn'ér q"* (*'not only not *p*; on the contrary, *q*').

Based on this typical form, this chapter first discusses the reversed progressive relationship, and sentences with and without adversative markers, and then summarizes the features of reversed progressive sentences.

8.1 Reversed progressive relationship

8.1.1 *Relationship between p and q*

In *"bùdàn bù p, fǎn'ér q"*, the reversed progressive relationship exists between p and q. If only p and q are considered, the movement from p to q is a progressive reversion.

Reversion means that what p states and what q states are opposite. The movement from p to q is reversion, to be exact. In some cases, p and q are complementary antonyms, and in other cases, p and q are temporary antonymous expressions formed by the connective *"bùdàn bù . . . fǎn'ér . . ."*. Compare the following two pairs of examples:

(1)   a 他不但不哭，反而笑了。
        Tā bùdàn bù kū, fǎn'ér xiào-le.
        he not only NEG cry on the contrary laugh-PEF
        {Instead of crying, he laughed.}

    b 他不但不笑，反而哭了。
        Tā bùdàn bù xiào, fǎn'ér kū-le.
        he not only NEG laugh on the contrary cry-PEF
        {Instead of laughing, he cried.}

DOI: 10.4324/9781003374237-8

154   *"bùdàn bù p, fǎn'ér q" and its adversative relationship*

(2)   a 他不但不哭，反而演得更加认真了。
Tā bùdàn bù kū, fǎn'ér yǎn de gèngjiā rènzhēn le.
he not only NEG cry on the contrary perform SP more serious PEF
{Not only did he not cry, but he performed even more seriously.}

b 他不但不笑，反而演得更加认真了。
Tā bùdàn bù xiào, fǎn'ér yǎn de gèngjiā rènzhēn le.
he not only NEG laugh on the contrary perform SP more serious PEF
{Not only did he not laugh, but he performed even more seriously.}

Progression means that *p* and *q* are not polar opposites. The denial of *p* does not result in *q*. The progression from *p* to *q* is a process of hierarchical change process, which can be described as follows:

$p \rightarrow$ neither *p* nor $q \rightarrow q$

The level "neither *p* nor *q*" refers to an invisible intermediate state between *p* and *q*, which can be termed as a "hierarchical distance" between *p* and *q*.

The following three points about the hierarchical distance need to be further clarified about the hierarchical distance.

First, the intermediate state between *p* and *q* in "*bùdàn bù p, fǎn'ér q*" can be obtained after the exclusion of *p* and *q*, i.e., i) "*jì bù (méi) p, yě bù (méi) q*" ('neither *p* nor *q*'); or ii) "*suīrán bù (méi) p, dàn yě bù (méi) q*" ('although not *p*, not *q*, either'). This can be illustrated by the following examples:

(3)   a 他既没哭，也没笑。
Tā jì ... yě ... méi kū, yě méi xiào.
he both ... and ... NEG cry NEG laugh
{He neither cried nor laughed.}

b 他虽然没哭，但也没笑。
Tā suīrán méi kū, dàn yě méi xiào.
he although NEG cry but also NEG laugh
{Although he didn't cry, he didn't laugh, either.}

(4)   a 他既没笑，也没哭。
Tā jì ... yě ... méi xiào, yě méi kū.
he both ... and ... NEG smile NEG cry
{He neither laughed nor cried.}

b 他虽然没笑，但也没哭。
Tā suīrán méi xiào, dàn yě méi kū.
he although NEG smile but also NEG cry
{Although he didn't laugh, he didn't cry, either.}

"bùdàn bù p, fǎn'ér q" and its adversative relationship   155

Second, if *p* and *q* have no intermediate state in between, then they cannot be linked by *"bùdàn bù . . . fǎn'ér . . ."*. Compare:

(5) a 我不想死，我想活！

    Wǒ   *bù*   *xiǎng*   *sǐ,*   *wǒ*   *xiǎng*   *huó!*
    I   NEG   want   die   I   want   live
    {I don't want to die; I want to live!}

    b 我不但不想死，反而想活！（？）

    Wǒ   *bùdàn*   *bù*   *xiǎng*   *sǐ,*   *fǎn'ér*   *xiǎng*   *huó!(?)*
    I   not only   NEG   want   die   on the contrary   want   live
    {Not only do I not want to die, but I want to live!} (?)

(6) a 我不想活，我想死！

    Wǒ   *bù*   *xiǎng*   *huó,*   *wǒ*   *xiǎng*   *sǐ!*
    I   NEG   want   live   I   want   die
    {I don't want to live; I want to die!}

    b 我不但不想活，反而想死！（？）

    Wǒ   *bùdàn*   *bù*   *xiǎng*   *huó,*   *fǎn'ér*   *xiǎng*   *sǐ!(?)*
    I   not only   NEG   want   live   on the contrary   want   die
    {Not only do I not want to live, but I want to die!} (?)

There is no intermediate state between *"xiǎng sǐ"* ('want to die') and *"xiǎng huó"* ('want to live'), thus it is pointless to use *"bùdàn bù . . . fǎn'ér . . ."*. If *"bùdàn bù . . . fǎn'ér . . ."* is to be used, *p* and *q* should be reworded so as to create a hierarchical distance. The following are two examples:

(7) a 我不但不想死，反而想活得比谁都好！

    Wǒ   *bùdàn*   *bù*   *xiǎng*   *sǐ,*   *fǎn'ér*   *xiǎng huó de bǐ shuí*
    I   not only   NEG   want   die   on the contrary   want   live SP than anyone
    dōu hǎo!
    all   good
    {Not only do I not want to die, but I want to live better than anyone else!}

    b 我不但不想活，反而想死得越早越好！

    Wǒ   *bùdàn*   *bù*   *xiǎng*   *huó,*   *fǎn'ér*   *xiǎng*   *sǐ*   *de*
    I   not only   NEG   want   live   on the contrary   want   die   SP
    yuè . . . yuè . . .   *zǎo*   *yuè*   *hǎo!*
    the more . . . the more . . .   early   good
    {Not only do I not want to live, but I want to die as soon as possible!}

Third, some hierarchical distances are bigger than others. The use of modifiers or some other grammatical elements can extend the hierarchical distance.

156 *"bùdàn bù p, fǎn'ér q"* and its adversative relationship

The modifier *gèngjiā* ('more') is often used in *q*, which increases the degree of *q*, extends the distance between *p* and *q*, and formally shows that *q* is at a higher level in the hierarchy. The following are two examples:

(8) 每当她来找孙如一，林素十回有九回在那里，他<u>不但不</u>尽快回避，让恋人们去温存亲热，<u>反而</u>谈兴更浓……
Měi   dāng   tā   lái   zhǎo Sūn Rúyī, Lín Sù   shí   huí   yǒu
always at (the time) she come find SUN Ruyi LIN Su ten time there be
jiǔ   huí   zài   nàli,   tā   bùdàn   bù   jǐnkuài   huíbì,   ràng
nine time be at there he not only NEG as quickly as possible avoid let
liànrén-men qù   wēncún qīnrè,   fǎn'ér   tán xìng   gèng nóng...
lover-PL   DC tender intimate on the contrary talk interest more strong
{LIN Su was there nine times out of ten when she came to SUN Ruyi. Instead of leaving the couple alone as quickly as possible so that they could make out, his interest in talking with them became even stronger.}

(9) 可是今天，陈炯明的心事也许是太沉重了，他一听侍妾提醒他该吃饭了，<u>不但不</u>像过去那样欣然领首，<u>反而</u>更加烦躁起来……
Kěshì   jīntiān,   Chén Jiǒngmíng   de   xīnshì
but   today   CHEN Jiongming SP   something weighing on one's mind
yěxǔ   shì   tài chénzhòng le,   tā yī   tīng shìqiè   tíxǐng   tā   gāi
perhaps COP too heavy   MP he once hear concubine remind him should
chīfàn le,   bùdàn   bù   xiàng guòqù   nàyàng xīnrán hànshǒu,
eat   MP not only NEG be like the past that joyful nod
fǎn'ér   gèngjiā   fánzào-qǐlái...
on the contrary more   start to be irritable
{But today, perhaps something was weighing too heavily on CHEN Jiongming's mind. When his concubine reminded him that it was time to eat, he didn't nod his head as joyfully as he used to; on the contrary, he got more irritable . . .}

8.1.2 *Relationship between "bù p" ('not p') and "q"*

In sentences in the form of *"bùdàn bù p, fǎn'ér q"*, if what is between *"p"* and *"q"* is a progressive reversion, then what is between *"bù p"* and *"q"* is a reversed progression.

First, there is no opposition between *"bù p"* and *"q"*; what exists in between is a hierarchical distance, which can be attested by replacing *"bù p"* with its synonym in the affirmative form. For example:

(10) 老师反复交代一定要把标语贴正，可是，你看他贴的，不但不正，反而歪得特别厉害！
Lǎoshī fǎnfù   jiāodài yīdìng   yào   bǎ biāoyǔ tiē-zhèng,
teacher repeatedly remind definitely must BA slogan put something up straight
kěshì, nǐ   kàn tā tiē   de, bùdàn bù   zhèng, fǎn'ér
but   you look he put something up SP not only NEG straight on the contrary
wāi   de tèbié   lìhai!
askew SP extremely badly

"bùdàn bù p, fǎn'ér q" and its adversative relationship 157

{The teacher repeatedly reminded him that the slogan must be put up at an even level, but look at what he did: not only isn't the slogan even, but it is terribly askew!}

The affirmative synonym of *"bù zhèng"* ('not straight') is *wāi* ('askew'). Obviously, *"wāi de tèbié lìhai"* ('extremely askew') is a higher level than *wāi* in the hierarchy. Sometimes it is not easy to find a ready-to-use affirmative synonym of *"bù p"*; for instance, *"bù xiào"* ('not laugh'). However, theoretically, any *"bù p"* must have an affirmative synonym, and therefore there must be a progressive relationship between the affirmative synonym of *"bù p"* and *"q"*.

Second, the progressive relationship between *"bù p"* and *"q"* is reversed in nature. Once *"bù p"* is replaced by its affirmative synonym, the reversion will no longer exist. For example, in (10), once *"bù zhèng"* is replaced by *wāi*, the reversion between the anterior clause and the posterior clause will disappear; only the progression remains. The loss of the reversion and the stay of the progression can be attested by the fact that once *"bù p"* is replaced by its affirmative synonym, the adversative connective *fǎn'ér* needs to be replaced by the progressive marker *érqiě*. Compare:

(11) a ⋯⋯你看他贴的，不但歪，<u>反而</u>歪得特别厉害！（–）

  ...Nǐ kàn tā tiē   de, bùdàn wāi, <u>fǎn'ér</u>   wāi
  you look he put something up SP not only askew on the contrary askew
  de tèbié   lìhai!
  SP extremely badly
  {. . . look at what he did: not only is the slogan askew, but on the contrary, it is terribly askew!}

  b ⋯⋯你看他贴的，不但歪，<u>而且</u>歪得特别厉害！（+）

  ...nǐ kàn tā tiē   de, bùdàn wāi, <u>érqiě</u> wāi de
  you look he put something up SP not only askew but also askew SP
  tèbié   lìhai!
  especially badly
  {. . . look at what he did: not only is it askew, but it is terribly askew!}

Thus, the relationship between *"bù p"* and *"q"* suffices to reveal the reversed progressive relationship indicated by *"bùdàn bù p, fǎn'ér q"*.

8.2 Four key elements in the reversed progressive sentences

8.2.1 *Progression precursor bùdàn and its synonyms*

The first key element in a reversed progressive sentence is the progression precursor *bùdàn* or its synonym. The most typical progression precursor is *bùdàn*. Other progression precursors include *bùjǐn*, *bùguāng*, *bùdàn*, *fēidàn*, and the like. The following are three examples:

158 *"bùdàn bù p, fǎn'ér q" and its adversative relationship*

(12)　……粮菜价钱<u>不光不降</u>, <u>反而</u>升高……

... *liáng cài*　　*jiàqián* <u>*bùguāng*</u> <u>*bù*</u>　*jiàng,* <u>*fǎn'ér*</u>　　*shēnggāo* ...
grain　vegetable price　not only NEG fall　on the contrary rise
{. . . the prices of food and vegetables are not just falling, but on the contrary, they are rising . . .}

(13)　死崔不像往常，<u>不单不怕他</u>，<u>反而</u>比他还横……

Sǐcuī bù　*xiàng wǎngcháng,* <u>*bùdān*</u>　<u>*bù*</u>　*pà tā,* <u>*fǎn'ér*</u>　　*bǐ*
Sicui NEG be like the past　　not only NEG fear him on the contrary than

tā hái hèng ...
him more tough
{Unlike before, not only isn't Sicui scared of him, but he is tougher than him . . .}

(14)　玻璃花<u>非但不动心</u>，<u>反而</u>把话凿死……

Bōlihuā <u>*fēidàn*</u>　<u>*bù*</u>　*dòngxīn,* <u>*fǎn'ér*</u>　　*bǎ*　*huà*
Bolihua　not only　NEG　be tempted　on the contrary　BA　words

záo-sǐ ...
fix something tightly
{Not only wasn't Bolihua tempted, but he said something that gave himself no way back . . .}

Progressive complex sentence markers include progression precursors, represented by *bùdàn*, and progression undertakers, represented by *érqiě*. A progressive complex sentence may include both the precursor and the undertaker, or either of them. Even if there is a semantic progression from one event to the other stated in the sentence, the sentence is not to be regarded as a progressive one with the absence of both the precursor and the undertaker. The following are some examples:

(15)　a 他<u>不仅</u>能作曲，<u>而且</u>能演唱。（progressive）

Tā <u>*bùjǐn*</u>　*néng zuòqǔ,* <u>*érqiě*</u>　　*néng yǎnchàng.*
he　not only can　compose music but also　can　sing in a performance
{Not only can he compose, but he can also perform songs.}

b 他<u>不仅</u>能作曲，也能演唱。（progressive）

Tā <u>*bùjǐn*</u>　*néng zuòqǔ,*　　***yě***　*néng yǎnchàng.*
he　not only can　compose music　also　can　sing in a performance
{Not only can he compose music, but he can also perform songs.}

c 他能作曲，<u>而且</u>能演唱。（progressive）

Tā néng zuòqǔ, <u>*érqiě*</u>　　*néng yǎnchàng.*
he　can　compose music　what's more　can　sing in a performance
{He can compose music, and what's more, he can perform songs.}

"bùdàn bù p, fǎn'ér q" and its adversative relationship   159

d 他能作曲，也能演唱。（coordinate）

Tā	*néng*	*zuòqǔ,*	***yě***	*néng*	*yǎnchàng.*
he	can	compose music	also	can	sing in a performance

{He can compose music and perform songs.}

Reversed progressive sentences are a subtype of progressive sentences. The progressive relationship in reversed progressive complex sentences is marked and highlighted by the progression precursor. Without the presence of the progression precursor *bùdàn* or its synonym as a progressive relationship marker, "*bù p, fǎn'ér q*" is not a progressive sentence form, because after all, *fǎn'ér* is not a progression undertaker.

8.2.2 *Reversion marker fǎn'ér and its synonyms*

The second key element in a reversed progressive sentence is the reversion marker *fǎn'ér* or its synonym. Reversion markers, represented by *fǎn'ér*, fall into three categories. The word *fǎn'ér* is different from the other markers in the other two categories in meaning and tone.

Category I: words meaning "in opposition", such as *fǎn'ér, fǎn, dǎo, fǎndào, dàofǎn, xiāngfǎn, fǎnguòlái,* and so on. The following are four examples:

(16) <u>不但不进</u>，<u>反</u>往外掏！

Bùdàn	*bù*	*jìn,*	*fǎn*	*wǎng*	*wài*	*tāo!*
not only	NEG	make money	on the contrary	toward	outside	pay out

{Not only (do we) not make money, but we pay out instead!}

(17) ……那妹子<u>非但不</u>像个站在街门口，搔首弄姿的风流女子，<u>倒</u>像是被哪家主人踢出屋的可怜的猫儿。

... nà mèizi <u>*fēidàn*</u> <u>*bù*</u> *xiàng gè zhàn zài jiē   ménkǒu, sāoshǒu-nòngzī*
that   girl   not only NEG be like CL stand in street doorway coquette
de fēngliú nǚzǐ, <u>*dào*</u>   *xiàng shì bèi   nǎ   jiā*
SP dissolute woman on the contrary be like COP PASSIVE certain household
zhǔrén tī-chū   wū   de kělián   de māor.
master kick out house SP pathetic SP cat

{Not only doesn't that girl look like a coquettish woman standing in the doorway, but, on the contrary, she's like a poor cat kicked out of the house by her owner.}

(18) 农民<u>不但没有</u>钱赚，<u>反倒</u>月月要从口袋里掏钱出来。

Nóngmín <u>*bùdàn*</u> <u>*méiyǒu*</u> *qián zhuàn,* <u>*fǎndào*</u>   *yuè-yuè   yào*
farmer   not only not have money earn on the contrary every month must
cóng kǒudài-li tāo-chūlái qián   chūlái.
from in pocket take out money

{Instead of being able to make money, farmers have to take it out of their pockets every month.}

160 *"bùdàn bù p, făn'ér q" and its adversative relationship*

(19) 这样捱到第二天，<u>不仅不</u>见好转，<u>相反</u>病得更沉重了。

Zhèyàng   ái   dào   dì'èr   tiān, <u>bùjǐn</u>   <u>bù</u>   jiàn   hǎozhuǎn,
so   hold on   reach   second day   not only   NEG   appear   get better

<u>xiāngfǎn</u>   bìng   de   gèng   chénzhòng   le.
on the contrary   be ill SP   more   serious   PEF

{(She) held on like this until the next day. Instead of getting better, on the contrary, (she) became more ill.}

Category II: adversative connective *què*, which is the only word that can be used in "*bùdàn bù p, făn'ér q*". The following are three examples:

(20) 回场后的哲学家<u>非但没</u>受到大家尊敬，<u>却</u>成了笑柄⋯⋯

Huí   chǎng   hòu   de   zhéxuéjiā   <u>fēidàn</u>   <u>méi</u>   shòudào   dàjiā   zūnjìng,
return farm   after   SP   philosopher   not only   NEG   receive   everyone respect

<u>què</u>   chéng-le   xiàobǐng . . .
however   become-PEF   laughingstock

{After returning to the (salt) farm, not only didn't the philosopher win anyone's respect, but he became a laughingstock . . .}

(21) 谁知道，三梆子<u>非但不</u>闹，<u>却</u>花钱买下这桌酒饭，<u>反过来</u>谢谢他。

Shuí   zhīdào, Sānbāngzi <u>fēidàn</u>   <u>bù</u>   nào,   <u>què</u>   huā   qián
who   know   Sanbangzi not only   NEG   make trouble however spend money

măi-xià   zhè   zhuō   jiǔfàn,   fănguòlái   xièxiè tā.
buy   this   table   food and drink on the contrary thank him

{Unexpectedly, not only didn't Sanbangzi make any trouble, but he thanked him with this feast.}

(22) 可厂长换了几届，<u>非但没</u>有救活厂子，银行的贷款<u>却</u>直线上升，几年时间就突破了千万大关。

Kě   chǎngzhǎng   huàn-le   jǐ   jiè, <u>fēidàn</u>   <u>méiyǒu jiù-huó chǎngzi,</u>
but   factory director change-PEF several CL not only   NEG   save   factory

yínháng de dàikuǎn <u>què</u>   zhíxiàn shàngshēng, jǐ   nián shíjiān jiù
bank   SP loan   however straight rise   several year time   quickly

tūpò   le   qiānwàn   dàguān.
break through PEF ten million mark

{The factory director has changed several times; however, not only did none of them save the factory, but the bank loan soared, having broken through the ten-million mark within a few years.}

Category III: words meaning "unexpectedly", including *piānpiān* ('deliberately'), *jìngrán* ('unexpectedly'), *jūrán* ('unexpectedly'), and so forth. The following are three examples:

(23) 他瞅玻璃花这架式，<u>非但没有</u>赶紧缩回去，<u>偏偏</u>觍着脸笑嘻嘻地说⋯⋯

Tā   chǒu   Bōlihuā   zhè   jiàshi,   <u>fēidàn</u>   <u>méiyǒu</u>   gǎnjǐn   suō-huíqù,
he   see   Bolihua   this   manner   not only   NEG   immediately draw back

"bùdàn bù p, fǎn'ér q" and its adversative relationship 161

piānpiān   tiǎn-zhe   liǎn   xiàoxīxī   de   shuō...
deliberately be brazen-PRG face   grin   SP   say
{He saw that Bolihua, instead of drawing back, grinned brazenly and said . . .}

(24)　……巡防士兵大声呼唤要他们靠岸，他们<u>不但不</u>听，<u>竟然</u>朝岸上开枪……

. . . xúnfáng shìbīng dàshēng hūhuàn yào tā-men kào   àn,   tā-men bùdàn
patrol   soldier loud   shout ask them come to shore they   not only
bù   tīng, jìngrán   cháo àn-shàng kāiqiāng . . .
NEG listen unexpectedly at   ashore   fire
{. . . the patrol shouted for them to come ashore; however, not only didn't they
listen, but they fired at the shore . . .}

(25)　可你老伴<u>非但没有</u>镇压这帮忤逆，<u>居然</u>用唱过歌的大嗓门说："……趁热
喝！……"

Kě   nǐ   lǎobàn   fēidàn   méiyǒu zhènyā zhè bāng wǔnì,
but your old spouse not only NEG   suppress this group disobedient people
jūrán   yòng chàng-guò gē de dà   sǎngmén shuō:" . . . Chèn rè
unexpectedly use sing-EXP   song SP loud voice   say   while   hot
hē! . . ."
drink
{But instead of suppressing these disobedient people, your better half even
said in a loud voice in which he/she had sung, ". . . drink it while it's
warm! . . ."}

Thus, the following three facts are worth noting.

First, reversion markers are employed to mark and highlight the reversion of
the posterior clause.

Second, reversion markers of the three categories can be used interchangeably.
Words in Category I emphasize that the situations are in opposition to each other,
words in Category II stress that the situation has greatly changed, and words in
Category III highlight unexpectedness. Words in Categories I and II usually cooccur to indicate the combination of reversion and opposition, as in the following
two examples:

(26)　朝鲜战场的战火……<u>不但不</u>使她感到恐惧，<u>相反</u>却有着使她马上投身战斗的
巨大吸引力。

Cháoxiǎn zhànchǎng de   zhànhuǒ . . . bùdàn   bù   shǐ   tā   gǎndào
Korea   battlefield SP   flames of war not only NEG   make her   feel
kǒngjù,   xiāngfǎn   què   yǒu-zhe shǐ   tā   mǎshàng   tóushēn
frightened on the contrary however have-PRG make her immediately devote
zhàndòu de jùdà   xīyǐnlì.
fight   SP great attraction
{The flames of war on the Korean battlefield . . . was a powerful attraction that
drew her into battle immediately rather than frightening her.}

162　*"bùdàn bù p, fǎn'ér q" and its adversative relationship*

(27) 好在他并没有逃走的迹象…… 不但没有逃走，相反，却直奔边防站而来。

Hǎozài　　tā bìng　　méiyǒu táozǒu de jìxiàng . . . bùdàn　　méiyǒu táozǒu,
fortunately he indeed NEG escape SP sign　　not only NEG escape

xiāngfǎn,　　què　　zhí　　bèn　　biānfáng zhàn ér　　lái.
on the contrary however directly rush border　　post and come

{Fortunately, there was no sign of him escaping . . . instead of running away, he came straight to the border post.}

In the above two aforementioned examples, *xiāngfǎn* precedes *què*. If *fǎn'ér* replaces *xiāngfǎn*, it needs to follow *què*. The following example is a rewrite of (26):

(28) 朝鲜战场的战火……不但不使她感到恐惧，却反而有着使她马上投身战斗的巨大吸引力。

Cháoxiǎn zhànchǎng de zhànhuǒ . . .　　bùdàn　　bù　　shǐ　　tā　　gǎndào
Korean　　battlefield　　SP flames of war not only NEG make her feel

kǒngjù,　　què　　fǎn'ér　　yǒu-zhe　　shǐ　　tā　　mǎshàng　　tóushēn
frightened however on the contrary have-PRG make her immediately devote

zhàndòu de jùdà xīyǐnlì.
fight SP great attraction

{The flames of war on the Korean battlefield . . . was a powerful attraction that drew her into battle immediately rather than frightening her.}

Compare (29) with *xiāngfǎn* preceding *què* and (30) with *fǎn'ér* following *què*:

(29) 它非但未落入人的圈套，相反，却用自己的超常行为嘲笑了高智商的人，使人在它的面前，陷入了惶惑不安和未知的可怕中。

Tā fēidàn　　wèi　　luò-rù rén　　de quāntào, xiāngfǎn,　　què　　yòng
it not only NEG drop in human SP trap　　on the contrary however use

zìjǐ　　de chāocháng　　xíngwéi cháoxiào-le gāo zhìshāng　　de
oneself SP extraordinary behavior ridicule-PEF high intelligence quotient SP

rén,　　shǐ　　rén　　zài tā de miànqián, xiànrù-le　　huánghuò-bù'ān hé
human make human in it SP front　　fall into-PEF panicking　　and

wèizhī　　de kěpà-zhōng.
unknown SP in terror

{Instead of falling into the trap set by humans, it ridiculed high-IQ human beings with its extraordinary behavior, which made them panic and fall into the fear of uncertainty in front of it.}

(30) 它非但未落入人的圈套，却反而用自己的超常行为嘲笑了高智商的人，……

Tā fēidàn　　wèi　　luò-rù rén　　de quāntào, què　　fǎn'ér　　yòng
it not only NEG drop in human SP trap　　however on the contrary use

zìjǐ　　de　　chāocháng　　xíngwéi　　cháoxiào-le gāo zhìshāng
oneself SP extraordinary behavior ridicule-PEF high intelligence quotient

de rén, . . .
SP human

"*bùdàn bù p, fǎn'ér q*" and its adversative relationship   163

{Instead of falling into the human trap, it ridiculed high-IQ human beings with its extraordinary behavior . . .}

Third, *fǎn'ér* is not a progression undertaker. If *fǎn'ér* were a progression undertaker, then its synonyms—such as *fǎndào, dǎo,* and *xiāngfǎn*—would all be progression undertakers and *fǎn'ér* could be used interchangeably with them. If *fǎndào, dǎo,* and *xiāngfǎn* were progression undertakers, then those that can cooccur with them—such as *què, piānpiāni*—would be progression undertakers as well. As a matter of fact, *fǎn'ér* has no intrinsic connection with the progressive relationship, but it is inevitably and absolutely related to reversion. The following are two examples:

(31) 在台上不一定什么都看得清，在台下<u>反面</u>看得清。

Zài tái-shàng bù yīdìng shénme dōu kàn de qīng, zài tái-xià
at on stage NEG definitely anything all can see clearly at off stage
<u>*fǎn'ér*</u>   *kàn de qīng.*
on the contrary   can see clearly

{You may not be able to see everything clearly when you are on stage, but you can see it clearly when you are off stage.}

(32) 在台下看得清，在台上<u>反面</u>不一定什么都看得清。

Zài tái-xià kàn de qīng, zài tái-shàng <u>*fǎn'ér*</u>   *bù yīdìng*
at off stage can see clearly at on stage on the contrary NEG definitely
shénme dōu kàn de qīng.
anything all can see clearly

{You can see everything clearly when you are off stage, but, on the contrary, you may not be able to see it clearly when you are on stage.}

There is no reason to regard these two examples, particularly (32), as progressive sentences. The following is another example:

(33) ……一个市委书记的千金小姐，怎么会看中一个下贱的罪犯，却<u>反面</u>看不上省委书记的儿子？

. . . yī gè shìwěi   shūjì de qiānjīn xiǎojiě, zěnme huì
one CL municipal party committee secretary SP daughter why can
kàn-zhòng yī gè xiàjiàn de zuìfàn, **què**   <u>*fǎn'ér*</u>   *kàn bù shàng*
favor one CL lowly SP criminal however on the contrary despise
shěngwěi   shūjì de érzi?
provincial party committee secretary SP son

{. . . how could the daughter of a municipal Party Secretary favor a lowly criminal, but despise the son of a provincial Party Secretary?}

There is no progressive relationship in this sentence, where the cooccurrence of *què* and *fǎn'ér* only indicates a reversion.

In "*bùdàn bù p, fǎn'ér q*", the progression from *p* to *q* is not marked or explicated by *fǎn'ér*. In this respect, "*bùdàn bù p, fǎn'ér q*" is similar to "*bùdàn p, yě*

164 *"bùdàn bù p, fǎn'ér q" and its adversative relationship*

q" in the sense that in both forms there is only a progression precursor, but no progression undertaker. In a grammar textbook, *"bù p, fǎn'ér q"*—in which no progressive precursor is present—is taken as a form of progressive sentences,[1] which is an obvious misunderstanding. The following two examples are reversed sentences with no progression involved.

(34) 他<u>不</u>因何伏兴的尖刻和发泄般的话语而生气，<u>反而</u>充满了对陈春梅夫妇的同情。

Tā	*bù*	*yīn*	*Hé Fúxīng*	*de*	*jiānkè*	*hé*	*fāxiè*	*bān*	*de*	*huàyǔ*	*ér*
he	NEG	because	HE Fuxing	SP	acrimonious	and	vent	like	SP	words	then

shēngqì,	*fǎn'ér*	*chōngmǎn-le*	*duì*	*Chén Chūnméi*	*fūfù*
become angry	on the contrary	be filled-PEF	with	CHEN Chunmei	couple

de	*tóngqíng.*
SP	sympathize

{Instead of being offended by the acrimony that HE Fuxing vented, he was filled with sympathy for CHEN Chunmei and his husband.}

(35) （老乔保）并<u>不</u>说责备他的话，<u>反而</u>自责自疚……

(Lǎo Qiáobǎo)	*bìng*	*bù*	*shuō*	*zébèi*	*tā*	*de*	*huà,*	*fǎn'ér*
old QIAO Bao	indeed	NEG	say	blame	him	SP	words	on the contrary

zìzé	*zìjiù* ...
blame oneself	ashamed of oneself

{[Old QIAO Bao] didn't blame him; on the contrary, he blamed himself and felt ashamed of himself . . .}

8.2.3 *Negator bù, méi, and its synonyms*

The third key element in a reversed progressive sentence is the negator, such as *bù*, *méi*, and its synonyms, among which *bù* is the most frequently used one, thus it is taken as the typical negator. However, other negators, such as *méi, méiyǒu, wèi*, and so on, are not uncommon in reversed progressive sentences. The following are two examples:

(36) 他<u>不仅没</u>能让最先的念头消失，<u>反而</u>又拖出第二个念头。

Tā	*bùjǐn*	*méi*	*néng*	*ràng*	*zuìxiān*	*de*	*niàntou*	*xiāoshī,*	*fǎn'ér*
he	not only	NEG	can	make	first	SP	thought	disappear	on the contrary

yòu	*tuō-chū*	*dì'èr*	*gè*	*niàntou.*
again	have	second	CL	thought

{Not only did he fail to give up the first thought, but he had a second one.}

(37) 他<u>非但未</u>能压倒这人，<u>反而</u>被这人来嘲笑。

Tā	*fēidàn*	*wèi*	*néng*	*yā-dǎo*	*zhè*	*rén,*	*fǎn'ér*	*bèi*	*zhè*
he	not only	NEG	can	overpower	this	person	on the contrary	PASSIVE	this

rén	*lái*	*cháoxiào.*
person	DC	ridicule

{Not only did he fail to overpower this man, but he was ridiculed by him.}

"bùdàn bù p, fǎn'ér q" and its adversative relationship   165

In *"bùdàn bù p, fǎn'ér q"*, the negator, i.e., *bù*, *méi*, or its synonyms, acts as the adverbial, and *p* is the predicative in the affirmative form and modified by the negator. The status and function of *bù*, *méi* or its synonyms are quite subtle. For one, the progression precursor *bùdàn* marks the progressive relationship between *"bù p"* and *q*, therefore the negator and *p* should be understood as a semantic unit in the negative form. For another, the collocation of the negator and *fǎn'ér* marks the reversed progressive relationship between *p* and *q*. In this sense, the negator introduces *p*, and *fǎn'ér* introduces *q*, hence a reversed sentence form *"bù /méi p, fǎn'ér q"*, as is illustrated by the following figure:

$$bùdàn \longrightarrow \quad \text{(progression with reversion)}$$
$$\boxed{bù\ p} \qquad \boxed{q}$$
$$bù \longrightarrow fǎn'ér \leftarrow \quad \text{(reversion with progression)}$$

Diagram 8.1 Formation of *"bùdàn bù p, fǎn'ér q"*

In some cases, the negator can be used repeatedly, with each occurrence introducing a different *p*, such as:

bùdàn bù p₁ bù p₂ bù p₃, fǎn'ér q.
bùdàn méi p₁ méi p₂ méi p₃, fǎn'ér q.

The following are two examples:

(38) 她不但不哭，不吵，不砸东西，反而变得温顺起来了。
  Tā bùdàn bù kū, bù chǎo, bù zá dōngxi, fǎn'ér
  she not only NEG cry NEG quarrel NEG smash thing on the contrary
  biàn de wēnshùn-qǐlái le.
  become SP start to be gentle PEF
  {Not only isn't crying, quarreling, or smashing things, but she's becoming meek.}

(39) 她不但没哭，没吵，没砸东西，反而变得温顺起来了。
  Tā bùdàn méi kū, méi chǎo, méi zá dōngxi, fǎn'ér
  she not only NEG cry NEG quarrel NEG smash thing on the contrary
  biàn de wēnshùn-qǐlái le.
  become SP start to be gentle PEF
  {Not only didn't she cry, quarrel, or smash things, but she became meek.}

In some cases, some other elements occur between *bùdàn* and the negator. The following are two examples:

(40) 水位不但一点没降，反而老在上升。
  Shuǐwèi bùdàn yīdiǎn méi jiàng, fǎn'ér lǎo zài
  water level not only a little NEG drop on the contrary always in progress
  shàngshēng.
  rise
  {Not only hasn't the water level dropped at all, but it keeps rising.}

166 *"bùdàn bù p, fǎn'ér q" and its adversative relationship*

(41) （香香）不但洗脚水不帮他倒，反叫他帮着去洗碗喂猪潲。

(Xiāngxiāng) bùdàn xǐ jiǎo shuǐ bù bāng tā dào, fǎn
Xiangxiang not only wash foot water NEG help him pour on the contrary
jiào tā bāng-zhe qù xǐ wǎn wèi zhūshào.
ask him help-PRG go wash dish feed swill

{Not only didn't [Xiangxiang] help him pour the foot washing water, but she asked him to help wash the dishes and feed the pigs with swill.}

In some sentences, the semantic unit containing the negator cannot be regarded as an "adverbial + predicative in the affirmative form": *bù* is a modifier in the complement or *méi/méiyǒu*, a verb meaning "not have", and acting as the predicate. In these sentences, the semantic unit containing *bù* or *méi* is not the typical "*bù p*" in "*bùdàn bù p, fǎn'ér q*", thus the entire unit should be understood as *p*. To put it another way, these sentences, although in the form of "*bùdàn bù p, fǎn'ér q*", are "*bùdàn p, fǎn'ér q*" in essence. What is worth noting is that semantically what *p* denotes in the former form is just the opposite of what *p* denotes in the latter form.

The following are four examples:

(42) 他苦苦思索着，"留有异物" 这念头<u>不但压不下去</u>，<u>反而</u>越来越强烈。

Tā kǔ-kǔ sīsuǒ-zhe, "liú yǒu yìwù" zhè niàntou <u>bùdàn</u>
he hard-REDP think-PRG remain there be foreign matter this thought not only
yā <u>bù</u> xiàqù, <u>fǎn'ér</u> yuèláiyuè qiángliè.
cannot suppress on the contrary more and more intense

{He thought hard. Not only couldn't the worry of "some foreign matter remaining there" be suppressed, but it became stronger and stronger.}

(43) 家里积攒的那点血汗钱，都被媳妇手拿把掐攥着，他<u>不仅</u>一个子抠<u>不出</u>来，<u>反倒</u>会惹一肚子气。

Jiā-lǐ jīzǎn de nà diǎn xuèhàn qián, dōu bèi xífu
in family save SP that bit blood and sweat money all PASSIVE wife
shǒuná-bǎqiā zuàn-zhe, tā <u>bùjǐn</u> yī gè zǐ kōu <u>bù</u> chūlái,
hold tightly in the hand grasp-PRG he not only one CL coin cannot get out
<u>*fǎndào*</u> *huì rě yī dùzi qì.*
on the contrary will get one stomach angry

{The hard-earned savings were tightly held by his wife. If he asked her for any, not only would he get nothing, but he would make himself angry.}

(44) 那张嘴，猝不及防，<u>不但开不出玩笑</u>，竟然冻住了。

Nà zhāng zuǐ, cùbù-jífáng, <u>bùdàn</u> kāi <u>bù</u> chū wánxiào,
that CL mouth sudden and unprepared not only cannot make jokes
jìngrán dòng-zhù le.
unexpectedly freeze PEF

{(He) was caught unprepared. Not only was (he) unable to make any jokes, but (he) became speechless.}

"*bùdàn bù p, fǎn'ér q*" and its adversative relationship   167

(45) ······ 他<u>不但</u>没有了听众，倒常常成了大家讥讽的对象······

...*tā*   ***bùdàn***   ***méiyǒu**-le*   *tīngzhòng,*   *dào*   *chángcháng*
he   not only   not have-PEF   audience   on the contrary   often

chéng-le   *dàjiā*   *jīfěng*   *de*   *duìxiàng* ...
become-PEF   everyone   ridicule   SP   object

{. . . not only did he lose his audience, but he often became the object of ridicule . . .}

8.2.4   Antonymous p and q

The fourth key element in a reversed progressive sentence is the antonymous parts "*p*" and "*q*", both of which are usually in the affirmative form. In certain cases, *p* can be in the negative form, but it is strictly restricted, as can be illustrated by the following examples.

(46) 这么敏感的问题，他不但没有避开不谈，反而一有机会就大讲特讲。

Zhème mǐn'gǎn de wèntí, tā bùdàn   *méiyǒu **bì-kāi bù**   **tán**, fǎn'ér*
such   sensitive SP issue he not only NEG   avoid NEG talk on the contrary

yī . . . jiù . . . yǒu jīhuì   *jiù dàjiǎng-tèjiǎng.*
as soon as   have chance   talk volubly

{Instead of shying away from such a sensitive issue, he talks volubly about it whenever he gets a chance.}

(47) 这种坏人，他不但没开除不用，反而让他当了伙食班班长。

Zhè zhǒng huài rén,   *tā bùdàn*   *méi **kāichú bù**   **yòng**, fǎn'ér*
this Kind bad person he not only NEG dismiss NEG employ on the contrary

ràng tā   *dāng-le huǒshíbān*   *bānzhǎng.*
make him be-PEF cooking team captain

{Not only didn't he fire such a villain, but, on the contrary, he made him the captain of the cooking team.}

(48) 碰了钉子，他不但没躺倒不干，反而信心越来越足。

Pèng dīngzi le   *dīngzi, tā bùdàn*   *méi **tǎng-dǎo bù**   **gàn**, fǎn'ér*
be rejected PEF   he not only NEG lie down NEG work on the contrary

xìnxīn   *yuèláiyuè*   *zú.*
Confidence more and more full

{After he was rejected, instead of lying down, he became more and more confident.}

Such sentences have three features.

First, if *p* is in the negative form, *q* cannot be in the negative form.

Second, if *p* is in the form of "V_1 *bù* V_2", "*bù* V_2" is a reiteration of V_1 and subordinate to V_1. The meaning of the sentence would remain the same even if "*bù* V_2" was removed. However, if V_1 was left out, the sentence would barely make sense. For example, (46) can be rewritten as (49a), but not as (49b).

168 *"bùdàn bù p, fǎn'ér q" and its adversative relationship*

(49) a 这么敏感的问题，他不但没有避开，反而一有机会就大讲特讲。

Zhème mǐn'gǎn de wèntí, tā bùdàn méiyǒu bì-kāi fǎn'ér
such sensitive SP issue he not only NEG avoid on the contrary
yī…jiù… yǒu jīhuì jiù dàjiǎng-tèjiǎng.
as soon as have chance talk volubly

{Instead of shying away from such a sensitive issue, he talks volubly about it whenever he gets a chance.}

b* 这么敏感的问题，他不但没有不谈，反而一有机会就大讲特讲。

Zhème mǐn'gǎn de wèntí, tā bùdàn méiyǒu bù tán, fǎn'ér
such sensitive SP issue he not only NEG NEG talk on the contrary
yī…jiù… yǒu jīhuì jiù dàjiǎng-tèjiǎng.
as soon as have chance talk volubly

Third, the negator before "V$_1$ *bù* V$_2$" needs to be *méi* or *méiyǒu* rather than *bù*. In some sentences, *q* can be negative in form, but these sentences have a number of distinct features. The following are two examples:

(50) 现在，不但没挣到新衣裳，反而连回家的车票钱也不够了。

Xiànzài, bùdàn méi zhèng-dào xīn yīshang, fǎn'ér lián…yě…
now not only NEG earn new clothes on the contrary even
*huí jiā de chēpiào qián yě **bù gòu** le.*
return home SP bus ticket money NEG enough MP

{Not only hasn't (he) earned enough to buy new clothes, but (he) doesn't even … have enough money to buy a bus ticket to go home.}

(51) 结果呢，不但不能当上什么"司令"，反而连自己的老婆也不肯听从"命令"了。

Jiéguǒ ne, bùdàn bù néng dāng-shàng shénme "sīlìng",
result MP not only NEG can become so-called commander
*fǎn'ér lián…yě… zìjǐ de lǎopo yě **bù kěn** tīngcóng*
on the contrary even… oneself SP wife NEG be willing obey
"mìnglìng" le.
order MP

{As a result, not only did he fail to become the so-called "commander", but even his wife won't obey his "orders".}

There are three distinctive features of sentences in which *q* is negative in form. First, *p* needs to be in the affirmative form and cannot be in the form of "V$_1$ *bù* V$_2$". Second, *q* is introduced by "*lián—yě*", which can make the situation sound extreme so as to stress the sharp contrast between *p* and *q* in the speaker's mind. Third, if "*lián—yě*" is absent, it can be added or the sentence can be rephrased to include "*lián—yě*". Among the following sentences, (52a) can be rewritten as (52b), and (53a) as (53b).

"bùdàn bù p, fǎn'ér q" and its adversative relationship **169**

(52) a 大家东奔西走全是为了她。可是，她不但不感激，反而不以为然。

dàjiā   dōngbēn-xīzǒu quán shì   wèile tā. Kěshì, tā   bùdàn   bù
everyone run around   all COP for   her but   she not only NEG
gǎnjī,   fǎn'ér   bùyǐwéirán.
be grateful on the contrary not regard it as right
{Everyone is running around for her sake, but instead of being grateful, she's not even impressed.}

→b ……反而连大家为她东奔西走也不以为然。

…fǎn'ér   lián … yě …   dàjiā   wèi   tā   dōngbēn-xīzǒu   yě
on the contrary even …   everyone for   her   run around   also
bùyǐwéirán.
not regard it as right
{… on the contrary, she's not even impressed by people running around for her sake.}

(53) a 吃了药，不但不见好转，反而下不了床了。

Chī-le   yào,   bùdàn   bù   jiàn   hǎozhuǎn,   fǎn'ér
take-PEF medicine not only NEG appear get better on the contrary
xià bù liǎo chuáng   le.
cannot get out of bed   MP
{After taking the medicine, not only didn't (he) get better; but (he) couldn't even get out of bed.}

→b ……反而连床也下不了了。

…fǎn'ér   lián … yě …   chuáng   yě   xià bù liǎo   le.
on the contrary even …   bed   cannot get out of   MP
{… on the contrary, (he) couldn't even get out of bed.]}

In order to highlight the sharp contrast between the two clauses, *fǎn'ér* can be added if it is absent in sentences where a negative form introduced by "*lián—yě*" occurs after "*bùdàn bù p*", or *fǎn'ér* can be used to replace *érqiě*. The following are two examples:

(54) 结果喜凤妈不仅没拍屁股骂街，连大门都没开，实在没一丝儿风雨。

Jiéguǒ Xǐfèng mā   bùjǐn   méi   pāi   pìgu   màjiē,
result Xifeng's mother not only NEG hit bottom shout abuse in the street
lián … dōu …   dàmén dōu méi   kāi,   shízài méi   yī   sīr   fēngyǔ.
even …   gate NEG open really NEG one CL storm
{As a result, instead of hitting her own bottom and shouting abuse in the street, Xifeng's mother didn't even open her door. Indeed, she didn't make a scene.}

170 *"bùdàn bù p, fǎn'ér q" and its adversative relationship*

(55) 时间一天一天过去了，他不但未按期回贵阳，而且连一封信也没有写给我。

    Shíjiān yī   tiān yī   tiān guòqù-le, tā bùdàn   wèi   àn
    time   one day one day pass-PEF he not only NEG according to
    qī   huí   Guìyáng, érqiě   lián . . . *yě* . . . *yī fēng xìn   yě méiyǒu*
    schedule return Guiyang but also even . . .   one CL   letter   NEG
    xiě-gěi wǒ.
    write to me
    {As time went by, not only did he fail to return to Guiyang on time, but he didn't even write a letter to me.}

    In (54), *fǎn'ér* can be present and placed before *"lián dàmén . . ."*, while in (55) *érqiě* can be replaced by *fǎn'ér*.

8.3 Marked and unmarked reversed progressive sentences

8.3.1 *Differences between the marked and the unmarked*

In terms of linguistic form, marked reversed progressive sentences are those in which *fǎn'ér* or its synonym is used to underline the reversed progressive relationship, whereas unmarked reversed progressive sentences are those in which no marker occurs to make the hidden reversed progressive relationship explicit. Compare the following two examples:

(56) 前些时，把吴越列为"揭、批、查"的对象，<u>他不但没有说清楚，最近却反而更加趾高气扬了</u>。

    Qián xiē   shí,   bǎ Wú Yuè liè wéi   "jiē, pī,   chá"   de
    before some time BA WU Yue list become expose criticize investigate SP
    duìxiàng, tā <u>bùdàn   méiyǒu</u> shuō-qīngchǔ, zuìjìn <u>què</u>   <u>fǎn'ér</u>
    target   he not only NEG   explain clearly lately however on the contrary
    gèngjiā zhǐgāo-qìyáng le.
    more   arrogant   MP
    {Some time ago, WU Yue was listed as a target of "exposing, criticizing, and investigating". Not only didn't he come clean about his problems, but he's even cockier lately.}

(57) 前些时，把吴越列为"揭、批、查"的对象，<u>他不但没有说清楚</u>，最近更加趾高气扬了……

    Qián xiē   shí,   bǎ Wú Yuè liè wéi   "jiē, pī,   chá"   de
    before some time BA WU Yue list become expose criticize investigate SP
    duìxiàng, tā <u>bùdàn</u>   <u>méiyǒu</u> shuō-qīngchǔ, zuìjìn gèngjiā zhǐgāo-qìyáng le . . .
    target   he not only NEG   explain clearly lately more   arrogant   MP
    {Some time ago, WU Yue was listed as a target of "exposing, criticizing, and investigating". Not only didn't he come clean about his problems, but he's even cockier lately.}

Example (56) is a marked reversed progressive sentence, whereas (57) is an unmarked one.

Strictly speaking, only marked reversed progressive sentences can be generalized as a reversed progressive sentence form due to the presence of a reversion marker. In comparison, unmarked ones lack a reversion marker that could distinguish them from general progressive sentences, but they can still be regarded as sentences in the "unmarked reversed progressive sentence forms" because the reversion marker *fǎn'ér* can be added or used to replace *érqiě*.

8.3.2 Two types of unmarked reversed progressive sentences

According to the occurrence or non-occurrence of a progression undertaker, unmarked reversed progressive sentences fall into two types.

Type I: with a progression undertaker

The most frequently-used progression undertaker is the conjunction *érqiě*. The following are two examples:

(58) 洗药瓶、倒痰盂、奔忙不停做"她"下手的杨兴中，不但不坏，而且好像是
受了某种冤枉的好人。

Xǐ   yào   píng, dào tányú, bēnmáng   bù   tíng zuò "tā" xiàshǒu
wash medicine bottle pour spittoon bustle about NEG stop be her assistant

de   Yáng Xīngzhōng,   bùdàn   bù   huài, érqiě   hǎoxiàng   shì
SP YANG Xingzhong   not only   NEG   bad   but also   seem   COP

shòu-le   mǒu   zhǒng   yuānwang   de   hǎo   rén.
suffer-PEF   certain   kind   wrong   SP   good   person

{Washing the medicine bottles and pouring the spittoons, YANG Xingzhong bustled about as "her" assistant. Not only wasn't he bad, but he seemed to be a good man who had been wronged in some way.}

(59) 从此，两个孩子不仅没有再得到一个父亲，而且又失去了自己的母亲，并
且，永远地失去了。

Cóngcǐ,   liǎng gè háizi bùjǐn   méiyǒu zài   dédào yī   gè   fùqīn, érqiě
since then two   CL child not only NEG   again get   one CL father but also

yòu   shīqù-le zìjǐ   de mǔqīn, bìngqiě, yǒngyuǎn de shīqù-le.
again lose-PEF oneself SP mother and   forever   SP lose -PEF

{From then on, the two children would not have a father anymore, but they also lost their mother, and forever.}

In some sentences, the progression undertaker is acted by the conjunction *shènzhì* ('even'), which, however, can be replaced by *érqiě*, as is illustrated by the following example:

(60) ⋯⋯光凭过去的本事和经验，在今天建设时期，不但未必能成为英雄，甚至
还有可能成为罪人。

... guāng píng guòqù de běnshì hé jīngyàn,   zài jīntiān jiànshè   shíqī,
just   rely the past SP skill   and experience in   today   construct period

172 *"bùdàn bù p, fǎn'ér q" and its adversative relationship*

bùdàn	wèibì		néng	chéngwéi	yīngxióng,	shènzhì	hái	yǒu
not only	unnecessarily	can	become	hero		even	still	there be

kěnéng	chéngwéi	zuìrén.
possible	become	sinner

{In today's construction period, not only may someone not become a hero, but they may even become a sinner if solely relying on past skills and experience.}

In any unmarked reversed progressive sentences with *"bùdàn bù . . . érqiě . . ."*, *érqiě* can be replaced by *fǎn'ér*. If in a sentence *érqiě* cannot be substituted by *fǎn'ér*, then there is no reversed progressive relationship in the sentence, and the sentence is not a reversed progressive one. The following is an example:

(61) 不但没有热情，而且显不出真诚。

Bùdàn	méiyǒu	rèqíng,	**érqiě**	xiǎn bù chū	zhēnchéng.
not only	not have	enthusiasm	but also	cannot show	sincere

{(He) is not only unenthusiastic but also insincere.}

That *fǎn'ér* can replace *érqiě* does not mean that the former can occur exactly in the position of the latter because the former is an adverb but the latter is a conjunction. To be specific, if the subject is present, *érqiě* needs to precede the subject, but if it is replaced by *fǎn'ér*, *fǎn'ér* needs to follow the subject.[2] The following are two examples:

(62) 这么做，不仅防风林不会长，而且橡胶树很可能都要死去。

Zhème zuò,	bùjǐn	fángfēng	lín	bù	huì	zhǎng,	**érqiě**	xiàngjiāoshù
so	do	not only windbreak	forest	NEG	will	grow	but also	rubber tree

hěn	kěnéng	dōu	yào	sǐqù.
quite	may	all	will	die

{If you do so, not only won't the windbreaks grow, but the rubber trees will probably die.}

(63) 这么做，不仅防风林不会长，橡胶树反而很可能都要死去。

Zhème	zuò,	bùjǐn	fángfēng	lín	bù	huì	zhǎng,	xiàngjiāoshù
so	do	not only	windbreak	forest	NEG	will	grow	rubber tree

fǎn'ér	hěn	kěnéng	dōu	yào	sǐqù.
on the contrary	quite	may	all	will	die

{If this is done, not only won't the windbreaks grow, but the rubber trees will probably die.}

That *érqiě* can be replaced by *fǎn'ér* does not mean the two words have identical functions. In fact, *"bùdàn . . . érqiě . . ."* indicates a progression, whereas *"bù . . . fǎn'ér . . ."* marks a reversion. The blending of the two creates the reversed progressive sentence form. Theoretically speaking, *érqiě* and *fǎn'ér* do not exclude each other because they each have their own functions. The occurrence of *érqiě*

"*bùdàn bù p, fǎn'ér q*" and its adversative relationship   173

implies that it can be followed by *fǎn'ér*, whereas the presence of *fǎn'ér* indicates that there is a vacancy for *érqiě* before it, i.e.,

> *bùdàn bù p, érqiě Ø q*
> *bùdàn bù p, Ø fǎn'ér q*

However, in actual language use, cooccurrence of *fǎn'ér* and *érqiě* is very rare. The following is an example in which *fǎn'ér* and *érqiě* cooccur:[3]

(64) 家丑不可外扬，而且说出去反而让人家笑他是傻瓜。

Jiāchǒu		*bù*	*kě*	*wài*	*yáng,*	*érqiě*	*shuō-chūqù*
domestic disgrace		NEG	can	outside	publicize	but also	tell . . . to others

fǎn'ér	*ràng*	*rénjiā*	*xiào*	*tā*	*shì*	*shǎguā.*
on the contrary	let	other people	laugh at	he	COP	idiot

{His family scandal is not to be disclosed. If it was disclosed, people would make a fool of him.}

Usually either *fǎn'ér* or *érqiě* occurs in a sentence, which is probably for the sake of conciseness. Moreover, the statement that *érqiě* can be replaced by *fǎn'ér* is just based on the fact that in one sentence either of them is present. Compare the following examples:

(65) 他不仅不后悔起用郎平，<u>而且</u>（反而）下大力锤炼她。

Tā	*bùjǐn*	*bù*	*hòuhuǐ*	*qǐyòng*	*Láng Píng,*	<u>*érqiě*</u>	*(fǎn'ér)*
he	not only	NEG	regret	line up	LANG Ping	but also	on the contrary

xiàdàlì	*chuíliàn*	*tā.*
made great efforts	hone	her

{Not only didn't he regret lining up LANG Ping (to play), but he made great efforts to hone her (skills) instead.}

(66) 林吟不但没吓唬住，（而且）脸上的表情<u>反而</u>更认真、更执拗了。

Lín Yín	*bùdàn*	*méi*	*xiàhu-zhù,*	*(érqiě)*	*liǎn-shàng*	*de*	*biǎoqíng*
LIN Yin	not only	NEG	be frightened	but also	on face	SP	expression

<u>*fǎn'ér*</u>	*gèng*	*rènzhēn,*	*gèng*	*zhíniù*	*le.*
on the contrary	more	serious	more	stubborn	MP

{Not only wasn't LIN Yin frightened, but he looked more serious and more stubborn instead.}

Type II: without a progression undertaker
There are three subtypes: i) "*hái* . . ." is used in *q*; ii) "*lián—yě* . . ." is used in *q*; iii) no connective is used in *q*. The following three are examples of each subtype.

(67) 他<u>不仅</u>不生气，<u>还</u>为它欢呼。

Tā	<u>*bùjǐn*</u>	*bù*	*shēngqì,*	<u>*hái*</u>	*wèi*	*tā*	*huānhū.*
he	not only	NEG	be angry	unusually	for	it	cheer

{Instead of being angry, he cheered for it.}

174   *"bùdàn bù p, fǎn'ér q" and its adversative relationship*

(68)   不但他没有"上去"，连已经升上去的陈淳安也"落"下来了。

      Bùdān   *tā*   *méiyǒu*   *"shàngqù"*,   *lián . . . yě . . .*   *yǐjīng*   *shēng-shàngqù*   *de*
      not only   he   NEG   go up   even . . .   already   promote
      Chén Chún'ān   *yě*   *"luò"-xiàlái*   *le.*
      CHEN Chun'an   fall down   PEF

      {Not only didn't he "go up", but even CHEN Chun'an, who had already been promoted, has "fallen down".}

(69)   这样，不仅不能成为建设"红色根据地"的力量，很可能成为贫下中农身上的负担。

      Zhèyàng, bùjǐn   *bù*   *néng chéngwéi jiànshè "hóngsè gēnjùdì" de lìliàng,*
      so   not only NEG can   become build   red   base area SP force
      hěn   *kěnéng*   *chéngwéi pínxiàzhōngnóng shēn-shàng de fùdān.*
      quite possible become   poor farmer   on body   SP burden

      {Therefore, instead of becoming a force for the construction of the "red base areas", (we are) even likely to become a burden on the poor farmers.}

A progression undertaker, for instance, *érqiě*, can be used and placed at the beginning of the posterior clause in each of these sentences.

Since the progression undertaker is absent in such unmarked reversed progressive sentences as in the three aforementioned examples, *fǎn'ér* can be used and placed at the beginning of the posterior clause, and thus an unmarked sentence will become a marked one.

Since both *érqiě* and *fǎn'ér* can be added to those unmarked reversed progressive sentences, and *érqiě* and *fǎn'ér* cannot occur in each other's syntactic position, there are two vacancies in the posterior clause, i.e., "*bùdàn bù p, Ø Ø q*". The first vacancy is for the progression undertaker and the second one is for the reversion marker.

8.3.3   *Uses of the marked and unmarked*

A marked reversed progressive complex sentence is usually used if it semantically disagrees with its preceding sentence. Between the two sentences, *dàn* or its synonym is either present or absent. The following are two examples:

(70)   艾蒿在我和柴禾走后，孤掌难鸣……　然而，他不但不肯揭发我的罪行，反倒为我鸣冤叫屈，留党察看仍不改口。

      Àihāo zài . . . hòu wǒ hé Cháihé zǒu hòu, gūzhǎng-nánmíng . . .
      Aihao after   I   and Chaihe leave after cannot clap with one hand
      rán'ér**, tā **bùdàn** **bù** **kěn** jiēfā wǒ de zuìxíng, **fǎndào
      however he not only NEG be willing expose I   SP guilt   on the contrary
      wèi wǒ míngyuān jiàoqū, liú dǎng
      for me complain of unfairness complain of being wronged remain party

"bùdàn bù p, fǎn'ér q" and its adversative relationship 175

chákàn réng bù gǎikǒu.
observe still NEG withdraw previous remarks
{After Chaihe and I left, Aihao was alone and helpless . . . however, he not only refused to expose my guilt, but also complained of the injustice done to me. He still wouldn't take back what he had said even when he was placed on probation within the Party.}

(71)   矮子贵二又叹一口气，莫奈何，说出了大狗送香草电子手表的事。（但是）香草非但不怕丑，反以此为荣耀，故意拿话来激他。
Ǎizi Guì'èr yòu tàn yī kǒu qì, mònàihé, shuō-chū le
dwarf Gui'er again sigh one CL breath have no way out say PEF
Dàgǒu sòng Xiāngcǎo diànzǐ shǒubiǎo de shì. (**Dànshì**) Xiāngcǎo
Dagou give Xiangcao electronic watch SP matter but Xiangcao
feidàn bù pàchǒu, fǎn yǐ cǐ wéi róngyào, gùyì
not only NEG be bashful on the contrary take this be honorable deliberately
ná huà lái jī tā.
use words DC provoke him
{Dwarf Gui'er sighed again, helpless, and told the story of Dagou giving an electronic watch to Xiangcao, who, far from being bashful, was proud of it and verbally provoked him.}

In some cases, some expressions, such as *bùliào* ('unexpectedly'), "*shéi liào*" ('unexpectedly'), "*méi xiǎng dào*" ('unexpectedly'), and so on, can be present between the two sentences to indicate both opposition and unexpectedness. The following are two examples:

(72)   这一天，按照工程指挥部党委的决定，本来是全面停工休息。不料, 围堰工区有一个民工中队在年终评比的红榜发布时，不但没能乘上火箭和飞机，偏偏骑上了小毛驴—当了下游……
Zhè yī tiān, ànzhào gōngchéng zhǐhuībù dǎngwěi de
this One day according to project headquarters party committee SP
juédìng, běnlái shì quánmiàn tínggōng xiūxi. **Bùliào,** wéiyàn
decision originally COP full-scale stop working rest unexpectedly cofferdam
gōng qū yǒu yī gè míngōng zhōngduì zài . . . shí niánzhōng
work area there be one CL migrant worker team at the time end of year
píngbǐ de hóngbǎng fābù shí, bùdàn méi néng chéng-shàng huǒjiàn
appraise SP honor roll release time not only NEG can catch rocket
hé fēijī, piānpiān qí-shàng le xiǎo máolú —dāng-le
and plane deliberately get on PEF small donkey be-PEF
xiàyóu . . .
backward position
{That day, according to the decision of the Party Committee of the project headquarters, was originally a full-scale shutdown. Unexpectedly, when the end-of-year appraisal was released, a migrant worker team in the cofferdam work area found itself not only not rated as advanced, but also as backward . . .}

176   *"bùdàn bù p, fǎn'ér q" and its adversative relationship*

(73)   ……没想玩过十天，蝎子<u>不但未死</u>，其中一个母的，<u>竟</u>在背部裂开，爬出六只小蝎。

. . . méi xiǎng wán guò shí tiān, xiēzi   <u>bùdàn</u>   <u>wèi</u>   sǐ,   qízhōng yī   gè
NEG   think play pass ten day scorpion not only NEG die there   one CL
mǔ   de,   <u>jìng</u>   zài bèibù liè-kāi, pá-chū   liù zhī xiǎo   xiē.
female SP unexpectedly at   back   crack   crawl out six CL young scorpion
{. . . After ten days of being played with, not only didn't the scorpion die, but one of the females cracked in her back and six young scorpions crawled out.}

If a reversed progressive complex sentence semantically agrees with its preceding sentence, it is usually unmarked. The semantic agreement can be either of the following two types:

The first type is parallel, which means that the progressive complex sentence is a semantic repetition of its preceding sentence, and that the former includes another meaning introduced by "*bùdàn bù . . . (érqiě) . . .*". The following are two examples:

(74)   只有一个人不笑。不但不笑，而且流露出不满的神色……

Zhǐyǒu yī   gè   rén   bù   xiào. Bùdàn   bù   xiào,   érqiě   liúlù-chū
only   one CL person NEG smile not only NEG smile but also show
bùmǎn   de shénsè . . .
dissatisfied SP look
{There was only one person who didn't smile. Not only didn't he smile, but he also looked dissatisfied . . .}

(75)   ……他稳坐摊前不去劝解。不仅不劝解，还捂着嘴偷偷地笑。

. . . tā wěn   zuò tān-qián   bù   qù quànjiě.   Bùjǐn
he   steady sit   in front of stall NEG go stop people from fighting not only
bù   quànjiě,   hái wǔ-zhe   zuǐ   tōutōu de xiào.
NEG stop people from fighting and cover-PEG mouth secretly SP laugh
{. . . sitting firm at his stall, he didn't stop those from fighting. Not only didn't he stop them, but he even covered his mouth and laughed secretly.}

The second type is causal, which means that the progressive complex sentence is an effect, and its preceding sentence is the cause. Due to the cause-and-effect relationship, *yīncǐ* ('therefore') or its synonym can be present between the two sentences. The following are two examples:

(76)   她要在各方面造成顾堃的坚定情绪。（因此）不仅不能让任何悲观的阴影侵袭他，而且要在他周围造成一个乐观的环境影响！

*Tā yào zài gè   fāngmiàn zàochéng Gù Kūn de jiāndìng qíngxù. (**Yīncǐ**)*
she want in every aspect   make   GU Kun SP stable   mood   therefore
bùjǐn   bù   néng ràng rènhé bēiguān   de yīnyǐng qīnxí tā, érqiě   yào
not only NEG can let   any   pessimistic SP shadow attack him but also will
zài tā zhōuwéi   zàochéng yī   gè   lèguān   de huánjìng
in   his surrounding area   create   one CL optimistic SP environment

yǐngxiǎng!
influence
{She wants to stabilize GU Kun's mood in all aspects. Therefore, not only can't she let him be pessimistic in any way, but she will create an optimistic environment around him!}

(77) ······化工厂生产的溴素，因违反操作规程出废品赔了本，（因此）非但不能给奖，还扣了分······

... huàgōng chǎng shēngchǎn de xiùsù, yīn   wéifǎn cāozuò guīchéng
chemical   plant produce SP bromine because violate operate regulation
*chū   fèipǐn péiběn   le   běn, (**yīncǐ**) fēidàn bù   néng gěi*
produce reject lose money PEF   therefore not only NEG can be given
jiǎng, hái kòu-le   fēn ...
bonus also deduct-PEF point
{... Because (the workers in the chemical plant) violated the operation regulations, some of the bromine produced turned out to be rejects, resulting in financial loss. For this reason, not only didn't (the workers) get the bonus, but (their) points were deducted ...}

Although the semantic agreement or disagreement between the reversed progressive complex sentence and its preceding one exerts influence on the speaker's choice of using a marked or unmarked sentence, the influence is not always decisive. In the final analysis, if the speaker intends to emphasize the adversative relationship between *p* and *q*, they will probably choose to use a marked sentence even though the sentence agrees with the preceding one. On the contrary, if the speaker means to highlight the progressive relationship between "*bù p*" and *q*, they are more likely to choose an unmarked sentence even if the sentence disagrees with the preceding one. The following are two examples:

(78) 果然，马守山这一步棋走对了，孙之翔成了市革委会副主任。（因此）马守山不仅没有被打倒，反而成了解放干部，进了三结合的班子。

Guǒrán,   Mǎ Shǒushān zhè yī bù qí   zǒu   duì le, Sūn Zhīxiáng
as expected MA Shoushan this one CL chess move right PEF SUN Zhixiang
*chéng-le   shì   géwěihuì   fù   zhǔrèn. (**Yīncǐ**)*
become-PEF municipal Revolutionary Committee deputy director therefore
Mǎ Shǒushān bùjǐn   méiyǒu bèi   dǎ-dǎo,   fǎn'ér
MA Shoushan not only NEG   PASSIVE overthrow on the contrary
chéng-le   jiěfàng gànbù, jìn-le   sān jiéhé   de
become-PEF liberate cadre enter-PEF   three in one combination SP
bānzi.
leadership
{Sure enough, MA Shoushan made the right move, and SUN Zhixiang became Deputy Director of the municipal Revolutionary Committee. Therefore, not only wasn't MA Shoushan overthrown, but he was reappointed and became a member of the three-in-one combination leadership.}

178 *"bùdàn bù p, fǎn'ér q" and its adversative relationship*

(79) 应保诚虽然对这一点恼火得要命，但他现在<u>非但</u>一点也<u>不能</u>发火，<u>而且</u>还应
处处表现轻松愉快才是。

Yìng Bǎochéng suīrán duì zhè yī diǎn nǎohuǒ de yàomìng, **dàn** *tā*
YING Baocheng although about this one point annoyed SP extreme but he

xiànzài <u>*fēidàn*</u> *yīdiǎn yě* <u>*bù*</u> *néng fāhuǒ,* <u>*érqiě*</u> *hái yīng*
now not only a little even NEG can lose temper but also also should

chùchù biǎoxiàn qīngsōng yúkuài cái shì.
all aspects behave relaxed happy then right

{Although YING Baocheng is very annoyed about this, not only shouldn't he lose his temper, but he needs to look relaxed and happy in all aspects.}

Summary

The reversed progressive sentence form is quite useful and frequently used. This form has some features that general progressive complex sentence forms do not have. Its unique features can be summarized as follows:

First, in terms of linguistic form, *"bùdàn bù p, fǎn'ér q"* is taken as the typical form, in which the role of *bùdàn* can be played by a synonym, such as *bùjǐn, bùguāng*, and so on, the role of *bù* can be played by a synonym, such as *méi, wèi*, and so forth, and the role of *fǎn'ér* can be played by a synonym, such as *fǎn, dǎo*, or even by *què, piān, jìng*, and so forth. Nevertheless, whatever synonym is used, the sentence can all be regarded as one in the form of *"bùdàn bù p, fǎn'ér q"*. In addition, apart from the marked form *"bùdàn bù p, fǎn'ér q"*, there are many sentences in the unmarked form. No matter whether they are marked or unmarked, they can also all be regarded as the form *"bùdàn bù p, fǎn'ér q"*.

Second, from the perspective of the inter-clausal relationship, *"bùdàn bù p, fǎn'ér q"* embodies both progression and reversion. Between *p* and *q*, there exists an obvious reversion as well as a hierarchical distance, hence a reversion with a progression. Between *"bù p"* and *q*, there exists an obvious progression as well as a reversion, hence a progression with reversion. This binary semantic feature of the inter-clausal relationship sets a unique logical ground for reversed progressive sentences, thus imposing restrictions on the variants of *"bùdàn bù p, fǎn'ér q"*.

Third, in light of the relation between the form and inter-clausal semantic relationship, *"bùdàn bù p, fǎn'ér q"* blends two structures that each have their own functions, i.e., the conjunction structure of *"bùdàn . . . (érqiě) . . ."* and the adverb structure of *"bù . . . fǎn'ér . . ."*. The former signals and explicates the progressive relationship between *"bù p"* and *q*, whereas the latter highlights the reversion. Usually, *érqiě* and *fǎn'ér* do not cooccur, but theoretically they can, i.e., *"bùdàn bù p, érqiě fǎn'ér q"*. In actual language use, reversed progressive sentences are either marked ones in the form *"bùdàn bù p, érqiě fǎn'ér q"*, or unmarked ones in the form *"bùdàn bù p, érqiě q"*, or in various other forms.

It should be pointed out that the anterior and the posterior clauses in a reversed progressive complex sentence usually share the same subject, which often occurs in the anterior clause. Nevertheless, there are a small number of sentences in which the two clauses each have their own subjects. If the subject is labeled as

S, marked reversed progressive complex sentences can be in the following three forms:

S bùdàn bù p, fǎn'ér q.
S₁ bùdàn bù p, S₂ fǎn'ér q.
Bùdàn S₁ bù p, S₂ fǎn'ér q.

The clauses in sentences in the last two forms have different subjects.

In some sentences, S_1 is in possession of S_2. The following are two examples:

(80)　他不但没有当上书记，他的科长职务反而被撸掉了。

Tā	*bùdàn*	*méiyǒu*	*dāng-shàng*	*shūjì,*	*tā*	*de*	*kēzhǎng*	*zhíwù*
he	not only	NEG	become	secretary	he	SP	section chief	post

fǎn'ér	*bèi*	*lū-diào*	*le.*
on the contrary	PASSIVE	remove	PEF

{Not only did he fail to be made secretary, but he was stripped of his post of section chief.}

(81)　她不仅不生气，脸上还挂着一种小姑娘似的顽皮。

Tā	*bùjǐn*	*bù*	*shēngqì,*	*liǎn-shàng*	*hái*	*guà-zhe*	*yī*	*zhǒng xiǎo gūniang*
she	not only	NEG	be angry	on face	still	hang-PRG	one kind	little girl

shìde	*wánpí.*
like	naughty

{Instead of getting angry, she had a look of a little naughty girl.}

In other sentences, S_1 and S_2 refer to two persons or matters that are opposite each other but have the same consequence, as in the following two examples:

(82)　不但台下的不能挤上去，台上的反而全部被赶了下来。

Bùdàn	*tái-xià*	*de*	*bù*	*néng*	*jǐ-shàngqù,*	*tái-shàng*	*de*
not only	under stage	SP	NEG	can	squeeze up there	on stage	SP

fǎn'ér	*quánbù*	*bèi*	*gǎn-xiàlái*	*le*	*xiàlái.*
on the contrary	all	PASSIVE	drive down	PEF	

{Not only did those under the stage fail to get on the stage, but all those on the stage were driven down.}

(83)　不但落水的没有救起来，救人的反而也跟着送了命。

Bùdàn	*luòshuǐ*	*de*	*méiyǒu*	*jiù-qǐlái,*	*jiù*	*rén*	*de*
not only	fall into the water	SP	NEG	rescue	rescue	person	SP

fǎn'ér	*yě*	*gēn-zhe*	*sòngmìng*	*le*	*mìng.*
on the contrary	aslo	follow-PRG	die	PEF	

{Not only wasn't the one who fell into the water saved, but the rescuer also died.}

It should also be pointed out that reversed progressive sentences are a subtype of progressive sentences, but their features are unique in varying degrees. The

180 *"bùdàn bù p, fǎn'ér q" and its adversative relationship*

classification of a complex sentence requires consideration of various factors. As for reversed progressive sentences, the following three situations need special consideration. First, since unmarked reversed progressive sentences do not formally have a reversion marker, they can be regarded as general progressive sentences. Second, although some reversed progressive sentences do not include an adversative connective, they can be regarded as (reversed) progressive sentences due to their peculiarities. Third, with the presence of a reversion marker, there is a cooccurrence of a progressive marker and an adversative marker in marked reversed progressive sentences, therefore they can be objectively classified as progressive-adversative complex sentences.

NB Some examples in this chapter are cited from literary works, political essays, articles, and so on. The sources are listed as follows:

1 *Changpian Xiaoshuo Xuankan* (《小说界-长篇小说专辑》) 1984(1), including (19), (20), (35), (45), (58), (60), (68), (71), (72), (77), and (79);
2 *Chunfeng* (《春风》) 1982(1), including (69);
3 *Dangdai* (《当代》) 1984(3) (Supplement), including (31); 1985(2), including (37) and (54);
4 *Fiction Monthly* (《小说月报》) 1997(6), including (29);
5 *Flower City* (《花城》) 1985(1), including (8), (59), and (76);
6 *Harvest* (《收获》) 1982(4), including (55); 1985(2), including (41);
7 *Lotus* (《芙蓉》) 1984(2), including (34); 1988(4), including (22);
8 *October* (《十月》) 1983(4), including (27) and (74); 1984(4), including (16); 1985(1), including (12) and (75); 1985(2), including (75);
9 *People's Literature* (《人民文学》) 1982(1), including (65); 1982(4), including (81);
10 *Qingming* (《清明》) 1983(3), including (33);
11 *Selected Stories* (《小说选刊》) 1996(11), including (67); 1998(11), including (43);
12 *Xiao Shuo Jia* (《小说家》) 1983(3), including (24) and (57); 1984(1), including (26); 1984(3), including (13), (14), (17), (21), (23), and (61); 1984(4), including (9) and (70); 1985(1), including (25) and (78); 1997 (3), including (36);
13 *Zhongpian Xiaoshuo Xuankan* (《中篇小说选刊》) 1984(5), including (42), (44), and (66); 1999(1), including (18).

Notes

1 Chinese (for Junior High School Students), Book 5, People's Education Press, 1957, p. 51.
2 The syntactic position of *xiāngfǎn* is the same as that of *fǎn'ér*, but different from that of *érqiě*. The word *xiāngfǎn* is an adjective. Although it can occur between two clauses and looks like a conjunction, it is still an adjective, or a weakened adjective. More details can be found in: XING Fuyi (邢福义), *Identification of Parts of Speech* (《词类辩难》). Gansu People's Education Press, 1981, p. 121.
3 It does not mean there is none.

9 Progressive *gèng*-sentences and adversative *gèng*-sentences

The *gèng* sentence form refers to a complex sentence form in which *gèng* is used to indicate a progressive relationship. For conciseness and preciseness, sentences in this form are referred to as "*gèng*" complex sentences.

As an adverb of degree, *gèng* has two functions in "*gèng*" complex sentences: indicating the degree of the VP/AP and marking the progressive relationship between the anteriorand posterior clauses.

Scholars have not paid much attention to "*gèng*" complex sentences. In some works on modern Chinese complex sentences, "*gèng*" complex sentences are only sporadically cited as examples.[1] In some works, the word *gèng* is mentioned only as a connective with no examples of "*gèng*" complex sentences.[2] In other works, "*gèng*" complex sentences are completely absent.[3]

In some "*gèng*" complex sentences, there is an adversative relationship.

9.1 "*p, gèng q*"

The simple form of "*gèng*" complex sentences is "*p, gèng q*", in which there is no connective in the anterior clause and *gèng* is located between the two clauses to signal a progressive relationship. Usually, *gèng* immediately precedes the VP/AP in the posterior clause. If the subject is present in the posterior clause, *gèng* needs to be placed after the subject. The following are five examples:

(1) 我爱北京，我更爱今天的北京。
    Wǒ ài Běijīng, wǒ gèng ài jīntiān de Běijīng.
    I love Beijing I more love today SP Beijing
    {I love Beijing, particularly today's Beijing.}

(2) 他的手术……动作轻快准确，缝合的技术更是全院少见的。
    Tā de shǒushù ... dòngzuò qīngkuài zhǔnquè, fénghé de jìshù gèng
    he SP operation movement light and quick precise suture SP skill more
    shì quán yuàn shǎojiàn de.
    COP entire hospital rare MP
    {His surgical . . . movements are light, quick, and precise, and his suturing skill is even more remarkable hospital-wide.}

DOI: 10.4324/9781003374237-9

182   *Progressive gèng-sentences and adversative gèng-sentences*

(3)   一路上, 他不说不笑，<u>更</u>不吵不闹，真让人别扭！

    Yīlù-shàng,   *tā bù   shuō bù   xiào, <u>gèng</u> bù   chǎo   bù*
    along the way he NEG talk NEG laugh more NEG make a noise NEG

    nào,   *zhēn ràng rén   bièniǔ!*
    make a trouble truly make person uncomfortable

    {Along the way, he didn't talk or laugh, not to mention that he didn't make any trouble. It really made people uncomfortable!}

(4)   ⋯⋯没有困难，<u>更</u>谈不上痛苦。

    . . . méiyǒu   kùnnán,   <u>gèng</u> tán-bùshàng   tòngkǔ.
    not have   difficulty   more be out of the question painful

    {. . . there is no difficulty, let alone pain.}

(5)   发现一篇好作品不容易，培养一个作者<u>更</u>不容易。

    Fāxiàn yī piān hǎo zuòpǐn bù   róngyì, péiyǎng yī gè zuòzhě <u>gèng</u>
    find   A CL   good work NEG easy   bring up one CL writer more

    bù   róngyì.
    NEG easy

    {It's not easy to find a good work, and it's even harder to cultivate a writer.}

Each of these sentences embodies one of the five semantic relationships between the anterior and posterior clauses in "*gèng*" complex sentences. Different semantic relationships are likely to be expressed by different non-simple forms, which will be elaborated in the following sections.

Whatever the inter-clausal semantic relationship is within a "*gèng*" complex sentence, any "*gèng*" complex sentence has the following three features:

First, the antecedent and the consequent, which are compared by *gèng*, both need to be present. For example, in (1) *gèng* compares "I love Beijing" and "I love today's Beijing". The same holds for (2), in which *gèng* compares "movements" and "suturing skill".

Two points should be made clear.

i) Sentences that do not contain both the antecedent and the consequent—even if *gèng* is present—are not "*gèng*" complex sentences. The following is an example:

(6)   在太阳难得照耀的地方，也有花有草，<u>更</u>需要温暖。

    Zài tàiyáng nándé zhàoyào de dìfang, yě   yǒu   huā   yǒu   cǎo, <u>gèng</u>
    in sun   rare shine SP place also there be flower there be grass more

    xūyào wēnnuǎn.
    need warm

    {Where there is no sunshine, there are also flowers and grass, which are more in need of warmth.}

In (6), *gèng* is followed by "*xūyào wēnnuǎn*" ('need warmth'), but there is nothing that can be regarded as the antecedent, thus it is not a "*gèng*" complex sentence.

Progressive gèng-sentences and adversative gèng-sentences 183

If (6) is rewritten to include the antecedent—which is to a lesser degree than the consequent—for example, "*xūyào shuǐfèn*" ('need water'), then it will become a "*gèng*" complex sentence, as (7):

(7) 在太阳难得照耀的地方，也有花有草，需要水分，更需要温暖。

Zài tàiyáng nándé zhàoyào de dìfang, yě yǒu huā yǒu cǎo, xūyào
in sun rare shine SP place also there be flower there be grass need

shuǐfèn, gèng xūyào wēnnuǎn.
water more need warm

{Where there is no sunshine, there are also flowers and grass, which are in need of water and more in need of warmth.}

ii) The word *gèng* can occur only once between the antecedent and the consequent. Any sentences with more than one occurrence of *gèng* are not "*gèng*" complex sentences. For example:

(8) 在太阳难得照耀的地方，也有花有草，更需要温暖，更需要细心照料。

Zài tàiyáng nándé zhàoyào de dìfang, yě yǒu huā yǒu cǎo, gèng
in sun rare shine SP place also there be flower there be grass more

xūyào wēnnuǎn, gèng xūyào xìxīn zhàoliào.
need warm more need careful look after

{Where there is no sunshine, there are also flowers and grass, which are more in need of warmth and more care.}

The aforementioned example is not a "*gèng*" complex sentence. However, if it is rewritten as (9), it will become a "*gèng*" complex sentence, in which *gèng* occurs between the antecedent "*xūyào wēnnuǎn*" ('need warmth') and the consequent "*xūyào xìxīn zhàoliào*" ('need care') to emphasize the progressive relationship.

(9) 在太阳难得照耀的地方，也有花有草，需要温暖，更需要细心照料。

Zài tàiyáng nándé zhàoyào de dìfang, yě yǒu huā yǒu cǎo, xūyào
in sun rare shine SP place also there be flower there be grass need

wēnnuǎn, gèng xūyào xìxīn zhàoliào.
warm more need careful look after

{Where the sun rarely shines, there are also flowers and grass, which are in need of warmth and more in need of care.}

Second, the antecedent and consequent are semantically comparable and formally symmetrical, like "*bùshuō-bùxiào*" ('neither talk nor laugh') and "*bùchǎo-bùnào*" ('neither make noise nor trouble') in (3), and "*méiyǒu kùnnán*" ('no difficulty') and "*tán-bùshàng tòngkǔ*" ('let alone pains') in (4).

Usually, the antecedent and the consequent in a "*gèng*" complex sentence are both in the affirmative form or the negative form. In (1) and (2), both clauses are in the affirmative form, and in (3), (4), and (5), both are in the negative form. In

184 *Progressive gèng-sentences and adversative gèng-sentences*

some sentences, one is affirmative and the other is negative, but both of them are semantically comparable. The following are two examples:

(10) 要尽量少激动，<u>更</u>不要过于疲劳。

Yào jìnliàng shǎo jīdòng, <u>gèng</u> bùyào guòyú píláo.
should to the best of one's abilities less excited more do not too tired
{Try not to be excited, and more importantly, not to be too tired.}

(11) 我不想听他唠叨，<u>更</u>担心这雨没完没了。

Wǒ bù xiǎng tīng tā láodao, <u>gèng</u> dānxīn zhè yǔ méiwán-méiliǎo.
I NEG want listen him chatter more worry this rain last forever
{I don't want to listen to his chatter, and I'm more worried that the rain will never stop.}

In (10), the antecedent is affirmative, but the consequent is negative. However, the sentence can be rewritten as (12a), in which both the antecedent and the consequent are negative, or as (12b), in which both are affirmative.

(12) a 不要太激动，更不要过于疲劳。

Bùyào tài jīdòng, gèng bùyào guòyú píláo.
do not too excited more do not too tired
{Don't be too excited, and more importantly, don't be too tired.}

b 要尽量少激动，更要尽量避免过于疲劳。

Yào jìnliàng shǎo jīdòng, <u>gèng</u> yào
should to the best of one's abilities less excited more should

jìnliàng bìmiǎn guòyú píláo.
to the best of one's abilities avoid too tired
{Try to avoid being excited, and more importantly, try to avoid being too tired.}

In (11), the antecedent is negative, but the consequent is affirmative, but both the negative expression "*bù xiǎng*" ('not want to') in the antecedent and the affirmative word *dānxīn* ('worry') can be replaced by *pà* ('be afraid') so that both the antecedent and consequent are more consistent and symmetrical, as is shown by (13).

(13) 我怕听他唠叨，更怕这雨没完没了。

Wǒ pà tīng tā láodao, gèng pà zhè yǔ méiwán-méiliǎo.
I afraid listen him chatter more afraid this rain last forever
{I'm afraid of listening to his chatter, and I'm more afraid that the rain will never stop.}

If in a sentence there are no two semantically comparable and formally symmetrical linguistic forms between which *gèng* is located, then the sentence is not a "*gèng*" complex sentence. For example:

Progressive gèng-sentences and adversative gèng-sentences 185

(14) 她这么一说，我更不能入梦了。

Tā	zhème	yī	shuō,	wǒ	<u>gèng</u>	bù	néng	rùmèng	le.
she	so	once	say	I	more	NEG	can	sleep	MP

{It was even more difficult for me to sleep after she said that.}

Third, syntactically, the two linguistic forms compared by *gèng* need to be clauses. For instance, the antecedent and the consequent in each of the "*gèng*" complex sentences mentioned here are both clauses.

Even if in a sentence the two linguistic forms related to *gèng* are semantically comparable or formally symmetrical, it is still not a "*gèng*" complex sentence if they are not clauses. For example:

(15) 本来是多眼白的眼睛，现在更白得怕人。

Běnlái	shì	duō	yǎnbái	de	yǎnjing,	xiànzài	<u>gèng</u>	bái	de
originally	COP	much	white	of eye	SP eye	now	more	white	SP

pàrén.
frightening

{The eyes had a lot of white, but now they are more frightening because of the whiteness.}

In the aforementioned example, what is related to *gèng* is "*běnlái shì duō yǎnbái*" ('originally having a lot of white') and "*bái de pàrén*" ('frightening because of the whiteness'), but the former acts as the attribute of *yǎnjīng* ('the eyes') rather than a clause. Nonetheless, if (15) is rewritten as (16), then it will become a "*gèng*" complex sentence.

(16) 眼睛本来多眼白，现在更白得怕人。

Yǎnjing	běnlái	duō	yǎnbái,	xiànzài	<u>gèng</u>	bái	de	pàrén.
eye	originally	much	white of eye	now	more	white	SP	frightening

{The eyes had a lot of white, but now they are more frightening because of the whiteness.}

There are four points worth noting.

i) In some cases, a "*gèng*" complex sentence can be compressed into a simple sentence through constituent sharing. For example, (17) is a complex sentence, but it can be compressed into (18), a simple sentence.

(17) 《辞海》中没有对"正常"的诠解，更没有对"正常人"的诠解。

Cíhǎi-zhōng	méiyǒu	duì	"zhèngcháng"	de	quánjiě,	<u>gèng</u>
in *Cihai*	there not be	of	normal	SP	interpret	furthermore

méiyǒu	duì	"zhèng cháng rén"	de	quánjiě.
there not be	of	normal person	SP	interpret

{There is no interpretation of "normal" in *Cihai*, let alone "normal person".}

186 *Progressive gèng-sentences and adversative gèng-sentences*

(18) 《辞海》中没有对 "正常" 更没有对 "正常人" 的诠解。

> *Cíhǎi-zhōng   méiyǒu   duì   "zhèngcháng"   <u>gèng</u>   méiyǒu   duì*
> in *Cihai*   there not be of   normal   furthermore there not be of
> *"zhèngcháng rén"   de   quánjiě.*
> normal   person SP   interpret
> {There is no interpretation of "normal" in *Cihai*, let alone "normal person".}

In some cases, the two linguistic forms related to *gèng* are located in different sentences in a sentence group. For example:

(19) 闯王听了，也很感动。周围的将士<u>更是</u>感动，有人知道此人活不成了，不禁感动得流出了眼泪。

> *Chuǎngwáng   tīng-le,   yě   hěn   gǎndòng.   Zhōuwéi   de*
> Dashing King   hear-PEF   also very   moved   surrounding area   SP
> *jiàngshì   <u>gèng shì</u> gǎndòng, yǒu   rén   zhīdào cǐ   rén*
> officer and soldier more   moved   there be person know this person
> *huó-bùchéng   le,   bùjīn   gǎndòng de   liú-chū le   yǎnlèi.*
> cannot survive MP   can't help doing ... moved   SP   shed   PEF tear
> {The Dashing King was also moved after he heard this. The surrounding officers and men were even more moved, and some couldn't help shedding tears, knowing that the man wouldn't be able to survive.}

Example (19) is a sentence group, in which "*chuǎngwáng gǎndòng*" ('the Dashing King was moved') and "*zhōuwéi de jiàngshì gǎndòng*" ('the surrounding officers and men were moved') are obviously located in two different sentences. If (19) is rewritten as (20), it will be a "*gèng*" complex sentence:

(20) 闯王听了很感动，周围的将士<u>更是</u>感动。

> *Chuǎngwáng   tīng-le   hěn   gǎndòng,   zhōuwéi   de*
> Dashing King   hear-PEF   very   moved   surrounding area   SP
> *jiàngshì   <u>gèng shì</u> gǎndòng.*
> officer and soldier more   moved
> {The Dashing King was moved after he heard this, and the surrounding officers and men were even more moved.}

ii) Some "*gèng*" complex sentences contain multiple layers, for example:

(21) 洪承畴第一次看见蒙古的男子舞蹈，感到很有刚健猛锐之气，但他并不喜爱；满洲的舞蹈有的类似跳神，有的模拟狩猎，他认为未脱游牧之风，<u>更不</u>喜欢。

> *Hóng Chéngchóu   dì-yī cì   kànjiàn Měnggǔ   de nánzǐ wǔdǎo, gǎndào hěn*
> HONG Chengchou   first time see   Mongolia SP male   dance   feel   very
> *yǒu gāngjiàn měngruì zhī qì,   dàn tā bìng bù   xǐ'ài; Mǎnzhōu*
> have vigorous robust   SP   manner but he indeed NEG like   Manchuria

Progressive gèng-sentences and adversative gèng-sentences 187

de	wǔdǎo	yǒude	lèisì	tiàoshén,	yǒude	mónǐ	shòuliè,	tā	rènwéi
SP	dance	some	be like	witch dance	some	simulate	hunt	he	think

wèi	tuō	yóumù	zhī	fēng,	*gèng*	bù	xǐhuān.
not yet	be separated	be nomadic	SP	style	more	NEG	like

{When HONG Chengchou first saw Mongolian men dance, he disliked it although he thought the dance was vigorous and robust. Some Manchurian dances were like witches jumping, and some simulated hunting, which he thought were still nomadic, so he disliked them even more.}

This example is a multi-layer complex sentence, with *gèng* marking the progressive relationship within the first layer, i.e., "... *bù xǐ'ài*; | ... *gèng bù xǐhuān* ...".

In this chapter, the so-called "*gèng*" complex sentences in the simple form refer to those that only use *gèng* to mark the progressive relationship. Thus, the sentences are simple only in the sense that the formal marker is simple as opposed to non-simple. If a "*gèng*" complex sentence in the simple form contains multiple layers, it is not simple at all in terms of the combination of clauses.

iii) A "*gèng*" complex sentence can sit in another "*gèng*" complex sentence as its component. For example:

(22)　有人同情慧梅, 更担心慧梅嫁给袁时中可能苦恼终身，都不免落泪, 红娘子和
　　　姑娘们更是忍不住泣不成声。

Yǒu	rén	tóngqíng	Huìméi,	*gèng*	dānxīn	Huìméi jià-gěi
there be	person	sympathize with	Huimei	more	worry about	Huimei marry

Yuán Shízhōng	kěnéng	kǔ'nǎo	zhōngshēn,	dōu	bùmiǎn	luòlèi,
YUAN Shizhong	may	distressed	lifetime	all	unavoidable	shed tears

Hóngniángzǐ	hé	gūniáng-men	*gèng shì*	rěn-bùzhù
Hongniangzi	and	girl-PL	more	can't help doing . . .

qìbùchéngshēng.
choke with sobs

{Some people sympathized with Huimei and were more worried that Huimei might be distressed for life after she married YUAN Shizhong, so they couldn't help but shed tears. Hongniangzi and the girls even choked with tears.}

In the aforementioned example, the first *gèng* and the second *gèng* are located within different layers. The first three sections, "some people sympathized with Huimei" and the last section "Hongniangzi and the girls even choked with tears" form the first layer, whereas the first section and the second section "(some people) were more worried that Huimei might be distressed for life after she married YUAN Shizhong" form the second layer.

iv) As a synonym of *gèng* and "*gèng shì*", *gèngjiā* is used in some *gèng* complex sentences, for example:

188 *Progressive gèng-sentences and adversative gèng-sentences*

(23) 他不能再忍受六十了，六十五或七十他<u>更加</u>无法面对！

Tā bù néng zài rěnshòu liùshí le, liùshíwǔ huò qīshí tā <u>gèngjiā</u>
he NEG can again bear sixty MP sixty-five or seventy he more

wú fǎ miànduì!
NEG method face

{He can't bear to be sixty anymore, and he is even less able to face sixty-five or seventy!}

9.2 "*bùdàn p, gèng q*"

One of the non-simple forms of "*gèng*" complex sentences is "*bùdàn p, gèng q*".

As one of the typical forms of progressive complex sentences, "*bùdàn p, gèng q*" indicates a forward progression, with *bùdàn* or its synonym acting as the progression precursor and *gèng* as the undertaker, the precursor and the undertaker collocate with each other and manifest a progression from a lower level to a higher one, from a lesser degree to a greater one, from a smaller size to a bigger one, or from inferiority to superiority. The following are two sentences in the form of "*bùdàn p, gèng q*":

(24) 那时，<u>不但</u>亏了自己，<u>更</u>亏了自己的先母。

Nà shí, <u>bùdàn</u> kuī-le zìjǐ, <u>gèng</u> kuī-le zìjǐ
that time, not only be unfair to-PEF oneself more be unfair to-PEF oneself

de xiāmǔ.
SP late mother

{At that time, (I) was not only unfair to (my)self, but more to (my) late mother.}

(25) 施正月<u>不但</u>刀快，暗器<u>更</u>快，（连我们唐门最精于使用暗器的唐干裘也不敢轻视他。）

Shī Zhēngyuè <u>bùdàn</u> dāo kuài, ànqì <u>gèng</u> kuài, (lián . . . yě . . .
SHI Zhengyue not only knife fast hidden weapon more fast, even . . .

wǒ-men Táng mén zuì jīng yú shǐyòng ànqì de
us TANG school most proficient in use hidden weapon SP

Táng Gānqiú yě bù gǎn qīngshì tā.)
TANG Ganqiu NEG dare ignore him

{SHI Zhengyue is not only a fast knifeman, but is even faster with hidden weapons[, so even TANG Ganqiu, who is the most skilled in using hidden weapons in our TANG school, dares not ignore him].}

The following are three more examples, among which (26) and (27) are in the form of "*bùjǐn p, gèng q*" and (28) in the form of "*bùguāng p, gèng q*":

(26) 她……<u>不仅</u>抚摸到他的形体，<u>更</u>能触摸到他的灵魂。

Tā . . . <u>bùjǐn</u> fǔmō-dào tā de xíngtǐ, <u>gèng</u> néng chùmō-dào tā de línghún.
she not only stroke he SP body more can touch his SP soul

{Not only can she stroke his body, but she can even touch his soul.}

Progressive gèng-sentences and adversative gèng-sentences **189**

(27) 一种象棋学派<u>不仅</u>首先要有科学的思想和理论，<u>更</u>需要实践运用的巨大成就。

Yī zhŏng xiàngqí xuépài <u>bùjĭn</u> shŏuxiān yào yŏu kēxué de sīxiăng hé
a kind chess school not only first of all need have science SP idea and

lĭlùn, <u>gèng</u> xūyào shíjiàn yùnyòng de jùdà chéngjiù.
theory more need practice use SP huge achievement

{A chess school needs scientific ideas and theories in the first place, but more importantly, great achievements in practical application.}

(28) 自己愿意用一些干部子弟，<u>不光</u>是为了用他们的"才"，<u>更</u>是用他们的"能"。他们能疏通上层联系，打通四面八方的关节。

Zìjĭ yuànyì yòng yīxiē gànbù zĭdì, <u>bùguāng</u> shì wèile yòng
oneself be willing use some cadre children not only COP in order to use

tā-men de "cái", <u>gèng</u> shì yòng tā-men de "néng". Tā-men néng
they SP talent more COP use they SP ability they can

shūtōng shàngcéng liánxì, dătōng sìmiàn-bāfāng de guānjié.
communicate upper level connect open up all directions SP relationship

{He himself was willing to employ some of the cadres' children, not only for their "talents", but more importantly for their "abilities". They were able to communicate with the upper echelons and build relationships in all aspects.}

Even if *gèng* is replaced by *yě*, "*bùdàn p, yě q*" is also a form of progressive sentences, because the progression precursor *bùdàn* or its synonym provides a clear momentum: the anterior progresses to the posterior clauses. However, *gèng* highlights the higher level, but *yě* does not have this function. Therefore, although formally *yě* can replace *gèng*, semantically it cannot. Compare the following two examples:

(29) 不但刀快，暗器也快。

Bùdàn dāo kuài, ànqì yě kuài.
not only knife fast hidden weapon also fast

{Not only the knife but also the hidden weapons are fast.}

(30) 不但刀快，暗器更快。

Bùdàn dāo kuài, ànqì gèng kuài.
not only knife fast hidden weapon more fast

{Not only is the knife fast, but the hidden weapons are even faster.}

These two examples are both progressive complex sentences. However, (29) is only about the progression of the scope of the matter, but (30) is not only about the progression of the scope but also the progression of the speed.

Three points should be noted:

i) "*bùdàn . . . gèng . . .*" can be followed by "*shènzhì . . .*", i.e., a three-layer form "*bùdàn p, gèng q, shènzhì r*", for example:

190 *Progressive gèng-sentences and adversative gèng-sentences*

(31) 人在生活中，<u>不仅仅</u>需要优裕和安适以及种种的物质上的满足，<u>更</u>需要精神上的一些冲击、一些警策、一些温暖、一些感染、一些慰藉和一些鼓舞，<u>甚至</u>还需要一点眼泪和一点战栗。

Rén   zài shēnghuó-zhōng, <u>bùjǐnjǐn</u> xūyào yōuyù   hé   ānshì
person in life   not only need affluent and quiet and comfortable
yǐjí zhǒngzhǒng de wùzhì-shàng de mǎnzú,   <u>gèng</u> xūyào jīngshén-shàng de
and all kinds   SP in material SP be satisfied more need in spirit   SP
yīxiē chōngjī, yīxiē jǐngcè, yīxiē wēnnuǎn, yīxiē gǎnrǎn, yīxiē wèijiè   hé
some impact some warn some warm   some infect some comfort and
yīxiē gǔwǔ,   <u>shènzhì</u> hái xūyào yīdiǎn yǎnlèi hé   yīdiǎn zhànlì.
some encourage even   also need a few tear   and a few shudder
{In life, people need not only affluence, comfort, and all kinds of material satisfaction, but more importantly, some spiritual impact, warning, warmth, infection, words of comfort, and encouragement, and even a few tears and shudders.}

In "*bùdàn p, gèng q, shènzhì r*", "*shènzhì r*" is a complement to "*gèng q*".

ii) If in a simple "*gèng*" complex sentence q is at a higher level than p, then the sentence can be rewritten as one in the form of "*bùdàn p, gèng q*". For example, (2) can be rewritten as (32):

(32) 他的手术<u>不仅</u>轻快准确，缝合的技术<u>更</u>是全院少见的。

Tā de shǒushù <u>bùjǐn</u> qīngkuài   zhǔnquè, fénghé de jìshù <u>gèng</u> shì
he SP operation not only light and quick precise suture SP skill more COP
quán yuàn   shǎojiàn de.
entire hospital rare   SP
{Not only are his surgical movements light, quick, and precise, but his suturing skill is more remarkable hospital-wide.}

The following are three more examples:

(33) 庄韬回到自己家了，西院二号，两间靠厕所的西房。阴，潮，臭。刚才硬着头皮钻进院，现在<u>更</u>硬着头皮钻进家。

Zhuāng Tāo huí-dào zìjǐ   jiā le, xī yuàn   èr-hào, liǎng
ZHUANG Tao return to oneself home PEF west courtyard homes No. 2 two
jiān kào   cèsuǒ de xī fáng. Yīn, cháo, chòu. Gāngcái yìng-zhe tóupí
CL be next to toilet SP west room cold damp stinky just now bite the bullet
zuān-jìn yuàn,   xiànzài <u>gèng</u> yìng-zhe tóupí zuān-jìn jiā.
get into courtyard now   more bite the bullet get into home
{Now ZHUANG Tao is back home, No. 2 in the west courtyard, two west rooms next to the bathroom. It's cold, damp, and stinky. If just now he forced himself into the courtyard very hard, now he is forcing himself into his house even harder.}

Progressive gèng-sentences and adversative gèng-sentences **191**

(34) 你用不着懊丧，<u>更</u>没必要失去对美好前程追求的信心和勇气。

Nǐ yòng-bùzháo àosàng, <u>gèng</u> méi bìyào shīqù duì měhǎo qiánchéng
you not need to depressed more NEG necessary lose in good future

zhuīqiú de xìnxīn hé yǒngqì.
pursue SP confidence and courage

{You don't need to be depressed, let alone lose the confidence and courage to pursue a better future.}

(35) （更难得的， 就是）慕容青烟毫不保留地把改良了的本门招式重新撰写记下，更将之归还给本门。

(Gèng nándé de, jiù shì) Mùróng Qīngyān háo bù bǎoliú de
more valuable SP just COP MURONG Qingyan a tiny bit NEG reserve SP

bǎ gǎiliáng-le de běn mén zhāoshì chóngxīn zhuànxiě
BA improve-PEF SP self school movement in martial arts afresh write

jì-xià, <u>gèng</u> jiāng zhī guīhuán-gěi běn mén.
note down furthermore BA it return to self school

{[What was even more valuable was that] MURONG Qingyan recorded the improved kung fu movements of the school without reservation, and more importantly, he returned the recording to the school.}

The three examples can all be rewritten as "*bùjǐn p, gèng q*", with *bùjǐn* placed before *gāngcái* in (33), after *nǐ* in (34), and after "*MURONG Qīngyān*" in (35).

Sometimes, to change the form of a sentence from "*p, gèng q*" to "*bùjǐn p, gèng q*", some word(s) need to be left out.

(36) 你当着老队长的面，可不能流露这样的情绪，<u>更</u>不能用这种词儿。

Nǐ dāng-zhe lǎo duìzhǎng de miàn, kě bù néng liúlù zhèyàng de
you face-PRG old captain SP face really NEG can show such SP

qíngxù, <u>gèng</u> bù néng yòng zhè zhǒng cír.
emotion more NEG can Use PRG kind word

{You can't show such emotion in front of the old captain, let alone use such words.}

(37) 你当着老队长的面，<u>不仅</u>不能流露这样的情绪，<u>更</u>不能用这种词儿。

Nǐ dāng-zhe lǎo duìzhǎng de miàn, <u>bùjǐn</u> bù néng liúlù zhèyàng de
you face-PRG old captain SP face not only NEG can show such SP

qíngxù, <u>gèng</u> bù néng yòng zhè zhǒng cír.
emotion more NEG can use PRG kind word

{You can't show such emotion in front of the old captain, let alone use such words.}

iii) The hierarchical levels of the antecedent and the consequent often reflect the facts in the real world and the logical relations between them, therefore *p* and

192 *Progressive gèng-sentences and adversative gèng-sentences*

q are not interchangeable at random. For example, in (33), "his home" and "the courtyard" cannot be swapped because his cold, damp, and stinky home is obviously even worse than the courtyard. The same holds for (34) and (35) for the same reason. However, in some cases, the hierarchy only reflects the speaker's personal perspective, and is subject to the speaker's state of mind or opinion. In these cases, *p* and *q* in Person A's sentence may be *q* and *p* respectively in Person B's sentence if the people hold opposite opinions about levels of *p* and *q* in the hierarchy. Compare:

(38) 不仅有必要学法语，更有必要学德语！
Bùjǐn yǒu bìyào xué fǎyǔ, gèng yǒu bìyào xué déyǔ!
not only there be necessary learn French more there be necessary learn German
{It is not only necessary to learn French, but more necessary to learn German!}

(39) 不仅有必要学德语，更有必要学法语！
Bùjǐn yǒu bìyào xué déyǔ, gèng yǒu bìyào xué fǎyǔ!
not only there be necessary learn German more there be necessary learn French
{It is not only necessary to learn German, but more necessary to learn French!}

Example (38) shows that the speaker lays emphasis on studying German, whereas (39) reveals that the speaker thinks that studying French is even more important.

9.3 "*jì p, gèng q*"

Another non-simple form of "*gèng*" complex sentences is "*jì p, gèng q*".

The collocation of *jì* and *yòu/yě* indicates a coordinate relationship, while the collocation of *jì* and *gèng* marks a coordinate relationship and a progressive relationship, emphasizing the second of the two juxtaposed matters. The following are two examples:

(40) 它既不是上海数量最多的民房，更不是水准最高的住宅。
Tā jì bù shì Shànghǎi shùliàng zuì duō de mínfáng, gèng bù
it both NEG COP Shanghai quantity most many SP private houses more NEG
shì shuǐzhǔn zuì gāo de zhùzhái.
COP level most high SP residence
{It is not even the most common kind of private house in Shanghai, let alone the highest standard one.}

(41) 咱们要找的既不是牛，更不是猪，（而是两匹好马。）
Zán-men yào zhǎo de jì bù shì niú, gèng bù shì zhū, (ér
we want look for SP both NEG COP cattle more NEG COP pig but
shì liǎng pǐ hǎo mǎ.)
COP Two CL good horse
{What we are looking for is not cattle, let alone pigs, [but two good horses.]}

Progressive gèng-sentences and adversative gèng-sentences 193

If *gèng* in (40) and (41) is replaced by *yě*, the coordinate relationship will remain, but the progressive relationship will be lost.

Six points should be noted.

i) In some cases, sentences in the form of "*jì p, gèng q*" can be rewritten as "*bùdàn p, gèng q*". However, the employment of *jì* in the anterior clause makes it clearer that *p* and *q* are two aspects of the same matter, for example:

(42) 对偏正式的合成词，<u>既</u>要了解两个字的意义，以帮助我们掌握词义，<u>更</u>要了解整个词的意义，不能只从字面上去了解。

Duì   piānzhèng   shì   de héchéngcí,   <u>jì</u>   yào   liǎojiě
about   modifier and modifyee   pattern SP compound word   both   need   know

liǎng gè zì   de yìyì,   yǐ   bāngzhù wǒ-men zhǎngwò
two   CL character SP meaning in order to help   us   master

cíyì,   <u>gèng</u> yào liǎojiě zhěnggè cí   de yìyì,   bù   néng
meaning of word   more   need know   whole   word SP meaning   NEG   can

zhǐ   cóng zìmiàn-shàng qù liǎojiě.
only from literal meaning go know

{For a compound word made up of a modifier and a modifyee, not only should we grasp the meaning of the two characters to help us understand the compound, but more importantly, we should understand the meaning of the word as a whole, rather than just the literal meaning (of each character).}

In this example, *bùjǐn* can replace *jì*, but it does not have the function of *jì*: making it clear that "understanding the meaning of the two characters" is just one aspect of studying compound words. In other words, while listing two aspects of a matter, "*jì p, gèng q*" emphasizes the second one.

ii) Some simple "*gèng*" complex sentences can be rewritten as "*jì p, gèng q*" if *p* and *q* are the two aspects of the same matter. For example, (3) can be rewritten as (43):

(43) 一路上，他<u>既</u>不说不笑，<u>更</u>不吵不闹，真让人别扭！

Yīlù-shàng,   tā <u>jì</u>   bù   shuō bù xiào, <u>gèng</u> bù   chǎo   bù
along the way he both NEG   talk   NEG laugh more   NEG make noise NEG

nào,   zhēn ràng rén   bièniǔ!
make trouble truly make person uncomfortable

{Along the way, he didn't talk or laugh, not to mention that he didn't make any trouble. It really made people uncomfortable!}

The following are three more examples:

(44) 是爱，还是恨？是爱，<u>更</u>是恨！

Shì ài,   háishi hèn? Shì ài,   <u>gèng</u> shì   hèn!
COP love or   hate COP love more   COP   hate

{Is it love or hate? It's love, but more of hate!}

194 *Progressive gèng-sentences and adversative gèng-sentences*

(45) 她的声调很怪，不是密云口音，更不是北京的口音。

Tā de shēngdiào hěn guài, bù shì Mìyún kǒuyīn, gèng bù shì
she SP tone very strange NEG COP Miyun accent more NEG COP

Běijīng de kǒuyīn.
Beijing SP accent

{Her tones are very strange, not Miyun accent, let alone Beijing accent.}

(46) 安适之毕竟是安适之，不是白天明，更不是你毛手毛脚的秦国祥。

Ān Shìzhī bìjìng shì Ān Shìzhī, bù shì Bái Tiānmíng, gèng bù
AN Shizhi after all COP AN Shizhi NEG COP BAI Tianming more NEG

shì nǐ máoshǒu-máojiǎo de Qín Guóxiáng.
COP you careless SP QIN Guoxiang

{AN Shizhi, after all, is AN Shizhi, not BAI Tianming, let alone you, careless QIN Guoxiang.}

These three examples above can be rewritten as the following ones respectively:

(47) ……既是爱，更是恨！

...Jì shì ài, gèng shì hèn!
both COP love more COP hate

{. . . it is love, but more of hate!}

(48) ……既不是密云口音，更不是北京的口音。

...Jì bù shì Mìyún kǒuyīn, gèng bù shì Běijīng de kǒuyīn.
both NEG COP Miyun accent more NEG COP Beijing SP accent

{. . . is not Miyun accent, let alone Beijing accent.}

(49) ……既不是白天明，更不是你毛手毛脚的秦国祥。

...jì bù shì Bái Tiānmíng, gèng bù shì nǐ máoshǒu-máojiǎo de
both NEG COP BAI Tianming more NEG COP you careless SP

Qín Guóxiáng.
QIN Guoxiang

{. . . is not BAI Tianming, let alone you, careless QIN Guoxiang.}

iii) "*jì . . . yòu . . .*" can cooccur with "*gèng . . .*", i.e., "*jì . . . yòu . . . gèng . . .*".
The following are two examples:

(50) 刘邦在垓下大战取得全胜之后，率领亲随巡视战场，既有天下初定的得
意，又有一生征战的回忆，更有满目疮痍的感慨。

Liú Bāng zài Gāixià dàzhàn qǔdé quánshèng zhīhòu, shuàilǐng
LIU Bang in Gaixia battle gain complete victory after lead

qīnsuí xúnshì zhànchǎng, jì . . . yòu . . . yǒu tiānxià chū dìng de
entourage inspect battleground both . . . and . . . have country just seize SP

déyì, yòu yǒu yī shēng zhēngzhàn de huíyì, gèng yǒu
complacent have whole lifetime fight wars SP recall more have

Progressive gèng-sentences and adversative gèng-sentences 195

mǎnmù-chuāngyí   de   gǎnkǎi.
devastation everywhere   SP   sigh with emotion
{After LIU Bang won the Gaixia battle, he led his followers to inspect the battle-field. He was not only proud of having seized the country, but also recalled his military career, and even lamented the devastation all over.}

(51) 突然杀出一个程咬金，以致功败垂成，<u>既</u>杀不了人，<u>又</u>夺不了玉山羊，<u>更</u>要狼狈逃回平阳城去。

Tūrán   shā-chū   yī   gè   Chéng Yǎojīn,   yǐzhì
sudden   appear   one   CL   CHENG Yaojin (someone unexpected) so that

gōngbàichuíchéng,   <u>jì . . . yòu . . .</u>   shā-bùliǎo   rén,   <u>yòu</u>
fail on the verge of success both . . . and . . . cannot kill   person

duó-bùliǎo   yù shānyáng,   <u>gèng</u> yào   lángbèi   táo-huíqù
cannot capture jade goat   more   must embarrassed flee back to

Píngyáng chéng   qù.
Pingyang city

{Something unexpected happened suddenly, so (he) failed on the verge of success. (He) could neither kill nor seize the jade goat, and to make matters worse, (he) had to flee helter-skelter back to Pingyang City.}

iv) "*jì . . . yě . . .*" and "*gèng . . .*" can also cooccur, i.e., "*jì . . . yě . . . gèng . . .*". The following are three examples:

(52) 说她是工农兵大学生，她的出身，<u>既</u>不是工人，<u>也</u>不是农民，<u>更</u>不是当兵的。

Shuō   tā   shì   gōng   nóng   bīng   dàxuéshēng,   tā   de   chūshēn,
say   she COP worker farmer soldier college student she SP background

<u>*jì . . . yě . . .*</u>   bù   shì   gōngrén,   <u>yě</u> bù   shì   nóngmín,   <u>gèng</u> bù
both . . . and . . .   NEG   COP   worker   NEG COP   COP   farmer   more NEG

shì   dāng   bīng   de.
COP   be   soldier SP

{Nominally, she is a college student with a worker, farmer, or soldier background, but she has neither been a worker nor a farmer, let alone a soldier.}

(53) 这小子当年在批斗会上<u>既</u>不打人，<u>也</u>不骂人，<u>更</u>不让你坐"喷气式"，（但他……往往问得你满头冒汗。）

Zhè   xiǎozi   dāngnián   zài pīdòuhuì-shàng <u>jì . . . yě . . .</u>   bù   dǎ   rén,
this   guy   the past   at criticism meeting both . . . and . . .   NEG   beat person

<u>*yě*</u> bù   mà   rén,   <u>gèng</u> bù   ràng   nǐ
   NEG curse person more NEG make   you

zuò "pēnqìshì",
be punished with the head and back being forcibly held down so that the arms and legs are mutually perpendicular

(dàn   tā   . . . wǎngwǎng   wèn   de   nǐ   mǎn   tóu   màohàn.)
but   he   often   ask   SP   you whole forehead sweat

196 *Progressive gèng-sentences and adversative gèng-sentences*

{At those criticism meetings this guy would neither beat nor swear at you, let alone twist your arms backwards and forcibly press your head and back down, [but ... often made you have sweat all over your face with tough questions.]}

(54) 年轻女强人佩如既没有熬成一名老处女，也没有故意当单身贵族拖延婚配时间，更没有说熬到最后绷不住劲了才屈尊下嫁给一个老头子或丑八怪什么的。

    Niánqīng   nǚqiángrén   Pèirú <u>jì</u> . . . <u>yě</u> . . .   méiyǒu áo-chéng yī míng
    young   strong woman   Peiru both . . . and . . . NEG become a CL
    lǎochǔnǚ, <u>yě</u> méiyǒu gùyì   dāng dānshēn guìzú   tuōyán hūnpèi
    spinster   NEG deliberately be   successful single person delay marry
    shíjiān, <u>gèng</u> méiyǒu shuō áo-dào   zuìhòu   běng-bùzhù jìn
    time   more NEG   say hold on until last moment cannot hold the breath
    le   cái qūzūn   xiàjià-gěi   yī gè lǎotóuzi huò chǒubāguài shénmede.
    PEF late condescend marry down one CL old man or ugly person and the like
    {Peiru, a strong young woman, did not become an old maid, nor did she deliberately delay her marriage to remain a successful single woman, not to mention that she didn't get married down to an old or ugly guy when she couldn't hold on.}

    Both "*jì . . . yòu . . . gèng . . .*" and "*jì . . . yě . . . gèng . . .*" highlight the third one among the three juxtaposed aspects. "*jì . . . yòu/yě . . . gèng . . .*" sentences manifest a coordinate relationship and a progressive relationship: coordination marked by "*jì . . . yòu . . .*" or "*jì . . . yě . . .*" and progression marked by *gèng*.

    v) In general, if two coordinate clauses occur before *gèng* in a simple "*gèng*" complex sentence, the sentence can be rewritten as "*jì . . . yòu/yě . . . gèng . . .*" The following are two examples:

(55) 没有一个人劝解他，没有一个人开导他，更没有一个人用什么办法把他那愤愤不满的情绪改变分毫。

    Méiyǒu   yī gè rén   quànjiě tā, méi yǒu   yī gè rén   kāidǎo
    there not be one CL person persuade him there not be one CL person guide
    tā, <u>gèng</u> méiyǒu   yī gè rén   yòng shénme bànfǎ bǎ tā nà fènfèn
    him more there not be one CL person use any   method BA his that angry
    bùmǎn   de qíngxù gǎibiàn fēnháo.
    dissatisfied SP mood change a tiny bit
    {There was no one to persuade him or to guide him, not to mention that there was no one to quell his indignation even a bit in any way.}

(56) 她绝不愿向任何人陈述痛苦，不需要别人的同情，更不愿让人把自己看成受害的弱者。

    Tā jué   bù   yuàn xiàng rènhé rén   chénshù tòngkǔ, bù   xūyào
    she absolutely NEG would to   any   person tell   painful NEG need
    biérén de tóngqíng, <u>gèng</u> bù   yuàn ràng rén   bǎ zìjǐ   kàn-chéng
    others SP sympathize more NEG would make person BA oneself regard . . . as
    shòuhài   de   ruòzhě.
    fall victim   SP   the weak

Progressive gèng-sentences and adversative gèng-sentences 197

{She never wants to tell anyone about her pain, nor does she need other people's sympathy, not to mention that she doesn't want to be seen as a helpless victim.}

In (55), *jì* can be added and placed at the beginning of the first clause, and *yòu/yě* can be put before *méiyǒu* in the second clause, hence a "*jì . . . yòu/yě . . . gèng . . .*" sentence. A similar change can be made to (56).

If *yě* is present between the two juxtaposed clauses before the *gèng*-clause, *jì* can be added and placed in the first clause. The following are two examples:

(57)　……有人用梯子爬上了大相国寺的大雄宝殿屋脊，也有人登上了钟楼和鼓楼，更有几个力气大一些的年轻人爬上了铁塔的第二层。

    . . . Yǒu rén   yòng tīzi   pá-shàng   le   Dàxiàngguósì   de
    there be person use   ladder climb up to PEF   Great Daxiangguo Temple SP
    dàxióngbǎodiàn wūjǐ,   yě   yǒu   rén   dēng-shàng le   zhōnglóu hé
    main hall   roof ridge also there be person go up to   PEF bell tower and
    gǔlóu,   <u>gèng</u>   yǒu   jǐ   gè   lìqi   dà   yīxiē de
    drum tower furthermore there be a few CL physical strength great some SP
    niánqīng rén   pá-shàng   le   tiětǎ   de   dì'èr   céng.
    young   person climb up to PEF iron tower SP the second level

    {. . . some used ladders to climb up onto the roof of the main hall of the Great Xiangguo Temple, some went up to the bell tower and drum tower, and some young people with more strength even climbed up to the second level of the iron tower.}

(58)　我不代表上帝，也不代表神明，更不代表什么奇迹。

    Wǒ bù   dàibiǎo shàngdì,   yě   bù   dàibiǎo shénmíng,   <u>gèng</u> bù
    I   NEG represent God   also NEG represent deities   more NEG
    dàibiǎo shénme qíjì.
    represent any   miracle

    {I don't represent God or deities, let alone any miracles.}

In (57) *jì* can be added and placed before "*yǒu rén*", and in (58) *jì* can be added and placed between *wǒ* and "*bù dàibiǎo*".

vi) There is a difference between "*jì p, yě q, gèng r*" and "*jì p, yòu q, gèng r*". In "*jì p, yě q*", *q* is less important than *p* and acts as a complement to *p*, whereas in "*jì p, yòu q*", *q* is more important than *p* and hence emphasized.[4] Due to this difference, the form "*jì p, yě q, gèng r*" highlights *r* after using *q* as a complement to *p*, while the form "*jì p, yòu q, gèng r*" highlights *r* after stressing the importance of *q*. Compare (59) and (60):

(59)　苏阿姨既是出色的医生，也是出色的护士，更是不可挑剔的出色的妻子！

    Sū āyí   jì . . . <u>yě</u> . . .   shì   chūsè   de yīshēng, <u>yě</u> shì   chūsè   de
    SU aunt both . . . and . . . COP excellent SP doctor   COP excellent SP
    hùshi, <u>gèng</u> shì   bù   kě   tiāoti   de   chūsè   de   qīzi!
    nurse   more COP NEG can nitpick SP outstanding SP wife

198 *Progressive gèng-sentences and adversative gèng-sentences*

{Aunt SU is an excellent doctor, as well as an excellent nurse, and even an impeccable wife!}

(60) 苏阿姨<u>既</u>是出色的医生，<u>又</u>是出色的护士，<u>更</u>是不可挑剔的出色的妻子！
Sū āyí <u>jì</u>...<u>yòu</u>... shì chūsè de yīshēng, <u>yòu</u> shì chūsè de
SU aunt both...and... COP excellent SP doctor   COP excellent SP
hùshi, <u>gèng</u> shì bù kě tiāoti de chūsè de qīzi!
nurse more COP NEG can nitpick SP outstanding SP wife
{Aunt SU is not only an excellent doctor but also an excellent nurse, and even an impeccable wife!}

In (59), "being an excellent nurse" is not as important as "being an excellent doctor" and it acts as a complement to "being an excellent doctor". In (60), "being an excellent nurse" is another aspect, which is more important than "being an excellent doctor". Compare (61) and (62):

(61) 这些年，<u>既</u>有喜悦，<u>也</u>有辛酸，<u>更</u>有说不清道不明的惆怅。
Zhèxiē nián, <u>jì</u>...<u>yě</u>... yǒu xǐyuè, <u>yě</u> yǒu xīnsuān, <u>gèng</u> yǒu
these year, both...and...there be joyous there be sad more there be
shuō-bùqīng dào-bùmíng de chóuchàng.
cannot be easily or clearly described SP melancholy
{Over the years, there have been joys, as well as sorrows, and even indefinable melancholy.}

(62) 这些年，<u>既</u>有喜悦，<u>又</u>有辛酸，<u>更</u>有说不清道不明的惆怅。
Zhèxiē nián, <u>jì</u>...<u>yòu</u>... yǒu xǐyuè, <u>yòu</u> yǒu xīnsuān, <u>gèng</u>
these year, both...and...there be joyous there be sad more
yǒu shuō-bùqīng dào-bùmíng de chóuchàng.
there be cannot be easily or clearly described SP melancholy
{Over the years, there have been not only joys but also sorrows, and even indefinable melancholy.}

It is obvious that "*yòu yǒu xīnsuān*" ('but also sorrows') in (62) is more emphatic than "*yě yǒu xīnsuān*" ('as well as sorrows') in (61).

9.4 "*shàngqiě p, gèng q*"

A third non-simple form of "*gèng*" complex sentences is "*shàngqiě p, gèng q*".

Different from "*bùdàn p, gèng q*", which shows an upward progression, "*shàngqiě p, gèng q*" marks a downward progression. This form indicates that the validity of *p* determines the validity of *q*. The word *gèng* shows that *p* progresses downward to *q*. The following are two examples:

Progressive gèng-sentences and adversative gèng-sentences 199

(63) 我阅读唐诗宋词<u>尚且</u>有困难，诗经、楚辞就<u>更</u>看不懂了。

Wǒ yuèdú tángshī   sòngcí   <u>shàngqiě</u> yǒu   kùnnán,
I   read   Tang Dynasty poem Song Dynasty poem even   have difficulty
Shījīng,   Chǔcí   jiù   <u>gèng</u> kàn-bùdǒng   le.
The Book of Songs The Songs of Chu just more can't understand MP
{I even have difficulty in reading Tang Dynasty and Song Dynasty poems, let
alone *The Book of Songs* and *The Songs of Chu*.}

(64) 阿Q<u>尚且</u>能不师自通叫"二十年后又是一个"，我江锋<u>更</u>不能蔫头蔫脑掉架丢
脑！

Ā Q <u>shàngqiě</u> néng bùshī-zìtōng jiào "èrshí nián hòu yòu shì yī gè",
Ah Q even   can be self-taught shout twenty year after again COP one CL
wǒ Jiāng Fēng   <u>gèng</u> bù   néng niāntóu-niānnǎo diàojià-diūnǎo!
I   JIANG Feng more NEG can   cowardly   lose self-control and face
{Even Ah Q was able to shout "(I) will be another (real man) 20 years after (I
die)" without being taught to say that by anyone; how can I, JIANG Feng, be a
coward and lose face!}

There are five notes to this form.
i) Sentences in the structure of "*shàngqiě . . . gèng . . .*" can be expressed
by "*lián X yě . . . gèng . . .*". The following are two examples. If expressed by
"*shàngqiě . . . gèng . . .*", (65a) can be rewritten as (65b), and (66a) as (66b).

(65) a 我站在茫茫的雨中，<u>连</u>一个马蹄子印<u>也</u>找不到，<u>更</u>说不准她具体是什么时
候走的，是我临睡之前，还是我睡了以后？
Wǒ zhàn zài mángmáng de yǔ-zhōng, <u>lián</u> . . . <u>yě</u> . . . yī gè mǎtízi   yìn
I   stand at heavy   SP in rain even . . .   one CL horse's hoof print
<u>yě</u> zhǎo-bùdào, <u>gèng</u> shuō-bùzhǔn tā   jùtǐ shì shénme shíhou zǒu de,
cannot find   more be unsure   she exact COP what   time   leave SP
shì wǒ lín   shuì zhīqián, háishi wǒ shuì-le   yǐhòu?
COP I   about to sleep before   or   I sleep-PEF after
{I stood in the rain and could not even find a single hoof print, not to mention
that I couldn't tell exactly when she was gone, before or after I fell asleep.}

b 我站在茫茫的雨中，一个马蹄子印<u>尚且</u>找不到，<u>更</u>说不准……
Wǒ zhàn zài mángmáng de yǔ-zhōng, yī gè mǎtízi   yìn <u>shàngqiě</u>
I   stand at heavy   SP in rain one CL horse's hoof print even
zhǎo-bùdào, <u>gèng</u> shuō-bùzhǔn . . .
cannot find   more be unsure
{I stood in the rain and could not even find a single hoof print, not to mention
that I couldn't tell exactly . . .}

200 *Progressive gèng-sentences and adversative gèng-sentences*

(66) a 我连爹爹是谁<u>也</u>不知道，奶奶是谁<u>更加</u>不知道，……

Wǒ <u>lián</u> . . . <u>yě</u> . . . diēdie shì   shéi <u>yě</u> bù   zhīdào, nǎinai shì   shéi <u>gèngjiā</u>
I   even . . .   dad COP who   NEG know nan   COP who more

bù   zhīdào, . . .
NEG know

{I don't even know who my dad is, let alone who my nan is . . .}

  b 爹爹是谁<u>尚且</u>不知道，奶奶是谁<u>更加</u>不知道，……

Diēdie shì   shéi <u>shàngqiě</u> bù   zhīdào, nǎinai shì   shéi <u>gèngjiā</u>
dad   COP who even . . .   NEG know   nan   COP who more

bù   zhīdào, . . .
NEG know

{I don't even know who my dad is, let alone who my nan is . . .}

In the following example, "*zòngshì* ('even') X *yě*" meaning the same as "*lián X yě*", is a concessive clause structure emphasizing X.

(67) 顺治在五台山出家，康熙瞒得极紧，<u>纵是</u>至亲的建宁公主<u>也</u>不让知道，群臣
自然<u>更加</u>不知。

Shùnzhì zài Wǔtáishān   chūjiā,   Kāngxī mán   de jí
Shunzhi at   Wutai Mountain become a monk Kangxi conceal SP extremely

jǐn, <u>zòngshì</u> . . . <u>yě</u> . . . zhìqīn   de Jiànníng gōngzhǔ <u>yě</u> bù   ràng zhīdào,
tight even   close kin SP Jianning princess NEG let   know

qúnchén zìrán   <u>gèngjiā</u> bù   zhī.
ministers natural more   NEG know

{(Emperor) Shunzhi had become a monk at Wutai Mountain, and (Emperor) Kangxi kept it a secret from everyone. He didn't even let his close kin Princess Jianning know about it, let alone the ministers.}

Therefore, if expressed by "*shàngqiě . . . gèng . . .*", (67) can be rewritten as (68):

(68) 顺治在五台山出家，康熙瞒得极紧，至亲的建宁公主<u>尚且</u>不让知道，群臣自
然<u>更加</u>不知。

Shùnzhì zài Wǔtáishān   · chūjiā,   Kāngxī mán   de jí
Shunzhi at   Wutai Mountain become a monk Kangxi conceal SP extremely

jǐn, zhìqīn   de Jiànníng gōngzhǔ <u>shàngqiě</u> bù   ràng zhīdào, qúnchén
tight close kin SP Jianning princess even   NEG let   know   ministers

zìrán   <u>gèngjiā</u> bù   zhī.
natural more   NEG know

{(Emperor) Shunzhi had become a monk at Wutai Mountain, and (Emperor) Kangxi kept it a secret from everyone. He didn't even let his close kin Princess Jianning know about it, let alone the ministers.}

ii) Sentences in the structure of "*shàngqiě . . . gèng . . .*" can be expressed by "*lián X dōu . . . gèng . . .*". The following are two examples:

Progressive gèng-sentences and adversative gèng-sentences 201

(69)　阿珂连父母都不认，我这老公自然更加不认了。

 Ākē <u>*lián*</u> ... <u>*dōu*</u> ... *fùmǔ* <u>*dōu*</u> *bù*   *rèn,*   *wǒ* *zhè* *lǎogōng* *zìrán*
 Ake even ...   parents NEG recognize I   this husband natural

 <u>*gèngjiā*</u> *bù*   *rèn*   *le.*
 more   NEG recognize MP

 {Ake doesn't even recognize her parents, let alone me, her husband.}

(70)　连我都没想到，你更没想到，我们的老队长竟然让你这一篇话说得抿不住嘴
 地乐！

 <u>*Lián*</u> ... *dōu* ... *wǒ* *dōu* *méi* *xiǎng-dào,* *nǐ* <u>*gèng*</u> *méi* *xiǎng-dào,* *wǒ-men*
 even ...   I   NEG expect   you more NEG expect   we

 de *lǎo* *duìzhǎng* *jìngrán*   *ràng*   *nǐ* *zhè* *yī* *piān* *huà*   *shuō* *de*
 SP old captain unexpectedly PASSIVE you this one CL words say SP

 mǐn-bùzhù   *zuǐ* *de* *lè!*
 can't compress lips SP laugh

 {Even I didn't expect, let alone you, that what you had said would make our old
 captain grin!}

  If "*shàngqiě* ... *gèng(jiā)* ..." is to be used, (69) can be rewritten as (71), and
(70) as (72):

(71)　父母尚且不认，我这老公自然更加不认了。

 Fùmǔ <u>*shàngqiě*</u> *bù*   *rèn,*   *wǒ* *zhè* *lǎogōng* *zìrán*   <u>*gèngjiā*</u> *bù*
 parent even   NEG recognize I this husband natural more   NEG

 rèn   *le.*
 recognize MP

 {Ake doesn't even recognize her parents, let alone me, her husband.}

(72)　我尚且没想到，你更没想到，……

 Wǒ <u>*shàngqiě*</u> *méi* *xiǎng-dào,* *nǐ* <u>*gèng*</u> *méi*   *xiǎng-dào,*...
 I   even   NEG expect   you more NEG expect

 {Even I didn't expect, let alone you, that what you had said would make our old
 captain grin!}

  Even if *lián* is removed from "*lián X dōu* ... *gèng* ...", "*X dōu* ... *gèng* ..."
still means the same as "*shàngqiě* ... *gèng* ...", for example:

(73)　我都不怕，你们更加不用怕。

 Wǒ <u>*dōu*</u> *bù*   *pà,*   *nǐ-men* <u>*gèngjiā*</u> *bùyòng*   *pà.*
 I   even NEG be frightened you-PL more   unnecessarily be frightened

 {Even I am not frightened, not to mention that you shouldn't be frightened.}

  In this example, "*wǒ dōu bù pà* ..." can be rewritten as "*lián wǒ dōu bù pà* ..."
or "*wǒ shàngqiě bù pà* ...".

202 *Progressive gèng-sentences and adversative gèng-sentences*

iii) In "*shàngqiě . . . gèng . . .*" sentences, what *gèng* modifies is usually a VP or an AP, but in some sentences, this is not the case.

First, some sentences in the form of "*shàngqiě p, gèng hékuàng q*". For example, (63) can be written as (74):

(74) 我阅读唐诗宋词<u>尚且</u>有困难，<u>更何况</u>诗经楚辞？

Wǒ yuèdú tángshī   *sòngcí*   *shàngqiě yǒu*   *kùnnán,*
I   read   Tang Dynasty poem   Song Dynasty poem   even   have   difficulty

gèng hékuàng Shījīng,   *Chǔcí?*
more   let alone   *The Book of Songs*   *The Songs of Chu*
{I even have difficulty in reading Tang Dynasty and Song Dynasty poems, let alone *The Book of Songs* and *The Songs of Chu*.}

The following is another example:

(75) 据我所知，就<u>连</u>北大那几位死去的名教授的书画古玩<u>尚且</u>在劫难逃，<u>更何况</u>苏伯伯那区区几柜书呢？

Jù   *wǒ suǒ zhī, jiù lián . . . shàngqiě . . . běidà*   *nà*
according to I   PAP know just even . . .   Peking University that

jǐ   *wèi sǐqù de míng jiàoshòu de shūhuà*   *gǔwán*
several CL die   SP famous professor SP painting and calligraphy work antique

shàngqiě zàijié-nántáo,   *gèng hékuàng Sū bóbo nà*   *qūqū*
impossible to escape the fate   more   let alone   SU uncle   that   only

jǐ   *guì*   *shū*   *ne?*
several   cabinet   book   MP
{As far as I know, it was even impossible for the paintings, calligraphy works, and antiques owned by those famous professors at Peking University who had passed away to escape the fate (of being destroyed), let alone those few cases of books that Uncle SU has.}

The word *gèng* before *hékuàng* is optional, but the presence of *gèng* emphasizes an upward progression. In actual use, there are "(*shàngqiě*) . . . *hékuàng* . . . . *gèng hékuàng* . . ." sentences, which include three levels with two progressions. The function of *gèng* in those sentences is even more obvious. For example:

(76) 结婚？谈何容易。现在黄花闺女还嫁不出去，<u>何况</u>她这离婚的四十岁的女人，<u>更何况</u>她还有一个儿子。

Jiéhūn? Tánhéróngyì.   *Xiànzài huánghuāguīnǚ hái*
marry   easier said than done   now   virgin girl   even

jià-bùchūqù,   *hékuàng tā zhè líhūn de sìshí suì de nǚrén,*
be unable to get married   let alone   she   this   divorce   SP   forty   year   SP   woman

gèng hékuàng tā hái yǒu yī gè érzi.
more   let alone   she   even   have   one   CL   son

Progressive gèng-sentences and adversative gèng-sentences 203

{Getting married? It's difficult. Nowadays, even a young girl is unable to get married, let alone a divorced 40-year-old woman, and to make things worse she has a son.}

Second, some sentences in the form of "*shàngqiĕ p, gèng biéshuō q*". For example, (63) can be written as (77):

(77) 我阅读唐诗宋词尚且有困难，更别说诗经楚辞了！

Wŏ yuèdú tángshī   sòngcí   <u>shàngqiĕ</u> yŏu   kùnnán,
I   read   Tang Dynasty poem Song Dynasty poem even   have difficulty

<u>gèng</u> <u>biéshuō</u> Shījīng,   Chŭcí   le!
more let alone *The Book of Songs The Songs of Chu* MP

{I even have difficulty in reading Tang Dynasty and Song Dynasty poems, let alone *The Book of Songs* and *The Songs of Chu*.}

Following is another example:

(78) ……他连科室那几个坐办公室的姑娘都分不清楚，更别说别的姑娘。

. . . tā lián . . . <u>dōu</u> . . . kēshì   nà jĭ   gè zuò bàngōngshì de gūniang
he   even . . .   department that several CL sit office   SP girl

<u>dōu</u> fēn-bùqīngchŭ, <u>gèng</u> <u>biéshuō</u> bié   de gūniang.
still can't tell apart more let alone other SP girl

{. . . he can't even tell apart those few girls who work in the office, let alone other girls.}

There are a number of similar expressions to "*gèng biéshuō*, such as "*gèng bùbì shuō*", "*gèng bùyào shuō*", "*gèng bùyòng shuō*". The following are two examples:

(79) 见面尚且怕，更不必说敢有托付了。

Jiànmiàn <u>shàngqiĕ</u> pà,   <u>gèng</u> <u>bùbì shuō</u>   găn yŏu   tuōfù   le.
meet   even   be afraid more needless to say dare make request MP

{(I) was even afraid to meet (them), needless to say that (I) dared not request (them) to do anything).}

(80) 丁山河连一个在外边搞工作的亲戚都没有，更不用说有职有权人的关系，（所以他绝无脱离农村的后门可走！）

Dīng Shānhé <u>lián</u> . . . <u>dōu</u> . . . yī gè zài wàibiān găo gōngzuò de qīnqi   <u>dōu</u>
DING Shanhe even . . .   a CL on outside do work   SP relative

méiyŏu, <u>gèng</u> <u>bùyòng shuō</u>   yŏu zhí   yŏu quán   rén   de guānxì,
not have more needlessly to say have position have authority person SP relation

(suŏyĭ   tā jué   wú   tuōlí nóngcūn de hòumén kĕ zŏu!)
therefore he absolutely not have leave countryside SP back door can go by

204 *Progressive gèng-sentences and adversative gèng-sentences*

{DING Shanhe does not even have a relative who works in town, let alone a relationship with someone in a position of authority, [so there is no back door for him to get out of the countryside!]}

If *"gèng biéshuō"* or its synonym is present in the posterior clause, the sentence is a downward progressive one, even though *shàngqiě* is absent in the anterior clause, for example:

(81)　这个余春生，从来就反对她到漠县来，<u>更不要说</u>到回水岗这样的山区了。

Zhè gè Yú Chūnshēng, cónglái jiù fǎnduì tā dào Mò xiàn lái, gèng
this CL YU Chunsheng, always just oppose her come Mo county DC more
bùyào shuō dào Huíshuǐgǎng zhèyàng de shānqū le.
let alone go to Huishuigang such SP mountainous area MP
{This YU Chunsheng has always opposed her coming to Mo County, let alone going to such a mountainous area as Huishuigang.}

vi) A simple *"gèng"* complex sentence can be rewritten as a downward progressive one, provided that in the sentence the movement from *p* to *q* is a downward progression. For example, (4) can be rewritten as (82a) or (82b):

(82)　a 困难尚且没有，痛苦（自然）更谈不上。

Kùnnán shàngqiě méiyǒu, tòngkǔ zìrán gèng tán-bùshàng.
difficulty even not have painful natural more be out of the question
{There is no difficulty, let alone pain.}

　　b 连困难都没有，（自然）更谈不上痛苦。

Lián . . . dōu . . . kùnnán dōu méiyǒu, (zìrán) gèng tán-bùshàng
even . . . difficulty not have natural more be out of the question
tòngkǔ.
painful
{There is no difficulty, let alone pain.}

In the following examples, (83) can be rewritten as (85), and (84) as (86).

(83)　友谊不是爱情，同情<u>更</u>不等于爱情。

Yǒuyì bù shì àiqíng, tóngqíng gèng bù děngyú àiqíng.
friendship NEG COP love sympathize more NEG equal love
{Friendship is not love, and sympathy is even less equal to love.}

(84)　咱们(是光知道改革的好处，)不理解改革的难处，<u>更</u>体会不到阻力有多大。

Zánmen (shì guāng zhīdào gǎigé de hǎochù,) bù lǐjiě gǎigé de
we COP only know reform SP benefit NEG understand reform *SP*
nánchù, gèng tǐhuì-bùdào zǔlì yǒu duō dà.
difficulty more can't realize resistance have how considerable

Progressive gèng-sentences and adversative gèng-sentences 205

{We [only know the benefits of reform,] do not even understand the difficulties of reform, not to mention that we cann't realize how considerable the resistance is.}

(85) 友谊尚且不是爱情，同情自然更不等于爱情!

Yŏuyì   shàngqiĕ bù   shì   àiqíng, tóngqíng   zìrán   gèng   bù   dĕngyú
friendship even   NEG COP love   sympathize natural more NEG equal

àiqíng!
love

{Friendship does not equal love, and sympathy is even less equal to love.}

(86) 咱们连改革的难处都不理解，自然更体会不到阻力有多大。

Zánmen lián ... dōu ...   gǎigé   de nánchù   dōu   bù   lĭjiĕ,   zìrán
we   even...   reform SP difficulty   NEG understand natural

gèng tĭhuì-bùdào zŭlì   yŏu   duō   dà.
more can't realize resistance have how considerable

{We do not even understand the difficulties of reform, not to mention that we can't realize how considerable the resistance is.}

v) The essential relationship between *p* and *q* in downward progressive sentences is "because *p* is valid, *q* is certainly valid". This relationship indicates that *q* is, as a matter of fact, inferred from *p*; therefore, downward progressive sentences have in common with inferential causal sentences. For this reason, "*shàngqiĕ* . . . *gèng* . . ." sentences can be paraphrased by "*jìrán* . . . (*nàme*) *jiù* . . ." sentences. The following is a paraphrase of (64):

(87) 阿Q既然能不师自通叫"二十年后又是一个"，那么，我江锋就更不能蔫头蔫脑掉架丢脑!

Ā Q   jìrán   néng bùshī-zìtōng jiào "èrshí nián hòu yòu shì yī
Ah Q now that can be self-taught shout twenty year after again COP one

gè", nàme, wǒ Jiāng Fēng jiù   gèng bù   néng niāntóu-niānnǎo
CL   Then I JIANG Feng just more NEG can   cowardly

diàojià-diūnǎo!
lose self-control and face

{Since even Ah Q was able to shout "(I) will be another (real man) 20 years after (I die)" without being taught (to say that) by anyone, then I, JIANG Feng, certainly can't be a coward and lose face!}

Since "*jìrán* . . . (*nàme*) *jiù* . . ."—a inferential sentence marker—is used, (87) is an inferential one rather than a progressive one. Compare the following examples:

(88) 刘毛妹都还没有能入党，小陶她自然更不能马上入党。

Liú Máomèi dōu   hái méiyŏu néng rù   dăng, Xiăo Táo tā   zìrán   gèng
LIU Maomei even still NEG   can join party little TAO she natural more

bù   néng măshàng   rù   dăng.
NEG can   immediately join Party

206 *Progressive gèng-sentences and adversative gèng-sentences*

{Even LIU Maomei can't join the party, not to mention that little TAO can't do it immediately.}

(89)　<u>既然</u>刘毛妹都还没有能入党，那（小陶）她<u>就更</u>······

<u>Jìrán</u>　　Liú Máomèi　dōu　hái　méiyǒu néng rù　dǎng,　nà　(Xiǎo Táo)
now that　LIU Maomei　even　still　NEG　can　join party　then　little TAO

tā　<u>jiù</u>　<u>gèng</u> . . .
she　just　more

{Since even LIU Maomei is not qualified to join the party yet, let alone [little TAO] her . . .}

In (88), the use of "*dōu . . . gèng . . .*" indicates that the sentence is a downward progressive sentence, whereas in (89) the use of "*jìrán . . . nà jiù . . .*" obscures the progressive relationship and marks the sentence as a general inferential-causal sentence. The following is another example:

(90)　师叔<u>既然</u>不知，我们<u>更加</u>不知了。

Shīshū　<u>jìrán</u>　bù　zhī,　wǒ-men　<u>gèngjiā</u>　bù　zhī　le.
master uncle　now that　NEG　know　we　more　NEG　know　MP

{Since Uncle doesn't know, let alone us.}

With the marker *jìrán*, (90) is an inferential-causal complex sentence. However, if *jìrán* is replaced by *shàngqiě*, the sentence will change into a downward progressive complex sentence, as (91):

(91)　师叔<u>尚且</u>不知，我们<u>更加</u>不知了。

Shīshū　<u>shàngqiě</u>　bù　zhī,　wǒ-men　<u>gèngjiā</u>　bù　zhī　le.
master uncle　even　NEG　know　we　more　NEG　know　MP

{Uncle doesn't even know, let alone us.}

9.5　"*gùrán p, gèng q*"

A fourth non-simple "*gèng*" complex sentence form is "*gùrán p, gèng q*".

In "*gùrán p, gèng q*", *gùrán* affirms *p*, and based on this affirmation *gèng* highlights *q*, which is at a higher level than *p*. Thus, "*gùrán p, gèng q*" can be regarded as a progressive sentence form based on an affirmation.[5] The following are three examples:

(92)　下头儿<u>固然</u>不可过于冒犯，上头儿<u>更</u>不能得罪。

Xiàtóur　<u>gùrán</u>　bù　kě　guòyú màofàn,　shàngtóur　<u>gèng</u>　bù
subordinate　admittedly　NEG　can　too　offend　superior　more　NEG

néng　dézuì.
can　offend

{Subordinates certainly can't be offended too much, let alone superiors.}

Progressive gèng-sentences and adversative gèng-sentences 207

(93) 虫子<u>固然</u>可怕，两条腿的虫子<u>更</u>可怕。

Chóngzi <u>gùrán</u>   kěpà, liǎng tiáo tuǐ de chóngzi <u>gèng</u> kěpà.
bug   admittedly scary two CL leg SP bug   more scary
{Scary as bugs are, two-legged bugs are even scarier.}

(94) 灰衣人的轻功姿势<u>固然</u>美妙，他用伞子杀人的招式<u>更</u>是好看。

Huī yī   rén   de   qīnggōng zīshì   <u>gùrán</u>   měimiào,   tā
gray clothes person SP light kung fu posture admittedly wonderful he

yòng sǎnzi   shā rén   de   zhāoshì <u>gèng</u> shì   hǎokàn.
use   umbrella kill people SP   move   more   COP   good-looking
{The light kung fu posture of the man in gray is certainly wonderful, and his move to kill with the umbrella is even better.}

Five points should be noted.

First, the word *zìrán* also indicates an affirmation, thus *gùrán* can be used interchangeably with *zìrán*. For example, *gùrán* in (92) can be substituted by *zìrán*. The following is another example, in which *zìrán* can be replaced by *gùrán*:

(95) 爱情<u>自然</u>令人销魂，权力<u>更</u>令人向往。

Àiqíng <u>zìrán</u>   lìng rén   xiāohún,   quánlì <u>gèng</u> lìng
love   admittedly make person be overwhelmed with joy power more make

rén   xiàngwǎng.
person desire
{While love is admittedly enchanting, power is even more desirable.}

Second, all complex sentences in the form of *"gùrán p, gèng q"* have a semantic commonality, i.e., an affirmation followed by a progression. Besides, there is a hidden adversative relationship in various degrees between the antecedent and the consequent.

Thus, some sentences in the form of *"gùrán p, gèng q"* can be rewritten as *"suīrán . . . dàn/què . . ."*. For example, (96) is a rewrite of (92):

(96) 下头儿虽然不可过于冒犯，上头儿却更不能得罪。

Xiàtóur   suīrán   bù   kě guòyú màofàn, shàngtóur què   gèng bù
subordinate although NEG can too   offend superior however more NEG

néng dézuì.
can offend
{Subordinates certainly can't be offended too much, let alone superiors.}

In some sentences in the form of *"gùrán p, gèng q"*, the word *gùrán* cannot be replaced by *suīrán*, but *dàn/què* can be used in the posterior clause. Among the following examples, (97) is a rewrite of (93), and (98) is a rewrite of (94).

208   *Progressive gèng-sentences and adversative gèng-sentences*

(97)   虫子固然可怕，两条腿的虫子却更可怕。

Chóngzi gùrán   kěpà, liǎng tiáo tuǐ de chóngzi què   gèng kěpà.
bug   admittedly scary two   CL leg SP bug   however more scary
{Scary as bugs are, two-legged bugs are even scarier.}

(98)   灰衣人的轻功姿势固然美妙，他用伞子杀人的招式却更是好看。

Huī yī   rén   de qīnggōng   zīshì   gùrán   měimiào, tā yòng
gray clothes person SP light kung fu posture admittedly wonderful he use

sǎnzi   shā rén   de zhāoshì què   gèng shì   hǎokàn.
umbrella kill people SP move   however more COP good-looking
{The light kung fu posture of the man in gray is certainly wonderful, but his move
to kill with the umbrella is even better.}

Here are two more examples, in which *gùrán* cannot be substituted by *suīrán*,
but *dàn/què* can be placed before *gèng/gèngjiā*:

(99)   此言一出，白衣尼<u>固然</u>一愕，躲在床后的韦小宝<u>更</u>是大吃一惊。

Cǐ yán   yī   chū,   báiyī ní   <u>gùrán</u>   yī è,
this remark as soon as come out nun in white clothing admittedly a be shcoked

duǒ zài chuáng-hòu de Wéi Xiǎobǎo <u>gèng</u> shì   dàchī-yījīng.
hide behind bed   SP WEI Xiaobao more COP shocked
{As soon as they heard the words, the white-clothing nun was shocked, while
WEI Xiaobao, who was hiding behind the bed, was even more shocked.}

(100)   韦小宝<u>固然</u>愁眉苦脸，陆先生<u>更加</u>惴惴不安。

Wéi Xiǎobǎo   <u>gùrán</u>   chóuméi-kǔliǎn,   Lù xiānshēng
WEI Xiaobao   admittedly   wearing a sad and worried face LU mister

<u>gèngjiā</u>   zhuìzhuì-bù'ān.
more   anxious and fearful
{While WEI Xiaobao looked sad and worried, Mr. LU was even more anxious
and fearful.}

Third, there is no adversative connective between the clauses in "*gùrán p, gèng
q*", and the word *gèng* acts as a progression undertaker, indicating a progression
from *p* to *q*. However, the presence of the adversative connective between the
clauses, such as *dàn, què*, or the like, highlights the adversative relationship, and
therefore the progressive relationship is obscured.

Any complex sentences with an adversative connective—whether in the form
of "*suīrán p, dàn/què gèng q*" or "*gùrán p, dàn/què gèng q*"—should be categorized as concessive complex sentences, i.e., a subtype of adversative complex
sentences. The following are two examples:

Progressive gèng-sentences and adversative gèng-sentences 209

(101) 这周围八百里的梁山泊，这被压迫者的"圣地"的梁山泊，<u>固然</u>需要一双铁臂膊，却<u>更</u>需要一颗伟大的头脑。

Zhè zhōuwéi   bābǎi   lǐ de Liángshān Pō,   zhè bèi
this surrounding area eight hundred CL SP Liangshan Marsh this PASSIVE

yāpò zhě   de "shèngdì" de Liángshān Pō,   <u>gùrán</u>   xūyào yī shuāng
oppress person SP holy land SP Liangshan Marsh admittedly need a pair

*tiě   bìbó, **què**   <u>gèng</u> xūyào yī kē wěidà de tóunǎo.*
iron arm however more need a CL great SP mind

{Liangshan Marsh, the "holy land" of the oppressed, covering an area of 800 *li*, not only needs a pair of iron arms, but more a great mind.}

(102) 说雍正是累死的<u>固然</u>有溢美之嫌，但说他自杀身亡就未免<u>更</u>离谱了。

Shuō Yōngzhèng shì lèi-sǐ   de <u>gùrán</u>   yǒu   yìměi
say Yongzheng COP die of exhaustion SP admittedly there be over praise

*zhī xián,   **dàn** shuō tā zìshā   shēnwáng jiù wèimiǎn <u>gèng</u>*
SP suspicion but say he commit suicide die   just truly   more

lípǔ   le.
ridiculous MP

{Admittedly, to attribute (Emperor) Yongzheng's death to hard work might be a glorification of him, but it is even more outrageous to say that he committed suicide.}

Examples (101) and (102) are concessive complex sentences. Only if *dàn* or *què* is removed can they be regarded as progressive complex sentences based on an affirmation.

The following are another two examples:

(103) 唐二十四少爷<u>虽然</u>不喜欢杀人，但更不喜欢看见自己欣赏的人被杀。

*Táng èrshísì shàoyé   <u>suīrán</u>   bù   xǐhuān shā rén, **dàn** <u>gèng</u>*
TANG Twenty-four young master although NEG like   kill person but more

bù xǐhuān kànjiàn zìjǐ   xīnshǎng de rén   bèi   shā.
NEG like see   himself like   SP person PASSIVE kill

{Young master TANG Twenty-four doesn't like to kill, but more than that, he doesn't want to see people he likes being killed.}

(104) 西门慕名轻功<u>虽然</u>不弱，但公孙我剑这一下急攻<u>更</u>是锋利无匹。

*Xīmén Mùmíng   qīnggōng   <u>suīrán</u>   bù   ruò,   **dàn** Gōngsūn Wǒjiàn*
XIMEN Muming light kung fu although NEG weak but GONGSUN Wojian

zhè yī xià jí   gōng <u>gèng</u> shì   fēnglì wúpǐ.
this one CL quick attack more COP sharp have no rivals

{XIMEN Muming is quite good at light kung fu, but this quick attack of GONGSUN Wojian is sharp and invincible.}

With "*suīrán . . . dàn . . .*", (103) and (104) are typical concessive sentences. If "*suīrán . . . dàn . . .*" is removed, they will be simple "*gèng*" complex sentences.

210 *Progressive gèng-sentences and adversative gèng-sentences*

Fourth, in some progressive sentences based on an affirmation there is no adversative relationship between *p* and *q*. There are two cases.

Case 1: In some sentences in the form of *"gùrán p, gèng q"*, the movement from *p* to *q* is an upward progression. Thus, those *"gùrán . . . gèng . . ."* sentences can be paraphrased as *"bùjǐn . . . gèng . . ."*, for example:

(105) 此去山西五台山，这条路<u>固然</u>从未走过，前途<u>更</u>是一人不识。

Cǐ qù Shānxī Wǔtáishān, zhè tiáo lù **gùrán** cóngwèi zǒu-guò,
this go Shanxi Wutai Mountain this CL road admittedly never travel-EXP

qiántú **gèng** shì yī rén bù shí.
future furthermore COP A person NEG know

{This time the road to Wutai Mountain in Shanxi has not only never been taken before, and more than that, there is no one (I) know along the way.}

Example (105) can be paraphrased as (106):

(106) 这条路不仅从未走过，前途更是一人不识。

Zhè tiáo lù bùjǐn cóngwèi zǒu-guò,
this CL road not only never travel-EXP

qiántú gèng shì yī rén bù shí.
future more COP one person NEG know

{This time the road to Wutai Mountain in Shanxi has not only never been taken before, and more importantly, there is no one (I) know along the way.}

The difference between (105) and (106) is that the former highlights the affirmation of "the road never been taken before" with *gùrán* but the latter does not.

Case 2: In some sentences in the form of *"gùrán p, gèng q"*, movement from *p* to *q* is a downward progression. Thus, those *"gùrán . . . gèng . . ."* sentences can be paraphrased as *"shàngqiě . . . gèng . . ."*, for example:

(107) （茅兄身上有伤，显不出真功夫。）老朽打赢了<u>固然</u>没什么光彩，打输了<u>更</u>是没脸见人。

（*Máoxiōng shēn-shàng yǒu shāng, xiǎn-bùchū zhēn gōngfu.*）
MAO brother on body there be injury can't show real kung fu

Lǎoxiǔ dǎ-yíng le **gùrán** méi shénme guāngcǎi, dǎ-shū
me an old man defeat PEF admittedly not have any glorious lose

le **gèng** shì méi liǎn jiàn rén.
PEF more COP not have face see people

{[Brother MAO has injuries, so he can't show his real kung fu.] There would be no glory in my win, and it would be even more shameful if I was defeated.}

Example (107) can be paraphrased as (108). The difference between (107) and (108) is that with *gùrán* the former highlights the affirmation of "no glory in my win".

Progressive *gèng*-sentences and adversative *gèng*-sentences 211

(108) 老朽打赢了尚且没什么光彩，打输了更是没脸见人。

Lǎoxiǔ   dǎ-yíng le   shàngqiě méi   shénme guāngcǎi, dǎ-shū
me an old man defeat PEF even   not have any   glorious   lose

le   gèng shì   méi   liǎn jiàn rén.
PEF more COP not have face see person

{There would be no glory in my win, and it would be even more shameful if I was defeated.}

In addition, it is generally assumed that there exists an innate adversative relationship between the clauses in a complex sentence introduced by *gùrán*.[6] However, as can be seen from this discussion, the assumption is not always ture. The following are three more examples:

(109) 两位施主年纪轻轻，武功如此了得，老衲<u>固然</u>见所未见，<u>而且</u>是闻所未闻，少年英雄，真了不起，了不起！

Liǎng wèi shīzhǔ niánjì qīng-qīng,   wǔgōng rúcǐ liǎodé,   lǎonà
two   CL donor age   young-REDP kung fu so   outstanding me an old monk

gùrán   jiànsuǒwèijiàn, érqiě   shì   wénsuǒwèiwén,   shàonián
admittedly have never seen furthermore COP have never heard of juvenile

yīngxióng, zhēn liǎobùqǐ,   liǎobùqǐ!
hero   truly amazing   amazing

{You two young people are so outstanding in kung fu. I have certainly never seen (such excellent kung fu), and I have never even heard of it. Young heroes, amazing, amazing!}

(110) 韦小宝平时说话，出口便是粗话，"他妈的"三字片刻不离口，但讲到沐英平云南的故事，学的是说书先生的口吻，粗话<u>固然</u>一句没有，偶然<u>还</u>来几句或通不通的成语。

Wéi Xiǎobǎo   píngshí   shuōhuà,   chūkǒu biàn shì   cūhuà,
WEI Xiaobao   normal times speak   speak just COP foul language

"tāmāde" sān zì   piànkè   bù   lí   kǒu,   dàn jiǎng-dào Mù Yīng
fuck   three character an instant NEG leave mouth but talk about MU Ying

píng Yúnnán de gùshì, xué de shì   shuōshū   xiānshēng de kǒuwěn,
pacify Yunnan SP story learn SP COP tell stories performer SP tone

cūhuà   gùrán   yī jù   méiyǒu, ǒurán   hái   lái jǐ   jù
foul language admittedly one CL not have occasionally even do a few CL

huòtōngbùtōng   de chéngyǔ.
barely make sense SP idiom

{WEI Xiaobao never speaks without foul language, and he can't do without saying "fuck". Nevertheless, when he told MU Ying's story of pacifying Yunnan, he imitated the storytelling performer's tone. Not only did he not use any rude words, but he even occasionally came up with some idioms that barely made sense.}

212   *Progressive gèng-sentences and adversative gèng-sentences*

(111) 这一来，庄家全家<u>固然</u>逮入京中，连杭州将军松槐、浙江巡抚朱昌祚以下所有大小官员，<u>也都</u>革职查办。

Zhèyīlái,   Zhuāng jiā   quán jiā   <u>gùrán</u>   dǎi   rù   jīng-zhōng,
as a result ZHUANG family whole family admittedly arrest enter in capital city

lián... yě...   Hángzhōu   jiāngjūn   Sōng Kuí,   Zhèjiāng   xúnfǔ
even...   Hangzhou   general   SONG Kui   Zhejiang   governor

Zhū Chāngzuò   yǐxià   suǒyǒu   dà   xiǎo   guānyuán,   <u>yě</u>   <u>dōu</u>
ZHU Changzuo   under   entire   senior   junior   official   all

gézhí   chábàn.
remove from office   investigate and charge

{As a result, the entire ZHUANG family was arrested and sent to the capital, and moreover, even Hangzhou General SONG Kui, Zhejiang Governor ZHU Changzuo, and all the senior and junior officials under them were dismissed to be investigated and charged accordingly.}

In the three aforementioned examples, the movement from the anterior clause introduced by *gùrán* to the posterior clause is an upward progression: a greater degree, or a higher level, or a wider range. There is no adversative relationship in these sentences.

Fifth, some simple "*gèng*" complex sentences can be rewritten as progressive complex sentences based on an affirmation or even as concessive complex sentences, providing that there exist a hierarchal distance and a contrast between *p* and *q*. For example, (5) can be rewritten as (112) and (113):

(112) 发现一篇好作品固然不容易，培养一个作者更不容易。

Fāxiàn yī piān hǎo   zuòpǐn gùrán   bù   róngyì, péiyǎng yī   gè   zuòzhě
find   a CL   good work admittedly NEG easy   bring up one CL writer

gèng bù   róngyì.
more NEG easy

{It's not easy to find a good work, and it's even harder to cultivate a writer.}

(113) 发现一篇好作品固然不容易，但培养一个作者却更不容易。

Fāxiàn yī piān hǎo   zuòpǐn gùrán   bù   róngyì, dàn péiyǎng yī   gè
find   a CL   good work admittedly NEG easy   but bring up one CL

zuòzhě què   gèng bù   róngyì.
writer   however more NEG easy

{It's not easy to find a good work, but it's even harder to cultivate a writer.}

The following are two more examples:

(114) 看来我不了解吴尘，吴尘<u>更</u>不了解我。

Kànlái   wǒ   bù   liǎojiě Wú Chén, Wú Chén <u>gèng</u> bù   liǎojiě wǒ.
it seems I   NEG know   WU Chen Wu Chen more NEG know   me

{It seems that I know little about WU Chen, and WU Chen knows even less about me.}

Progressive gèng-sentences and adversative gèng-sentences   213

(115)   ……祖国需要我，我<u>更</u>需要祖国啊！

… *Zŭguó   xūyào   wŏ,   wŏ   **gèng**   xūyào   zŭguó   a!*
motherland   need   me   I   more   need   motherland   MP
{… my motherland needs me, and I need my motherland even more!}

Example (114) can be rewritten as (116a) and (116b), and (115) as (117a) and (117b):

(116)   a   我固然不了解吴尘，吴尘更不了解我。

Wŏ   gùrán   bù   liăojiĕ   Wú Chén,   Wú Chén   gèng   bù   liăojiĕ   wŏ.
I   admittedly   NEG   know   WU Chen   Wu Chen   more   NEG   know   me
{It is true that I know little about WU Chen, and WU Chen knows even less about me.}

b   我固然不了解吴尘，吴尘却更不了解我。

Wŏ   gùrán   bù   liăojiĕ   Wú Chén,   Wú Chén   què   gèng   bù   liăojiĕ
I   admittedly   NEG   know   WU Chen   Wu Chen   however   more   NEG   know
wŏ.
me
{It is true that I know little about WU Chen, but WU Chen knows even less about me.}

(117)   a   祖国固然需要我，我更需要祖国！

Zŭguó   gùrán   xūyào   wŏ,   wŏ   gèng   xūyào   zŭguó!
motherland   admittedly   need   me   I   more   need   motherland
{My motherland needs me, and I need my motherland even more!}

b   祖国固然需要我，我却更需要祖国！

Zŭguó   gùrán   xūyào   wŏ,   wŏ   què   gèng   xūyào   zŭguó!
motherland   admittedly   need   me   I   however   more   need   motherland
{My motherland needs me, but I need my motherland even more!}

In such simple "*gèng*" complex sentences, the progressive relationship is explicit. The adversative relationship, by comparison, is implicit. If *gùrán* is present, these sentences will become progressive sentences based on an affirmation, and despite the overall progressive relationship, an adversative relationship starts to emerge. If the adversative connective *dàn* or *què* is present in these progressive sentences, it will mark them as concessive adversative ones.

Summary

First, "*gèng*" complex sentences in modern Chinese can be in various forms, as in the following table:

214 *Progressive gèng-sentences and adversative gèng-sentences*

Table 9.1 "gèng" complex sentences in modern Chinese

"gèng" complex sentences	
Simple form	*Non-simple forms*
p, gèng q	*bùdàn p, gèng q*
	jì p, gèng q
	shàngqiě p, gèng q
	gùrán p, gèng q

Second, there are semantic commonalities between simple "*gèng*" complex sentences and non-simple "*gèng*" complex sentences. However, the semantic relationships in the former are more complicated than that in the latter. For example, the five sentences listed at the beginning of this chapter represent the five possible semantic relationships embodied in the sentence form "*p, gèng q*", among which the last four can be rewritten respectively as "*bùdàn p, gèng q*", "*jì p, gèng q*", "*shàngqiě p, gèng q*", and "*gùrán p, gèng q*". Only the first relationship cannot be expressed by any non-simple form; therefore example (118a), a sentence indicating the first relationship, cannot be rewritten as any of the other four forms (118b—118e).

(118) a 我爱北京，我更爱今天的北京。
      Wǒ   ài   Běijīng, wǒ gèng ài   jīntiān de Běijīng.
      I   love Beijing I   more love today SP Beijing
      {I love Beijing, particularly today's Beijing.}

      b* 我不但爱北京，我更爱今天的北京。
      Wǒ bùdàn   ài   Běijīng, wǒ gèng ài   jīntiān de Běijīng.
      I   not only love Beijing I   more love today SP Beijing

      c* 我既爱北京，我更爱今天的北京。
      Wǒ jì   ài   Běijīng, wǒ gèng ài   jīntiān de Běijīng.
      I   both love Beijing I   more love today SP Beijing

      d* 北京我尚且爱，今天的北京我更爱。
      Běijīng wǒ shàngqiě ài,   jīntiān de Běijīng wǒ gèng ài.
      Beijing I   even   love today SP Beijing I   more love

      e* 我固然爱北京，我更爱今天的北京。
      Wǒ gùrán   ài   Běijīng, wǒ gèng ài   jīntiān de Běijīng.
      I   admittedly love Beijing I   more love today SP Beijing

Those simple "*gèng*" complex sentences that cannot be rewritten as non-simple ones have a semantic feature: what is stated in the posterior clause is part of what is stated in the anterior clause, i.e., *q* is included in *p*. In those sentences, *gèng* is used to show progression and to emphasize *q*. Furthermore, no connectives

Progressive gèng-sentences and adversative gèng-sentences 215

indicating progression can occur in the anterior clause. The following are another two examples of those sentences:

(119) 我害怕回忆十年动乱的岁月，更害怕回忆1967年夏季的那段时间。

Wǒ hàipà huíyì shí nián dòngluàn de suìyuè, gèng hàipà huíyì 1967 nián
I fear recall ten years of turmoil SP time more fear recall 1967 year

xiàjì de nà duàn shíjiān.
summer SP that period Time

{I'm terrified to recall those ten years of turmoil, in particular the summer of 1967.}

(120) 我无法忘怀家乡的一切，更无法忘怀家乡的那条小河。

Wǒ wúfǎ wànghuái jiāxiāng de yīqiè, gèng wúfǎ
I be unable to forget hometown SP everything more be unable to

wànghuái jiāxiāng de nà tiáo xiǎo hé.
forget hometown SP that CL small river

{I can't forget anything in my hometown, especially the small river.}

Third, different from conjunctions, such as *érqiě, dànshì, suǒyǐ, gèng* is an adverb, thus it cannot always be used as a complex sentence (or sentence group) relationship marker. The same holds for other adverbs, such as *dōu, hái, yě, jiù*. It is important to understand when *gèng* can be used as a connective, for example, both the antecedent and the consequent need to be present and the relationship between them need to have particular features. The study of all these characteristics of *gèng* will have implications for the research on other adverbs that can act as connectives.

NB Some examples in this chapter are cited from literary works, political essays, articles, and so on. The sources are listed as follows:

1 *Changjiang Literature* (《长江》) 1988(1), including (6), (14), (15), (26), (44), and (81); 1989(3), including (5) and (114);
2 *Changpian Xiaoshuo Xuankan* (《长篇小说专辑》) 1984(2), including (3), (11), (34), (36), (45), (55), (70), and (80);
3 *Chinese* for Junior High School Students, Book 1, including (42);
4 *Dangdai* (《当代》) 1984(1), including (2), (10), (31), (46), (56), (58), (65a), (83), (84), and (92); 1988(1), including (28) and (33);
5 *Eight Hundred Words in Modern Chinese* (《现代汉语八百词》), including (63);
6 *Fiction Monthly* (《小说月报》) 1997(6), including (54);
7 *Flower City* (《花城》) 1983(3), including (52);
8 *Harvest* (《收获》) 1982(2), including (76); 1987(6), including (18) and (40);
9 *I Love New Beijing* (《我爱新北京》) by LAO She, including (1);
10 *In Memory of the Forgotten* (《为了忘却的纪念》) by LU Xun (鲁迅), including (79);

11 *Li Zicheng* (《李自成》) written by YAO Xueyin (姚雪垠) and published in 1981, including (19), (21), and (22);
12 *Lotus* (《芙蓉》) 1984(2), including (34); 1988(4), including (18) and (40);
13 *Love and Tramp* (《爱情与陷阱》) by GAO Fang (高放), including (63);
14 *Northern Literature* (《东北文学》) 1988(57)(总第57期), including (24);
15 *October* (《十月》) 1983(4), including (53) and (75); 1987(5), including (64);
16 *Qingming* (《清明》) 1983(3), including (50);
17 *Selected Stories* (《小说选刊》) 1996(11), including (93);
18 *Selected Works of Excellent Chinese Short Stories in 1980*(《1980年全国优秀短篇小说评选获奖作品集》), including (89);
19 *Selected Works of MAO Dun* (《矛盾文集》), including (101);
20 *Shenzhen Economic Daily* (《深圳商报》), 1999 (August 25), including (27); 1999(August 26), including (102);
21 *The Deer and the Cauldron* (《鹿鼎记》) by JIN Yong (金庸), including (66a), (67), (69), (70), (90), (99), (100), (105), (107), (109), (110), and (111);
22 *Wolongji* (《卧龙记》) by an unknown author, including (25), (35), (41), (51), (94), (103), and (104);
23 *Zhongshan* (《钟山》) 1983(4), including (78);
24 *Zhuhai* (《珠海》) 1988(总第10期), including (23).

Notes

1 LI Jinxi (黎锦熙) and LIU Shiru (刘世儒). *Coorinated Phrases and Cooridinated Complex Sentences* (《联合词组和联合复句》). New Knowledge Press, 1958; LIU Yuehua (刘月华). *Practical Grammar of Chinese* (《实用汉语语法》). Foreign Language and Teaching Research Press, 1983.
2 HU Yushu (Ed.) (胡裕树). *Modern Chinese* (《现代汉语》). Shanghai Education Press, 1981.
3 ZHANG Zhigong (张志公) (Ed.). *Chinese Knowledge* (《汉语知识》). Beijing: People's Education Press, 1979. In addition, in another book (HUANG Borong (黄伯荣) and LIAO Xudong (廖旭东). *Modern Chinese* (《现代汉语》). Gansu People's Press, 1983.), "*gèng*" complex sentences are completely absent, and only "*gèng bùbì shuō*" and "*gèng bùyòng shuō*" are mentioned.
4 More information about the comparisons between "*jì . . . yě . . .*" and "*jì . . . yòu . . .*" can be found in another book written by the author, i.e.: XING Fuyi (邢福义). *Complex Sentences and Connectives* (《复句与关系词语》). Heilongjiang People's Press, 1985, pp. 74–75.
5 The word *gùrán* shows affirmation, more information can be found in another book, i.e., LV Shuxian (吕叔湘). *Eight Hundred Words in Modern Chinese* (《现代汉语八百词》). The Commercial Press, 1980, pp. 206–207.
6 More information can be found in the following two books:

   (i) LV Shuxian (吕叔湘). Eight Hundred Words in Modern Chinese (《现代汉语八百词》). Beijing: The Commercial Press, 1980.
   (ii) Department of Chinese Language and Literature, Peking University (Ed.). *Interpretations of Grammatical Words in Modern Chinese* (《现代汉语虚词例释》). The Commercial Press, 1982, p. 216.

10 Factive "*jíshĭ p, yĕ q*"

It is generally assumed that *p* in sentences in the form of "*jíshĭ p, yĕ q*" is a hypothesis, but it can also refer to a fact. This chapter makes a special study on factive sentences in the form of "*jíshĭ p, yĕ q*". For convenience, sentences in the form of "*jíshĭ p, yĕ q*" are termed as hypothetical *jíshĭ*-sentences if what is stated in *p* is a hypothesis, and as factive *jíshĭ*-sentences if what is stated in *p* is a fact.

This chapter is divided into four sections, each devoted to the discussion of one of the four basic forms of factive *jíshĭ*-sentences. Whether or not a *jíshĭ*-sentence can be regarded as factive depends on the context. The basic forms aforementioned refer to those "*jíshĭ p, yĕ q*" forms based on a specific context. The examples used in this chapter include typical complex sentences, non-typical ones, and compacted ones.

Synonyms of *jíshĭ* include *jíbiàn, jílìng, zòngshĭ*, and so on, which are not differentiated in this chapter.

10.1 "*nàshí . . . jíshĭ p, yĕ q*"

The first sentence form is "*nàshí . . . jíshĭ p, yĕ q*". In this form, "*nàshí*" is not literally "then", but the sum of the time reference and the fact reference; *jíshĭ* introduces an amended wording *p*. Thus, this form can be termed as an amended form. The following is an example:

(1)　那时，他们很少交谈。<u>即使</u>交谈，<u>也</u>只是工作上的联系，干干巴巴，三言两语。

　　Nàshí,　tā-men　hěn　shǎo　jiāotán.　Jíshĭ . . . yĕ . . . jiāotán,　yĕ zhĭshì
　　that time　they　very　rare　converse　even if . . .　converse　only

　　gōngzuò-shàng　de　liánxì,　gāngānbābā,　sānyán-liǎngyǔ.
　　in work　SP　contact　dry　only a few words

　　{At that time, they rarely talked to each other. Even if they did, their conversation was only work-related, brief, and dry.}

In the aforementioned example, *jiāotán* ('talk') is a past event, while "*jíshĭ jiāotán . . .*" ('even if they talked to each'), meaning that they only talked occasionally, amends the wording "*hěn shǎo jiāotán*" ('rarely talked to each other').

DOI: 10.4324/9781003374237-10

218 *Factive "jíshǐ p, yě q"*

10.1.1 Time-referential expression

The word *nàshí* ('back then') or its equivalent is used as the time reference in sentences in the form of "*jíshǐ p, yě q*". Equivalents to *nàshí* include *píngrì* ('normally') or *xiànglái* ('always'), but in the context what these words refer to is when the event took place. The following are two examples:

(2) 大革命失败后，这些工人组织都被摧垮了，<u>即使</u>有留下来的工会，会员数目与党员差不多，已经很少。

Dàgémìng   shībài   hòu, zhèxiē gōngrén zǔzhī   dōu   bèi
great revolution fail   after   these   worker   organization all   PASSIVE

cuīkuǎ-le,   <u>jíshǐ</u>   yǒu   liú-xiàlái de gōnghuì, huìyuán shùmù   yǔ
destroy-PEF even if there be remain   SP trade union member number as

dǎngyuán   chàbùduō,   yǐjīng   hěn   shǎo.
party member roughly the same already very   few

{After the failure of the First Civil Revolutionary War, those workers' organizations were destroyed. Even if some trade unions survived, the number of their members was roughly as small as that of the Party members.}

(3) 平日, 他少言寡语, 只把心操在编辑工作上, <u>即使</u>有点小小的不顺心，<u>也</u>常常就在肚子里消化了。(可这一回，他实在无法冷静了。)

Píngrì,   tā shǎoyán-guǎyǔ, zhǐ bǎ cāoxīn   cāo zài biānjí
normal times he taciturn   only BA focus attention   at   edit

gōngzuò-shàng, <u>jíshǐ</u> . . . <u>yě</u> . . . yǒu diǎn xiǎo-xiǎo   de bù   shùnxīn,   <u>yě</u>
on work   even if . . .   have a bit small-REDP SP NEG satisfactory

chángcháng jiù zài . . . lǐ dùzi   lǐ xiāohuà-le. (Kě zhè yī   huí,   tā
often   just in   stomach digest-PEF but this one time he

shízài   wúfǎ   lěngjìng le.
really   be unable to calm   MP

{In normal times, he is quiet and only focuses on his editorial work. Even if he is a little upset, he often bottles up his unhappiness. [However, this time, he can't keep calm.]}

In (2), "after the failure of the First Civil Revolutionary War" means "the time after the First Civil Revolutionary War failed", whereas in (3) *píngrì* refers to the days before "this time".

If the time of the occurrence of the event is self-evident or does not need to be emphasized, the time-referential expression can be absent. The following are two examples:

(4) 皇帝倒是每天一早必到永和宫请安，但见到太后的时候甚少，<u>即使</u>见到了，太后<u>也</u>脸无笑容，沉默寡言。

Huángdì dàoshì   měi   tiān yīzǎo   bì   dào   Yǒnghé Gōng
emperor although every day   early morning surely go to   Yonghe Palace

qǐng'ān,   dàn   jiàn-dào tàihòu   de shíhou shèn   shǎo,
pay respects to but   see   empress dowager SP time   very   little

Factive "jíshǐ p, yě q" 219

jíshǐ . . . yě . . .	jiàn-dào	le,	tàihòu		yě	liǎn	wú
even if . . .	see	PEF	empress dowager			face	not have

xiàoróng,	chénmò	guǎyán.
smiling expression	silent	quiet

{Although the Emperor went to Yonghe Palace every morning to greet the Empress Dowager, he seldom saw her. Even if he got to see her, she was unsmiling and silent.}

(5)　工棚里，没有了往日的欢笑。即使歪诗杜和苟玉田能设法引出一点笑声，听来也是干巴巴的让人难受。

Gōngpéng-lǐ,	méiyǒu-le		wǎngrì	de	huānxiào.	Jíshǐ . . . yě . . .
in work shed	there not be-PEF		the past	SP	laugh heartily	even if . . .

Wāishī Dù	hé	Gǒu Yùtián	néng	shèfǎ	yǐnchū	yīdiǎn	xiàoshēng,
Doggerel DU	and	GOU Yutian	can	manage to	elicit	a little	laughter

tīng-lái	yě	shì	gānbābā	de	ràng	rén	nánshòu.
sound	COP	dry		SP	make	person	uncomfortable

{In the work shed there was no longer the hearty laughter you would hear in the past. Even if DU—the doggerel writer—and GOU Yutian managed to elicit a bit of laughter, it would sound uncomfortably dull.}

It is understood that in both (4) and (5), the temporal setting is "those days".

10.1.2　Fact-referential expression

In sentences in the form of "jíshǐ p, yě q", the fact-referential expression, which can be short or long, is written in declarative language. The following are two examples:

(6)　那时……"勇士们"大打出手，不由分说地乒乒乓乓砸烂了许多人家送给表叔油漆的家具，痛心如煎的表叔公，面对这场横祸的解决办法是用一根宽宽的毛蓝布腰带结束了自己的生命，即使是无力的反抗，表叔公也使用了他的独特的表示愤怒的方式！

Nàshí . . .	"yǒngshì-men"	dàdǎchūshǒu,	bùyóufēnshuō		de
that time	warrior-PL	attack brutally	allow no explanation		SP

pīngpīngpāngpāng	zálàn-le	xǔduō	rénjiā	sòng-gěi	biǎoshū	yóuqī
banging	smash-PEF	many	others	give	uncle	paint

de	jiājù,	tòngxīnrújiān	de	biǎoshūgōng,	miànduì	zhè	chǎng
SP	furniture	grieved	SP	uncle's father	face	this	CL

hènghuò		de	jiějué	bànfǎ	shì	yòng	yī	gēn	kuān-kuān
unexpected calamity		SP	resolve	way	COP	use	one	CL	wide-REDP

de	máolánbù	yāodài	jiéshù-le	zìjǐ	de	shēngmìng,
SP	indigotine fabric	belt	end-PEF	oneself	SP	life

jíshǐ . . . yě . . .	shì	wúlì		de	fǎnkàng,	biǎoshūgōng	yě	shǐyòng-le	tā
even if . . .	COP	have no strength		SP	resist	uncle's father		use-PEF	he

de	dútè	de	biǎoshì	fènnù	de	fāngshì!
SP	distinctive	SP	express	indignant	SP	way

220 *Factive "jíshǐ p, yě q"*

{At that time the "warriors" struck and smashed a lot of painted furniture given to Uncle by others. Uncle's father, who was sorely grieved, killed himself with a wide indigotin belt. That was his way to face the unexpected calamity. Even though it was a feeble protest, he expressed his indignation in a unique way!}

(7) 我记得那时北方的许多临铁路的小城，都是汽车站紧挨着火车站，这无疑是为了使旅客搭乘换车较为方便，可是其脏乱程度就加倍了，两个车站以及相连接的地带也成了简易"旅社"，特别是夏末秋初之交，气候尚能容人露宿时，很多无钱或舍不得花钱住店的旅客，都横七竖八地倚坐或躺卧在候车室的地上休息，⋯⋯ 即使有人带了被卷，那被卷也通常用一块自织的土布包着，那包布虽有点暗红土绿的条纹，也脏污得辨不出颜色。

Wǒ jìde **nàshí** běifāng de xǔduō lín tiělù de xiǎo chéng,
I remember that time north SP many be close to railway SP small town

dōu shì qìchēzhàn jǐn āi-zhe huǒchēzhàn, zhè wúyí
all COP coach station very close be adjacent-PRG railway station this have no doubt

shì wèile shǐ lǚkè dāchéng huànchē jiàowéi fāngbiàn, kěshì qí
COP in order to make passenger travel by transfer relatively convenient but its

zāng luàn chéngdù jiù jiābèi-le, liǎng gè chēzhàn yǐjí xiāng
dirty messy degree then double-PEF two CL station as well as mutually

liánjiē de dìdài yě chéng-le jiǎnyì "lǚshè", tèbié shì xiàmò
join SP area also become-PEF simple hostel particularly COP end of summer

qiūchū zhī jiāo, qìhòu shàng néng róng rén lùsù
beginning of fall SP join climate still can allow human being sleep outdoors

shí, hěn duō wú qián huò shěbùde huā qián zhù diàn
time very many not have money or be reluctant to spend money stay at hostel

de lǚkè, dōu héngqī-shùbā de yǐzuò huò tǎngwò zài hòuchēshì de
SP passenger all disorderly SP recline or lie down at waiting room SP

dì-shàng xiūxi, ... jíshǐ ... yě ... yǒu rén dài-le bèijuǎn, nà bèijuǎn yě
on floor rest even if ... there be person bring-PEF quilt that quilt

tōngcháng yòng yī kuài zì zhī de tǔbù bāo-zhe, nà
usually use one piece self weave SP homemade fabric wrap-PRG that

bāobù suī yǒu diǎn ànhóng tǔlǜ de tiáowén, yě
homemade fabric although have a little dull red brownish green SP stripe still

zāngwū de biàn-bùchū yánsè.
dirty SP cannot make out color

{I remember that back then, in many small northern cities near the railway line, the bus station was located next to the railway station. This was undoubtedly to make it easier for passengers to transfer between the bus and train, but the area was even dirtier and messier because of that—the two stations and the connecting area thus became a simple "hostel". Particularly at the turn of late summer and early autumn, when the climate allowed people to sleep in the open, many passengers who couldn't afford to or didn't want to pay to stay in a hostel leaned back or lay down on the floor in the waiting room to rest. Even if someone brought a quilt, it was usually wrapped with a piece of homemade fabric. Although the fabric had dull red and brownish green stripes, it was so dirty that the colors couldn't be made out.}

Factive "jíshǐ p, yě q" 221

In (6) and (7), the content between *nàshí* and the section of "*jíshǐ p, yě q*" is the fact-referential expression. The ellipsis dots are used to refer to what is omitted, but the remaining part is still quite long. Sentences (6) and (7) can be respectively compacted into (8) and (9) so that the sentence structure will become clear.

(8)　那时，痛心如煎的表叔公用一根腰带结束了自己的生命，<u>即使</u>是无力的反抗，他<u>也</u>使用了自己表示愤怒的方式！

Nàshí,　tòngxīnrújiān de biǎoshūgōng yòng yī　gēn yāodài jiéshù-le zìjǐ
that time grieved　　SP uncle's father use　one CL belt　　end-PEF oneself

de　shēngmìng, jíshǐ . . . yě . . . shì　wúlì　　　de fǎnkàng, tā　yě
SP　life　　　even if . . .　COP　have no strength　SP resist　he　also

shǐyòng-le　zìjǐ　　biǎoshì　fènnù　　de　fāngshì!
use-PEF　　oneself　express　indignant　SP　way

{At that time Uncle's father, who was sorely grieved, killed himself with a belt. Even though it was a feeble protest, he expressed his indignation in his unique way!}

(9)　那时，很多无钱或舍不得花钱住店的旅客都在候车室的地上休息，<u>即使</u>有人带了被卷，那被卷<u>也</u>通常用一块自织的土布包着，脏污得辨不出颜色。

Nàshí,　hěn duō　wú　　qián　huò shěbùde　　huā　qián　zhù
that time very many not have money or　be reluctant to spend money stay at

diàn de lǚkè　　dōu zài hòuchēshì　　de dì-shàng xiūxi, jíshǐ . . . yě . . .
hotel SP passenger all　at waiting room SP on floor rest　even if . . .

yǒu　rén　dài-le　　bèijuǎn, nà　bèijuǎn yě tōngcháng yòng yī　kuài
there be person bring-PEF quilt　that quilt　also usually　use one piece

zì　zhī　de tǔbù　　　bāo-zhe, zāngwū de biàn-bùchū　　yánsè.
self weave SP homemade fabric wrap-PRG dirty　SP cannot make out color

{Back then, many passengers who couldn't afford to or didn't want to pay to stay in a hostel leaned back or lay down on the floor in the waiting room to rest. Even if someone brought a quilt, it was usually wrapped with a piece of homemade fabric, which was so dirty that the colors couldn't be made out.}

10.1.3　*p restricted by time reference and in opposition to fact reference*

First, *p* in "*jíshǐ p, yě q*" is restricted by the time reference. Second, there is a semantic conflict between what is stated in *p* and the fact reference. The fact reference refers to a general situation, but what is stated in *p* is inconsistent with that situation. Therefore, *p* is an amendment to the generation situation. In (1) "rarely talk to each other" and "talked", and in (2) "those workers' organizations were destroyed and "some trade unions survived" are two examples of inconsistency between what is stated in *p* and the fact reference. The following is another example:

222 Factive *"jíshǐ p, yě q"*

(10) ……（向来）小镇的男女青年百分之九十九点九，都是一到婚龄都自然而然地"树上的鸟儿成双对"，<u>即使</u>不能说对对都是美满姻缘，<u>却也</u>大多如意。

...(Xiànglái) xiǎo zhèn de nánnǚ　　　qīngnián bǎi fēn zhī jiǔshíjiǔ diǎn jiǔ,
always　　　 small town SP male and female youth　　ninety-nine point nine percent
dōu shì　yī　dào　hūnlíng　　dōu zìrán-érrán de "shù-shàng de niǎor
all　 COP once reach age of marriage all　natural　 SP on tree　　SP bird
chéng　shuāngduì", *jíshǐ* . . . *yě* . . . bù　　néng shuō duì-duì　 dōu shì
become　pair　　　 even if . . .　　NEG can　say　every pair　all　 COP
měimǎn　yīnyuán, *què*　*yě*　dàduō　rúyì.
perfect　marriage however　　　mostly　be satisfactory

{In the small town, 99.9% of the young men and women [always] naturally get "paired up like the birds in the tree" as soon as they reach the age of marriage. Most of the couples are happy, even if not all marriages are perfectly satisfactory.}

In the aforementioned example, there is an obvious conflict between "get paired up" and "not all marriages are perfectly satisfactory". In some sentences, the conflict is literally expressed, but in other sentences it is between the lines. Whether the conflict is explicit or implicit, *p* and *q* are restricted by the time reference: since *nàshí* can be used, both *p* and *q* are realis. If, on the other hand, *nàshí* cannot be used, *"jíshǐ p, yě q"* is hypothetical. The following are two examples.

(11) 他说，"文革前"，……不敢打听，<u>即使</u>问了<u>也</u>没用……

Tā　shuō, "wéngé　　　　qián", . . . bù gǎn　dǎting,　　*jíshǐ* . . . *yě* . . .
he　say　 Cultural Revolution before　NEG　dare　ask about　even if . . .
wèn-le　*yě* méi　　yòng . . .
ask-PEF　　 there not be　use

{He said, "Before the Cultural Revolution . . . I dared not ask about it, and even though I had asked, it would have been useless . . ."}

(12) 面子撕不开啊！<u>即使</u>撕开了，杨喜堂拍屁股一跑，又得花多少钱去铺这条路啊。

Miànzi　sī bù kāi　　　　a! *Jíshǐ*　sī-kāi　le,　Yáng Xǐtáng　pāipìgu
face　　cannot be torn apart MP　even if　tear apart PEF YANG Xitang　throw up job
yī　pǎo, yòu　děi　huā　duōshǎo qián　qù pū　zhè tiáo lù　a.
once leave again must spend how much money go pave this CL road MP

{(I) can't fall out with YANG Xitang! Even if (I) did, how much would it cost to pave the road if he quit and left!}

In (11), although the time reference—"before the Cultural Revolution"—is present, both "asking" and "being useless" are irrealis. In (12), the time reference is absent, and "falling out with YANG Xitang" and "YANG Xitang leaving" are irrealis. Thus, the two examples are both hypothetical sentences in the form of *"jíshǐ p, yě q"*.

Factive "*jíshǐ p, yě q*"   223

10.1.4   Postpositional "*jíshǐ p*" in factive *jíshǐ*-sentences

To emphasize *p* in factive *jíshǐ*-sentences, "*jíshǐ p*" can be placed after *q*. Compare (13) and (14):

(13)   那些日子，你对大哥太冷漠。即使他从来没有埋怨一句，但你确实伤了他的心。

  Nàxiē   rìzi,   nǐ   duì   dàgē   tài   lěngmò.   Jíshǐ   tā   Cónglái
  those   day   you   to   eldest brother   too   indifferent   even if   he   ever

  méiyǒu   mányuàn   yī   jù,   dàn   nǐ   quèshí   shāng-le   tā   de   xīn.
  NEG   complain   one   CL   but   you   indeed   hurt-PEF   he   SP   heart

  {In those days, you were too indifferent to (your) eldest brother. You really hurt his feelings, even though he never complained.}

(14)   不过，碧桐说你对大哥冷漠，这是事实。你确实伤了大哥的心——即使他从来没有埋怨一句。

  Bùguò,   Bìtóng   shuō   nǐ   duì   dàgē   lěngmò,   zhè   shì   shìshí.
  but   Bitong   say   you   to   eldest brother   indifferent   this   COP   truth

  Nǐ   quèshí   shāng-le   dàgē   de   xīn—   jíshǐ   tā   cónglái   méiyǒu
  you   indeed   hurt-PEF   eldest brother   SP   heart   even if   he   ever   NEG

  mányuàn   yī   jù.
  complain   one   CL

  {However, Bitong said that you were too indifferent to (your) eldest brother, and it is true. You really hurt his feelings, even if he never complained.}

The postpositioned *p in* (14) is more prominent than the pre-positioned *p* in (13).

10.1.5   Alternatives to *jíshǐ*

In general, *jíshǐ* can be replaced by *suīrán* ('although'), or by *suīrán ǒu'ěr* ('although occasionally'). Two examples are (1) and (2). In (1), "even if they talked" can be replaced by "although they talked occasionally'" and in (2), "even if some trade unions survived" can be rewritten as "although some trade unions survived".

In sentences in the form of "*nàshí . . . jíshǐ p, yě q*", *jíshǐ* can deflate or play down *p*, the supplementary fact. However, if *suīrán* replaces *jíshǐ*, the deflation of *p* will become a recognition of *p*. Compare (15) and (16):

(15)   ……（那时）（船员们）进国货商店就没有那种窝囊气。虽然有的店员不客气，他们心里也坦然。

  . . . (nàshí)   (chuányuán-men)   jìn   guóhuò   shāngdiàn   jiù   méiyǒu
  that time   mariner-PL   enter   domestic goods   shop   just   not have

  nà   zhǒng   wōnangqì.   Suīrán   yǒude   diànyuán   bù   kèqì,   tā-men
  that   kind   annoyance   although   some   shop assistant   NEG   polite   they

  xīn-lǐ   yě   tǎnrán.
  in heart   still   calm

224 *Factive "jíshǐ p, yě q"*

{. . . [At that time] [the seafarers] didn't have that type of petty annoyances when they visited domestic goods stores. Although some shop assistants were rude, the seafarers were at ease.}

(16)　……（那时）（船员们）进国货商店就没有那种窝囊气。<u>即使</u>有的店员不客气，他们心里<u>也</u>坦然。

　　. . . (nàshí) (chuányuán-men) jìn　guóhuò　　shāngdiàn jiù　méiyǒu
　　that time　　mariner-PL　　　enter　domestic goods　shop　　 just　not have
　　nà　zhǒng　wōnangqì.　Jíshǐ . . . yě . . .　yǒude　diànyuán　　bù　　kèqi,
　　that　kind　　annoyance　even if . . .　　some　shop assistant　NEG　polite
　　tā-men　xīn-lǐ　　yě　tǎnrán.
　　they　　in heart　　calm

　　{. . . [At that time] [the seafarers] didn't have that type of petty annoyances when they visited domestic goods stores. Even though some shop assistants were rude, the seafarers were at ease.}

In (15), *suīrán* marks *p* as a fact and concedes it. In (16), *jíshǐ* plays down *p* and concedes it.

10.2　*"jíshǐ p (zài . . . shíhòu/dìfāng/zhōng/lǐ), yě q"*

In *"jíshǐ p (zài . . . shíhòu/dìfāng/zhōng/lǐ), yě q"*, *p* is acted by the prepositional structure *"zài . . . shíhòu/dìfāng/zhōng/lǐ"*, which specifies a point of time or a location. The following are two examples:

(17)　中国的民族资产阶级，<u>即使</u>在革命时, <u>也</u>不愿意同帝国主义完全分裂，……

　　Zhōngguó de　mínzú zīchǎnjiējí, jíshǐ . . . yě . . . zài . . . shí gémìng shí, yě bù
　　China　　SP nation bourgeoisie even if . . .　　when　　revolt　　NEG
　　yuànyì　　tóng dìguózhǔyì wánquán　fēnliè, . . .
　　be willing to　with imperialism completely separate

　　{China's national bourgeoisie was unwilling to be completely separated from imperialism even during the revolution . . .}

(18)　否则，（让吊脚弓）吊死了一个不应该吊死的人，<u>即使</u>在这一片蛮荒之地，<u>也</u>没有你的立足之地了。

　　Fǒuzé,　　(ràng　diàojiǎogōng)
　　otherwise　allow　 a trap that hangs the prey by the arch of the foot
　　diào-sǐ　　　le　yī　gè　bù　　yīnggāi　diào-sǐ　　　de　rén,
　　kill by hanging　PEF　one　CL　NEG　should　kill by hanging　SP　person
　　jíshǐ . . . yě . . . zài zhè yī　piàn　mánhuāng zhī dì,　yě méiyǒu　　nǐ
　　even if . . .　　in this one piece　wild　　SP land　　 there not be　you
　　de　lìzú　　　zhī　dì　　le.
　　SP　keep a foothold　SP　place　MP

　　{Otherwise, if the trap killed someone who should not be killed, there would be no place for you even in this wild land.}

In (17), "even during the revolution" specifies the time, and in (18), "even in this wild land" specifies the location.

Factive "jíshǐ p, yě q" 225

10.2.1 Specificity of the zài-structure

In *"jíshǐ p (zài . . . shíhòu/dìfāng/zhōng/lǐ), yě q"*, the *zài*-structure acting as *p* needs to refer to a particular time or location related to a realis event. What the *zài*-structure refers to must have been mentioned in the preceding context, unless it refers to a well-known event, such as "those three years of economic difficulties" and "the Cultural Revolution". The following are two examples:

(19) 看到的，总是那单调而往复不息的推拉刨锯的动作；听到的，总是木头和
金属撞击啃咬的错杂而刺耳的嘈音。若不是有了千曲，他早都厌烦了这单
调无味的劳动，而现在，一切都由于她的存在，她的身影而百物生辉
了。⋯⋯因此，<u>即使</u>在劳作漫长的白日中，他<u>也</u>从内心感应到一种和谐韵
律，⋯⋯

Kàn-dào de,   zǒng   shì   nà   dāndiào   ér   wǎngfù   bù   xī   de
see   SP   always COP that monotonous and repeat   NEG stop SP

tuī   lā   bàojù de   dòngzuò,   tīng-dào de, zǒng   shì   mùtou hé   jīnshǔ
push pull saw SP movement hear   SP   always COP wood and metal

zhuàngjī kěnyǎo de cáo   yīn.   Ruò bùshì yǒu-le   Qiānqǔ, tā zǎo
bang   gnaw   SP noisy sound if NEG there be-PEF Qianqu he early

dōu   yànfán-le   zhè dāndiào-wúwèi de láodòng, ér xiànzài, yīqiè
already be sick of-PEF this monotonous SP labor   but now   everything

dōu yóuyú tā   de   cúnzài, tā   de   shēnyǐng ér   bǎi   wù
all due to she SP exist she SP figure   then numerous object

shēnghuī-le. . . . Yīncǐ, jíshǐ . . . yě . . . zài . . . zhōng láozuò màncháng de
brighten-PEF therefore even if . . .   during   work   long   SP

báirì   zhōng, tā yě cóng nèixīn gǎnyìng-dào yī zhǒng héxié yùnlǜ, . . .
daytime he from heart feel   one kind harmonious rhythm

{What you see is always the monotonous and repeated movement of saw pushing and pulling, and what you hear is always the mixed and harsh noise of the banging and gnawing of wood and metal. If it had not been for Qianqu, he would have become tired of this monotonous labor a long time ago, but now, everything is shining because of her existence and her figure . . . Therefore, even during the long day of work, he still feels a kind of harmonious rhythm from the bottom of his heart . . .}

(20) 广州东峰湖新溪浦
Guǎngzhōu Dōngfēng Hú   Xīnxīpǔ
Guangzhou Dongfeng Lake Xinxipu
{Xinxipu, Dongfeng Lake, Guangzhou

十一月二十日二十点
Shíyī yuè   èrshí rì   èrshí   diǎn
November the twentieth twenty o'clock
8 pm November 20

南国的夜晚，<u>即使</u>在冬天吧，<u>也</u>仍是旖旎和浪漫的。
Nánguó   de   yèwǎn jíshǐ . . . yě . . . zài dōngtiān ba, yě réng shì
the South SP night even if . . .   in winter   MP   still COP

226 *Factive "jíshǐ p, yě q"*

yǐnǐ	hé	làngmàn	de.
charming	and	romantic	SP

Evenings in the South, even in winter, are still charming and romantic.}

In these two examples, the context makes it clear which day "the long day of work" refers to and which winter "the winter" refers to.

If the *zài*-structure lacks specificity, the sentence cannot be regarded as a factive *jíshǐ*-sentence even though the *zài*-structure is present after *jíshǐ*; for example:

(21) 我感到有几分悲凉, 这几棵称为 "响杨" 的树，二十年前还是我和张茹亲手栽的呐，树苗是行政处长从新疆运来的，响杨名符其实，即使在微风中也威武地抖动着，⋯⋯

Wǒ gǎndào yǒu jǐ fēn bēiliáng, zhè jǐ kē chēng-wéi
I feel have several CL desolate this several CL be called
"xiǎngyáng" de shù, èrshí nián qián háishì wǒ hé Zhāng Rú
ringing poplar SP tree twenty year before actually I and ZHANG Ru
qīnshǒu zāi de ne, shùmiáo shì xíngzhèng chùzhǎng
with one's own hands plant SP MP sapling COP administration section chief
cóng Xīnjiāng yùn-lái de, xiǎngyáng míngfúqíshí, *jíshǐ*...*yě*...
from Xinjiang transport SP ringing poplar live up to the name even if...
zài...*zhōng* wēifēng zhōng *yě* wēiwǔ de dǒudòng-zhe,...
in breeze powerful SP shake-PRG

{I feel a little desolate. These trees, which are called "ringing poplar", were actually planted by ZHANG Ru and me, with our own hands, twenty years ago. The saplings had been transported from Xinjiang by Director of Administration. The ringing poplars deserve their name, shaking powerfully even in the breeze . . .}

This example is not a factive *jíshǐ*-sentence, as "the breeze" is not specifically related to a realis event.

10.2.2 *Function of demonstrative pronouns in the zài-structure*

If the *zài*-structure includes a demonstrative pronoun, such as *zhè* or *nà*, the time or location that the structure refers to is usually specific. For instance, *zhè* in *"jíshǐ zài zhè yī piàn mánhuāng zhī dì"* in (18) is a specific location. Example (21) will become a factive *jíshǐ*-sentence if rewritten as (22) with *zhèyàng* specifying the location:

(22) "响杨" 名符其实，即使在这样的微风中，也威武地抖动！

"Xiǎngyáng" míngfúqíshí, *jíshǐ*...*yě*... *zài*...*zhōng* **zhèyàng**
ringing poplar live up to the name even if... in such
de wēifēng zhōng, *yě* wēiwǔ de dǒudòng!
SP breeze powerful SP shake

{The ringing poplars deserve their name, shaking powerfully even in such a breeze . . .}

Factive "jíshǐ p, yě q" 227

In some sentences, only a demonstrative pronoun is present before the temporal or locative expression without descriptive expressions in the *zài*-structure. In these sentences, the *zài*-structure has a very clear reference. The following is an example:

(23) （徐彦文：）"……那些年，什么正直，什么良心，什么道德，早都被践踏了。……"（刘迟：）<u>即使</u>在那个年代，大多数<u>人也</u>并没有泯灭自己的良知！"
(Xú Yànwén): …"nàxiē nián, shénme zhèngzhí, shénme liángxīn, shénme
XU Yanwen those year what righteous what conscience what
dàodé, zǎo dōu bèi jiàntà-le…." (Liú Chí:) <u>Jíshǐ</u>…<u>yě</u>… zài
morality early already PASSIVE destroy-PEF LIU Chi even if… in
nà gè niándài, dàduōshù rén <u>yě</u> bìng méiyǒu mǐnmiè zìjǐ de liángzhī!"
that CL time majority person indeed NEG lose oneself SP conscience
{[XU Yanwen,] ". . . In those years, everything was destroyed, be it integrity, conscience, or morality . . ." [LIU Chi,] "Even back then, most people didn't leave their conscience behind!"}

10.2.3 Supplementary information after the zài-structure

In some sentences in the form of "*jíshǐ p (zài . . . shíhòu/dìfāng/zhōng/lǐ), yě q*", supplementary information about the related fact follows the *zài*-structure. The following are two examples.

(24) 其实，牛福对儿子管教极为严格，<u>即使</u>在三年经济困难时期，市场上买不到煤油，牛福<u>也</u>不惜高价弄几斤，不让儿子闲着。
Qíshí, Niú Fú duì érzi guǎnjiào jíwéi yángé, jíshǐ…<u>yě</u>… zài sān
actually NIU Fu with son discipline extremely strict even if… in three
nián jīngjì kùnnan shíqī, shìchǎng-shàng mǎibùdào méiyóu, Niú Fú <u>yě</u>
year economy difficult period on market cannot buy kerosene NIU Fu
bùxī gāojià nòng jǐ jīn, bù ràng érzi xián-zhe.
not begrudge high price get several 500 grams NEG let son idle-PRG
{In fact, NIU Fu was very strict with his son. Even in those three years of economic difficulties, when kerosene was not on the market, NIU Fu would not hesitate to buy some at a high price to keep his son from being idle. (Without a lamp, his son wouldn't be able to study at night.)}

(25) 所以，<u>即使</u>在今天，面对这血淋淋的现实，有谁敢去怀疑它的合理性呢？
Suǒyǐ, jíshǐ zài jīntiān, miànduì zhè xiělínlín de xiànshí,
therefore even if at today face this dripping with blood SP reality
yǒu shéi gǎn qù huáiyí tā de hélǐxìng ne?
there be who dare go doubt it SP rationality MP
{Therefore, even today, in the face of this bloody reality, who dares to doubt its rationality?}

In (24), the fact that "kerosene was not on the market" is supplemented and placed after the *zài*-structure "in those three years of economic difficulties", and

228 *Factive "jíshǐ p, yě q"*

in (25), the fact of "being in the face of the bloody reality" is provided and placed after "*zài jīntiān*" ('today').

In these sentences, the supplementary information can be present inside the *zài*-structure and act as an attribute, as in the following two examples:

(26) 即使在市场上买不到煤油的三年经济困难时期, 牛福也不惜高价弄几斤, 不让儿子闲着。

Jíshǐ . . . yě . . . zài shìchǎng-shàng mǎibùdào méiyóu de sān nián
even if . . . in on market cannot buy kerosene SP three year

jīngjì kùnnan shíqī, Niú Fú yě bùxī gāojià nòng jǐ
economy difficult period NIU Fu not begrudge high price get several

jīn, bù ràng érzi xián-zhe.
500 grams NEG let son idle-PRG

{Even in those three years of economic difficulties, when kerosene was not on the market, NIU Fu would not hesitate to buy some at a high price to keep his son from being idle. (Without a lamp, his son wouldn't be able to study at night.)}

(27) 即使在面对这血淋淋的现实的今天, 有谁敢去怀疑它的合理性呢?

Jíshǐ zài miànduì zhè xiělínlín de xiànshí de jīntiān, yǒu
even if at face this dripping with blood SP reality SP today there be

shéi gǎn qù huáiyí tā de hélǐxìng ne?
who dare go doubt it SP rationality MP

{Even today, in the face of this bloody reality, who dares to doubt its rationality?}

In (26), "kerosene was not on the market" followed by *de* acts as an attribute of "those three years of economic difficulties". In (27), "be in the face of this bloody reality" followed by *de* functions as an attribute of *jīntiān*.

In those sentences, the *zài*-structure can be moved to the front of *jíshǐ*; hence the section about the fact will act as a clause, as in the following two examples:

(28) 在三年经济困难时期, 即使市场上买不到煤油, 牛福也不惜高价弄几斤, 不让儿子闲着。

Zài sān nián jīngjì kùnnan shíqī, jíshǐ . . . yě . . . shìchǎng-shàng
in three year economy difficult period even if . . . on market

mǎibùdào méiyóu, Niú Fú yě bùxī gāojià nòng jǐ
cannot buy kerosene NIU Fu not begrudge high price get several

jīn, bù ràng érzi xián-zhe.
500 grams NEG let son idle-PRG

{In those three years of economic difficulties, even kerosene was not on the market, NIU Fu would not hesitate to buy some at a high price to keep his son from being idle.}

(29) 在今天, 即使面对这血淋淋的现实, 有谁敢去怀疑它的合理性呢?

Zài jīntiān, jíshǐ miànduì zhè xiělínlín de xiànshí, yǒu shéi
at today even if face this dripping with blood SP reality there be who

gǎn qù huáiyí tā de hélǐxìng ne?
dare go doubt it SP rationality MP

{Today, even in the face of this bloody reality, who dares to doubt its rationality?}

Factive "jíshǐ p, yě q" 229

In (28), the part "kerosene was not on the market" turns into a clause introduced by *jíshǐ*, and in (29), "be in the face of this bloody reality" also becomes a clause introduced by *jíshǐ*.

10.2.4 *q in factive "jíshǐ p, yě q"*

In factive "*jíshǐ p, yě q*", what is stated in *q* usually refers to an event that took place at a certain time and in a certain place, but it can be an inference. In other words, what *q* states in a factive *jíshǐ*-sentence is not always a reality. Compare (30) and (31):

(30)　（又是四十度高温了！可是）<u>即使</u>在这么个大热天，他<u>也</u>一天工作十小时。
　　　(*Yòu shì sìshí dù gāowēn le! Kěshì*) <u>*jíshǐ*</u>...<u>*yě*</u>... *zài zhème*
　　　again COP forty degree high temperature MP but　　even if...　　on such
　　　gè dà rè tiān, tā <u>yě</u> yī tiān gōngzuò shí xiǎoshí.
　　　CL real hot day he　　one day work　　ten hour
　　　{[It's 40 degrees again! However,] he still works ten hours a day even on such a hot day.}

(31)　（又是四十度高温了！可是）<u>即使</u>在这么个大热天，他<u>也</u>不会放下笔的。
　　　(*Yòu shì sìshí dù gāowēn le! Kěshì*) <u>*jíshǐ*</u>...<u>*yě*</u>... *zài zhème*
　　　again COP forty degree high temperature MP but　　even if...　　on such
　　　gè dà rè tiān, tā <u>yě</u> bù huì fàng-xià bǐ de.
　　　CL real hot day he　　NEG will put down pen SP
　　　{[It's 40 degrees again! However,] he won't take a rest from writing even on such a hot day.}

In the two aforementioned examples, each *p*, which specifies the time, is factive, but the two *q*'s are different: in (30) it refers to a fact, whereas in (31) it is an inference. Compare two more examples:

(32)　（他来得不是时候。因此，）<u>即使</u>在这里，他<u>也</u>总是愁眉苦脸的。
　　　(*Tā lái de bù shì shíhou. Yīncǐ,*) <u>*jíshǐ*</u>...<u>*yě*</u>... *zài zhèlǐ, tā <u>yě</u>*
　　　he come SP NEG COP time　　therefore even if...　　at here he
　　　zǒngshì chóuméi-kǔliǎn de.
　　　always worried and painful SP
　　　{[He came at a bad time, therefore,] even at here, he always looks worried and miserable.}

(33)　（他来得不是时候。因此，）<u>即使</u>在这里，他的病<u>也</u>不可能很快治好的。
　　　(*Tā lái de bù shì shíhou. Yīncǐ,*) <u>*jíshǐ*</u>...<u>*yě*</u>... *zài zhèlǐ, tā de*
　　　he come SP NEG COP time　　therefore even if...　　at here he SP
　　　bìng <u>yě</u> bù kěnéng hěn kuài zhì-hǎo de.
　　　illness NEG possible very soon cure SP
　　　{[He came at a bad time, therefore,] even at here, his illness won't be cured soon.}

In the two aforementioned examples, each *p*, which specifies the location, is factive, but the two *q*'s are different: in (32) it refers to a fact, whereas in (33) it is an inference.

230 *Factive "jíshǐ p, yě q"*

10.2.5 *Absence of jíshǐ*

In sentences in the form of "*jíshǐ p (zài . . . shíhòu/dìfāng/zhōng/lǐ), yě q*", *jíshǐ* is absent. For example, *jíshǐ* in (17) can be omitted. If the word *zài* acts more like a verb than a preposition, *jíshǐ* can be replaced by *suīrán*. For example, *jíshǐ* in (33) can be omitted or replaced by "*suīrán*".

In sentences in the form of "*jíshǐ p (zài . . . shíhòu/dìfāng/zhōng/lǐ), yě q*", *jíshǐ* highlights the specified time or location with a tone of exaggeration. If "although at this time/in this place" is used, the speaker means "it would be the same at other times/in other places". If "even at this time/in this place" is used, the speaker means "let alone other times/other places". If the particle *ba* is used, for instance, "*jíshǐ zài dōngtiān ba*" in (20), the sentence will have a more exaggerated effect. The following is an example:

(34) <u>即使</u>在病中，她的信仍然是八天一封……

> *Jíshǐ*   zài . . . *zhōng* bìng zhōng, tā de xìn réngrán shì bā tiān yī fēng...
> even if during   be ill   she SP letter still   COP eight day one CL
> {Even during her illness, she wrote a letter every eight days.}

If "even during her illness" in (34) is changed into "during her illness" or "although she was ill", the speaker means that she normally writes a letter every eight days. However, "*jíshǐ zài bìng zhōng . . .*" (or "*jíshǐ zài bìng zhōng ba . . .*") implies that "since she wrote a letter every eight days even when she was ill, she might write more frequently when she is well".

10.3 *"quèshí y, yīncǐ jíshǐ p, yě q"*

In the sentence form "*quèshí y, yīncǐ jíshǐ p, yě q*", *y* refers to a reason, and *p* acts as the foil for *q*; for example:

(35) 杨老是奋斗发家的，<u>因此即使</u>他后来家财万贯，<u>也</u>还始终保留着节俭的本色，有时未免给人有些过分的感觉。

> *Yáng lǎo   shì   fèndòu   fājiā   de,   **yīncǐ**   <u>jíshǐ</u> . . . <u>yě</u> . . .*
> YANG old   COP   work hard   make family fortune SP   therefore   even if . . .
>
> *tā hòulái   jiācái-wànguàn,   <u>yě</u> shǐzhōng bǎoliú-zhe jiéjiǎn de běnsè,*
> he afterwards extremely wealthy   all along   keep-PRG   frugal   SP nature
>
> *yǒushí   wèimiǎn   gěi   rén   yǒuxiē   guòfèn   de gǎnjué.*
> sometimes unavoidably give person some   excessive SP feeling
> {Old Yang had made a fortune by working hard, so even though he was extremely wealthy, he still retained his thrifty nature, which sometimes unavoidably made him appear stingy.}

In this example, "Old Yang had made a fortune by working hard" is the reason for what is stated in the following part of the sentence, therefore it should be understood as "because Old Yang had made a fortune by working hard". The part "he was extremely wealthy" introduced by *jíshǐ* is a real fact that serves as the foil for "retained his thrifty nature".

Factive "jíshǐ p, yě q"   231

10.3.1   *"(quèshí) y"*

In sentences in the form of *"quèshí y, yīncǐ jíshǐ p, yě q"*, *"quèshí y"* presents a certain fact as the reason for *"jíshǐ p, yě q"*, but the word *quèshí* is optional. However, for the preceding context, *"(quèshí) y"* is likely to be the result. The following is an example:

(36) 他原以为要颇费周折，没想到竟然这样轻易地如愿以偿，一到这省城，一打
听便着。他简直不相信自己的好运气了，因此，即使现在到了她的家门口，
那种恍如梦中的感觉，依然未曾消失。

Tā   yuán   yǐwéi   yào   pō   fèi   zhōuzhé,   méi   xiǎng-dào
he   original   mistakenly think   need   quite cost   trouble   NEG   expect

jìngrán   zhèyàng qīngyì de rúyuànyǐcháng,   yī   dào   zhè
unexpectedly so   easy   SP have one's wish granted   as soon as arrive   this

shěngchéng,   yī   dǎtīng   biàn zháo.   Tā jiǎnzhí   bù
provincial capital   as soon as ask about then   achieve goal he completely NEG

xiāngxìn zìjǐ   de   hǎo   yùnqi le, yīncǐ,   jíshǐ   xiànzài dào-le   tā
believe   oneself SP   good   luck MP therefore even if now   arrive-PEF she

de jiā   ménkǒu,   nà   zhǒng huǎngrú   mèng-zhōng de gǎnjué, yīrán
SP home   doorway   that kind   as if   in dream   SP feeling   still

wèicéng   xiāoshī.
not yet   disappear

{He had thought that it would take a lot of trouble, but it turned out that he succeeded so easily. When he arrived in the provincial capital, he got the answer as soon as he inquired. He could hardly believe his good luck, and even now, when he arrived at her door, he still felt as if he was in a dream.}

In this example, *"y"* is acted by "he could hardly believe his good luck", and *yīncǐ* indicates that it is the reason for the *jíshǐ*-sentence that follows. However, it is also the result of the preceding context, i.e., *"yī dǎtīng biàn zháo . . ."* ('he got to know the answer as soon as he inquired').

In some cases, a rhetorical question act as *"y"* to reinforce the tone, as in the following example:

(37) 谁不是打姑娘时过来的？即使命运不济，让当年的窈窕少女田映薇变成个不
争气的、整日介围着饭单在厨房转的沈家姆妈，可她，还是有意无意地期
待着、盼望着，在她那可能不再会发出光彩的"灰太太"生活中，出现一
点奇迹！

Shéi bù   shì dǎ gūniang shí guòlái   de? Jíshǐ   mìngyùn bùjì, ràng
who   NEG COP from girl   time experience SP   even if fate   bad make

dāngnián de yǎotiǎo   shàonǚ Tián Yìngwēi   biàn-chéng gè bù
the past   SP gentle and beautiful girl   TIAN Yingwei   become   CL NEG

zhēngqì   de, zhěng rì   jiè wéi-zhe   fàndān zài chúfáng zhuàn de
be aggressive SP entire day so   wear-PRG   apron   in   kitchen   turn   SP

Shěn jiā   mǔmā,   kě tā, háishi yǒuyì   wúyì   de qīdài-zhe,
SHEN family mom   but she still   intentionally unintentionally SP expect-PRG

232 *Factive "jíshǐ p, yě q"*

pànwàng-zhe,	*zài ... zhōng*	*tā*	*nà*	*kěnéng*	*bù*	*zài*	*huì*	*fāchū*
look forward to-PRG	in	she	that	may	NEG	again	will	emit

guāngcǎi	*de*	*"huī tàitai"*	*shēnghuó zhōng,*	*chūxiàn*	*yìdiǎn*	*qíjì!*
light	SP	Cinderella wife	life	happen	a little	miracle

{Who hasn't been a young girl? Even though fate turned the fair lady TIAN Yingwei into an unambitious Mrs. Shen, who wears an apron and cooks in the kitchen all day, she still hopes, consciously or unconsciously, for some miracle in her Cinderella-like-wife life, which might no longer shine.}

A rhetorical question is used in the aforementioned example, i.e., "who hasn't been a young girl?", which means the same as "every woman has been a young girl". The connective *yīncǐ* can occur between this rhetorical question ("*y*") and the *jíshǐ*-sentence that follows.

10.3.2 *p introduced by jíshǐ*

In *"quèshí y, yīncǐ jíshǐ p, yě q"*, *p* introduced by *jíshǐ* is usually a present situation. For example, *xiànzài* ('right now') is used in (36). In (35), what *hòulái* ('later') really means is *xiànzài* ('te present'). The following is another example:

(38) 工作上有崔惠平，即使贡存义差些，也不会出大差错。

Gōngzuò-shàng	*yǒu*	*Cuī Huìpíng,*	*jíshǐ ... yě ...*	*Gòng Cúnyì*	*chà*
in work	there be	CUI Huiping	even if ...	GONG Cunyi	poor

xiē,	*yě*	*bù*	*huì*	*chū*	*dà*	*chācuò.*
some	NEG	will	make	big	mistake

{With CUI Huiping being a colleague, even if GONG Cunyi is not so good, he won't make big mistakes.}

In the example above, although the word "now" or its synonym is absent, it can occur before *jíshǐ*, i.e., "even if GONG Cunyi is not so good now".

10.3.3 *yīncǐ/suǒyǐ between "(quèshí) y" and "jíshǐ p, yě q"*

In sentences in the form of *"quèshí y, yīncǐ jíshǐ p, yě q"*, *yīncǐ* or *suǒyǐ* can be present between *"quèshí y"* and *"jíshǐ p, yě q"*, as in (35) and (36). In the following sentence, *yīncǐ /suǒyǐ* is implied:

(39) 而我们党采取了毛泽东同志的建党路线，即使工人成分还不占多数，也能够建设并已经建成一个工人阶级的马克思列宁主义政党。

Ér	*wǒ-men*	*dǎng*	*cǎiqǔ-le*	*Máo Zédōng tóngzhì*	*de*	*jiàn*	*dǎng*	*lùxiàn,*
but	our	party	adopt-PEF	MAO Zedong comrade	SP	build	party	ground rules

jíshǐ ... yě ...	*gōngrén*	*chéngfèn*	*hái*	*bù*	*zhàn*	*duōshù,*	*yě*
even if ...	worker	background	still	NEG	account for	majority	

nénggòu	*jiànshè*	*bìng*	*yǐjīng*	*jiàn-chéng*	*yī*	*gè*	*gōngrénjiējí*	*de*
can	build	and	already	complete	one	CL	working class	SP

Mǎkèsī-Lièníng zhǔyì zhèngdǎng.
Marxist-Leninism political party
{We have adopted Comrade MAO Zedong's ground rules for building our party. Even if workers are not in the majority of the party members yet, we can build and have built a working-class Marxist-Leninist party.}

In "*quèshí y, yīncǐ jíshǐ p . . .*", the causality actually exists between "*y*" and "*q*". What *q* denotes can be a factual result of "*y*", or a result inferred from "*y*", or a combination of both. In (35), "he still retained his thrifty nature" is a realis effect; in (38), "he won't make big mistakes" is an inference; while in (39), "we can build and have built a . . ." is both a real fact and an inference. The following is another example:

(40) 他是很有才干的，眼下<u>即使</u>技术还不够熟练，大家<u>还是</u>乐意选举他。

Tā shì hěn yǒu cáigàn de, yǎnxià jíshǐ jìshù hái bùgòu
he COP very have ability SP the present even if skill still not enough

shúliàn, dàjiā háishi lèyì xuǎnjǔ tā.
skillful everybody still be willing to elect he

{He is very talented. Even if he's not skillful enough at the moment, people are still willing to vote for him.}

In the aforementioned examples, *q*, i.e., "people are still willing to vote for him", is a fact. If the wording of *q* changes into something like "he will do great things in the future", it will be an inference. If *q* is worded as "people are still willing to vote for him, and will work hard under his leadership", it will be both a fact and an inference.

In some sentences, *q* is in the form of a rhetorical question indicating an inference; for example:

(41) 一个（是）待嫁女，一个（是）未婚男，<u>即使</u>过了格，既不犯重婚罪，又没有破坏家庭罪的嫌疑，有什么关系呢？

Yī gè (shì) dàijià nǚ, yī gè (shì) wèihūn nán, jíshǐ
one CL COP marriageable female one CL COP unmarried male even if

guògé-le gé jì . . . yòu . . . bù fàn chónghūnzuì, yòu
cross the line-PEF both . . . and . . . NEG commit bigamy

méiyǒu pòhuài jiātíng zuì de xiányí, yǒu shénme guānxì ne?
NEG destroy family offence SP suspicion there be what matter MP

{One is a woman to be married and the other is an unmarried man. Even though they have crossed the line, will it matter? After all, they are not guilty of bigamy, nor are they suspected of undermining anyone's family.}

Given the preceding context, "cross the line" is a fact, and *q* is acted by a rhetorical question, i.e., "will it matter?".

Even if *q* is a rhetorical question, "*y*" can still be a rhetorical question. In this case, the two rhetorical questions work together to achieve a more emphatic effect as the cause and the effect echo each other. The following is another example:

234 *Factive "jíshǐ p, yě q"*

(42) 谁不知道他是个小人？<u>即使</u>眼下当了什么"革委会主任"，难道群众会打心眼
里拥护他吗？

Shéi bù zhīdào tā shì gè xiǎorén? Jíshǐ yǎnxià dāng-le
who NEG know he COP CL vile character even if the present be appointed as-PEF
shénme "géwěihuì zhǔrèn", nándào qúnzhòng huì dǎ
what revolutionary committee director surely not the masses will from
xīnyǎn-lǐ yōnghù tā ma?
in bottom of heart support he MP
{Who doesn't know he is a snob? Even if he is now the director of the Revolutionary Committee, will the masses support him from the bottom of their hearts?}

In this example, "*y*" is the rhetorical question "who doesn't know he is a snob?" and *q* is also the rhetorical question "will the masses support him from the bottom of their hearts?".

10.3.4 *suīrán vs. jíshǐ*

In "*quèshí y, yīncǐ jíshǐ p, yě q*", *p* refers to a fact acting only as a foil, and *jíshǐ* downplays the fact referred to by *p*, making the fact less important. Therefore, *jíshǐ* has a stronger tone of concession than *suīrán*.

Since *jíshǐ* can downplay the influence of the fact, "*quèshí y, yīncǐ jíshǐ p, yě q*" sounds relatively gentle and indirect when the speaker uses this form to offer advice while needing to point out the listener's fault or weakness. Compare (43) and (44):

(43) 你的能力是不错的，<u>虽然</u>只有中专文凭，也不能自己小看自己！

Nǐ de nénglì shì bùcuò de, suīrán zhǐyǒu zhōngzhuān
you SP Ability COP not bad SP although only technical secondary school

wénpíng, yě bù néng zìjǐ xiǎokàn zìjǐ!
diploma still NEG can oneself look down onesome
{You are quite capable. Although you only have a secondary technical school diploma, you can't look down on yourself!}

(44) 你的能力是不错的，<u>即使</u>只有中专文凭，也不能自己小看自己！

Nǐ de nénglì shì bùcuò de, jíshǐ...yě... zhǐyǒu zhōngzhuān
you SP ability COP not bad SP even if... only technical secondary school

wénpíng, yě bù néng zìjǐ xiǎokàn zìjǐ!
diploma NEG can oneself look down onesome
{You are quite capable. Even although you only have a secondary technical school diploma, you can't look down on yourself!}

Both examples are well-formed. However, in terms of rhetorical effect, (44) is better than (43). In (43), *suīrán* recognizes the listener's weakness, therefore the listener might feel uncomfortable. However, in (44), although *jíshǐ* acknowledges the speaker's weakness but tones it down, hence the listener will feel less uncomfortable than if *suīrán* is used. Obviously, if one needs to show respect, love, or care, it is more appropriate to use "*quèshí y, yīncǐ jíshǐ p, yě q*".

10.4 *"quèshí p, dànshì jíshǐ p (rúcǐ/zhèyàng), yě q"*

In sentences in the form of *"quèshí p, dànshì jíshǐ p (rúcǐ/zhèyàng), yě q"*, *p* occurs before the *jíshǐ*-clause showing a fact, and a pronoun occurs in the *jíshǐ*-clause, referring back to *p*. Thus, this form can be termed as co-referential. The following is an example:

(45) 她 变 得 比 过 去 丰 腴，因 而 也 显 得 更 加 白 净，比 他 想 象 中 要 年 轻 得 多。但是，即使如此，也无法掩盖岁月留下的痕迹——还是这双眼睛！

Tā biàn-de bǐ guòqù fēngyú, yīn'ér yě xiǎnde gèngjiā
she become COMP the past buxom therefore also appear more

báijing, bǐ tā xiǎngxiàng-zhōng yào niánqīng de duō. Dànshì,
fair and clear COMP he in imagination might young SP much but

jíshǐ . . . yě . . . rúcǐ, yě wúfǎ yǎn'gài suìyuè liú-xià de hénjì– hái shì
even if . . . so be unable to cover up time leave SP imprint still COP

zhè shuāng yǎnjing!
this pair eye

{She became plumper, and therefore she looks fairer and much younger than he had imagined. However, even so, it can't cover up the traces left by the years—her eyes are the same!}

In this example, *p* is the fact that "she has become plumper . . . younger than he had imagined", and *rúcǐ* ('so') introduced by *jíshǐ* is a co-reference of *p*.

10.4.1 Co-reference in *"quèshí p, dànshì jíshǐ p (rúcǐ/zhèyàng), yě q"*

In *"quèshí p, dànshì jíshǐ p (rúcǐ/zhèyàng), yě q"*, *"quèshí p"* denotes a fact which is a topic for the rest of the form. The inclusion of *quèshí* in this form indicates that *p* is a fact, but *quèshí* can be absent in factive sentences. However, if what is stated in *"quèshí p"* is a hypothesis, then *"jíshǐ p, yě q"* is not factive, either. Compare (46) and (47):

(46) 她狠狠地打他，狠狠地咬他，…… 然而，即使这样，也未能消除她心头深深的怨恨。

Tā hěn-hěn de dǎ tā, hěn-hěn de yǎo tā, . . . rán'ér, jíshǐ . . . yě . . .
she hard-REDP SP hit him hard-REDP SP bite him however even if . . .

zhèyàng, yě wèi néng xiāochú tā xīntóu shēn-shēn de yuànhèn.
so NEG can eliminate her in heart deep-REDP SP resentment

{She hit and bit him hard . . . however, even so, she still failed to eliminate her deep resentment at him.}

(47) 假如让他见到他，她一定狠狠地打他，狠狠地咬他！……然而，即使这样，也不能消除她心头深深的怨恨。

Jiǎrú ràng tā jiàn-dào tā, tā yīdìng hěn-hěn de dǎ tā, hěn-hěn
if let she see him she definitely hard-REDP SP hit him hard-REDP

236 *Factive "jíshǐ p, yě q"*

de yǎo tā! . . . Rán'ér, jíshǐ . . . yě . . . zhèyàng, yě bù   néng xiāochú tā
SP bite him however   even if . . .   so   NEG can eliminate her

xīntóu shēn-shēn de yuànhèn.
in heart deep-REDP SP resentment

{If she sees him, she will beat and bite him hard!. . . however, even so, she won't be able to eliminate her deep resentment at him.}

The *jíshǐ*-sentence in (46) is a factive one, for what precedes *jíshǐ* refers to a fact, whereas the *jíshǐ*-sentence in (47) is a hypothetical one, for what occurs before *jíshǐ* is only a hypothesis.

10.4.2   Pronoun *rúcǐ* or *zhèyàng* acting as p in "*jíshǐ p*"

In sentences in the form of "*quèshí p, dànshì jíshǐ p (rúcǐ/zhèyàng), yě q*", p in "*jíshǐ p*" is often acted by the pronoun *rúcǐ* or *zhèyàng*, or by a phrase including *rúcǐ* or *zhèyàng*. If the other elements in the phrase are removed and only *rúcǐ* or *zhèyàng* remains, the sentence will still make sense. The following are two examples:

(48)   她教三个班的课，又当班主任，还要参加各种各样的社会活动，忙得没有年
       节假，没有星期天，可是，即使如此辛苦，她也没有一句怨言。

Tā jiāo sān gè bān de kè,   yòu dāng bānzhǔrèn,   hái yào cānjiā
she teach three CL class SP course and be   class teacher and must attend

gèzhǒng-gèyàng de shèhuì huódòng, máng de méiyǒu   niánjiéjià, méiyǒu
various   SP society activity   busy SP not have holiday   not have

xīngqītiān, kěshì, jíshǐ . . . yě . . . rúcǐ xīnkǔ   tā yě méiyǒu yī jù yuànyán.
Sunday   but   even if . . .   so laborious she   not have one CL complaint

{She teaches three groups of students and works as a class teacher, and besides, she must participate in all kinds of social activities. She is too busy to have any holidays or have Sundays off. However, even if she works so hard, she doesn't complain at all.}

(49)   他发了，又是盖房子，又是打家具，彩电、冰箱样样有。但是，即使日子如
       此红火，他还是不感到满足。

Tā fā-le,   yòushì . . . yòushì . . . gài   fángzi, yòushì dǎ
he   make a fortune-PEF both . . . and . . .   build house   make

jiājù,   cǎidiàn, bīngxiāng yàng-yàng yǒu. Dànshì, jíshǐ rìzi rúcǐ
furniture color TV fridge   every kind have but   even if life so

hónghuo,   tā háishi bù   gǎndào mǎnzú.
prosperous he still   NEG   feel   satisfied

{He made a fortune, so he built a house and made furniture, and now has everything, including a color TV set and a refrigerator. However, even if he lives a prosperous life, he is still not contented.}

In (48), *xīnkǔ* ('works hard') can be removed, and in (49), "*rìzi . . . hónghuǒ*" ('lives a prosperous life') can be omitted.

Factive "jíshǐ p, yě q"   237

10.4.3   *dàn or its synonym between "quèshí p" and "jíshǐ p (rúcǐ/zhèyàng), yě q"*

In sentences in the form of *"quèshí p, jíshǐ p (rúcǐ/zhèyàng), yě q"*, *dàn* or its synonyms can be used and placed between *"quèshí p"* and *"jíshǐ p (rúcǐ/zhèyàng), yě q"*. For instance, *dànshì* is present in (45). Even if *dànshì* or its synonym is absent, it can be used. The following is an example:

(50)   她不是不知道，李珊现在绝不会构成对她的任何实际威胁，<u>即使</u>如此，她也不能善罢甘休。

   Tā bù shì bù zhīdào, Lǐ Shān xiànzài jué   bù   huì gòuchéng
   she NEG COP NEG know   LI Shan now   absolutely NEG will pose

   duì tā de rènhé shíjì wēixié, <u>jíshǐ . . . yě</u> . . . rúcǐ, tā   yě   bù   néng
   to her SP any   real threaten even if . . .   so   she still NEG can

   shànbà-gānxiū.
   be willing to let go
   {She certainly knows that LI Shan will definitely not pose any real threat to her now, but even so, she can't let her go.}

In this example, *dànshì, kěshì* or *rán'ér* can be used and placed before *jíshǐ*. As a matter of fact, there is an innate opposition between *"quèshí p"* and *q*. If *dàn* or its synonym is present, *"jíshǐ rúcǐ/zhèyàng"* can be omitted, and the remaining parts *"quèshí p"* and *q* will form a general adversative sentence. For example:

(51)   她不是不知道，李珊现在绝不会构成对她的任何实际威胁，然而，她也不能善罢甘休。

   Tā bù   shì   bù   zhīdào, Lǐ Shān xiànzài jué   bù   huì gòuchéng
   she NEG COP NEG know   LI Shan now   absolutely NEG will pose

   *duì tā de rènhé shíjì wēixié, **rán'ér**, tā yě bù   néng shànbà-gānxiū.*
   to her SP any   real threaten however she still NEG can   be willing to let go
   {She certainly knows that LI Shan will definitely not pose any real threat to her now, but she still can't let her go.}

In these sentences where the pronoun used in *"jíshǐ p"* is *zhèyàng*, if *"jíshǐ zhèyàng"* is removed, the remaining will be a general adversative sentence. Moreover, if only *jíshǐ* is removed, the remaining will still be a general adversative sentence. The following is an example:

(52)   二年前，……他这项收入一年不过三千多元。<u>即使</u>这样，<u>也</u>引起四邻乡亲的惊羡。

   Èr nián qián, . . . tā zhè xiàng shōurù yī   nián bùguò sānqiān   duō
   two year before he   this item income one year only   three thousand over

   yuán. <u>Jíshǐ . . . yě</u> . . . zhèyàng, yě yǐnqǐ sìlín   xiāngqīn   de
   yuan   even if . . .   so   cause neighbor fellow villager SP

   jīngxiàn.
   envy with surprise

238 *Factive "jíshǐ p, yě q"*

{Two years ago . . . his income from this project was merely over three thousand *yuan* a year. Even so, it aroused his neighbors and fellow villagers' surprise and envy.}

If *dàn* or its synonym is present in (52), it will be an adversative sentence, as (53). Then, if *jíshǐ* is removed, the remaining is still an adversative sentence, as (54).

(53) 他这项收入一年不过三千多元, 但是，即使这样，也引起四邻乡亲的惊羡。
      Tā   zhè xiàng shōurù yī   nián bùguò sānqiān   duō yuán,   **dànshì,**
      he   this item   income one year only   three thousand over yuan but
      jíshǐ . . . yě . . . zhèyàng, yě yǐnqǐ   sìlín   xiāngqīn   de jīngxiàn.
      even if . . . so   cause neighbor fellow villager SP envy with surprise
      {His income from this project was merely over three thousand yuan a year; however,
      even so, it aroused surprise and envy among his neighbors and fellow villagers.}

(54) 他这项收入一年不过三千多元, 但是，这样也引起四邻乡亲的惊羡。
      . . . tā   zhè xiàng shōurù yī   nián bùguò sānqiān   duō *yuan,*
      he   this item   income one year only   three thousand over yuan
      dànshì, *zhèyàng yě   yǐnqǐ   sìlín   xiāngqīn   de jīngxiàn.*
      but   so   also cause neighbor fellow villager SP envy with surprise
      {His income from this project was merely over three thousand yuan a year, but
      this aroused his neighbors and fellow villagers' surprise and envy.}

10.4.4 *suīrán and jíshǐ*

In *"quèshí p, dànshì jíshǐ p (rúcǐ/zhèyàng), yě q"*, *jíshǐ* emphasizes a given fact in a tone of exaggeration full of emotion. If *jíshǐ* is replaced by *suīrán*, the sentence will turn into an objective statement that analyzes the relationship between matters. Compare the following two examples:

(55) ⋯⋯ 在表叔公的熏陶下，我从小学会了一点油漆和木匠的手艺，虽然如此，
      我却无力继承更无力开张⋯⋯
      . . . zài . . . xià . . . biǎoshūgōng de   xūntáo   xià, wǒ cóngxiǎo
      under   uncle's father SP   influence   I   from childhood
      xuéhuì-le yīdiǎn yóuqī hé   mùjiàng de shǒuyì, suīrán   rúcǐ, wǒ
      learn-PEF a little painter and carpenter SP skill   although so   I
      què   wúlì   jìchéng   gèng wúlì   kāizhāng . . .
      however be unable to take . . . on more be unable to open a business
      {Under the influence of Uncle's father, I learned a little bit of painting and car-
      pentry when I was a child; however, despite this, I wasn't able to take on the
      work, let alone open up a business . . .}

(56) 和许多 "黑五类" 子弟一样，我身上也有一个 "黑烙印"，⋯⋯母亲去世前把
      我托给了在镇上当油漆匠的表叔公，即使这样,也未能擦掉我的 "印记"，⋯⋯
      Hé xǔduō "hēiwǔlèi"   zǐdì   yīyàng, wǒ shēn-shàng yě   yǒu
      as many Five Black Categories children same I   on body   also there be

Factive "jíshǐ p, yě q" 239

yī	gè	"*hēi*	*làoyìn*" ...	*mǔqīn*	*qùshì*	*qián*	*bǎ*	*wǒ*
one	CL	black	brand	mother	pass away	before	BA	I

tuō-gěi ... *le* *zài zhèn-shàng dāng yóuqījiàng de*
leave someone to the care of ... PEF at in town work as painter SP

biǎoshūgōng, jíshǐ ... *yě* ... *zhèyàng, yě wèi néng cā-diào wǒ de "yìnjì",* ...
uncle's father even if ... so NEG can erase I SP brand

{Like many of the children of those who fell into "Five Black Categories", I also had a "black brand" . . . Before my mother had passed away, she left me in the care of my uncle's father, who was a painter in town, but even so, my "brand" couldn't be erased . . .}

These two example are cited from the same page of the same short story, but *suīrán* is used in the former and *jíshǐ* is used in the latter. Although these words can be used interchangeably in the two sentences, the sentences wouldn't sound as good as the original ones if the two words were swapped. In (55), *suīrán* is a better choice than *jíshǐ* because the former can better reflect the speaker's inadequate capability. In (56), *jíshǐ* can better express a helpless and desperate mood than *suīrán*.

10.4.5 *A similar form to "quèshí p, jíshǐ p (rúcǐ/zhèyàng), yě q"*

In conversational Chinese, there is a form similar to "*quèshí p, jíshǐ p (rúcǐ/ zhèyàng), yě q*", i.e.:

A: *Quèshí p.*
B: *Jíshǐ p (rúcǐ/zhèyàng), yě q".*

The following is an example:

(57) 小羊吃了一惊, 温和地说: "我怎么会把您的水弄脏呢？您站在上游，水是从您那儿流到我这儿来的，不是从我这儿流到您那儿去的。" 狼气冲冲地说:"就算这样吧，你总是坏家伙！……"

Xiǎo yáng chījīng-le yī jīng, wēnhé de shuō: "Wǒ zěnme huì bǎ
little lamb be surprised-PEF one gentle SP say I how can BA

nín de shuǐ nòng zāng ne? Nín zhàn zài shàngyóu, shuǐ shì
you SP water make dirty MP you stand in upper reaches water COP

cóng nín nàr liú-dào wǒ zhèr lái de, bù shì cóng wǒ zhèr liú-dào
from your there flow to my here come SP NEG COP from my here flow to

nín nàr qù de." Láng qìchōngchōng de shuō: "Jiùsuàn zhèyàng ba, nǐ
your there go SP wolf furious SP say even if so MP you

zǒngshì huàijiāhuo! . . ."
always bad guy

{The little lamb was surprised and said gently, "How can I possibly make your water dirty? You are standing upstream. The water flows from you to me, not from me to you." The wolf replied furiously, "Even so, you are always a bad guy! . . ."}

240 *Factive "jíshǐ p, yě q"*

In the aforementioned example, *zhèyàng* refers to the fact stated by the little lamb, and *"jiùsuàn zhèyàng"* equals *"jíshǐ zhèyàng"*. In some cases, no pronoun is used to refer to the fact; instead, the fact is reiterated by the other speaker. For example:

(58)　（朱泉山：）"顾书记，我没那样想过……"（顾荣：）<u>即使</u>没想过，现在<u>也</u>可以想想嘛。"

(Zhū Quánshān:) "Gù shūjì,　wǒ　méi　nàyàng　xiǎng-guò. . ." *(Gù róng:)*
ZHU Quanshan GU secretary I NEG that think GU Rong

<u>jíshǐ</u> . . . <u>yě</u> . . .　méi　xiǎng-guò,　xiànzài　<u>yě</u>　kěyǐ　xiǎng-xiǎng　ma."
even if . . . NEG think-EXP now can think-REDP MP

{[ZHU Quanshan,] "Secretary GU, I didn't think that way . . ." [GU Rong,] "Even if you haven't thought about it, you can think about it now."}

In this example, "even if you haven't thought about it" can be rephrased as "even so".

This is also a co-referential sentence form, but what is co-referred to is the fact stated by the other speaker, and clearly *jíshǐ* is used to downplay the fact. To be specific, the speaker uses *jíshǐ* to imply: I will concede that this is true and do not want to delve into the matter.

If what is stated by the other speaker is a fact, *"jíshǐ p, yě q"* is factive, and if what is stated is a hypothesis, the *jíshǐ*-sentence is a hypothetical one. The following is an example:

(59)　A: <u>如果</u>他再来，我<u>就</u>把他抓起来。

<u>Rúguǒ</u>　tā　zài　lái,　wǒ　<u>jiù</u>　bǎ　tā　zhuā-qǐlái.
if he again come I then BA he arrest

{If he comes again, I will arrest him.}

B: <u>即使</u>这样，<u>也</u>不能解决问题呀！

<u>Jíshǐ</u> . . . <u>yě</u> . . .　zhèyàng,　<u>yě</u>　bù　néng　jiějué　wèntí　ya!
even if . . . so NEG can resolve problem MP

{Even so, the problem won't be solved!}

Summary

First, a *jíshǐ*-sentence can be factive, i.e., *"jíshǐ p, yě q"* is not always a form of hypothetical complex sentence because *"jíshǐ p, yě q"* does not always indicate a hypothetical relationship.[1,2]

Second, in sentences in the factive form of *"jíshǐ p, yě q"*, what *p* states is always a fact, and only in *"nàshí . . . jíshǐ p, yě q"* is what *q* states a fact. In all other forms, such as *"jíshǐ p (zài . . . shíhòu/dìfāng/zhōng/lǐ), yě q"*, *"quèshí Y, yīncǐ jíshǐ p, yě q"*, and *"quèshí p, dànshì jíshǐ p (rúcǐ/zhèyàng), yě q"*, what *q* states can refer to a fact or an inference. It is *p* that determines whether a *jíshǐ*-sentence is factive or hypothetical, for what *p* states can be a concessive adversativity from one fact to the other, or a concessive adversativity from a fact to an inference.

Third, only in a clear context can a sentence in the form of "*jíshǐ p, yě q*" be a factive one. Without a clear context, a *jíshǐ*-sentence is usually regarded as a hypothetical one, or it is uncertain whether it is factive or hypothetical. It should be noted that by default "*jíshǐ p, yě q*" indicates a hypothetical relationship, and only when certain conditions are met can "*jíshǐ p, yě q*" be factive.

Fourth, there are some commonalities between factive *jíshǐ*-sentences and factive *suīrán*-sentences; thus the former can be rewritten as the latter. However, the two sentence forms have different effects in expression. Factive *suīrán*-sentences state the fact objectively, whereas factive *jíshǐ*-sentences carry a concessive tone, and usually with emotion because they state a fact as if it was a hypothesis.

Fifth, factive *jíshǐ*- sentences can be generalized into certain forms, and the present chapter discusses four of them:

I   The amendment form: "*nàshí . . . jíshǐ p, yě q*"
II The specificity form: "*jíshǐ p (zài . . . shíhòu/dìfāng/zhōng/lǐ), yě q*"
III The foil form: "*quèshí y, yīncǐ jíshǐ p, yě q*"
IV The co-reference form: "*quèshí p, dànshì jíshǐ p (rúcǐ/zhèyàng), yě q*"

These four forms might not cover all factive *jíshǐ*-sentences. There might be more complicated and subtle cases that need further research.

Sixth, quite a number of sentence forms in Chinese are similar to each other and can be used interchangeably. However, since they are different forms, they have different functions and different effects in expression. Exposition of certain rules about the Chinese language during teaching will greatly benefit students who study Chinese, particularly those who study it as a foreign language or second language.

NB Some examples in this chapter are cited from literary works, political essays, articles, and so on. The sources are listed as follows:

1   *Chinese* for Primary School Students, Book 3, including (3);
2   *Dangdai* (《当代》) 1984(3), including (58); 1985(3), including (35);
3   *Fiction Monthly* (《小说月报》) 1985(6), including (3) and (37);
4   *Flower City* (《花城》) 1984 (3), including (1); 1985(1), including (50); 1985(2), including (24) and (52); 1985(3), including (6), (7), (10), (11), (21), (36), (45), (47), (55), and (56);
5   *Lotus* (《芙蓉》) 1985(2), including (5), (16), (20), and (34); 1985(3), including (12), (14), (18), (19), (25), and (41);
6   *Romantic Stories of Emperor Qianglong* (《乾隆韵事》) by GAO Yang (高阳), including (4);
7   *Selected Stories* (《小说选刊》) 1999(9), including (38);
8   *Selected Works of LIU Shaoqi* (《刘少奇选集》), including (39);
9   *Selected Works of MAO Tse-tung* (《毛泽东选集》), including (17);
10 *Selected Works of ZHOU Enlai* (《周恩来选集》), including (2);
11 *Woodpecker* (《啄木鸟》) 1994(2), including (23).

Notes

1 It is stated in another book (Department of Chinese Language and Literature, Peking University (Ed.). *Interpretations of Grammatical Words in Modern Chinese* (《现代汉语虚词例释》). The Commercial Press, 1982, p. 262.) that *p* introduced by *jíshǐ* refers to a fact
2 It has been claimed in many grammar works that complex sentences in the form of "*jíshǐ p, yě q*" are categorized as hypothetical ones and that the sentences show a hypothetical relationship.

11 Investigation into concessive complex sentence forms

In the previous chapters, four concessive sentence forms have been discussed, i.e., "*suīrán p, dàn q*", "*jíshǐ p, yě q*", "*nìngkě p, yě q*", and "*wúlùn p, dōu q*". This chapter further investigates these four concessive forms, exploring the commonalities among concessive forms as well as the scope and types of concessive forms and discussing concessive complex sentences marked by *rènpíng* ('no matter').

11.1 Commonalities among concessive sentences

The so-called concessive sentences refer to those in which the relationship between the clauses is concessive first and adversative second; therefore "concessive sentences" is short for "concessive-adversative sentences". The following are two examples:

(1) 虽然他说确有其事，我还是不相信。

Suīrán	*tā*	*shuō*	*quèyǒuqíshì*,	*wǒ*	*háishi*	*bù*	*xiāngxìn.*
although	he	say	it be true	I	still	NEG	believe

{Although he said it was true, I still don't believe it.}

(2) 即使他说确有其事，我还是不相信。

Jíshǐ	*tā*	*shuō*	*quèyǒuqíshì*,	*wǒ*	*háishi*	*bù*	*xiāngxìn.*
even though	he	say	it be true	I	still	NEG	believe

{Even though he said it was true, I still don't believe it.}

Example (1) is in the form of "*suīrán p, dàn q*", hence it is a *suīrán*-sentence for short, whereas (2) is in the form of "*jíshǐ p, yě q*", hence it is a *jíshǐ*-sentence for short.

In comparing between *suīrán* and *jílìng*, LI Jingxi pointed out that *suīrán* stresses the speaker's concession of a fact, and *jílìng* highlights the speaker's reluctance to recognize the fact.[1] LV Shuxiang wrote, "*suīrán*-sentences and *jíshǐ*-sentences are both concessive sentences. The word 'concede' means to recognize reluctantly".[2] Both scholars regarded *suīrán*-sentences and *jílìng*-sentences as

DOI: 10.4324/9781003374237-11

244   *Investigation into concessive complex sentence forms*

subtypes of concessive complex sentences. (LI Jinxi mentioned some synonyms of *jíshǐ*, such as *jílìng*, *zònglìng*, and so on, but not *jíshǐ*.)

The commonalities among concessive complex sentences can be concluded from the subtypes *suīrán*-sentences and *jíshǐ*-sentences in the following table:

Table 11.1 Commonalities among concessive sentences

Concessive complex sentence		*suīrán p, dàn q*	*jíshǐ p, yě q*
Concession	Meaning: *p* is conceded	+	+
	Form: concessive marker	+ (*suīrán*)	+ (*jíshǐ*)
Adversativity	Meaning: *p* contrasts with *q*	+	+
	Form: adversative connective such as *dàn*	+	+ (to intensify)

From the table, it can be seen that all concessive complex sentences—*suīrán*-sentences or *jíshǐ*-sentences—involve concession and adversativity expressed in some form. Since the middle of the 1950s, the term "concessive sentence" has hardly been used in grammar teaching at middle school and in some unversity grammar textbooks. Besides, *suīrán*-sentences are separated from *jíshǐ*-sentences to be categorized as adversative complex sentences and hypothetical complex sentences respectively. Why is this? The reason is that *p* in *suīrán*-sentences denotes a fact, whereas *p* in *jíshǐ*-sentences refers to a hypothesis. Why are *jíshǐ*-sentences classified as hypothetical sentences and thus have an equal status with *rúguǒ*-sentences? The logic is that *p* in both *jíshǐ*-sentences and *rúguǒ*-sentences refers to a hypothesis. In all, the classification of *jíshǐ*-sentences is based on the assumption that *p* is a hypothesis. However, this assumption is not tenable.

First, in some *jíshǐ*-sentences *p* refers to a fact rather than a hypothesis. Even though factive "*jíshǐ p, yě q*" depends on the context and is subject to the restrictions of certain conditions, *p* is not an actual hypothesis, which has been discussed in the preceding chapter. The following are two more examples:

(3)   他说得很随意，……但对我来说，却永远无法忘记。…… 即使如此，我们的
       交往依然是淡淡的，或者说形式大于内容。
       Tā shuō de hěn suíyì, ... dàn duì ... lái shuō wǒ lái shuō, què   yǒngyuǎn
       he   say SP very casual but   for ...   me   however forever
       wúfǎ   wàngjì.   ... Jíshǐ   rúcǐ, wǒ-men de jiāowǎng yīrán shì
       be unable to forget   even though so   we   SP interact still COP
       dàn-dàn   de, huòzhě shuō xíngshì dà   yú   nèiróng.
       indifferent-REDP SP   or   say   form   great than content
       {He said it casually . . . but for me, I can never forget it . . . Even so, we still don't know each other well, or, to put it another way, our interaction is just a formality.}

Investigation into concessive complex sentence forms   245

(4)   我的20岁，是在昌都度过的。……转眼到了3月。即使在昌都这样的地方，
春天的气息也日渐浓了起来。

Wǒ   de   20   suì,   shì   zài Chāngdū   dùguò   de.   ... Zhuǎnyǎn
I   SP   twenty   year of age   COP   in Changdu   spend   SP   eye blinks
dào-le   3 yuè.   Jǐshǐ ... yě ...   zài   Chāngdū   zhèyàng   de   dìfang,   chūntiān
arrive-PEF   March   even if   in   Changdu   such   SP   Place   spring
de   qìxī   yě   rìjiàn   nóngle-qǐlái.
SP   smell   day by day   become stronger

{The year I turned 20 was spent in Changdu . . . In the blink of an eye, it was
already March. Even in such a place like Changdu, the smell of spring was getting
stronger day by day.}

In (3), the anaphoric *rúcǐ* refers to "he said it casually . . . but for me, I can never
forget it", which is a fact. In (4), what follows *jíshǐ* is also a fact. It is obviously
incorrect to regard these two "*jíshǐ . . . yě . . .*" sentences as hypothetical complex
sentences.

Second, even if *p* in all *jíshǐ*-sentences indicated a hypothesis, the aforementioned classification would be inconsistent. Compare the following four
examples:

Table 11.2 Inconsistency in classification

		Relation between p *and* q	
		Causal succession	*Reversed succession*
Relationship between *p* and the fact	*p* referring to a fact	Example (5)	Example (6)
	p referring to a hypothesis	Example (7)	Example (8)

(5)   因为下雨，不能施工。
Yīnwèi   xiàyǔ,   bù   néng   shīgōng.
because   rain   NEG   can   construction
{Because of the rain, the construction cannot be carried out.}

(6)   虽然下雨，也能施工。
Suīrán   xiàyǔ,   yě   néng   shīgōng.
although   rain   still   can   construction
{Although it is raining, the construction can be carried out.}

(7)   如果下雨，不能施工。
Rúguǒ   xiàyǔ,   bù   néng   shīgōng.
if   rain   NEG   can   construction
{If it rains, the construction cannot be carried out.}

246 *Investigation into concessive complex sentence forms*

(8) 即使下雨，也能施工。

 Jíshǐ *xiàyǔ,* *yě* *néng* *shīgōng.*
 even if rain still can   construction
 {Even if it rains, the construction can be carried out.}

One way to examine the similarities and differences between *jíshǐ*-sentences and *rúguǒ*-sentences is to look at the relationship between *p* and *q*. The other way is to look at the relationship between *p* and the real fact. However, if these two ways are taken as the classification criteria, they are in conflict with each other. Compare:

Table 11.3 Conflicts between classification criteria

	Based on the relationship between p *and* q	*Based on the relationship between* p *and the real fact*
yīnwèi-sentences and *suīrán*-sentences	Different types	Same type
yīnwèi-sentences and *rúguǒ*-sentences	Same type	Different types
rúguǒ-sentences and *jíshǐ*-sentences	Different types	Same type
jíshǐ-sentences and *suīrán*-sentences	Same type	Different types

Therefore, complex sentences should be classified according to the relationship between *p* and *q*. This classification criterion can be applied to all the complex sentences, including coordinate sentences, alternative sentences, progressive sentences, and so on. If the criterion in the same classification system is not consistent, the classification will be chaotic. For instance, when sentences are classified according to the relationship between *p* and *q*, "*yīnwèi p, suǒyǐ q*" is regarded as a cause-effect complex sentence form, and "*suīrán p, dàn q*" as a adversative complex sentence form. However, when sentences are classified based on the relationship between *p* and the fact, "*rúguǒ p, jiù q*" and "*jíshǐ p, yě q*" are both taken as hypothetical sentence forms and "*zhǐyǒu p, cái q*" and "*wúlùn p, dōu q*" as conditional sentence forms.

From the perspective of the relationship between *p* and *q*, *suīrán*-sentences and *jíshǐ*-sentences have obvious commonalities which determine their status in the complex sentence classification system:

Investigation into concessive complex sentence forms 247

Diagram 11.1 Position of *suīrán*-sentences and *jíshǐ*-sentences in tripartite classification

248 *Investigation into concessive complex sentence forms*

11.2 Scope of concessive complex sentences

The commonalities among concessive complex sentences have been concluded from the comparison between *suīrán*-sentences and *jíshǐ*-sentences, and these commonalities can be used as the criterion for judging whether a sentence is a concessive one or not, from which sub-categories of concessive sentences can be identified and the scope of concessive sentences can be defined.

If R = concession + adversativity, then the following deductive reasoning can be used to determine whether a non-*suīrán*-sentence or non-*jíshǐ*-sentence is a concessive one:

> Any complex sentence with Feature R is a concessive complex sentence.
> X is characterized by R,
> Therefore, X is a concessive complex sentence.

11.2.1 *"wúlùn p, dōu q"*

First, as *wúlùn, bùlùn, bùguǎn* and the like are concession markers, *"wúlùn p, dōu q"* involves concession. "When a concession is made before a turn is taken, a tendency has developed to turn around".[3] In fact, *p* by itself has no implication as to whether *p* and *q* are in a causal relationship or in an adversative relationship. However, as long as *wúlùn* precedes *p*, the tendency to reverse will develop, and the listener will soon become aware that what has been said is only a concession and that what is going to be said will surely be the opposite of or at least in conflict with *p*. The details have been discussed in Chapter 4 of this volume. Compare the following two pairs of examples:

(9) a 天气多好，让我带玲玲到公园去玩玩吧！（causal）
Tiānqì duō hǎo, ràng wǒ dài Línglíng dào gōngyuán qù wán-wán ba!
weather how nice let me take Lingling to park DC play-REDP MP
{What a beautiful day, so let me take Lingling to the park!}

b 天气多好，我和玲玲却只能整天整天地呆在家里！（adversative）
Tiānqì duō hǎo, wǒ hé Línglíng què zhǐ néng zhěng tiān zhěng tiān
weather how nice I and Lingling however only can whole day whole day
de dāi zài jiā-lǐ!
SP stay at home
{What a beautiful day, but I have to stay at home with Lingling all day long.}

(10) a 无论天气多好，（-）（no causal clause can follow）
Wúlùn tiānqì duō hǎo,
regardless of weather how nice
{No matter how beautiful the day is,}

Investigation into concessive complex sentence forms 249

b 无论天气多好，我和玲玲都只能整天整天地呆在家里!（Adversative）
Wúlùn   tiānqì   duō hǎo, wǒ hé Línglíng dōu zhǐ   néng zhěng tiān
regardless of weather how nice I   and Lingling still only can   whole day
zhěng tiān de dāi   zài jiā-lǐ!
whole day SP stay at home
{No matter how beautiful the day is, I must stay at home with Lingling all day long.}

In this aspect, *wúlùn*-sentences, *suīrán*-sentences, and *jíshǐ*-sentences are similar to each other. They are similar in the sense that none of them can include clauses linked by a causal relationship, but all of them can include clauses linked by an adversative relationship. The following are three more pairs of examples:

(11)   a 无论环境怎么险恶，（−）(no causal clause can follow)
Wúlùn   huánjìng   zěnme xiǎn'è,
regardless of environment how   hostile
{No matter how hostile the situation is,} (−)

b 无论环境怎么险恶, 我们都愿意去。
Wúlùn   huánjìng   zěnme xiǎn'è, wǒ-men dōu yuànyì   qù.
regardless of environment how   hostile we   still be willing to go
{No matter how hostile the situation is, we are willing to go.}

(12)   a 虽然环境特别险恶，（−）(no causal clause can follow)
Suīrán   huánjìng   tèbié xiǎn'è,
although   environment how   hostile
{Though the situation is hostile,}(−)

b 虽然环境特别险恶， 我们都坚持写作。
Suīrán   huánjìng   tèbié xiǎn'è, wǒ-men dōu jiānchí   xiězuò.
although   environment how   hostile we   still insist   write
{Though the situation is hostile, we keep on writing.}

(13)   a 即使环境再险恶, (−) (no causal clause can follow)
Jíshǐ   huánjìng   zài   xiǎn'è,
even though environment more   hostile
{Even if the situation is more hostile,} (−)

b 即使环境再险恶, 我们都能挺得住。
Jíshǐ   huánjìng   zài   xiǎn'è, wǒ-men dōu néng tǐngdezhù.
even though environment more   hostile we   still can   bear
{Even if the situation is more hostile, we can hold up.}

250 *Investigation into concessive complex sentence forms*

Second, "*wúlùn p, dōu q*" entails adversativity, which can best be proven by the occurrence of adversative connective *dàn* or its synonym between the clauses. An adversative conjunction, such as *dàn* or *kě*, can be present, as in (14a); or the adversative adverb *què* can be present, as in (14b); or there can be a combination of an adversative adverb and an adversative conjunction, as in (14c).

(14)   a 无论天气多好，但我和玲玲都只能整天整天地呆在家里！

Wúlùn   tiānqì   duō hǎo, dàn wǒ hé Línglíng dōu zhǐ   néng zhěng
regardless of weather how nice but I   and Lingling still only can   whole
tiān zhěng tiān de dāi zài jiā-lǐ!
day whole day SP stay at home
{No matter how beautiful the weather is, I must stay at home with Lingling all day long!}

b 无论天气多好，我和玲玲却都只能整天整天地呆在家里！

Wúlùn   tiānqì   duō hǎo, wǒ hé Línglíng què   dōu zhǐ   néng
regardless of weather how nice I   and Lingling however still only can
zhěng tiān zhěng tiān de dāi zài jiā-lǐ!
whole day whole day SP stay at home
{No matter how nice the weather is, I must stay at home with Lingling all day long!}

c 无论天气多好，但我和玲玲却都只能整天整天地呆在家里！

Wúlùn   tiānqì   duō hǎo, dàn wǒ hé Línglíng què   dōu zhǐ
regardless of weather how nice but I   and Lingling however still only
néng zhěng tiān zhěng tiān de dāi zài jiā-lǐ!
can   whole day whole day SP stay at home
{No matter how nice the weather is, I must stay at home with Lingling all day long!}

Details about the occurrence of adversatives in "*wúlùn p, dōu q*" have been discussed in Chapter 4 of the present volume. The following are four more examples. In (15) and (16), only *dàn* or *kě* is present:

(15)   敌人<u>无论</u>怎样对党进行恶毒攻击，造谣中伤，<u>但</u>铁一般的事实是怎样诬蔑也改变不了的。

Dírén <u>wúlùn</u>   zěnyàng duì dǎng jìnxing èdú   gōngjī, zàoyáo
enemy no matter how   to   party conduct vicious attack spread rumors
zhòngshāng, <u>dàn</u> tiě yìbān de shìshí shì   zěnyàng wūmiè yě
slander   but iron same SP fact   COP how   slander still
gǎibiàn-bùliǎo de.
cannot change SP
{No matter how viciously the enemy attacks the Party with rumors, the hard facts cannot be changed by any slander.}

(16) <u>不管</u>身上有些什么毛病，<u>可</u>干起工作来那股玩命劲，就像着了魔似的。

Bùguǎn   shēn-shàng   yǒu   xiē   shénme   máobìng,   kě   gàn-qǐlái
no matter   on body   there be   some   any   illness   but   start to do

gōngzuò   lái   nà   gǔ   wánmìng   jìn,   jiù   xiàng ... shìde
work   that   CL   not care about any risks   strength   just   like

zháomó-le   mó   shìde.
be possessed-PEF

{No matter where (he) was not feeling well, (he) was like being possessed once (he) started to work.}

In (17), only *què* is present:

(17) <u>不管</u>虼蚤在床上的遗迹究竟是什么，它在雯雯身上留下的<u>却</u>是非常明确：雯雯浑身都是疙瘩。

Bùguǎn   gèzǎo zài chuáng-shàng   de   yíjì   jiūjìng   shì   shénme,   tā
no matter   flea   on bed   SP   mark   exactly   COP   what   it

zài ... shēnshàng   Wénwén   shēnshàng   liúxià   de   què   shì   fēicháng
on one's body   Wenwen   leave   SP   however   COP   very

míngquè: Wénwén   húnshēn   dōu   shì   gēda.
clear   Wenwen   all over   all   COP   lump

{Whatever what the flea left on the bed was exactly, what the flea left on Wenwen's body was very clear: she had lumps all over her body.}

In (18), both *dàn* and *què* are present:

(18) <u>不管</u>她平时对大学生有多少抱怨，<u>但</u>在这"外人"面前, 她<u>却</u>忍不住反唇相讥了……

Bùguǎn   tā   píngshí   duì   àxuéshēng   yǒu   duōshǎo
no matter   she   normal times   about   university student   have   how much

bàoyuàn,   dàn   zài ... miànqián   zhè   "wàirén"   miànqián,   tā   què
complain   but   in front of ...   this   outsider   she   however

rěn-buzhù   fǎnchún-xiāngjī   le ...
cannot help doing something   sneer back   MP

{No matter how much she usually complains about college students, in front of this "outsider", she can't help but sneer back at them ...}

Third, a confirmed concessive complex sentence can often be rewritten as a *wúlùn*-sentence if there is a semantic ground for the change of form, and this can be regarded as circumstantial evidence. To be rewritten, only the concessive connective and the elements collocating with the concessive connective need to be changed. The following are two examples:

(19) 他<u>虽然</u>笨，也晓得共产党历来主张集体化。

Tā suīrán   bèn,   yě xiǎode Gòngchǎndǎng   lìlái   zhǔzhāng jítǐhuà.
he although stupid still know Communist Party always advocate collectivization

{Stupid as he is, he knows that the Communist Party has always advocated collectivization.}

(20) 即便别人对他说露骨的恭维话，他也毫无反应。

Jíbiàn *biérén* *duì tā shuō lùgǔ de gōngwéi* *huà, tā yě*
even if other people to he say explicit SP compliment words he still

háo *wú* *fǎnyìng.*
a tiny bit not have response

{He wouldn't respond at all even if others flattered him.}

If *suīrán* in (19) and *jíshǐ* in (20) are replaced by *wúlùn* (or its synonym) and *bùguǎn* (or its synonym) respectively, and *zěnme* and *duōshǎo* are added respectively, (19) and (20) will become *wúlùn*-sentences, i.e., (21) and (22):

(21) 他不管怎么笨，也晓得共产党历来主张集体化。

Tā bùguǎn *zěnme bèn, yě xiǎode Gòngchǎndǎng lìlái zhǔzhāng*
he regardless of how stupid still know Communist Party always advocate

jítǐhuà.
collectivization

{However stupid he is, he knows that the Communist Party has always advocated collectivization.}

(22) 无论别人对他说多少露骨的恭维话，他也毫无反应。

Wúlùn *biérén* *duì tā shuō duōshǎo lùgǔ de gōngwéi* *huà,*
no matter other people to he say how much explicit SP compliment words

tā yě háo wú *fǎnyìng.*
he still a tiny bit not have response

{No matter how much others flattered him, he had no response at all.}

11.2.2 "*nìngkě p, yě q*"

First, the sentence form "*nìngkě p, yě q*" involves a concession, and such words as *nìngkě*, *nìngyuàn*, *nìngkěn*, *níng*, and the like are the markers for concession. As a matter of fact, *p* by itself does not imply whether *p* and *q* are in a causal relationship or in an adversative relationship. Nonetheless, if *nìngkě* precedes *p*, the tendency to reverse will develop, and the audience will soon realize that what has been said is just a concession and that what is going to be said will definitely contrast with *p*. Compare the following examples:

(23) a 别人不义，我们不仁。（causal）

Biérén bù *yì,* *wǒ-men bù* *rén.*
others NEG righteous we NEG benevolent

{Since they are not righteous, we are not benevolent.}

b 别人不义，我们不可不仁。（adversative）

Biérén bù *yì,* *wǒ-men bùkě bù* *rén.*
others NEG righteous we cannot NEG benevolent

{Others are not righteous, but we cannot be malevolent.}

Investigation into concessive complex sentence forms   253

(24)   a 宁可别人不义，（-）（no causal clause can follow）
Nìngkě   *biérén*   *bù*   *yì,*
would rather   others   NEG   righteous

b 宁可别人不义，我们不可不仁。（adversative）
Nìngkě   *biérén*   *bù*   *yì,*   *wǒ-men*   *bùkě*   *bù*   *rén.*
would rather   others   NEG   righteous   we   cannot   NEG   benevolent
{It is better for others to be unrighteous than for us to be malevolent.}

In this aspect, *nìngkě*-sentences are similar to *suīrán*-sentences and *jíshǐ*-sentences. They are similar in the sense that none of them can include clauses linked by a causal relationship but all of them can include clauses linked by an adversative relationship. Compare:

(25)   a 当时，他<u>宁可</u>被捕入狱，（−）(no causal clause can follow)
Dāngshí,   *tā*   <u>*nìngkě*</u>   *bèi*   *bǔ*   *rùyù,*
that time   he   would rather   PASSIVE   arrest   be put in prison
{At that time, he would rather be arrested and put in prison,}(−)

b 当时，他<u>宁可</u>被捕入狱，也不出卖朋友。
Dāngshí,   *tā*   <u>*nìngkě*</u> *... yě ...*   *bèi*   *bǔ*   *rùyù,*   *yě*   *bù*
that time   he   would rather ...   PASSIVE   arrest   be put in prison   NEG

chūmài   *péngyǒu.*
betray   friend
{At that time, he would rather be arrested and put in prison, (he) would not betray his friends.}

(26)   a 当时，他<u>虽然</u>被捕入狱，（−）(no causal clause can follow)
Dāngshí,   *tā*   <u>*suīrán*</u>   *bèi*   *bǔ*   *rùyù.*
that time   he   although   PASSIVE   arrest   be put in prison
{At that time, although he was arrested and put in prison,} (−)

b 当时，他<u>虽然</u>被捕入狱，也不违背良心说瞎话。
Dāngshí,   *tā*   <u>*suīrán*</u>   *bèi*   *bǔ*   *rùyù,*   *yě*   *bù*   *wéibèi*
that time   he   although PASSIVE arrest be put in prison   still   NEG   betray

liángxīn   *shuō*   *xiāhuà.*
conscientiousness   say   lie
{At that time, although he was arrested and put in prison, (he) would not betray his conscientiousness and tell lies.}

(27)   a 当时，他<u>即使</u>被捕入狱，（−）(no causal clause can follow)
Dāngshí,   *tā*   <u>*jíshǐ*</u>   *bèi*   *bǔ*   *rùyù.*
that time   he   even if PASSIVE arrest be put in prison
{At that time, even if he was arrested and put in prison,} (−)

254 *Investigation into concessive complex sentence forms*

b 当时，他即使被捕入狱，也要把这部小说写下去。

Dāngshí, *tā* *jíshǐ* *bèi* *bǔ* *rùyù,* *yě* *yào* *bǎ*
that time he even if PASSIVE arrest be put in prison still will BA

zhè *bù* *xiǎoshuō* *xiě-xiàqù.*
this CL novel keep writing

{At that time, even if he had been arrested and put in prison, (he) would have kept on writing this novel.}

Second, "*nìngkě p, yě q*" entails adversativity, which can best be proven by the occurrence of adversative connective *dàn* or its synonym between the clauses. The conjunction *dàn* or *kě* can occur, as in (28a), or the adverb *què* can be present, as in (28b). Related issues has been discussed in Chapter 3 of the present volume.

(28) a 宁可别人不义，但我们不可不仁。

Nìngkě *biérén bù* *yì,* *dàn wǒ-men* *bùkě* *bù* *rén.*
would rather others NEG righteous but we cannot NEG benevolent

{It is better for others to be unrighteous than for us to be malevolent.}

b 宁可别人不义，我们却不可不仁。

Nìngkě *biérén bù* *yì,* *wǒ-men* *què* *bùkě* *bù* *rén.*
would rather others NEG righteous we however cannot NEG benevolent

{It is better for others to be unrighteous than for us to be malevolent.}

In the following two examples, *dàn* is present in (29), and *què* in (30).

(29) 他宁愿承担舆论和道德的谴责，但不能眼睁睁地葬送自己和莲莲未来的幸福。

Tā *nìngyuàn* *chéngdān yúlùn* *hé* *dàodé* *de qiǎnzé,* *dàn bù*
he would rather bear public opinion and morality SP condemn but NEG

néng yǎnzhēngzhēng de zàngsòng zìjǐ *hé* *Liánlián wèilái de xìngfú.*
can helpless SP ruin oneself and Lianlian future SP happiness

{He would rather bear the condemnation of public opinion and morality than stand by and allow the future happiness of himself and Lianlian to be ruined.}

(30) 宁肯让工期一拖再拖，经济效益受到损害，他的权威和尊严却不能有丝毫动摇。

Nìngkěn *ràng* *gōngqī* *yī tuō zài tuō,* *jīngjì*
would rather allow time limit for a project delay again and again economy

xiàoyì *shòu-dào* *sǔnhài,* *tā* *de* *quánwēi* *hé* *zūnyán* *què*
benefit suffer damage he SP authority and dignity however

bù *néng* *yǒu* *sīháo* *dòngyáo.*
NEG can have slightest shake

Investigation into concessive complex sentence forms   255

{He would rather allow the construction period to be delayed again and again and the economic benefits be damaged than allow his authority and dignity to be shaken in the slightest.}

Third, a confirmed concessive complex sentence can often be rewritten as a *nìngkě*-sentence if there is a semantic basis for the change, and this can be regarded as circumstantial evidence. The rewriting only involves the change of the concessive connective. The following are two examples:

(31) <u>虽然</u>多花钱，他也不肯放过这个机会。
     <u>*Suīrán*</u> *duō* *huā* *qián,* *tā* *yě* *bù* *kěn*   *fàngguò zhè gè*
     although more spend money he still NEG be willing miss   this CL
     jīhuì.
     opportunity
     {Although it would cost more money, he didn't want to miss this opportunity.}

(32) <u>即使</u>少睡点儿觉，也要把这篇文章写完。
     Jíshǐ *shǎo shuìjiào diǎnr jiào,* *yě* *yào bǎ zhè piān wénzhāng xiě-wán.*
     even if less sleep a bit   still will BA this CL essay   finish writing
     {(I) will finish writing this essay even if (I) lose some sleep.}

If the word *suīrán* in (31) and the word *jíshǐ* in (32) are replaced by *nìngkě*, or *nìngkěn*, or the like, these two sentences will become *nìngkě*-sentences.

11.2.3   *Expanded scope of concessive sentences*

Since *wúlùn*-sentences and *nìngkě*-sentences are similar to *suīrán*-sentences and *jíshǐ*-sentences in the sense that they all involve concession and adversativity, *wúlùn*-sentences and *nìngkě*-sentences should be categorized as concessive complex sentences. In other words, there are four subtypes of concessive complex sentences in modern Chinese: i) *suīrán*-sentences; ii) *jíshǐ*-sentences; iii) *wúlùn*-sentences; and iv) *nìngkě*-sentences. Therefore, the scope of concessive complex sentences is justifiably expanded on the basis of logic.

11.3   Four subtypes of concessive complex sentences

The four subtypes of concessive complex sentences can be respectively termed as factual concessive sentences, hypothetical concessive sentences, unconditional concessive sentences, and preferable concessive sentences. In spite of the commonalities, they have their own characteristics in form and function, as shown in the following table:

256 *Investigation into concessive complex sentence forms*

Table 11.4 Subtypes of concessive complex sentences

Subtypes of concessive sentences	Representative form	Function	Example
Factive	*suīrán p, dàn q*	Factive concession	(33)
Hypothetical	*jíshǐ p, yě q*	Hypothetical concession	(34)
Unconditional	*wúlùn p, dōu q*	Unconditional concession	(35)
Preferable	*nìngkě p, yě q*	Preferable concession	(36)

(33) 他们虽然自己挨饿，也要把口粮省下来。

Tāmen suīrán zìjǐ ái'è, yě yào bǎ kǒuliáng shěng-xiàlái.
they although themselves starve still will BA rations save up
{Although they themselves are starving, they will still save up their rations.}

(34) 他们即使自己挨饿，也要把口粮省下来。

Tāmen jíshǐ zìjǐ ái'è, yě yào bǎ kǒuliáng shěng-xiàlái.
they even if themselves starve still will BA rations save up
{Even if they themselves starve, they will still save up their rations.}

(35) 他们无论自己怎么挨饿，也要把口粮省下来。

Tāmen wúlùn zìjǐ zěnme ái'è, yě yào bǎ kǒuliáng shěng-xiàlái.
they no matter themselves how go hungry still will BA rations save up
{They will save their rations no matter how they starve themselves.}

(36) 他们宁可自己挨饿，也要把口粮省下来。

Tāmen nìngkě . . . yě . . . zìjǐ ái'è, yě yào bǎ kǒuliáng shěng-xiàlái.
they would rather . . . themselves starve will BA rations save up
{They would rather starve themselves to save up their rations.}

11.3.1 *Factive concession*

A factive concession is a concession to a real fact. In factive concessive complex sentences, the existence of the fact that *p* states is recognized, but *p*'s influence on *q* is unrecognized. What *p* states serves as a foil for what *q* states; in other words, *q* is highlighted and becomes prominent. Compare the following examples:

(37) 李晖是高干子女，干起活来有那种自视清高的娇气劲儿。

Lǐ Huī shì gāogàn zǐnǚ, gàn qǐ huó lái yǒu nà zhǒng zìshì
LI Hui COP senior official child start to work have that kind regard oneself as
qīnggāo de jiāoqì jìnr.
noble and virtuous SP pampered look
{LI Hui is a child from a senior official family, so at work she has the expression of having high self-esteem and being pampered.}

Investigation into concessive complex sentence forms 257

(38) 李晖是高干子女，<u>但是</u>干起活来没有那种自视清高的娇气劲儿。

Lǐ Huī   shì   gāogàn   zǐnǚ, <u>dànshì</u> gàn qǐ huó lái méiyǒu nà   zhǒng
LI Hui COP senior official child but start to work not have that kind

zìshì   qīnggāo   de jiāoqì   jìnr.
regard oneself as noble and virtuous SP pampered look

{LI Hui is a child from a senior official family, but at work she doesn't have the expression of having high self-esteem or being pampered.}

(39) 李晖<u>虽说</u>是高干子女，干起活来<u>却</u>没有那种自视清高的娇气劲儿。

Lǐ Huī <u>suīshuō</u> shì   gāogàn   zǐnǚ, gàn qǐ huó lái <u>què</u>   méiyǒu
LI Hui although COP senior official child start to work however not have

nà   zhǒng zìshì   qīnggāo   de jiāoqì   jìnr.
that kind regard oneself as noble and virtuous SP pampered look

{Although LI Hui is a child from a senior official family, at work she doesn't have the expression of having high self-esteem or being pampered.}

Among these three examples, (37) is a cause-effect sentence, showing people's general impression of children with a senior official family background. Example (38) is a general/direct adversative sentences, indicating that LI Hui, a child from a senior official family, is different from other children with a similar family background. Example (39) is a factive concessive sentence, in which *suīshuō* is used to concede the fact that LI Hui is a child from a senior official family, and then *què* is used to make a 180-degree turn; therefore, *p* functions as a foil for *q*—LI Hui is different from other children with a similar family background.

All factive concessive sentences are based on a fact. To achieve an empathetic effect, the wording of sentences can be varied. However, whatever the situation is, factive concession sentences are based on an objective fact. For this reason, a factual concession is a reasonable concession.

11.3.2 Hypothetical concession

A hypothetical concession is a concession to a hypothetical situation, or to a real fact as if it were a hypothesis. Similar to a factive concession, a hypothetical concession also uses *p* as a foil for *q* so as to highlight *q* and emphasize that *q* is not influenced by *p*. The difference between a factive concession and a hypothetical concession is that in the former *p* is a real fact, whereas in the latter *p* is a hypothesis, or a real fact treated as if it were a hypothesis.

There are two types of hypothetical concession: total-hypothetical concession and quasi-hypothetical concession.

Total-hypothetical concessions are purely hypothetical concessions, including rational hypothetical concessions and exaggerated hypothetical concessions. The hypothesis in a rational hypothetical concession can turn into a reality despite some possible exaggerated factors. The hypothesis in an exaggerated hypothetical concession cannot become a fact because it is a pure exaggeration. Just because the hypothesis in a total-hypothetical concession is completely or partially

258 *Investigation into concessive complex sentence forms*

an exaggeration, total-hypothetical concessive sentences carry a very strong emphatic tone. The following are four examples:

(40) 即使你头发全白了，我照样可以认得出来。（rational hypothetical concession）（can become a reality）

Jíshǐ nǐ   tóufa quán bái-le,   wǒ zhàoyàng kěyǐ rèn de chūlái.
even if your hair entirely white-PEF I   still   can can recognize
{Even if your hair has turned all white, I can still recognize (you).}

(41) 即使你烧成了灰，我照样可以认得出来。（exaggerated hypothetical concession）（cannot be a reality）

Jíshǐ nǐ   shāo chéng-le   huī, wǒ zhàoyàng kěyǐ rèn de chūlái.
even if you burn become-PEF ash I   still   can can recognize
{I could still recognize (you) even if you were burned to a crisp.}

(42) 你即使讨个哑巴，我也不拦你！（rational hypothetical concession）（can be a reality）

Nǐ jíshǐ tǎo gè yǎba, wǒ yě bù lán nǐ!
you even if marry CL mute I   still NEG stop you
{I won't stop you even if you marry a mute!}

(43) 你即使讨个猪婆，我也不拦你！（exaggerated hypothetical concession）（cannot be a reality）

Nǐ jíshǐ tǎo gè zhūpó, wǒ yě bù lán nǐ!
you even if marry CL sow I   still NEG stop you
{I wouldn't stop you even if you married a sow!}

Quasi-hypothetical concessions are mock hypothetical concessions, in which *p* is a reality but sounds as if it were a hypothesis because of the use of *jíshǐ*. In general, *jíshǐ* in quasi-hypothetical concessive sentences can be replaced by *suīrán*, but they have different expressive effects. In short, with *suīrán* the reality is presented as a reality, while with *jíshǐ* the reality sounds somewhat like a hypothesis and can be regarded as a hypothesis if de-contextualized. Details about factive "*jíshǐ p, yě q*" have been discussed in Chapter 10 of the present volume. Compare the following two examples:

(44) 康伟业这枚链坠，唯一的遗憾是有两道若隐若现的条纹，<u>尽管</u>是这样，至少也值人民币万元以上。

Kāng Wěiyè zhè méi liànzhuì, wéiyī de yíhàn shì yǒu liǎng dào
KANG Weiye this CL pendant only SP pity COP have two CL
ruòyǐn-ruòxiàn   de tiáowén, jǐnguǎn   shì zhèyàng,
partly hidden and partly visible SP stripe even though COP so
zhìshǎo yě zhí   rénmínbì wàn   yuán yǐshàng.
at least still be worth RMB   ten thousand yuan above
{The only flaw in KANG Weiye's pendant is the two looming lines, but it is still worth more than ten thousand RMB *yuan* in spite of the flaw.}

Investigation into concessive complex sentence forms 259

(45) 康伟业这枚链坠，唯一的遗憾是有两道若隐若现的条纹，<u>即使</u>是这样，至少
也值人民币万元以上。

Kāng Wěiyè   zhè   méi   liànzhuì,   wéiyī   de   yíhàn   shì   yǒu   liǎng   dào
KANG Weiye   this   CL   pendant   only   SP   pity   COP   have   two   CL

ruòyǐn-ruòxiàn   de tiáowén, <u>jíshǐ</u>   shì   zhèyàng, zhìshǎo yě
partly hidden and partly visible SP stripe   even if COP so   at least still

zhí   rénmínbì wàn   yuán yǐshàng.
be worth RMB   ten thousand yuan above

{The only flaw in KANG Weiye's pendant is the two looming lines, but even so, it is still worth more than ten thousand RMB *yuan.*}

In these two examples, *zhèyàng* refers to the fact that there are two looming lines in the pendant. However, in (44) with *jǐnguǎn* ('although'), the fact is stated as a fact, thus the sentence is a factive concessive one, whereas in (45) with *jíshǐ*, the fact is stated as if it were a hypothesis, and thus the concession is more obvious in this sentence.

11.3.3   Unconditional concession

An unconditional concession is a concession to all conditions. In an unconditional concessive sentence, "*wúlùn p*" presents and concedes all possible conditions, and then the posterior clause states that none of the conditions will affect the validity of *q*. The anterior clause in an unconditional concessive sentence needs to be arbitrary or alternative in form. The arbitrary feature is expressed by an interrogative pronoun, such as *shéi, shénme, zěnme*, and so on. The alternative feature is exhibited by a conjunction linking alternatives, such as *huòzhě, háishì*, and so forth. These two features entail each other, i.e., the arbitrary feature includes the alternative feature, and vice versa. In other words, regardless of which form is used, both of the two features are included.

In an unconditional concessive sentence, whether what *p* states is hypothetical or factive does not matter. It is pointed out in *Eight Hundred Words in Modern Chinese* that "*bùguǎn* . . . indicates a hypothesis . . .",[4] which means that *p* in all unconditional concessive sentences is hypothetical. This is obviously contrary to the fact. The following are two examples:

(46) <u>不管</u>别人再拿什么玩笑打岔，我也没兴致了。

<u>Bùguǎn</u>   biérén zài   ná   shénme wánxiào dǎchà,   wǒ   yě   méi
regardless of   others again with what   joke   interrupt   I   still NEG

xìngzhì   le.
interest   MP

{No matter with what jokes people interrupt me, I won't be interested anymore.}

(47) <u>不管</u>明天下不下雪，咱们起个大早，每人带上一件工具，到解放路集合——
扫雪！

<u>Bùguǎn</u>   míngtiān xià bù   xià xuě, zán-men qǐ   gè dà zǎo, měi
regardless of tomorrow fall NEG fall snow we   get up CL very early every

260 *Investigation into concessive complex sentence forms*

Rén   dài-shàng yī   jiàn gōngjù, dào Jiěfàng Lù   jíhé—   sǎo   xuě!
person take along one CL tool   go Jiefang Road assemble sweep snow
{Whether it snows tomorrow or not, let's get up early, bring a tool each, and gather on Jiefang Road—to remove the snow!}

In (46), "with what jokes people interrupt me" is a hypothesis, and in (47) "whether it snows tomorrow or not" is also a hypothesis.

The following are another two examples:

(48) 不管姐姐怎么数落、怨恨, 小伙子只是低着头, 不敢还腔。

Bùguǎn   jiějie   zěnme   shǔluo,   yuànhèn,   xiǎohuǒzi
no matter... elder sister how   scold   hold a grudge against lad

zhǐshì   dī-zhe   tóu,   bù   gǎn   huánqiāng.
merely   bend-PRG   head   NEG dare   answer back

{No matter how his elder sister scolded him and complained about him, the young man just kept his head lowered and dared not talk back.}

(49) （但又不是普通的平面镜，而是一面不寻常的 "哈哈镜", ）不管镜子里怎样变形、夸张、失真，照在镜子里的总是你这个人。

(Dàn yòu bù   shì   pǔtōng de píngmiànjìng, ér shì   yī miàn bù
but   also NEG COP common SP plane mirror   but COP one CL NEG

xúncháng de "hāhājìng",)   bùguǎn   jìngzi-lǐ zěnyàng biànxíng,
usual   SP distorting mirror regardless of in mirror how   deform

kuāzhāng, shīzhēn, zhào zài jìngzi-lǐ de zǒng shì nǐ zhè gè rén.
exaggerate distort reflect in mirror   SP always COP you this CL person

{[However, (it) is not an ordinary plain mirror, but an unusual "distorting mirror",] no matter how the person in the mirror is deformed, exaggerated, or distorted, the one reflected in the mirror is always you.}

In (48), "no matter how his elder sister scolded him and complained about him", and in (49) "no matter how the person in the mirror is deformed, exaggerated, or distorted" are either an ongoing action or something that has already happened.

In an unconditional concessive sentence, all the possible conditions are first conceded and then disregarded; therefore this type of sentence is the best choice for expressing a situation in which the occurrence of a result is not affected by any conditions. Compare the following two examples:

(50) 在白色恐怖弥漫的年代里，尽管环境十分险恶，鲁迅先生（也）一直把密信和文稿珍藏着。

Zài   báisè kǒngbù   mímàn   de   niándài-lǐ,
in   white terror (mass killing, mass arrest, etc.) pervade SP   during years

jǐnguǎn   huánjìng   shífēn   xiǎn'è,   Lǔ Xùn xiānsheng (yě)
even though condition   extremely treacherous   LU Xun mister   still

yīzhí   bǎ   mìxìn   hé   wén'gǎo   zhēncáng-zhe.
always   BA   confidential letter   and   manuscript treasure-PRG

{During the years of white terror, Mr. LU Xun still treasured the confidential letters and manuscripts, despite the dangerous conditions.}

Investigation into concessive complex sentence forms   261

(51)　在白色恐怖弥漫的年代里，<u>无论</u>环境怎样险恶，鲁迅先生（也）一直把密信
　　　和文稿珍藏着。

　　　Zài   báisè kǒngbù   mímàn   de   niándài-lǐ,
　　　in   white terror (mass killing, mass arrest, etc.) pervade SP   during years
　　　wúlùn   huánjìng   zěnyàng   xiǎn'è,   Lǔ Xùn xiānsheng (yě)   yīzhí
　　　no matter condition   how   treacherous LU Xun mister   still   always
　　　bǎ   mìxìn   hé   wén'gǎo   zhēncáng-zhe.
　　　BA   confidential letter and   manuscript treasure-PRG
　　　{During the years of white terror, Mr. LU Xun still treasured the confidential let-
　　　ters and manuscripts, no matter how dangerous the situation was.}

Example (50) is a factive concessive sentence, whereas (51) is an unconditional
concessive sentence. The latter is a more powerful expression of how "treasuring the
confidential letters and manuscripts" is not affected by any of the dangerous situations.

11.3.4　Preferable concession

A preferable concession, marked by *nìngkě*, is a concession to an undesirable
choice when there are no better ones. If in the posterior clause "*yě q*" is in the
affirmative form, the sentence emphasizes that the subject resolves to do something; if "*yě q*" is in the negative form, the sentence emphasizes that the subject is
determined not to do something. The following are four examples:

(52)　<u>宁可</u>孤注一掷，<u>也要</u>弄个明白。

　　　Nìngkě . . . yě . . . gūzhù-yīzhì,   yě yào nòng gè míngbai.
　　　would rather . . .   put all one's eggs in one basket   will make CL clear
　　　{(I) would rather put all (my) eggs in one basket to get to the bottom of it.}

(53)　我<u>宁可</u>死了，<u>也要</u>娶她。

　　　Wǒ nìngkě . . . yě . . . sǐ   le,   yě yào qǔ   tā.
　　　I   would rather . . . die MP   will marry she
　　　{I would rather die to marry her.}

(54)　<u>宁可</u>自己一个人担风险，<u>也不能</u>让王主任有个三长两短。

　　　Nìngkě . . . yě . . . zìjǐ   yī gè rén   dān fēngxiǎn, yě bù   néng ràng
　　　would rather . . .   oneself one CL person take risk   NEG can let
　　　Wáng zhǔrèn   yǒu gè sāncháng-liǎngduǎn.
　　　WANG director have CL accident
　　　{I would rather take the risk myself than let anything happen to Director WANG.}

(55)　看你那副脸孔、那个神气，<u>宁可</u>饿死，<u>也不</u>吃你的饭。

　　　Kàn nǐ   nà fù liǎnkǒng, nà gè shénqì, nìngkě . . . yě . . .
　　　look at your that CL face   that CL manner would rather . . .
　　　è-sǐ,   yě bù   chī nǐ de fàn.
　　　starve   NEG eat you SP food
　　　{Look at your face and manner. (I) would rather starve than eat your food.}

262 *Investigation into concessive complex sentence forms*

In (52) and (53), "*nìngkě . . . yě yào . . .*" is used, i.e., *q* is in the affirmative form; whereas in (54) and (55), "*nìngkě . . . yě bù . . .*" is used, i.e., *q* is in the negative form.

There are three points to be noted.

First, just as in unconditional concessions, *p* in preferable concessions can be a hypothesis or a reality. Compare (56) and (57):

(56)   在必要的时候，我们宁可自己挨饿，也要让孩子们吃饱。

    Zài   bìyào   de shíhou,   wǒ-men nìngkě . . . yě . . . zìjǐ   ái'è,
    at   necessary SP time   we   would rather . . . oneself go hungry

    yě yào ràng háizi-men chī-bǎo.
    will let   child-PL   have enough to eat

    {When necessary, we would rather starve ourselves to make sure our children have enough to eat.}

(57)   三年困难时期，他们宁可自己挨饿，把省下的口粮留给向红。

    Sān   nián kùnnan shíqī,   tā-men nìngkě   zìjǐ   ái'è,   bǎ
    three year difficult period they   would rather oneself go hungry BA
    shěng-xià de kǒuliáng liú-gěi   Xiàng Hóng.
    save   SP rations   keep . . . for XIANG Hong

    {During the three years of hardship, they would rather starve themselves to save their rations for XIANG Hong.}

In (56), "starving ourselves" is a hypothesis, whereas in (57), "starving themselves" is a fact. The following is an example:

(58)   可是一灯抱着舍身度人的大愿大勇，宁受铁掌撞击之祸，也决不还手，只盼他终于悔悟。

    Kěshì Yīdēng bào-zhe shěshēn   dù   rén   de dà   yuàn
    but   Yideng have-PRG sacrifice oneself enlighten others SP great willing
    dà   yǒng,   nìng . . . yě . . . shòu tiězhǎng zhuàngjī zhī huò,
    great courageous would rather . . . suffer iron palm Hit   SP misfortune
    yě jué   bù   huánshǒu, zhǐ   pàn   tā zhōngyú huǐwù.
    definitely NEG fight back only hope he Finally repent

    {However, Yideng, who had the great wish and courage to sacrifice his life for the enlightenment of others, would rather be hit by the "iron palm" than fight back, only hoping that the other one would finally repent.}

Example (58) is cited from a novel. From the preceding context it is known that "hitting by the iron palm" has happened.

Second, there are similarities between quasi-preferable concessions and quasi-hypothetical concessions. As in rational quasi-hypothetical concessions, the hypothesis in rational quasi-preferable concessions can turn into a reality despite some possible exaggerated factors; as in exaggerated quasi-hypothetical

Investigation into concessive complex sentence forms   263

concessions, the hypothesis in exaggerated quasi-preferable concessions cannot become a fact because it is a pure exaggeration. The following are two examples:

(59)   宁肯死，宁肯跳进山洪，也不让那俩坏蛋逮住。

Nìngkěn . . . *yě* . . . *sǐ,   nìngkěn* . . . *yě* . . . *tiào-jìn   shānhóng,   yě bù*
would rather . . .   die would rather . . .   jump into mountain torrent   NEG
ràng   nà   liǎ   huàidàn   dǎi-zhù.
let   that two   bad person   catch
{(I) would rather die, or jump into the mountain torrents, than let those two bad guys catch (me).}

(60)   宁可自己进地狱，也要成全她上天堂！

Nìngkě . . . *yě* . . . *zìjǐ   jìn   dìyù, yě yào chéngquán*
would rather... oneself enter hell   will help other people get what they want
tā   shàng   tiāntáng!
she go up to   paradise
{To help her go to heaven, (I) would rather go to hell myself!}

The anterior clause in each of these two examples means "would rather die". In (59), "jumping into the mountain torrents" can be realized despite the tone of exaggeration, whereas, in (60), "going to hell" is a pure exaggeration that cannot be realized.

Third, in terms of expression, a preferable concessive sentence is the ideal choice for a determination to concede an undesirable choice when no better options are available. However, if there is no need to make a choice, the preferable concessive sentence is not to be used. The following are two examples:

(61)   宁可少生产一些，也一定要把设备维修好。

Nìngkě . . . *yě* . . . *shǎo shēngchǎn yīxiē, yě   yīdìng   yào   bǎ   shèbèi*
would rather . . . less   produce   some still definitely must BA equipment
wéixiū   hǎo.
maintain   good
{(We) would rather produce less to make sure that the equipment is well maintained.}

(62)   * 宁可少生产一些，他也不会有意见。

nìngkě . . . *yě* . . . *shǎo shēngchǎn yīxiē, tā yě bù   huì   yǒu   yìjiàn.*
would rather . . . less   produce   some he   NEG will have objection

The use of *nìngkě* in (61) emphasizes the concession to the thought of "producing less" in order to stress the speaker's resolution to "make sure that the equipment is well maintained". Admittedly, *nìngkě* can be replaced by *jíshǐ*, but if it is, the sense of concession will be lost. Example (62) makes no sense, because it is

264 *Investigation into concessive complex sentence forms*

impossible to achieve the effect of "him having no objection" by resolving to concede "producing less". If *jíshǐ* replaces *nìngkě* in (62), the sentence will become a well-formed hypothetical concessive sentence that reveals the relationship or connection between matters and has nothing to do with subjective concessions.

11.4 Concessive sentence form "*rènpíng p, (dōu/yě) q*"

Another form of concessive complex sentences is "*rènpíng p, (dōu/yě) q*", but it does not belong to any subtype of concessive sentences.

First, in some sentences in the form of "*rènpíng p, (dōu/yě) q*", the concession is an unconditional one, *rènpíng* means the same as *wúlùn* or *bùguǎn*, and the anterior clause includes an interrogative pronoun, such as *zěnme*, *nǎlǐ*, and so on. The following are three examples:

(63) <u>任凭</u>我们怎么说，她依然走了。
<u>Rènpíng</u> wǒ-men ***zěnme*** shuō, tā yīrán zǒu-le.
no matter we how say she still leave-PEF
{No matter what we said, she still went away.}

(64) <u>任凭</u>马俊友怎么喊她，她也不回头。
<u>Rènpíng</u> Mǎ Jùnyǒu ***zěnme*** hǎn tā, tā yě bù huítóu.
no matter MA Junyou how call her she still NEG look back
{No matter how hard MA Junyou called her, she did not look back.}

(65) <u>任凭</u>沈云娥怎样苦苦哀求，他丝毫不再动心。
<u>Rènpíng</u> Shěn Yún'é ***zěnyàng*** kǔkǔ āiqiú, tā sīháo bù zài dòngxīn.
no matter SHEN Yun'e how hard plead he slightest NEG again waver
{No matter how hard SHEN Yun'e pleaded, he no longer wavered in the slightest.}

In some sentences, what occurs in the position of *rènpíng* is *rèn* or *rènsuí*, both of which are synonyms of *rènpíng*. The following are two examples:

(66) <u>任</u>你怎样诬害，陈毅同志的光辉形象永远屹立在我们心中。
<u>Rèn</u> nǐ ***zěnyàng*** wūhài, Chén Yì tóngzhì de guānghuī xíngxiàng
no matter you how frame CHEN Yi comrade SP glorious image
yǒngyuǎn yìlì zài wǒ-men xīn-zhōng.
forever stand still at we in heart
{No matter how you frame it, Comrade CHEN Yi's glorious image will stand still in our hearts forever.}

(67) <u>任随</u>走到哪里，拿鼻子闻一闻，都有浓浓的红苕干烧酒和蒜苗炒回锅肉的香味。
<u>Rènsuí</u> zǒu dào ***nǎlǐ***, ná bízi wén yī wén, dōu yǒu nóng-nóng
no matter walk arrive wherever with nose sniff all there be strong-REDP

Investigation into concessive complex sentence forms   265

de   *hóngsháogān*   *shāojiǔ hé*   *suànmiáo*   *chǎo*   *huíguōròu*
SP   dried sweet potato   arrack   and   garlic shoots   stir fry   twice-cooked pork slices
de   *xiāngwèi.*
SP   aroma

{No matter where you go, you can always smell the strong aroma of sweet potato arrack and twice-cooked pork with garlic shoots.}

Second, in some sentences in the form of "*rènpíng p, (dōu/yě) q*", the concession is factive, *rènpíng* means the same as *suīrán* or *jǐnguǎn*, and no interrogative pronouns are present. The following are two examples:

(68)   任凭老赵满头大汗地使尽了他的本领，车子还是颠簸着。

    Rènpíng Lǎo Zhào mǎntóu-dàhàn de shǐ-jìn le   tā de běnlǐng, chēzi   háishi
    although old ZHAO sweat all over   SP use up PEF he SP skill   vehicle still
    diānbǒ-zhe.
    bump-PRG

    {Although old ZHAO tried his best and was sweating profusely, the cart still kept bumping.}

(69)   （卢华……望着一片充满绿意的荒野。）荒原实在太辽阔了，任凭卢华极目眺望，仍然看不见它的边缘。

    (*Lú Huá . . . wàng-zhe   yī   piàn   chōngmǎn   lǜyì   de   huāngyě.*)
    LU Hua   look at-PRG one   CL   be filled with   greenery   SP   wilderness
    Huāngyuán shízài tài liáokuò le,   rènpíng   Lú Huá jímù
    wilderness   really too vast   MP   although   LU Hua   look as far as possible
    tiàowàng,   réngrán kàn-bùjiàn tā de biānyuán.
    look into the distance still   can't see   it SP edge

    {[Lu Hua . . . looked at a wilderness full of greenery.] The wilderness was so vast that LU Hua could not see the edge, although he gazed into the distance as far as he could.}

Third, in some sentences in the form of "*rènpíng p, (dōu/yě) q*", the concession is a hypothetical one, *rènpíng* means the same as *jíshǐ*, and no interrogative pronouns are present. The following are two examples:

(70)   哪怕他是我爷，任凭丢了我这乌纱帽，我也不能违章背理，假公济私！

    Nǎpà   tā   shì   wǒ   yé,   rènpíng   diū-le   wǒ   zhè   wūshāmào,   wǒ
    even if   he COP   my   father   even if   lose-PEF   my   this   official post   I
    yě   bù   néng wéizhāng-bèilǐ,
    still NEG can   break rules and go against conscience
    jiǎgōng-jìsī!
    exploit public offices for private gain

    {Even if he was my father, even if I lost this official position, I can by no means exploit public offices for my private gain by violating the rules or going against conscience!}

266 *Investigation into concessive complex sentence forms*

(71)　任他黄河说成旱滩，还是县官不如现管哩，……

Rèn　　tā　Huánghé　　shuō-chéng　　　hàn　tān,　hái　shì　xiànguān
even if　he　Yellow River　describe . . . as . . .　dry　beach　still　COP　head of county

bùrú　　　　xiànguǎn　　　li, . . .
not be as good as　person in charge　MP

{Even if he described the Yellow River as a dry beach, it is still better to go to the person directly in charge than a senior official.}

It should be noted that in some sentences *rènpíng* acts as a verb, meaning almost the same as *ràng* ('let'). Besides, *rènpíng* and the words that follow usually form a pivotal construction, and the *rènpíng*-clause can be the last clause in the sentence. The following is an example:

(72)　百无聊赖地依在门框上，任凭黄昏的冷风扑打着，连晚饭也没有力气去做了。

Bǎiwú-liáolài　de　yī　　zài　　　ménkuàng-shàng,　rènpíng
bored stiff　　　SP　lean　against　on doorframe　　　　allow . . . to do as they please

huánghūn　de　lěng　fēng　pūdǎ-zhe,　lián . . . yě . . .　wǎnfàn　yě　　méiyǒu
dusk　　　　SP　cold　wind　beat-PRG　even . . .　　　　dinner　still　not have

lìqi　　qù　zuò　le.
strength　go　make　MP

{(She) leaned against the doorframe in boredom, letting the cold dusk wind blow against (her), and didn't even have the energy to prepare dinner.}

In this example, the clause introduced by *rènpíng* is a pivotal construction, and "the cold dusk wind" acts as the object of *rènpíng* and as the subject of "blow against her". Even if the clause after the *rènpíng*-clause is deleted, the sentence will still be grammatically correct, as can be shown by (73):

(73)　百无聊赖地依在门框上，任凭黄昏的冷风扑打着。

Bǎiwú-liáolài　de　yī　　zài　　　ménkuàng-shàng,　rènpíng
bored stiff　　　SP　lean　against　on doorframe　　　　allow . . . to do as they please

huánghūn　de　lěng　fēng　pūdǎ-zhe.
dusk　　　　SP　cold　wind　beat-PRG

{(She) leaned against the doorframe in boredom, letting the cold dusk wind blow against (her).}

The following is another example, in which the *rènpíng*-clause, i.e., "*rènpíng gūniáng qiǎngbái*" is a pivotal construction followed by no clauses:

(74)　他哑口无言，好像做错事的孩子，任凭姑娘抢白。

Tā　yǎkǒuwúyán,　　　　hǎoxiàng　zuò　cuò　shì　de　háizi,
he　be reduced to silence　as if　　　do　wrong　thing　SP　child

rènpíng   *gūniang*   *qiǎngbái.*
allow . . . to do as they please   make   satirize
{Like a child who did something wrong, he was speechless and allowed the girl to satirize him as much as she pleased.}

Summary

First, all concessive complex sentences are both concessive and adversative. The concession and adversativity both have formal features and semantic properties. The concession is formally expressed by a concessive marker, and the adversativity by a frequently-used adversative marker or a particular concessive marker under a corresponding condition.

Second, concessive complex sentences fall into four subtypes: factive, hypothetical, unconditional, and preferable. Their features are exhibited in two aspects: different concessive markers in form and different semantic meanings (factive concession, hypothetical concession, unconditional concession, and preferable concession) in function.

Third, "*rènpíng p, (dōu/yě) q*" is also a form of concessive complex sentences, separate from the four aforementioned sub-types.

NB Some examples in this chapter are cited from literary works, political essays, articles, and so on. The sources are listed as follows:

1 *Changcheng* (《长城》) 1982(1), including (54);
2 *Changjiang Literature* (《长江》) 1984(1), including (19);
3 *Chinese* for Junior High School Students, Book 1, including (55); Book 2, including (53), (57), and (61); Book 3, including (72);
4 *Dangdai* (《当代》) 1982(3), including (58); 1982(5), including (36); 1983(3), including (60); 1983(4), including (17) and (80);
5 *Divine Eagle, Galant Knight* (《神雕侠侣》) by JIN Yong (金庸), including (59) and (64);
6 *Fiction Monthly* (《小说月报》) 1982(3), including (73); 1982(6), including (35); 1983(4), including (52); 1999(9), including (3) and (4);
7 *Flower City* (《花城》) 1983(3), including (66);
8 *Harvest* (《收获》) 1983(3), including (70); 1983(4), including (75); 1984(4), including (20) and (21);
9 *My Thirty Years* (《我这三十年》) by JIN Yong (金庸), including (59) and (64);
10 *October* (《十月》) 1983(1), including (58) and (75);
11 *People's Literature* (《人民文学》) 1982(3), including (22), (23), and (78);
12 *Qinghai Hu* (《青海湖》) 1983(6), including (20) and (76);
13 *Selected Short Stories Published in 1958* (《1958年短篇小说选》), including (74);

14 *Selected Works of CHI Li* (《池莉精品文集》), including (50);
15 *Selected Works of DENG Xiaoping* (1975–1982) (《邓小平文选(1975–1982年)》), including (67);
16 *Zhongshan* (《钟山》) 1983(4), including (71).

Bibliography

1 LI Jinxi (黎锦熙). *The New Chinese Grammar* (《新著国语文法》). The Commercial Press, 1992[1924].
2 LV Shuxiang (吕叔湘). *Sketches of Chinese Grammar* (《中国文法要略》). The Commercial Press, 1956, p. 43.
3 ZHANG Xichen (章锡琛). *Collation and Annotation on Ma's Grammar* (《马氏文通校注》). Zhonghua Book Company, 1956, p. 397.
4 LV Shuxiang (吕叔湘). *Eight Hundred Words in Modern Chinese* (《现代汉语八百词》). The Commercial Press, 1980, p. 272.

12 Outline of adversative sentence forms

This chapter presents an outline of adversative complex sentence forms marked by *dàn* or its synonym from various perspectives.

Strictly speaking, adversative complex sentence forms include "(*yīnwèi/chúfēi/yàome*)...*fǒuzé*..." constructions, but the word *fǒuzé* and its synonyms are a different type of adversative words from *dàn*, *què*, or their synonyms. Thus, adversative complex sentence forms in this chapter are limited to the various forms marked by *dàn* or its synonym. The form of "*p, fǒuzé q*" has been discussed in Chapter 2 in this volume.

12.1 Conventional and unconventional forms

Among adversative complex sentence forms marked by *dàn* or its synonym, some are conventional and some are unconventional, both of which need to be well understood.

12.1.1 Conventional forms

Conventional forms refer to those in which an adversative marker is used in a conventional way, including "...*dàn/què*..." sentences, and "*suīrán*...*dàn /què*..." sentences, as *suīrán* often collocates with *dàn/què*. These forms are recognized as adversative sentence forms by grammar books and most people.

As markers for the adversative relationship, "...*dàn/què*..." and "*suīrán*...*dàn /què*..." are two different subtypes of adversative markers.

Subtype I: *dàn* and its synonyms, including such conjunctions as *dàn*, *dànshì*, *kěshì*, *rán'ér*, *bùguò*, *zhǐshì*, and the adverb *què*. These are direct adversative markers, occurring in the posterior clause and clearly showing that the posterior clause is in opposition to the anterior clause.

Subtype II: *suī* and its synonyms, including *suī*, *suīrán* and *jǐnguǎn*. These are indirect markers, usually present in the anterior clause, suggesting an adversative relationship between the anterior clause and the posterior clause.

Adversative connectives of Subtype I are typical adversative markers. The presence of these markers in various other complex sentence forms can

DOI: 10.4324/9781003374237-12

270 *Outline of adversative sentence forms*

transform them into adversative ones. In contrast, *suī* and its synonyms are concessive connectives and can only be present in conventional adversative complex sentences. Despite this difference, all markers of these two subtypes can be used to form conventional adversative complex sentences. The cooccurrence of *suīrán/jǐnguǎn* and *dàn/què*, or the occurrence of *dàn/què* by itself, can indicate the adversative relationship. Even the occurrence of *suīrán/jǐnguǎn* alone can indicate the adversative relationship. The following are four examples:

(1) 我<u>虽</u>笨，<u>但</u>也晓得应该分清是非。

    Wǒ <u>*suī*</u>   *bèn,*   <u>*dàn*</u> *yě* *xiǎode yīnggāi fēn-qīng*   *shìfēi.*

    I   although stupid but   also   know   should   distinguish   right and wrong

    {I'm not smart, but I know that I should distinguish between right and wrong.}

(2) 我很笨，<u>但</u>也晓得应该分清是非。

    Wǒ *hěn*   *bèn,*   <u>*dàn*</u> *yě*   *xiǎode yīnggāi fēn-qīng*   *shìfēi.*

    I   very   stupid but   also   know   should   distinguish   right and wrong

    {I'm not smart, but I know that I should distinguish between right and wrong.}

(3) 我<u>虽然</u>笨，也晓得应该分清是非。

    Wǒ <u>*suīrán*</u>   *bèn,*   *yě* *xiǎode yīnggāi fēn-qīng*   *shìfēi.*

    I   although stupid also   know   should   distinguish clearly   right and wrong

    {Although I'm not smart, I know that I should distinguish between right and wrong.}

(4) 我晓得应该分清是非，<u>虽然</u>我很笨。

    Wǒ xiǎode yīnggāi fēn-qīng   *shìfēi,*   <u>*suīrán*</u>   *wǒ hěn bèn.*

    I   know   should   distinguish clearly right and wrong although I   very stupid

    {I know that I should distinguish between right and wrong, though I'm not smart.}

Each of these four examples are complex sentences showing an adversative relationship. The first two examples use "*suī* . . . *dàn* . . ." and ". . . *dàn* . . ." to show the adversative relationship between clauses, whereas the latter two examples only employ "*suī*. . . (*yě*) . . ." and ". . . *suīrán* . . ." respectively, showing an obvious adversative relationship even though *dàn* or its equivalent does not occur.

12.1.2 Unconventional forms

Unconventional forms refer to those in which an adversative marker would normally not occur but is deliberately used. Thus, an unconventional form is a conventional adversative form and a non-adversative form combined, and it is a special phenomenon in which markers of different types cooccur in the same sentence. To be specific, there are two different combinations.

Outline of adversative sentence forms 271

First, the presence of *dàn* or its synonym in non-adversative complex sentence forms. Non-adversative forms include those that are coordinate, progressive, hypothetical, correlative conditional, or cause-effect inferential, etc. In some cases, adversative connective *dàn* or its synonym can occur in those non-adversative sentence forms, as has been discussed in previous chapters. The following is a brief outline:

Case 1: *jì p, yòu q + dàn (què)*
        = *jì p, dàn (què) yòu q*

The following are examples of Case 1:

(5)   a 既想照顾他，又怕别人风言风语。
     Jì . . . yòu . . .   xiǎng   zhàogù   tā,   yòu pà   biérén   fēngyán-fēngyǔ.
     both . . . and . . .   want to   look after   him   fear   others   slanderous gossip
     {(She) wanted to look after him, and at the same time (she) was afraid that people would whisper.}

     →b 既想照顾他，<u>但</u>又怕别人风言风语。
     Jì . . . yòu . . .   xiǎng   zhàogù   tā,   <u>dàn</u> yòu pà   biérén fēngyán-fēngyǔ.
     both . . . and . . .   want to   look after   him   but   fear   others   slanderous gossip
     {(She) wanted to look after him, but at the same time (she) was afraid that people would whisper.}

     →c 既想照顾他，<u>却</u>又怕别人风言风语。
     Jì . . . yòu . . .   xiǎng   zhàogù   tā,   <u>què</u>   yòu   pà   biérén
     both . . . and . . .   want to   look after   him   however   fear   others
     fēngyán-fēngyǔ.
     slanderous gossip
     {(She) wanted to look after him, but at the same time (she) was afraid that people would whisper.}

Case 2: *jì p, yě q + dàn (què)*
        = *jì p, dàn (què) yě q*

The following are examples of Case 2:

(6)   a 既有天伦之乐，也有纠纷烦恼。
     Jì . . . yě . . .   yǒu   tiānlúnzhīlè,   yě yǒu   jiūfēn   fánnǎo.
     both . . . and . . .   have   family relationships   have   dispute   annoyance
     {(He) enjoys his family relations, and at the same time (he) is bothered by disputes.}

     →b 既有天伦之乐，<u>但</u>也有纠纷烦恼。
     Jì . . . yě . . .   yǒu   tiānlúnzhīlè,   <u>dàn</u> yě yǒu   jiūfēn   fánnǎo.
     both . . . and . . .   have   family relationships   but   have   dispute   annoyance
     {(He) enjoys his family relations, but at the same time (he) is bothered by disputes.}

272 *Outline of adversative sentence forms*

→c 既有天伦之乐，却也有纠纷烦恼。

Jì . . . *yě* . . . *yǒu tiānlúnzhīlè,* ___*què*___ ___*yě yǒu jiūfēn fánnǎo.*___
both . . . and . . . have family relationships however have dispute annoyance
{(He) enjoys his family relations, but at the same time (he) is bothered by disputes.}

Case 3: *yīmiàn p, yīmiàn q + dàn (què)*
= *yīmiàn p, dàn yīmiàn què q*

The following are examples of Case 3:

(7) a 一面摆酒接待，一面派人报告警察局。

___*Yīmiàn*___ . . . *yīmiàn* . . . *bǎijiǔ jiēdài,* ___*yīmiàn*___ *pài rén bàogào*
. . . meanwhile . . . host a banquet receive send person report
jǐngchájú.
police station
{While (he) hosted a banquet for (them), (he) sent someone to report it to the police.}

→b 一面摆酒接待，一面却派人报告警察局。

___*Yīmiàn*___ . . . *yīmiàn* . . . *bǎijiǔ jiēdài,* ___*yīmiàn*___ *què pài rén*
. . . meanwhile . . . host a banquet receive however send person
bàogào jǐngchájú.
report police station
{(He) hosted a banquet for (them), but meanwhile he sent someone to report it to the police.}

→c 一面摆酒接待，但一面又派人报告警察局。

___*Yīmiàn*___ . . . *yīmiàn* . . . *bǎijiǔ jiēdài,* ___*dàn*___ ___*yīmiàn*___ *yòu pài rén*
. . . meanwhile . . . host a banquet receive but also send person
bàogào jǐngchájú.
report police station
{(He) hosted a banquet for (them), but meanwhile he sent someone to report it to the police.}

Case 4: *yī fāngmiàn p, lìng yī fāngmiàn q + dàn (què)*
= *yī fāngmiàn p, dàn lìng yī fāng miàn què q*

The following are examples of Case 4:

(8) a 一方面承认我有才干，另一方面又说我不能重用。

___*Yī fāngmiàn*___ *chéngrèn wǒ yǒu cáigàn,* ___*lìng yī fāngmiàn*___ *yòu shuō wǒ*
on the one hand acknowledge I have talent on the other one hand also say I
bù néng zhòngyòng.
NEG can be put in an important position
{On the one hand, (he) acknowledged my talent, and on the other hand, (he) said
that I could not be put in any important position.}

Outline of adversative sentence forms　273

→b 一方面承认我有才干，<u>但另</u>一方面又说我不能重用。

Yī fāngmiàn　chéngrèn　wǒ yǒu　cáigàn, <u>dàn</u> **lìng yī fāngmiàn**　yòu
on the one hand acknowledge I have talent but on the other one hand also

shuō wǒ　bù　néng zhòngyòng.
say I NEG can be put in an important position

{On the one hand, (he) acknowledged my talent, but on the other hand, (he) said that I could not be put in any important position.}

→c 一方面承认我有才干，<u>另</u>一方<u>面却</u>又说我不能重用。

Yī fāngmiàn　chéngrèn　wǒ yǒu　cáigàn, **lìng yī fāngmiàn**　<u>què</u>
on the one hand acknowledge I have ability on the other one hand however

yòu　shuō wǒ bù　néng zhòngyòng.
also say I NEG can put someone in an important position

{On the one hand, (he) acknowledged my talent, but on the other hand, (he) said that I could not be put in any important position.}

Case 5: *yī biān p, yī biān q + dàn (què)*
= *yī biān p, dàn (què) yī biān q*

The following are examples of case 5:

(9)　a 一边不停地说恭喜，一边随时准备拔出手枪。

Yībiān ... *yībiān* ... bùtíng　de shuō gōngxǐ,　**yībiān** suíshí
as ... continue SP say congratulate at any moment

zhǔnbèi　bá-chū　shǒuqiāng.
be ready pull out pistol

{(He) was ready to draw his pistol as he kept saying congratulations.}

→b 一边不停地说恭喜，<u>但一</u>边随时准备拔出手枪。

Yībiān ... *yībiān* ... bùtíng　de shuō gōngxǐ,　<u>dàn</u> **yībiān** suíshí
as ... continue SP say congratulate but at any moment

zhǔnbèi bá-chū shǒuqiāng.
be ready pull out pistol

{He kept saying congratulations, but he was ready to draw his pistol at any time.}

→c 一边不停地说恭喜，<u>却一</u>边随时准备拔出手枪。

Yībiān ... *yībiān* ... bùtíng　de shuō　gōngxǐ,　<u>què</u>　**yībiān**
as ... continue SP say congratulate however

suíshí　zhǔnbèi　bá-chū　shǒuqiāng.
at any moment be ready pull out pistol

{He kept saying congratulations, but he was ready to draw his pistol at any time.}

→d 一边不停地说恭喜，一<u>边却</u>随时准备拔出手枪。

Yībiān ... *yībiān* ... bùtíng　de shuō　gōngxǐ,　**yībiān**　<u>què</u>
as ... continue SP say congratulate however

274 *Outline of adversative sentence forms*

suíshí *zhǔnbèi* *bá-chū* *shǒuqiāng.*
at any moment be ready pull out pistol
{He kept saying congratulations, but he was ready to draw his pistol at any time.}

Case 6: *jì p, gèng q + què*
= *jì p, què gèng q*

The following are examples of Case 6:

(10) a 既有爱，更有恨！
Jì *yǒu* *ài,* **gèng** *yǒu* *hèn!*
both there be love more there be hate
{There is love and, more importantly, there is hate.}

→b 既有爱，却更有恨！
Jì *yǒu* *ài,* <u>*què*</u> **gèng** *yǒu* *hèn!*
both there be love however more there be hate
{There is love but, more importantly, there is hate.}

Case 7: *bùdàn bù p, érqiě (fǎn'ér) q + què*
= *bùdàn bù p, què (fǎn'ér) q*

The following are examples of Case 7:

(11) a 不但不害怕，而且（反而）显得更加执拗了。
Bùdàn *bù* *hàipà,* *érqiě* **(fǎn'ér)** *xiǎnde gèngjiā* *zhíniù* *le.*
not only NEG fear but also on the contrary seem even more obstinate MP
{Instead of being afraid, he seemed even more obstinate.}

→b 不但不害怕，却（反而）显得更加执拗了。
Bùdàn **bù** *hàipà,* <u>*què*</u> **(fǎn'ér)** *xiǎnde* *gèngjiā*
not only NEG fear however on the contrary seem even more
zhíniù *le.*
obstinate MP
{Instead of being afraid, he seemed even more obstinate.}

Case 8: *rúguǒ shuō p, nàme q + què*
= *rúguǒ shuō p, nàme què q*

The following are examples of case 8:

(12) a 如果说过去还有点糊涂，那么，今天已经是完全清醒了。
Rúguǒ shuō *guòqù* *hái* *yǒudiǎn hútu,* **nàme,** *jīntiān yǐjīng* *shì*
if say the past still a little confused then today already COP

Outline of adversative sentence forms   275

wánquán   qīngxǐng le.
completely clear   MP
{If he was still a little confused before, then he is completely clear today.}

→b 如果说过去还有点糊涂，那么，今天却已经是完全清醒了。
Rúguǒ shuō *guòqù   hái yǒudiǎn hútu,   **nàme**, jīntiān <u>què</u>   yǐjīng*
if   say   the past still a little   confused then   today however already
shì   wánquán   qīngxǐng le.
COP   completely clear   MP
{If he was still a little confused before, then he is completely clear today.}

Case 9: *yuè p, yuè q + què*
     = *yuè p, què yuè q*

The following are examples of Case 9:

(13)   a 声音越低，越有威慑力。
       *Shēngyīn **yuè**...yuè...   dī,   **yuè** yǒu   wēishè   lì.*
       voice   the more...the more...   low   have intimidate force
       {The lower the voice, the more intimidating it is.}

       →b 声音越低，却越有威慑力。
       *Shēngyīn **yuè**...yuè...   dī,   <u>què</u>   **yuè** yǒu wēishè   lì.*
       voice   the more...the more...   low however   have intimidate force
       {The lower the voice, however the more intimidating it is.}

Case 10: *jìrán p, (jiù) q + què*
      = *jìrán p, què q*

The following are examples of Case 10:

(14)   a 既然解决不了问题，就不要累死累活地干了。
       Jìrán *jiějué bù liǎo wèntí,   **jiù**   bùyào lèisǐ-lèihuó   de gàn le.*
       since cannot solve problem then   do not work oneself to death SP do MP
       {Since the problem can't be solved, don't work (yourself) to death.}

       →b 既然解决不了问题，为什么还要累死累活地干呢？
       Jìrán *jiějué bù liǎo wèntí,   **wèishénme** hái   yào   lèisǐ-lèihuó*
       since cannot solve problem   why   still   will work oneself to death
       de   gàn ne?
       SP   do   MP
       {Since the problem can't be solved, why (are you) still working yourself to death?}

276 *Outline of adversative sentence forms*

→c 既然解决不了问题，为什么却还要累死累活地干呢？

***Jìrán** jiějué bù liǎo wèntí,   **wèishénme** què   hái yào lèisǐ-lèihuó*
since cannot solve problem why   however still will work oneself to death

de gàn ne?
SP do MP

{Since the problem can't be solved, why (are you) still working yourself to death?}

Second, the presence of adversative connective *dàn* or its synonym in special adversative complex sentence forms.

Special adversative complex sentence forms refer to those in which a concessive-adversative relationship exists between the clauses, but *dàn* or its synonym is usually absent. Special adversative complex sentence forms include hypothetical concessive forms, preferable concessive forms, and unconditional concessive forms. In some cases, *dàn* or its synonym can occur in these concessive adversative complex sentences to achieve a particular pragmatic effect, such as highlighting the adversativity, or demarcating the opposition boundary while emphasizing the adversativity. However, the collocation of *dàn* or its synonym and *suīrán* and the like is the norm, and the occurrence of *dàn* or its synonym in *jíshǐ*-sentences, *nìngkě*-sentences, and *wúlùn*-sentences is unconventional. Related issues have been discussed in the previous chapters. Here is an outline:

Case 11: *jíshǐ p, yě q + dàn (què)*
    = *jíshǐ p, dàn (què) yě q*

The following are examples of Case 11:

(15) a 即使自己有很多好的意见，也应该听听大家的意见。

***Jíshǐ** . . . yě . . . zìjǐ   yǒu hěn duō hǎo de yìjiàn, **yě** yīnggāi*
even if   oneself have very many good SP opinion   should

tīng-tīng   dàjiā   de yìjiàn.
listen to-REDP everyone SP opinion

{Even if (you) have a lot of good ideas, (you) should listen to other people's opinions.}

→b 即使自己有很多好的意见，但是也应该听听大家的意见。

***Jíshǐ** . . . yě . . . zìjǐ   yǒu hěn duō hǎo de yìjiàn, **dànshì** yě yīnggāi*
even if   oneself have very many good SP opinion but   should

tīng-tīng   dàjiā   de yìjiàn.
listen to-REDP everyone SP opinion

{Even if (you) have a lot of good ideas, (you) should still listen to other people's opinions.}

Case 12: *nìngkě p, yě q + dàn (què)*
    = *nìngkě p, dàn (què) yě q*

Outline of adversative sentence forms 277

The following are examples of Case 12:

(16) a 宁可慢些，也要好些！

    Nìngkě ... *yě* ... *màn* *xiē,* **yě** *yào* *hǎo* *xiē!*
    would rather ... slow a little need good a little
    {It's better to be slower!}

    →b 宁可慢些，但要好些！

    Nìngkě *màn* *xiē,* <u>*dàn*</u> *yào* *hǎo* *xiē!*
    would rather slow a little but need good a little
    {It's better to be slower!}

    →c 宁可慢些，却要好些！

    Nìngkě *màn* *xiē,* <u>*què*</u> *yào* *hǎo* *xiē!*
    would rather slow a little however need good a little
    {It's better to be slower!}

Case 13: *wúlùn p, dōu q + dàn (què)*
        = *wúlùn p, dàn (què) (dōu) q*

The following are examples of case 13:

(17) a 无论他们怎么造谣中伤，都影响不了我老爸的形象！

    Wúlùn ... *dōu* ... *tā-men* *zěnme* *zàoyáo* *zhòngshāng,* **dōu**
    no matter ... they how spread rumors slander

    yǐngxiǎng bù liǎo *wǒ* *lǎobà* *de* *xíngxiàng!*
    cannot affect my father SP image
    {No matter how they slander my dad, they can't ruin his image at all!}

    →b 无论他们怎么造谣中伤，但都影响不了我老爸的形象！

    Wúlùn ... *dōu* ... *tā-men* *zěnme* *zàoyáo* *zhòngshāng,* <u>*dàn*</u> **dōu**
    no matter ... they how spread rumors slander but

    yǐngxiǎng bù liǎo *wǒ* *lǎobà* *de* *xíngxiàng!*
    cannot affect my father SP image
    {No matter how they slander my dad, they can't ruin his image at all!}

    →c 无论他们怎么造谣中伤，却都影响不了我老爸的形象！

    Wúlùn ... *dōu* ... *tā-men* *zěnme* *zàoyáo* *zhòngshāng,* <u>*què*</u> **dōu**
    no matter ... they how spread rumors slander however

    yǐngxiǎng bù liǎo *wǒ* *lǎobà* *de* *xíngxiàng!*
    cannot affect my father SP image
    {No matter how they slander my dad, they can't ruin his image at all!}

278 *Outline of adversative sentence forms*

12.2 Linguistic form and semantic meaning

Linguistic form is an exterior and visible form, and semantic meaning is an invisible relationship implied by the linguistic form. It is necessary to observe the linguistic form and semantic meaning in order to understand adversative sentences.

12.2.1 *Validity of adversative sentence forms*

The validity of an adversative sentence form is determined by the existence of a logical basis for an adversative relationship between matters. Specifically, it depends on the opposition, contrast, or difference between matters, and even on the correspondence between the employed sentence form and the logical basis.

If there is no logical basis for an adversative relationship between matters, no adversative sentence forms can be used. The following are two examples:

(18) *这样极可珍贵的作品，<u>虽</u>只剩了很不完整的一段，<u>但是</u>很可惜的。

Zhèyàng jí   kě   zhēnguì de zuòpǐn, <u>suī</u>   zhǐ   shèng-le   hěn
such   extremely very precious SP work   although only leave-PEF very

bù   wánzhěng de   yī   duàn,   <u>dàn</u> <u>shì</u>   hěn   kěxī   de.
NEG   complete   SP   one   section   but   COP   very   regrettable   SP

(19) *这种教育方式<u>虽则</u>是受 "刘介梅的今昔对比展览会" 的启发，<u>但</u>在上海<u>却</u>得到了推广。

Zhè   zhǒng   jiàoyù   fāngshì   <u>suīzé</u>   shì   shòu   "Liú Jièméi de
this   type   educate   method   although   COP   receive   LIU Jiemei   SP

jīnxī   duìbǐ   zhǎnlǎnhuì" de qǐfā,   <u>dàn</u> zài Shànghǎi <u>què</u>
past and present   compare   exhibition   SP inspire   but   in   Shanghai   however

dédào-le   tuīguǎng.
receive-PEF   promote

These two examples are cited from *Selections of Chinese Short Reviews*.[1] There is no adversative relationship between ". . . *zhī shèng le hěn bù wánzhěng de yī duàn*" ('only an incomplete section remains') and "*shì hěn kěxī de*" ('is a pity') in (18); neither does an adversative relationship exist between "*zhè zhǒng jiàoyù fāngshì shì shòu . . . qǐfā*" ('this education method was inspired by . . .') and "*zài shànghǎi dé dào le tuīguǎng*" ('was promoted in Shanghai') in (19). Therefore, the two sentences are ill-formed, and the adversative connective "*suī (suīzé) . . . dàn/què . . .*" should be removed.

If there is no logical basis for the adversative relationship required by a particular adversative sentence form, that form cannot be used. Compare the following two examples:

(20) 有三个同志坐下来抱在一起想暖和一下，<u>但</u>他们再也没有站起来。

Yǒu   sān   gè   tóngzhì   zuò-xiàlái bào   zài yīqǐ   xiǎng   nuǎnhuo
there are three CL comrade sit down   cuddle at   together   want to warm up

Outline of adversative sentence forms   279

yīxià, <u>dàn</u> tā-men zài yě   méiyǒu zhàn-qǐlái.
a bit   but   they   for ever NEG   stand up
{Three comrades sat down and cuddled up to each other to try to warm up, but they never stood up again.}

(21)   *有三个同志<u>虽然</u>坐下来抱在一起想暖和一下，<u>但</u>他们再也没有站起来。

Yǒu   sān   gè   tóngzhì   <u>suīrán</u>   zuò-xiàlái bào   zài yīqǐ   xiǎng
there are three CL   comrade   although   sit down   cuddle at   together   want to
nuǎnhuo yīxià, <u>dàn</u> tā-men zài yě   méiyǒu zhàn-qǐlái.
warm up a bit   but   they   for ever NEG   stand up

In (20), there is an adversative relationship between "sat down . . ." and "never stood up again"; therefore ". . . *dàn* . . ." is used, and the sentence is a well-formed one. However, (21) is an ill-formed sentence due to the use of "*suīrán* . . . *dàn* . . .". The logical basis for "*suīrán* . . . *dàn* . . ." sentences is contrastive causality, but there is no such relationship between "sat down . . . to warm up" and "never stood up again" in (21).

In the contrastive causality relationship, the result/effect is the opposite of the anticipated result/effect of the cause. The following are two examples:

(22)   因为黑夜笼罩着他，所以我看不到他脸上的忧伤。（causality）
Yīnwèi   hēiyè   lǒngzhào-zhe tā,   suǒyǐ   wǒ kàn bù dào tā   liǎn-shàng de
because night   shroud-PRG   him therefore I   cannot see   his on face   SP
yōushāng.
sadness
{I couldn't see the sadness on his face because he was covered by the darkness of the night.}

(23)   虽然黑夜笼罩着他，但我仍然看到了他脸上的忧伤。（contrastive causality）
Suīrán   hēiyè lǒngzhào-zhe tā,   dàn wǒ réng rán kàn-dào-le tā   liǎn-shàng de
although night shroud-PRG him but I   still   see-PEF   his on face   SP
yōushāng.
sadness
{Although he was covered by the darkness of the night, I still saw the sadness on his face.}

If there is no contrastive causality, "*suīrán* . . . *dàn* . . ." cannot be used, which is why (21) is an ill-formed sentence. Compare another pair of sentences:

(24)   俗话说，左眼跳财；<u>但</u>俗话又说，右眼跳祸……
Súhuà shuō, zuǒ yǎn tiào   cái;   <u>dàn</u> súhuà yòu shuō, yòu   yǎn tiào
saying say   left eye twitch fortune but   saying also say   right eye twitch
huò . . .
disaster
{Twitching on the left eye foretells fortune, as the saying goes, but twitching on the right eye forecasts disaster, says the same saying.}

280 *Outline of adversative sentence forms*

(25)   * <u>虽然</u>俗话说，左眼跳财；<u>但</u>俗话又说，右眼跳祸……

<u>*Suīrán*</u> *súhuà shuō, zuǒ yǎn tiào   cái;   <u>*dàn*</u> *súhuà yòu shuō, yòu yǎn*
although saying say   left eye twitch fortune but saying also say   right eye

tiào   huò . . .
twitch disaster

    In (24), ". . . *dàn* . . ." is correctly used, for there is an opposition between "twitching on the left eye foretells fortune" and "twitching on the right eye forecasts disaster". However, in (25), "*suīrán* . . . *dàn* . . ." is incorrectly used, for "twitching on the left eye foretells fortune" and "twitching on the right eye forecasts disaster" cannot influence each other, i.e., there is no logical basis for contrastive causality.

    It is also the logical basis that determines the validity of a sentence in the unconventional form. Take, for example, the unconventional form "*wúlùn p, dàn (dōu) q*". Three conclusions can be drawn from the observation of the logical basis for the relationship between *p* and *q*.

    First, in some cases there is contrastive causality between *p* and *q*, hence an unconventional form can be used. The following are three examples:

(26)   <u>不管</u>是属于哪种情况，黎子流<u>却</u>绝对不会是脑袋一热、灵机一动或一时的意气用事而辞职的。

<u>*Bùguǎn*</u> *shì   shǔyú   nǎ   zhǒng qíngkuàng, Lí Zǐliú <u>*què*</u>   *juéduì*
no matter COP belong to which type   situation   LI Ziliu however absolutely

bù   huì shì   nǎodàiyīrè,   língjīyīdòng   huò yīshí
NEG   can COP lose one's mind have a sudden inspiration or   a short moment

de   yìqì-yòngshì   ér   cízhí   de.
SP   act on impulse without due consideration then   resign SP

{Whatever the case it was, LI Ziliu would never have resigned because he lost his mind, or had a sudden inspiration, or acted on impulse.}

(27)   <u>不管</u>这些神话怎样荒唐可笑，<u>但</u>在日本人的心理上有着深固的根底，正足以满足其夸大的心理，助长其征服别国的强烈野心。

<u>*Bùguǎn*</u> *zhèxiē shénhuà zěnyàng huāngtáng kěxiào,   <u>*dàn*</u> zài . . . shàng*
no matter these   myth   how   absurd   ridiculous but   in

rìběnrén   de xīnlǐ   shàng yǒu-zhe   shēngù   de gēndǐ,
Japanese person SP psyche   there be-PRG deep and solid SP foundation

zhèng zúyǐ   mǎnzú qí   kuādà   de xīnlǐ, zhùzhǎng qí   zhēngfú bié
just   suffice satisfy their exaggerate SP psyche increase   their conquer other

guó   de qiángliè yěxīn.
country SP strong   fierce ambition

{However absurd and ridiculous these myths may be, they have deep roots in the Japanese psyche, just enough to satisfy their inflated mentality and fuel their fierce ambition to conquer other countries.}

(28)   他想给妻子谈一谈，<u>不管</u>有什么分歧，多大的分歧，<u>但</u>为了孩子，就把这一切暂时放下吧。

Tā xiǎng   gěi   qīzi tán yī tán, <u>bùguǎn</u>   yǒu shénme fēnqí,   duō dà
he want to with wife have a talk no matter have what   disagreement how big

Outline of adversative sentence forms 281

de fēnqí, **dàn** wèile háizi, jiù bǎ zhè yīqiè zànshí fàng-xià ba.
SP disagreement but for kid just BA this all temporary put aside MP
{He wanted to have a talk with his wife and ask her to put everything aside for now for the child's sake, no matter what disagreements they had or how serious the disadvantages were.}

In all the three examples, "*bùguǎn . . . dàn/què . . .*" is used. From the perspective of a logical basis, they are similar to "*suīrán . . . dàn/què . . .*" sentences, and all of them can be rewritten as "*suīrán . . . dàn/què . . .*" sentences if such words as *nǎzhǒng, zěnyàng, shénme,* or *duō* are changed. Examples (29)—(31) are the respective rewrites of (26)—(28):

(29) 虽然是属于那种情况，黎子流却绝对不会是⋯⋯ 意气用事而辞职的。
*Suīrán shì shǔyú nà zhǒng qíngkuàng, Lí Zǐliú **què** juéduì*
although COP belong to that type situation LI Ziliu however absolutely
bù huì shì yìqì-yòngshì ér cízhí de.
NEG can COP act on impulse without due consideration then resign SP
{Although it was the case, LI Ziliu would never have resigned because he lost his mind . . .}

(30) 虽然这些神话十分荒唐可笑，但在日本人的心理上有着深固的根底，⋯⋯
*Suīrán zhèxiē shénhuà shífēn huāngtáng kěxiào, **dàn** zài . . . shàng*
although these myth very absurd ridiculous but in
Rìběn rén de xīnlǐ shàng yǒu-zhe shēngù de gēndǐ, . . .
Japanese SP psyche there be-PRG deep and solid SP foundation
{Although these myths may be absurd and ridiculous, they have deep roots in the Japanese psyche . . .}

(31) 虽然有分歧，很大的分歧，但为了孩子，就把这一切暂时放下吧。
*Suīrán yǒu fēnqí, hěn dà de fēnqí, **dàn** wèile háizi,*
although have disagreement very big SP disagreement but for kid
jiù bǎ zhè yīqiè zànshí fàng-xià ba.
just BA this all temporary put aside MP
{Put everything aside for now for the child's sake, though we have some disagreements, very serious disagreements.}

Second, in some cases there is a partial contrastive causality between *p* and *q*. In those cases, if the speaker wishes to emphasize that what is stated in *p* contradicts every aspect of what is stated in *q* in order to show a completely positive or negative attitude, the adversative connective *dàn* can be used in "*wúlùn . . . (dōu) . . .*" sentences, hence is an unconventional form. The following example has been used in Chapter 4, Volume III:

(32) 不管你是不是指我，但不许你这样说！
*Bùguǎn nǐ **shì bù shì** zhǐ wǒ, **dàn** bù xǔ nǐ zhèyàng shuō!*
no matter... you whether refer to me but NEG allow you so say
{Whether you refer to me or not, you are not allowed to say so!}

282   *Outline of adversative sentence forms*

In (32), if "you refer to me", certainly "you are not allowed to say so", but even if "you refer to someone else", "you mustn't say so, either!" Therefore, there is a partial adversative relationship between *p* and *q*. The following is another example:

(33)   廉兴！<u>甭管</u>团支部是<u>不是</u>个有用的衙门，<u>但</u>它毕竟是个衙门!你怎么敢把它当成你家仓库！

   Lián Xīng! <u>*Béngguǎn*</u> *tuán*   *zhībù*   **shì bù shì**   *gè*   *yǒuyòng de*
   LIAN Xing no matter league branch whether . . . or not CL   useful   SP
   yámen,   <u>*dàn*</u> *tā bìjìng*   *shì*   *gè*   *yámen!*   *Nǐ   zěnme gǎn*
   government office but   it   after all COP CL   government office you how   dare
   bǎ   tā dāng-chéng nǐ   jiā   cāngkù!
   BA   it   treat as   your household warehouse
   {LIAN Xing! Whether the League branch is a useful government office or not, it is, after all, a government office! How dare you take it as your household warehouse!}

If "the League branch" is "a useful government office", then it obviously deserves its name; even if it is "a useless government office", it is still a government office. Thus, there is a partial adversative relationship between *p* and *q* in (33). In conclusion, there is a corresponding logical basis for the use of *dàn* in those two sentences.

Third, if there is no contrastive causality at all between the clauses, unconventional forms, such as "*wúlùn . . . dàn/què (dōu) . . .*", cannot be used. The following is an example:

(34)   假使这佛手原种系遗传突变所造成，<u>无论</u>截枝引种，还是采籽育苗，<u>都</u>能使之繁衍新种。

   Jiǎshǐ   zhè   fóshǒu   yuán   zhǒng   xì   yíchuán tūbiàn   suǒ   zàochéng,
   if   this choko   original species COP inherit   mutate PAP cause
   <u>*wúlùn*</u>   *jié*   *zhī*   *yǐnzhòng,*   *háishi   cǎi   zǐ*
   no matter cut   branch introducer a fine variety or   harvest seed
   yùmiáo,   <u>*dōu*</u> *néng shǐ*   *zhī*   *fányǎn*   *xīn   zhǒng.*
   raise seedlings both can   make   it   reproduce   new   species
   {If this original choko species is the result of a genetic mutation, it will be possible to reproduce the new species either by using the branches or by using the seeds to raise seedlings.}

No adversative connectives can be used in this example because there is no opposition between "reproducing the new species" and "using the branches" or between "reproducing the new species" and "using the seeds".

12.2.2   *Selection of adversative sentence forms*

The selection of a particular adversative sentence form is determined by the speaker's choice of adversative relationships.

Outline of adversative sentence forms   283

The semantic relationship within a complex sentence reflects both the objective reality and the speaker's subjective view, and the subjective view outweighs the objective reality in the selection of the sentence form. (More details can be found in Chapter 1, Volume IV.) This is also the case for sentence form selection. The validity of a sentence form certainly depends on the various adversative relationships in the objective reality, but the speaker's subjective view determines whether a particular adversative sentence form should be selected or which adversative sentence form should be selected. There are three possible choices for the speaker.

First, there is an implied adversative relationship in the sentence, but the speaker ignores it. In this case, the speaker is most likely to choose a non-adversative form. The following are three examples:

(35)   老人家<u>不仅</u>经常接济穷苦人家，<u>而且</u>从不希望得到些微的回报。

　　　 Lǎorénjiā <u>*bùjǐn*</u> *jīngcháng jiējì* 　　　　　　　 *qióngkǔ rénjiā,* <u>*érqiě*</u>
　　　 old person not only often 　　give material assistance 　poor 　 family 　 and

　　　 cóng bù 　 *xīwàng dédào xiēwēi de huíbào.*
　　　 ever NEG expect receive a little SP return

　　　 {The old person often helped the poor and needy and never expected even a small return.}

(36)   军官们<u>一面</u>"哈依哈依"地接受训斥，<u>一面</u>不失时机地推卸自己的责任。

　　　 Jūnguān men <u>*yīmiàn*</u> . . . <u>*yīmiàn*</u> . . . "*hāyī hāyī*" *de jiēshòu xùnchì,* <u>*yīmiàn*</u>
　　　 officer-PL 　　. . . meanwhile . . . 　　yes 　yes 　SP accept rebuke

　　　 bù 　*shī* 　*shíjī* 　　 *de tuīxiè zìjǐ* 　 *de zérèn.*
　　　 NEG miss opportunity SP shirk oneself SP responsibility

　　　 {While saying "yes, sir, yes, sir" to respond to the reprimand, the officers lost no time to pass the buck.}

(37)   <u>如果说</u>年青的一代有着更多的勇敢，<u>那么</u>父亲一代则有着更多的成熟。

　　　 <u>*Rúguǒ shuō*</u> *niánqīng de yī dài* 　　 *yǒu-zhe gèng duō de yǒnggǎn,*
　　　 if 　　say young 　SP one generation have-PRG more a lot of SP brave

　　　 <u>*nàme*</u> *fùqīn yī dài* 　　 *zé yǒu-zhe gèng duō de chéngshú.*
　　　 then father one generation but have-PRG more a lot of SP mature

　　　 {If the younger generation has more courage, then the father generation has more maturity.}

Example (35) is marked as a progressive sentence, but if the speaker took the implied opposition into account, the sentence could be marked as an adversative one as (38). Example (36) is marked as a coordinate sentence, but it could be marked as an adversative one if the speaker considered the conflict as (39). Example (37) is marked as a hypothetical sentence, but it could be marked as an adversative one if the speaker wished to emphasize the contrast as (40).

284 *Outline of adversative sentence forms*

(38) 老人家经常接济穷苦人家，<u>但是</u>从不希望得到些微的回报。

Lǎorénjiā jīngcháng jiējì qióngkǔ rénjiā, <u>dànshì</u> cóng
old person often give material assistance poor family but ever
bù xīwàng dédào xiēwēi de huíbào.
NEG expect receive a little SP return
{The old person often helped the poor and needy, but he never expected even a small return.}

(39) 军官们"哈依哈依"地接受训斥，却不失时机地推卸自己的责任。

Jūnguān men "hāyī hāyī" de jiēshòu xùnchì, què bù shī shíjī
officer-PL yes yes SP accept rebuke however NEG miss opportunity
de tuīxiè zìjǐ de zérèn.
SP shirk oneself SP responsibility
{The officers said "yes, sir, yes, sir" to respond to the reprimand, but they still lost no time to pass the buck.}

(40) 年青的一代有着更多的勇敢，父亲一代却有着更多的成熟。

Niánqīng de yī dài yǒu-zhe gèng duō de yǒnggǎn, fùqīn yī
young SP one generation have-PRG more a lot of SP brave father one
dài què yǒu-zhe gèng duō de chéngshú.
generation however have-PRG more a lot of SP mature
{The younger generation has more courage; however, the father generation has more maturity.}

Second, there is an adversative relationship in the sentence, and the speaker chooses to highlight this relationship; thus the sentence is marked as an adversative one. The following are two examples:

(41) 但直到现在，总还是没有得到，<u>但</u>也没有遇见过赤练蛇和美女蛇。

Dàn zhídào xiànzài, zǒng háishi méiyǒu dédào, <u>dàn</u> yě méiyǒu yùjiàn-guò
but be up to now always still NEG get but also NEG meet-EXP
chìliànshé hé měinǚshé.
crimson snake and beauty snake
{Yet until now, I still haven't gotten (a box of flying centipedes), but I haven't met a crimson snake or a "beauty snake", either.}

(42) 那时我的祖母<u>虽然</u>还康健，<u>但</u>母亲也已分担了些家务，……

Nà shí wǒ de zǔmǔ <u>suīrán</u> hái kāngjiàn, <u>dàn</u> mǔqīn yě yǐ
that time I SP grandmother although still healthy but mother also already
fēndān-le xiē jiāwù, ...
share-PEF some housework
{Although my grandmother was still healthy then, my mother had already shared some of the household chores . . .}

Outline of adversative sentence forms   285

The two aforementioned examples could be rewritten as coordinate sentences as (43) and (44) respectively, if the speakers put the emphasis on the coordinate relationship.

(43)   但直到现在，总还是没有得到，也没有遇见过赤练蛇和美女蛇。
   Dàn zhídào   xiànzài, zǒng   háishi méiyǒu dédào,   yě   méiyǒu yùjiàn-guò
   but   be up to now   always still   NEG   get   also NEG   meet-EXP
   chìliànshé   hé   měinǚshé.
   crimson snake and beauty snake
   {Yet until now, I still haven't gotten (a box of flying centipedes), nor have I met a crimson snake or a "beauty snake".}

(44)   那时我的祖母还康健，母亲也已分担了些家务。
   Nà   shí   wǒ de zǔmǔ   hái kāngjiàn, mǔqīn yě   yǐ   fēndān-le
   that time I   SP grandmother still healthy   mother also already share-PEF
   xiē   jiāwù.
   some housework
   {My grandmother was still healthy then, and my mother had already shared some of the household chores.}

Again, it can be seen that the speaker's subjective view determines the sentence form. The following are another two examples:

(45)   肚子很饿，气力不够，但是必须鼓着勇气前进。
   Dùzi   hěn è,   qìlì   bù   gòu,   dànshì bìxū gǔ-zhe   yǒngqì
   stomach very hungry energy NEG be enough but   must muster-PRG courage
   qiánjìn.
   move forward
   {Although he was hungry and weak, he had to move forward with courage.}

(46)   荔枝林深处，隐隐露出一角白屋，那是温泉公社的养蜂场，却起了个有趣的名儿，叫"养蜂大厦"。
   Lìzhī   lín   shēn chù,   yǐnyǐn lùchū yī   jiǎo   bái   wū,   nà   shì
   lychee forest deep place faint   appear one corner white house that COP
   wēnquán gōngshè de yǎng fēng chǎng, què   qǐ-le   gè yǒuqù
   hot spring commune SP keep bee farm   however be give-PEF CL interesting
   de míng r, jiào "yǎng fēng dàshà".
   SP name   call keep bee mansion
   {Deep in the lychee forest, a corner of a white house peeked out. It was the bee farm of the Hot Spring Commune, but it had an interesting name—"Bee-keeping Mansion".}

Example (45) could be rewritten as a causal sentence as (47), and (46) could be transformed into an annotative sentence as (48).

286   *Outline of adversative sentence forms*

(47)   肚子很饿，气力不够，<u>因此</u>必须鼓着勇气前进。

Dùzi   hěn   è,   qìlì   bù   gòu,   <u>yīncǐ</u>   bìxū   gǔ-zhe
stomach   very hungry energy NEG   be enough therefore must   muster-PRG

yǒngqì   qiánjìn.
courage   move forward

{He was hungry and weak, so he had to move forward with courage.}

(48)   那是温泉公社的养蜂场，(这个养蜂场)起了个有趣的名儿，叫"养蜂大厦"。

Nà   shì   wēnquán gōngshè   de yǎng fēng chǎng, (zhè gè yǎng fēng chǎng)
that COP hot spring commune SP keep bee farm   this CL keep bee farm

qǐ-le   gè yǒuqù   de míng r, jiào "yǎng fēng dàshà".
be give-PEF CL interesting SP name   call keep bee mansion

{It was the bee farm of the Hot Spring Commune, and (this bee farm) had an interesting name—"Bee-keeping Mansion".}

However, the speakers of (45) and (46) choose to use an adversative complex sentence form instead of a cause-effect one or an annotative one, most likely because they regard the implied opposition as extremely important. The following is another example:

(49)   桥脚上站着一个人，<u>却</u>是我的母亲，双喜便是对伊说着话。

Qiáojiǎo-shàng zhàn-zhe yī gè rén,   <u>què</u>   shì   wǒ de mǔqīn,
on pier   stand-PRG one CL person however COP   I   SP mother

Shuāngxǐ biàn shì duì yī   shuōhuà zhe   huà.
Shuangxi just COP to her talk   PRG

{On the pier someone was standing. It wasn't anyone else but my mother, to whom Shuangxi was talking.}

The adversative connective *què* is used in (49), for the speaker wishes to emphasize that "the person standing one the pier" was not "anyone else" but "my mother", but it can also be rewritten as an annotative sentence, as (50).

(50)   桥脚上站着一个人，(这个人)是我的母亲。

Qiáojiǎo-shàng zhàn-zhe yī gè rén,   (zhè gè rén) shì wǒ de mǔqīn.
on pier   stand-PRG one CL person this CL person COP I   SP mother

{On the pier someone was standing, and it was my mother.}

Third, there exist multiple semantic relationships in a sentence, and the speaker chooses to present them all, then the chosen sentence form will be marked as unconventional, such as "*jì p, dàn (què) yě q*"; "*yuè p, què yuè q*"; "*jìrán p, què q*"; "*jíshǐ p, què yě q*"; and so on. The selection of these forms reveals that the speaker wishes to emphasize the coexistence of the coordinate, or conditional, or hypothetical relationship and the adversative relationship. Compare the following examples:

Outline of adversative sentence forms 287

(51) a 既要讲数量，也要讲质量！

Jì . . . yě . . . yào jiǎng shùliàng, yě yào jiǎng
both . . . and . . . must pay attention to quantity must pay attention to
zhìliàng!
quality
{(We) should pay attention to both quantity and quality!}

b 既要讲数量，更要讲质量！

Jì yào jiǎng shùliàng, gèng yào jiǎng zhìliàng!
both must pay attention to quantity more must pay attention to quality
{(We) should pay attention to quantity and, more importantly, to quality!}

c 既要讲数量，却更要讲质量！

Jì yào jiǎng shùliàng, què gèng yào jiǎng
both must pay attention to quantity however more must pay attention to
zhìliàng!
quality
{(We) should pay attention to quantity, but more importantly, to quality!}

In (51a), "*jì . . . yě . . .*" indicates a coordinate relationship. In (51b), "*jì . . . gèng . . .*" marks a combination of coordinate and a progressive relationships; therefore (51b) is in an unconventional form including progressive and coordinate relationships. In (51c), "*jì . . . què gèng . . .*" marks three relationships: coordinate, adversative, and progressive.

If a sentence includes two semantic relationships respectively labeled as X and Y, then X can be formally invisible and Y is formally visible, or vice versa, or both are visible. Unconventional sentence forms are those in which both X and Y are visible, reflecting the speaker's double perspectives. If there are three semantic relationships contained in a sentence, they can be labeled as X, Y, and Z, and the relationships can be formally presented as: X; Y; Z; XY; XZ; YZ; or XYZ.

12.3 Linguistic form and pragmatic value

The pragmatic value refers to the pragmatic effect of a linguistic form. Investigations into the pragmatic value of adversative sentence forms offer another perspective to understand adversative sentences.

12.3.1 Form and value of conventional forms

First, the pragmatic values of adversative and non-adversative sentence forms with the same logical basis are different. Compare the following examples:

(52) a 第一炮一定要打响，必须认真准备。

Dì'yī pào yīdìng yào dǎ-xiǎng, bìxū rènzhēn zhǔnbèi.
beginning definitely must succeed have to careful prepare
{The beginning must be successful, and careful preparation needs to be made.}

288 *Outline of adversative sentence forms*

b 第一炮一定要打响，<u>因此</u>，必须认真准备。

Dì'yī pào   yídìng   yào   dǎ-xiǎng,   <u>yīncǐ,</u>   bìxū   rènzhēn   zhǔnbèi.
beginning definitely must   succeed   therefore have to careful prepare
{The beginning must be successful, so careful preparation needs to be made.}

c 第一炮一定要打响，<u>但是</u>，必须认真准备。

Dì'yī pào   yídìng   yào   dǎ-xiǎng,   <u>dànshì,</u>   bìxū   rènzhēn   zhǔnbèi.
beginning definitely must   succeed   but   have to careful prepare
{The beginning must be successful, but careful preparation needs to be made.}

In (52a), with no markers present, the cause-effect relationship is implied between the two clauses. In (52b), with the presence of *yīncǐ*, the cause-effect relationship between the two clauses is visible. In (53c), with occurrence of the adversative connective *dànshì*, the implied cause-effect relationship between the two clauses is transformed into an adversative relationship. Examples (52a) and (52b) develop in the direction indicated by the logical relationship between the clauses, expose the causal relationship between the matters and emphasize that "careful preparation" is a necessary condition for "a successful beginning". Example (52c) is an adversative sentence with a reminding and warning tone, which not only indicates that "careful preparation" is a necessary condition for "a successful beginning", but also emphasizes that there might be negative consequences if otherwise. Compare:

(53)   她希望逢着一个可以把一切献给自己的男人，<u>因此</u>她不能轻易把自己交付给他。

Tā   xīwàng féng-zhe   yī   gè   kěyǐ   bǎ   yīqiè xiàn-gěi zìjǐ   de nánrén,
she hope   meet-PRG one CL   can   BA   all   give to   oneself SP man
<u>yīncǐ</u> tā   bù   néng   qīngyì   bǎ   zìjǐ   jiāofù-gěi   tā.
so   she NEG can   easily   BA oneself entrust . . . to him
{She hopes that the man she is meeting can give everything to her; she can't, therefore, entrust herself to him easily.}

(54)   她希望逢着一个可以把一切献给自己的男人，<u>但她却</u>不能轻易把自己交付给他。

Tā   xīwàng féng-zhe   yī   gè   kěyǐ   bǎ   yīqiè xiàn-gěi zìjǐ   de nánrén, <u>dàn</u>
she hope   meet-PRG one CL   can   BA   all   give to   oneself SP man   but
tā   <u>què</u>   bù   néng   qīngyì   bǎ   zìjǐ   jiāofù-gěi   tā.
he however NEG can   easily   BA oneself entrust . . . to him
{She hopes that the man she is meeting can give everything to her, but she can't entrust herself to him easily.}

What (53) means is that "she hopes that the man she is dating is someone who can give everything to her, but she is uncertain whether he is such a man, therefore she can't entrust herself to him easily". The use of the connective *yīncǐ* in (53) marks the sentence as a cause-effect complex sentence and indicates that "she does not trust him at the moment". What (54) means is that "she hopes that the

Outline of adversative sentence forms 289

man she is dating is someone who can give everything to her, and she feels that he is such a man, but she still can't entrust herself to him easily". In (54), with *dàn* and *què*, the posterior clause implies that "she tends to trust him, but yet not to the degree that she can entrust herself to him", which is quite the opposite of the meaning of the posterior clause in (53).

Second, the pragmatic values of different adversative sentence forms with the same logical basis are different. Compare the following examples:

(55) 你做得对，<u>但是</u>不应该吵架。

Nǐ	*zuò*	*de*	*duì,*	*<u>dànshì</u>*	*bù*	*yīnggāi*	*chǎojià.*
you	do	SP	right	but	NEG	should	quarrel

{You did the right thing, but you shouldn't have quarreled.}

(56) 你做得对，<u>只是</u>不应该吵架。

Nǐ	*zuò*	*de*	*duì,*	*<u>zhǐshì</u>*	*bù*	*yīnggāi*	*chǎojià.*
you	do	SP	right	only	NEG	should	quarrel

{You did the right thing, only you shouldn't have quarreled.}

In (55), the speaker seriously criticizes "the quarrel", as *dànshì* carries a serious tone, whereas in (56), the speaker tactfully criticizes "the quarrel", as *zhǐshì* carries a mild tone. In other words, *dànshì* stresses an absolute opposition between the matters, while *zhǐshì* indicates a partial conflict. The posterior clause in any adversative sentence with *zhǐshì* is meant to revise what is stated in the anterior clause to some degree or from certain perspective, and it can end with such words as *bàle* and *jiùshìle*, which carry a mild tone. The following are two examples:

(57) a 你做得对，只是不应该吵架罢了。

Nǐ	*zuò*	*de*	*duì,*	*zhǐshì*	*bù*	*yīnggāi*	*chǎojià*	*bàle.*
you	do	SP	right	only	NEG	should	quarrel	MP

{You did the right thing, only you shouldn't have quarreled.}

b 你做得对，只是不应该吵架就是了。

Nǐ	*zuò*	*de*	*duì,*	*zhǐshì*	*bù*	*yīnggāi*	*chǎojià*	*<u>jiùshìle</u>.*
you	do	SP	right	only	NEG	should	quarrel	MP

{You did the right thing, only you shouldn't have quarreled.}

Compare another two examples:

(58) 张为已经五十几，<u>但是</u>李正才有二十六。(他们之间可有"代沟"呀!)

Zhāng Wéi yǐjīng wǔshí jǐ, <u>dànshì</u> Lǐ Zhèng cái yǒu èrshíliù. (Tā-men
ZHANG Wei already fifty odd but LI Zheng just have twenty-six they
zhījiān kě yǒu "dàigōu" ya!)
between indeed there be generation gap MP

{ZHANG Wei is already in his fifties, but LI Zheng is only twenty-six. [There is indeed a "generation gap" between them!]}

290   *Outline of adversative sentence forms*

(59)   <u>虽然</u>张为已经五十几，<u>但是</u>李正才有二十六。(他们那个班子可是有后劲的呀!)

    <u>Suīrán</u>   Zhāng Wéi   yǐjīng   wǔshí jǐ,   <u>dànshì</u> Lǐ Zhèng cái yǒu èrshíliù.
    although ZHANG Wei already fifty   odd but   LI Zheng just have twenty-six

    (*Tā-men nà gè bānzi kě   shì yǒu hòujìn de ya!*)
    their   that CL team indeed COP have stamina SP MP

    {Although ZHANG Wei is already in his fifties, LI Zheng is only twenty-six. [Their team really has staying power!]}

In (58), *dànshì* is used to emphasize the big age difference between ZHANG Wei and LI Zheng, thus *suīrán* cannot be added. In (59), "*suīrán . . . dànshì . . .*" is used to emphasize that the validity of one matter does not depend on the validity of another, i.e., "although ZHANG Wei is already in his fifties, it does not matter to the whole team, because LI Zheng is only twenty-six, which suggests that their team really has staying power". Thus, *dànshì* stresses the opposition between matters, while "*suīrán . . . dànshì . . .*" first concedes a matter and then emphasizes that this matter does not affect the validity of the other matter.

The form "*suīrán p, dànshì q*" denotes an inevitable adversative relationship between *p* and *q*, which can be illustrated by a comparison between (60) and (61).

(60)   张为喜欢跳舞，<u>但是</u>李正喜欢看电影，所以星期六他们不会在一起。

    Zhāng Wéi   xǐhuān   tiàowǔ,   <u>dànshì</u>   Lǐ Zhèng   xǐhuān   kàn   diànyǐng,
    ZHANG Wei like   dance   but   LI Zheng like   watch   movie

    suǒyǐ   xīngqīliù tā-men bù   huì zài yīqǐ.
    therefore Saturday they   NEG can be together

    {ZHANG Wei likes dancing, but LI Zheng enjoys going to the movies, so they can't be together on Saturdays.}

If ZHANG Wei and LI Zheng are just friends, who cannot "force" each other to do anything, then *dànshì* emphasizes the difference between their hobbies, and *suīrán* cannot be used. However, the following example is felicitous:

(61)   <u>虽然</u>张为喜欢跳舞，<u>但是</u>李正喜欢看电影，所以星期六他们不会在一起。

    <u>Suīrán</u>   Zhāng Wéi   xǐhuān   tiàowǔ,   <u>dànshì</u>   Lǐ Zhèng   xǐhuān   kàn
    although   ZHANG Wei like   dance   but   LI Zheng like   watch

    diànyǐng,   suǒyǐ   xīngqīliù   tā-men bù   huì zài yīqǐ.
    movie   therefore Saturday   they   NEG can be together

    {While ZHANG Wei likes dancing, LI Zheng enjoys going to the movies, so they can't be together on Saturdays.}

Interestingly, from "*suīrán . . . dànshì . . .*" in (61), it can be inferred that ZHANG Wei and LI Zheng are either husband and wife or in a special relationship. Example (61) indicates that ZHANG Wei and LI Zheng each enjoy their own recreational activities freely on Saturdays despite their intimacy.

Outline of adversative sentence forms   291

12.3.2 *Form and value of unconventional forms*

First, the pragmatic values of unconventional and non-adversative sentence forms with the same logical basis are different. Compare the following two examples in "*rúguǒ shuō p, nàme q*" and "*rúguǒ shuō p, nàme què q*" respectively:

(62) <u>如果说张为是猛虎，那么</u>，李正就是雄鹰！
    Rúguǒ shuō Zhāng Wéi   shì   měng hǔ,   nàme,   Lǐ Zhèng   jiù   shì
    if   say   ZHANG Wei   COP   fierce tiger then   LI Zheng   thus   COP
    xióngyīng!
    powerful eagle
    {If Zhang Wei is a fierce tiger, then Li Zheng is a powerful eagle!}

(63) <u>如果说张为是猛虎，那么</u>，李正却是雄鹰！
    Rúguǒ shuō Zhāng Wéi   shì   měng hǔ,   nàme,   Lǐ Zhèng   què   *shì*
    if   say   ZHANG Wei   COP   fierce tiger then   LI Zheng   however COP
    xióngyīng!
    powerful eagle
    {If Zhang Wei is only a fierce tiger of the earth, then Li Zheng is a powerful eagle of the air!}

In a hypothetical form of "*rúguǒ shuō p, nàme q*", (62) compares ZHANG Wei and LI Zheng and praises both of them for their own advantages and powerfulness. In an unconventional form of "*rúguǒ shuō p, nàme què q*", (63) indicates both a hypothesis and an opposition. The adversative connective *què* is used to reflect the speaker's personal viewpoint: although the tiger and the eagle are both very strong, the eagle can fly high in the sky while the tiger can only run on the ground. From the comparison between (62) and (63), it can be concluded that ZHANG Wei and LI Zheng are both praised in the former, but LI is praised and ZHANG is belittled in the latter. Compare "*yuè p, yuè q*" and "*yuè p, què yuè q*":

(64) 日子越红火，他心里越感到不安。
    Rìzi yuè . . . yuè . . .   *hónghuo,   tā xīn-lǐ   yuè gǎndào bù'ān.*
    life the more . . . the more . . .   prosperous   he in heart   feel   uneasy
    {The more prosperous his life is, the more uneasy he feels.}

(65) 日子越红火，他心里却越感到不安。
    Rìzi yuè . . . yuè . . .   *hónghuo,   tā xīn-lǐ   què   yuè gǎndào*
    life the more . . . the more . . .   prosperous   he in heart   however   feel
    bù'ān.
    uneasy
    {The more prosperous his life is, but the more uneasy he feels.}

In the form of "*yuè p, yuè q*", Example (64) is a correlative conditional sentence, with the anterior clause referring to a condition or ground with indefinite variability, and the posterior clause showing a result with corresponding indefinite

292 *Outline of adversative sentence forms*

variability. In the unconventional form of "*yuè p, què yuè q*", Example (65) indicates a correlative condition and an opposition. Stressing the conflict between the condition and the result, *què* shows that the correlation between the condition and the result is a negative one. In actual language use, "*yuè . . . què yuè . . .*" is often employed to emphasize the negative correlation, which has been discussed in Chapter 7 of Volume III.

Second, the pragmatic values of unconventional and special adversative sentence forms with the same logical basis are different. Compare the following two examples in the forms of "*nìngkě p, yě q*" and "*nìngkě p, què q*" respectively:

(66) 他宁可别人负他，自己也不肯负人。

Tā nìngkě . . . yě . . . biérén fù tā, zìjǐ yě bù kěn fù rén.
he would rather . . . others betray him oneself NEG want to betray others
{He would rather be betrayed by others than betray others.}

(67) 他宁可别人负他，自己却不肯负人。

Tā nìngkě biérén fù tā, zìjǐ què bù kěn fù rén.
he would rather others betray him oneself however NEG want to betray others
{He would never betray others even if others betray him.}

The "*nìngkě p, yě q*" form emphasizes that the subject makes a choice with forbearance. In some cases, an adversative connective is used to achieve the pragmatic effect of highlighting the opposition. A comparison between these two examples shows that in (67), *què* stresses the opposition between the two clauses: "never betraying others" is not affected by "others betraying him" at all. Compare another two examples in the forms of "*jíshǐ p, yě q*" and "*jíshǐ p, dàn q*" respectively:

(68) 即使他心底恼怒得恨不得把我一口咬碎，脸上还是展露出一副友好的笑容。

Jíshǐ tā xīndǐ nǎonù de hènbùde bǎ wǒ yī kǒu
even if he deep down inside be angry SP can't wait BA me one mouth
yǎo-suì, liǎn-shàng háishi zhǎnlù-chū yī fù yǒuhǎo de xiàoróng.
bite . . . to pieces on face still show one CL friendly SP smile
{Even though deep down inside he was so angry that he wished he could bite me to pieces, he put on a friendly smile.}

(69) 即使他心底恼怒得恨不得把我一口咬碎，但脸上还是展露出一副友好的笑容。

Jíshǐ tā xīndǐ nǎonù de hènbùde bǎ wǒ yī kǒu
even if he deep down inside be angry SP can't wait BA me one mouth
yǎo-suì, dàn liǎn-shàng háishi zhǎnlù-chū yī fù yǒuhǎo de
bite . . . to pieces but on face still show one CL friendly SP
xiàoróng.
smile
{Even though deep down inside he was so angry that he wished he could bite me to pieces, yet he put on a friendly smile.}

Outline of adversative sentence forms 293

The form of "*jíshǐ p, yě q*" emphasizes a hypothetical concession, and with the occurrence of an adversative connective, two pragmatic effects can be achieved. First, the adversative connective can emphasize that the posterior clause is contrary to the anterior clause, especially the conclusion in the posterior clause contrasts with or negates the hypothesis stated in the anterior clause. Second, if the structures of the two clauses are complex, the adversative connective can mark the boundary between the opposing items, which has been mentioned in Chapter 3, Volume III. Moreover, Example (69) puts more emphasis on the adversative relationship than (68). If the two clauses in (69) are expanded, the sentence will be something like (70):

(70) 即使他心底恼怒得恨不得把我一口咬碎，希望有朝一日我从现在这个位置上
跌落下去，掉到他的掌心里，听任他摆布作弄，但脸上还是展露出一副友好
的笑容，一再举杯祝贺我鹏程万里。

Jíshǐ   tā   xīndǐ   nǎonù   de   hènbùde   bǎ   wǒ   yī   kǒu
even if he   deep down inside be angry SP   can't wait   BA   me   one mouth
yǎo-suì,   xīwàng yǒuzhāo-yīrì wǒ cóng xiànzài zhè gè wèizhì-shàng
bite . . . to pieces hope   someday   I   from now   this CL in position
diēluò-xiàqù,   diào-dào tā   de   zhǎngxīn-lǐ,   tīngrèn   tā   bǎibù
fall down   fall to   he   SP   in palm of hand allow   he   manipulate
zuònòng, dàn liǎn-shàng háishi zhǎnlù-chū yī   fù   yǒuhǎo de xiàoróng,
distress   but on face   still   show   one CL   friendly SP smile
yīzài   jǔ   bēi   zhùhè   wǒ péngchéng-wànlǐ.
repeatedly raise glass congratulate me have a bright future
{Even though deep down inside he was so angry that he wished he could bite me to pieces and hoped that someday I would fall from my current position into his hands, at his mercy and manipulation, yet he put on a friendly smile, and toasted my bright future again and again.}

In this example, both clauses are more complex. The word *dàn* not only emphasizes the adversative relationship, but also marks the boundary between the two opposing items.

12.4 Research and Teaching

The discussions in this chapter offer suggestions for the research and teaching of adversative sentence forms.

12.4.1 On research

Special attention should be paid to two aspects of the study of adversative complex sentences.

First, more effort should be devoted to the research of the triangular relationship: form-meaning-value.

Adversative complex sentences should be studied from three perspectives: linguistic form (Perspective A), semantic meaning (Perspective B), and pragmatic value (Perspective C).

294 *Outline of adversative sentence forms*

Three steps can be taken to study adversative complex sentences. An investigation into Perspective A is the first step: make clear all the possible conventional and unconventional forms, based on the formal markers represented by *dàn* or *què*. An integrated investigation into of Perspectives A and B is the second step: verify the correspondence between the linguistic form and semantic meaning from both directions and identify the logical ground, general rules, and special conditions for adversative complex sentences. An integrated examination of Perspectives A and C is the third step: distinguish the different pragmatic values of synonymous linguistic forms, as the same semantic relationship expressed by different linguistic forms must have different pragmatic values. In other words, the study of adversative sentences should be furthered from the perspectives of pragmatic production and comprehension. The author holds that the research on the triangular form-meaning-value relationship will push forward the research of complex sentences on the adversative type.

Second, strive for the three adequacies.

The three adequacies refer to adequacy of observation, adequacy of description, and adequacy of explanation. To begin with, various forms of complex sentence types should be observed adequately. The perspective of observation should be established in a broad field of vision. To achieve adequacy of observation, a very important method is to test whether *dàn* or *què* is compatible with each complex sentence form. Then, within the research scope, all the rules, particularly the hidden rules about adversative sentence forms, should be summarized and described to the full extent. Depth and detail are the requirements for adequate description. Last, sentence forms of the adversative type should be fully explained. A theoretical explanation of grammatical facts should be developed based on a thorough observation and elaborate description. Adequacy of explanation is characterized by accuracy and depth rather than extensiveness or meticulousness. Take, for example, *dàn* and its synonyms. Statically, they function as a marker for the adversative relationship, whereas dynamically, they can be used in various adversative sentence forms with the same logical ground. Thus, the relationship between the linguistic form and the logical basis is not a simple one-to-one correspondence, but a complex one. Obviously, theoretical explanations of the similarities and differences between the static function and dynamic function of *dàn* and its synonyms can facilitate the understanding of adversative complex sentences. As for the procedure of the research, i.e., whether explanation first or description first depends on the property and requirements of the theme of the research.

The three adequacies are the requirement of in-depth research, and the triangular relationship among the form, the meaning, and the value is the methodology. The requirement and the methodology prove and supplement each other.

12.4.2 On teaching

In the teaching of adversative complex sentences, special attention should be paid to two issues:

Outline of adversative sentence forms   295

First, the one-sided approach should be avoided.

If prototypical adversative sentence forms are regarded as the only ones in which *dàn* or its synonyms can occur, it is a one-sided teaching approach, which not only prevents students from understanding adversative complex sentences comprehensively and accurately, but may also lead to self-contradiction in teaching.

The following is a typical example.

An article about grammar in Textbook 6 of *Chinese* for Junior Middle School Students claims, "Connectives should be used correctly, and mistakes should be avoided in connective collocation".[2] Example (71) is an ill-formed sentence listed in the book, and it is followed by an explanation: "The word *jíshǐ* should be replaced by *suīrán*, for only *suīrán* can collocate with *dàn*, which marks an adversative relationship."

(71)   *我们在学习上即使取得了一定的成绩，但这仅仅是第一步，决不能自满。
    Wǒmen zài ... shàng xuéxí shàng jíshǐ   qǔdé-le   yídìng de chéngjì,
    we   in   study   even if gain-PEF definite SP achievement
    dàn zhè jǐnjǐn shì   dìyī bù, jué   bù   néng zìmǎn.
    but this only COP first step absolutely NEG can   complacent
    {Even though we have made some progress in our studies, it is only the beginning and we should not be complacent.}

In this sentence, *suīrán* would be more appropriate than *jíshǐ*, because what follows *jíshǐ* is a real fact rather than a hypothetical situation, and it is unnecessary to treat the fact as a hypothesis for emphasis. If the sentence can be rewritten as (72), it will be a well-formed one:

(72)   即使我们在学习上取得了很大的成绩，但是，这仅仅是第一步，决不能自满！
    Jíshǐ   wǒmen zài ... shàng xuéxí shàng qǔdé-le   hěn dà de chéngjì,
    even if we   in   study   gain-PEF very big SP achievement
    dànshì, zhè jǐnjǐn shì   dìyī bù, jué   bù   néng zìmǎn!
    but   this only COP first step absolutely NEG can   complacent
    {Even though we have made great progress in our studies, this is just the first step, thus we should not be complacent.}

Therefore, the reason that (71) is an imperfect sentence is not that *jíshǐ* and *dàn* cannot cooccur. In that textbook, "*jíshǐ . . . yě . . .*" sentences are categorized as hypothetical complex sentences, and the occurrence of *dàn* in a "*jíshǐ . . . yě . . .*" sentence is regarded as incorrect, which is clearly a one-sided view.

In the same textbook, after the article is an essay written by LU Xun, in which there is a sentence:

(73)   即使所举的罪状是真的罢，但这些事情，是无论哪一个"友邦"也都有的，
    他们的维持他们的"秩序"的监狱，就撕掉了他们的"文明"的面具。
    Jíshǐ   suǒ jǔ de zuìzhuàng shì   zhēn de ba, dàn zhèxiē shìqíng, shì
    even if PAP list SP accusation COP real SP MP but these matter   COP

296 *Outline of adversative sentence forms*

wúlùn		*nǎ*	*yī*	*gè*	*"yǒubāng"*		*yě*	*dōu yǒu*	*de,*	*tā-men de*
no matter ...		which	one	CL	friendly nation		also	all have	SP	they SP

wéichí   tā-men de   "zhìxù"   de   jiānyù,   jiù   sīdiào-le   tā-men de
maintain   they   SP   order   SP   prison   just tear off-PEF   they   SP

"wénmíng"   de   miànjù.
civilization SP   mask

{Even if the accusations listed are true, these matters are common to any "friendly nation". Their prisons that maintain their "order" have just torn off their mask of "civilization".}

In the above example, "*jíshǐ . . . dàn . . .*" is used.

In Book 3 of *Chinese for Senior Middle School Students*, there is another essay by LU Xun, from which (74) is cited:

(74) 即使无人豢养，饿的精瘦，变成野狗了，但还是遇见所有的阔人都驯良，遇见所有的穷人都狂吠的，不过这时它就愈不明白谁是主子了。

Jíshǐ   wú   rén   huànyǎng, è   de   jīngshòu, biànchéng
even if   there not be person   feed   hungry   SP   wiry   become

yěgǒu   le,   dàn háishì yùjiàn suǒyǒu de kuòrén dōu xùnliáng, yùjiàn
wild dog PEF   but still   meet   all   SP the rich all gentle   meet

suǒyǒu de qióngrén dōu kuángfèi   de,   bùguò   zhèshí   tā jiù
all   SP the poor   all bark furiously MP   however this time it then

yù   bù   míngbai shuí shì   zhǔzi le.
more   NEG   know   who   COP   master MP

{Even if ("a running dog") has been deserted, lean and hungry, and has become a stray dog, yet whenever it meets a rich person, it is gentle, and whenever it meets a poor one, it barks furiously, but at this time it will become more confused as to who is its master.}

In the aforementioned example, "*jíshǐ . . . dàn . . .*" is also used.

Second, superficiality should be avoided in teaching.

In teaching, the explanation of phenomena cannot stay at the level of "conventionally" or "sometimes". Instead, teachers should help students find out the unconventional cases and the situations and conditions that "sometimes" really refers to; otherwise the teaching of adversative sentences is superficial.

As to how to avoid being superficial in teaching adversative complex sentence forms, it is most important to timely apply the research findings to teaching to so as guide students to master the rules. Take, for example, the two sentences in the author's *Modern Chinese*:[3]

(75) 如果你是牛郎，我就是织女！[4]

Rúguǒ   nǐ   shì   niúláng,   wǒ jiù   shì   zhīnǚ!
if   you   COP   cowherd   I   just   COP   weaving maiden

{If you were the Cowherd, I would be the Weaving Maiden!}

(76) 如果你是老虎，我就是武松！
Rúguǒ nǐ shì lǎohǔ, wǒ jiù shì Wǔ Sōng!
if   you COP tiger I then COP WU Song
{If you were a tiger, I would be WU Song!}[5]

At first glance, there does not seem to be much difference between the two sentences. However, *què* cannot replace *jiù* in (75), but it can do so in (76). Thus, it can be concluded that some hypothetical sentences with *rúguǒ* allow the occurrence of *què*, but some do not. Then, which hypothetical complex sentences with *rúguǒ* do? In teaching, students can be guided to combine the linguistic form with the semantic meaning in order to find the answer. The process generally goes as follows:

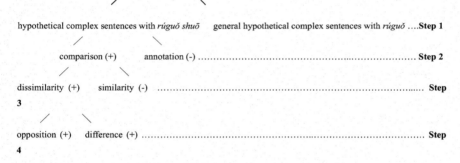

Diagram 12.1 Steps of checking whether *què* can be present in hypothetical sentences with *rúguǒ*

In Step 1, it can be seen that *què* can be present in "*rúguǒ shuō . . . nàme . . .*" (In some "*rúguǒ . . . nàme . . .*" sentences *shuō* can be added and placed after *rúguǒ*.) In Step 2, it can be observed that *què* can only occur in hypothetical complex sentences with "*rúguǒ shuō*" to make a comparison. Step 3 reveals that *què* can occur in those that present dissimilarities. Step 4 concludes that *què* can appear in those that present dissimilarities, be the dissimilarities a contrast or a difference. In conclusion, a condition for the occurrence of *què* in hypothetical sentences can be found if these steps are taken.

Apart from "*rúguǒ shuō p, nàme q*", there is another special form of hypothetical complex sentences—"*rúguǒ p, wèishénme q*"—that allows the occurrence of *què*, hence "*rúguǒ p, què wèishénme q*" or "*rúguǒ p, wèishénme què q*". The following are three examples:

(77) 如果他真是留苏学生，为什么却一句俄语也不会说？
Rúguǒ tā zhēn shì liú   Sū   xuéshēng, **wèishénme** *què*
if   he really COP study abroad Soviet student   why   however

298 *Outline of adversative sentence forms*

yī . . . yě bù . . . jù   éyǔ   yě bù huì shuō?
not even one sentence Russian   can say
{If he really studied in the Soviet Union, why doesn't he speak a word of Russian?}

(78) 若想武林中知道他的厉害，却为什么又要装死呢？

Ruò xiǎng   wǔlín-zhōng   zhīdào tā de lìhai,   què wèishénme yòu
if   want to in martial arts circle know   he SP power yet   why   really

yào   zhuāng sǐ   ne?
need pretend dead MP

{If he wanted people in the martial arts circle to know how powerful he is, then why did he have to play dead?}

(79) 倘若真是我杀的，却何必不认？

Tǎngruò zhēn   shì   wǒ shā de, què hébì   bù   rèn?
if   really COP I   kill SP yet   why necessarily NEG admit

{If I really was the killer, would I need to deny it?}

This form is similar to "*jìrán p, què wèishénme q*" and "*jìrán p, wèishénme què q*", in which "*wèishénme q*" is often used to disprove the validity of *p*, the basis for the hypothesis. More details can be found in Chapter 5, Volume III.

The author of the present book understands that it is impossible to teach everything about adversative sentence forms profoundly and thoroughly due to the limitations of teaching time, research quality, and student capabilities. However, if teachers can help students have a thorough understanding of one or two questions, students' analytical thinking will be developed.

Summary

This chapter re-examines sentence forms of adversative types from four perspectives: the conventional and unconventional forms, the linguistic form and the semantic meaning, the linguistic form and the pragmatic value, and research and teaching.

Questions about adversative complex sentence forms and the related issues cannot be fully answered in one or two chapters. It takes time to make a thorough investigation to find all the answers. As a matter of fact, the author is still puzzled by many questions.

For example, what are the differences between conventional ". . . *dàn* . . ." sentences and ". . . *què* . . ." sentences in structure and meaning? What rules can be thus discovered?

Another example is unconventional "*wúlùn . . . dōu* . . ." sentences, which allow the occurrence of *dàn* or *què* under certain conditions. However, are there any rules about the absence of *dàn/què* and *dōu*? Are there any differences among various forms of "*wúlùn . . . dōu* . . ." in acceptance of *dàn/què*?

A third example: what are the principles governing the judgment of the pragmatic value of various forms of adversative complex sentences? What are the rules?

Outline of adversative sentence forms 299

There are more questions than the aforementioned ones. All the questions can only be possibly solved after long-term and in-depth study by the joint efforts of a large number of researchers and scholars.

NB Some examples in this chapter are cited from literary works, political essays, articles, and so on. The sources are listed as follows:

1 *Chinese* for Junior High School Students, Book 1, including (41) and (45); Book 2, including (20), (42), (46), and (49); Book 6, including (71) and (73);
2 *Dangdai* (《当代》) 1984(1), including (54);
3 *Flower City* (《花城》) 1983 (4), including (32);
4 *Hongyan* (《红岩》) 1983(2), including (33);
5 *October* (《十月》) 1982(3), including (56) and (34);
6 *Review on Short Stories Published in FLOWER CITY in 1978* (《一九七八<花城>中篇小说》评述) by YE Xiaofan (叶小帆), including (37)
7 *Selected Stories* (《小说选刊》) 1997(1) (supplement), including (28);
8 *State of Divinity* (《笑傲江湖》) by JIN Yong (金庸), including (79);
9 *The Semi-Gods and Semi-Devils* (《天龙八部》) by JIN Yong (金庸), including (67) and (78);
10 *Xiao Shuo Jia* (《小说家》) 1998(4), including (24);
11 *Zhongpian Xiaoshuo Xuankan*(《中篇小说选刊》) 1994(6), including (27) and (36); 1997(4), including (26) and (69).

Notes

1 Editorial Office of Zhongguo Yuwen (Ed.). *Selections of Chinese Short Reviews* (《语文短评选辑》). Zhonghua Book Company, 1959, pp. 103–104.
2 On Pages 27–28 in *Chinese* for Junior High School Students, Book 6, published by People's Press in 1980, there is a sentence as follows:

> "we should try to use conjunctions correctly, and to avoid the collocation mistakes of paired conjunctions".

3 XING Fuyi (邢福义) (Ed.). *Modern Chinese* (《现代汉语》). Higher Education Press, 1991.
4 Translators' note: The story of the Cowherd and the Weaving Maiden is a sad and beautiful legend about love. After a lot of hardships, the couple finally broke through the resistance and were able to enjoy an annual reunion.
5 Translator's note: WU Song is a legendary hero who fought a man-eating tiger and eventually defeated it.

Index

abnormal correlation 142, 143, 144, 146, 148, 149, 151

abnormal correlative sentence 144

adversative complex sentence 1, 26, 28, 57, 58, 73, 153, 180, 208, 244, 246, 269, 270, 271, 276, 293, 294, 295, 296, 298

adversative conjunction 5, 250

adversative connective 19, 21, 22, 67, 81, 95, 97, 100, 110, 142, 144, 149, 151, 157, 160, 180, 208, 213, 244, 250, 254, 269, 271, 276, 278, 281, 282, 288, 291, 292, 293

adversative relationship 1, 8, 25, 47, 59, 61, 62, 65, 66, 69, 71, 72, 73, 75, 78, 81, 83, 86, 87, 88, 89, 90, 93, 119, 153, 154, 177, 181, 207, 208, 210, 211, 213, 248, 249, 252, 253, 269, 270, 276, 278, 279, 282, 283, 284, 286, 288, 290, 292, 294, 295

adversative sentence form 73, 269, 271, 278, 282, 283, 287, 289, 291, 292, 293, 294, 295, 298

concession 20, 21, 22, 24, 25, 67, 72, 90, 234, 243, 244, 248, 252, 255, 256, 257, 259, 261, 263, 264, 265, 267

concessive complex sentence 17, 208, 209, 212, 243, 244, 245, 248, 251, 255, 256, 264, 267

concessive connective 19, 251, 255, 270

concessive sentence 21, 26, 209, 243, 244, 248, 255, 257, 258, 264

contrastive causality 4, 17, 19, 23, 30, 31, 33, 36, 279, 280, 282

conventional form 269, 287

coordinate complex sentence 59, 60, 63, 67

correlation 128, 129, 130, 137, 138, 142, 144, 146, 148, 149, 150, 151, 292

counter-hypothetical sentence 247

dàn or its synonym 59, 60, 62, 63, 64

direct contrast 4, 9, 57

downward progression 198, 204, 210

factive concession 256, 257, 267

factive concessive sentence 247, 257, 261

forward progression 188

hierarchical distance 154, 155, 156, 178

hypothetical concession 256, 257, 258, 262

inferential sentence marker 205

isomorphic form 127

linguistic form 19, 179, 178, 184, 185, 186, 278, 287, 293, 294, 297, 298

marked reversed progressive sentence 170, 171, 172, 174, 180

negative correlation 128, 129, 130, 140, 149, 150, 151, 252

negator 164, 165, 168

normal correlation 142, 146, 148, 149, 151

partial adversative relationship 83, 86, 87, 282

partial contrast 10, 12, 13, 14, 15, 281

positive correlation 128, 129, 130

pragmatic significance 97, 111, 113

pragmatic value 287, 289, 291, 292, 294, 298

preferable concession 256, 261, 262, 263

progression precursor 157, 158, 159, 164, 165, 188, 189

progression undertakers 158, 163

progressive relationship 165, 170, 172, 177, 178, 181, 183, 187, 192, 193, 196, 206, 208, 213, 287

Index   301

reduced contrast 12, 13
reversed progressive relationship 153, 165,
  170, 172
reversed progressive sentence 153, 170,
  171, 172, 174, 178, 180
reversion marker 159, 161, 171, 180

semantic basis 4, 255
slight contrast 5, 10
subdivision I 75, 76, 78, 83, 86, 87, 88, 89, 93
subdivision II 75, 76, 77, 78, 83, 86, 87,
  88, 89, 93
subdivision III 75, 77, 78, 81, 88, 89, 91,
  92, 93
sufficient condition 113, 124, 125, 152

total adversative relationship 87,
  88, 89
typical marker 1, 17, 95

unconditional concession 256, 259,
  262, 267
unconditional concessive sentence 91, 251,
  259, 260
unconditional concessive sentence 91, 259,
  260, 261
unconventional form 269, 270, 280, 281,
  282, 287, 291, 292, 294, 298
unmarked reversed progressive sentence
  170, 171, 172, 174, 180

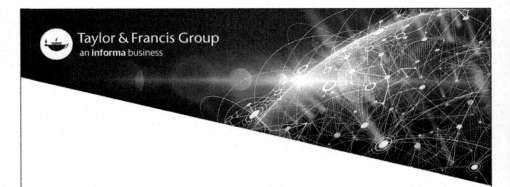

Taylor & Francis eBooks

www.taylorfrancis.com

A single destination for eBooks from Taylor & Francis with increased functionality and an improved user experience to meet the needs of our customers.

90,000+ eBooks of award-winning academic content in Humanities, Social Science, Science, Technology, Engineering, and Medical written by a global network of editors and authors.

TAYLOR & FRANCIS EBOOKS OFFERS:

- A streamlined experience for our library customers
- A single point of discovery for all of our eBook content
- Improved search and discovery of content at both book and chapter level

REQUEST A FREE TRIAL
support@taylorfrancis.com